Guiding Human Development

**The Counselor and the
Teacher in the Elementary School**

June Grant Shane
Harold G. Shane
Robert L. Gibson
Paul F. Munger

Indiana University

Charles A. Jones Publishing Company
Worthington, Ohio

In appreciation of the able teachers and counselors
who have deepened our insights and extended our vision
as to the potentially powerful force for good
that resides in childhood education.

Preface

Guiding Human Development: The Counselor and the Teacher in the Elementary School presents foundations and procedures of counseling and guidance that have been carefully selected to help strengthen modern educational programs. Counselors, supervisors, and teachers will find throughout the book unifying concepts and practices that will help them encourage maximum child development. As the subtitle indicates, the book is designed to acquaint these educators more fully with the workings of an insightfully planned program conceived explicitly for elementary school age children.

With stress on goal identification for behavioral growth, observation techniques, evaluation processes, and record keeping, *Guiding Human Development* outlines procedures for organizing, supervising, and administering guidance services. It also examines ways in which guidance and curriculum planning can be coordinated. Finally, it is written to sensitize the classroom or "teamed" teacher and elementary principal to the new opportunities and responsibilities which are implicit in guidance at an early age.

Part I of the book is concerned with *knowledge* and presents an overview of backgrounds, theory, and research that are important to counselors and teachers working with children of elementary school age. Part II deals with *functions* and translates the counselor's knowledge into proposals that offer promise for improving the effectiveness of his practices. Part III—*milieu*—recognizes that the counselor not only applies his skills but does so in a physical setting and in various psychologically significant ways that mediate or otherwise influence his opportunities and procedures.

The task of attaining truly fine programs in elementary education—including a unified concept of counseling and guidance—is a demanding and an arduous one. We hope that our proposals for improving the guidance of human development will encourage counselors and teachers to work with continued confidence, with clearer perspectives, and with a renewed sense of urgency and purpose as they seek to increase the effectiveness of American education.

Indiana University
Bloomington, Indiana
January 1971

June Grant Shane
Harold G. Shane
Robert L. Gibson
Paul F. Munger

Contents

Part
ONE

1

Backgrounds of Guidance During the Elementary School Years

If it were possible to have transported Julius Caesar from 50 B.C. to 1920 A.D. and to put him down on a small midwestern farm, little that he saw would have been unfamiliar. Muscle power was still used to do most of the work. Coal burned in the stove, food was crudely preserved, and water was hand pumped. The "outdoor plumbing" was inferior to that in the home of a well-to-do Roman of 2000 years ago.

But put Caesar and an American adult of 1920 into the world of the 1970's and both would be mystified by most of what they saw. The world of computers, atomic energy, space travel, and television would be almost as alien to the man of 1920 as to the man of 50 years before the birth of Christ. In the past 50 years, man's environment has changed more than it did the past 2000 years—or for that matter, in the past 50,000!

Hundreds of books and articles of the past decade have dealt with the phenomenon of a change so rapid that is has carried mankind into technically advanced societies, such as the U.S., from yesterday to tomorrow! Technological advances have dramatically affected all aspects of our living: work, leisure, travel, health, homes, food, and clothing. This rate of change has become so extraordinarily rapid that many people are ill-equipped to cope with the consequences. Indeed, we may have moved so rapidly that "this sudden collision with the future and its influences on our behavior may well be seen in retrospect as one of the great forces shaping the last half of the twentieth century." (53)

3

Kenneth Boulding, the economist, makes the point that within the memory of people now living is the point at which the history of the human race may be divided into two parts (7). During the first part man moved from a pre-civilized to a civilized society. Now, according to Boulding, he approaches a second great transition—the move from a civilized to a post-civilized society. This second transition in terms of historic continuity will be so great that its magnitude can only be compared to the first great change that occurred when man ascended from barbarism to civilization. Accordingly, many persons alive today have crossed a great watershed in human history. They have moved into an almost entirely new world—one that, according to Sir George Thompson, parallels the invention of agriculture in the neolithic age (61).

In this new era, despite its potentiality, education has not moved as rapidly as many other social institutions in accepting the challenge to help individuals understand and accept change and to deal creatively with new ways of life in a society that will continue to change rapidly. We seem to find it much easier to utilize the products of change—prepared foods, miracle drugs, computers, space ships, paper clothing—than to alter some of our ways of life that were designed for another time.

In an era such as this, the field of counseling and guidance has become one of important opportunities and impressive responsibilities. For some years it has been recognized that this is true at the secondary and university level, and at various times in life for purposes of rehabilitation or vocational guidance. Only more recently has it begun to become evident that counseling has an equally important role to fill at the elementary school level.

Elementary Education
and the Dynamics of Change

Most professions concerned with the study of human beings and their behavior agree that the early years of childhood are important ones. So critical are they that these years are generally conceded to be the most influential period of all in shaping personality. Nonetheless, these first years of life have not received the attention that has been given in the past to the period that adolescents spend in secondary schools and colleges. The upper levels of schooling have received support for specialized personnel and for program development far more extensively than at the elementary level. Yet would there not be fewer educational and human misfits during adolescence and adult years if greater attention were focused on the early years of childhood? As George Leonard put it:

> No sane investor in humans would pour the most dollars and effort into the upper end of the student's age scale, especially

since any constructive change accomplished at the lower end will accrue to our advantage throughout all the school years that follow (35).

Leonard is not alone in his opinions. For decades, a few prescient educators have emphasized the critical and formative nature of early childhood years. They contended that greater concern for younger children would contribute to greater fulfillment of human potentiality. However, they were often paid little heed. Only recently has it begun to be realized that a vast increase in support during these early years is desirable. Such support is of especial importance because elementary education is the one period in the American educational system when *all* children are reached. Since the base of the "human pyramid" of students is broadest where the youngest children are enrolled, money spent at this level reaches the largest possible segment of the population.

In addition, changes in human behavior made during these years with respect to attitudes and skills can sometimes be accomplished in hours or days. Later, in adolescence, comparable behavioral changes may take months, years, or may even be impossible to achieve. Clearly, the return on money invested in early childhood carries the highest rate of interest on the investment being made in American education. It is this investment in boys and girls with which *Guiding Human Development: The Counselor and the Teacher in the Elementary School* is concerned.

Guidance in the Elementary School

Writers in the field of counseling and guidance and in elementary education frequently have acknowledged that guidance services can play an important role in improving the education of young children. This viewpoint is reflected in some books on elementary education, a larger number of books dealing with the general field of counseling and guidance which incorporate a chapter or two on elementary programs, and in a variety of articles that usually editorialize or treat some narrow aspect of the topic.

There is a need for current literature which provides a comprehensive background and specific suggestions for students in the field of counseling and guidance who plan to work in the elementary schools. Such literature should help educators who are involved in a continuous program extending from the preschool or kindergarten through twelve to fourteen years of public education. It is the writers' purpose to present a carefully drawn picture of elementary education *as the school counselor must see and understand it* and to bring into this picture *those relevant professional contributions to early and middle childhood* that guidance program personnel can make.

The chapters that follow should be equally useful to elementary teachers, supervisors, and administrators who are striving to understand how they can work more effectively with counselors in serving both children and pre-adolescents.

Guiding Human Development: The Counselor and the Teacher in the Elementary School

This book has been organized into three parts that are of direct concern to the counselor in the elementary school: 1) knowledge, 2) function, and 3) milieu (environment).

PART I is concerned with KNOWLEDGE. It presents an overview of backgrounds, theory, and research that applies to children of elementary school age. In addition, it provides a digest of professional knowledge that the counselor should bring to his task of helping young learners.

PART II is concerned with FUNCTIONS. It translates the counselor's knowledge into proposals that offer promise for improving the effectiveness of his practices. It carefully describes his activities in the elementary school.

PART III is concerned with MILIEU (environment). It recognizes that the counselor not only applies his skills but that he does so in a physical setting and in various psychologically significant ways that mediate or otherwise influence his opportunities and procedures.

Problems in Communicating Ideas

Before turning to the background information presented in Chapter 1, attention is directed toward the increasing problems involved in communicating ideas—of conveying accurately to others the "meaning of the meaning." Since elementary school guidance is a newly developed field it is extremely important that meaning be communicated with clarity, precision, and reasonable rapidity.

Increasingly, the language and its related symbols used in the context of our culture are creating severe difficulties among, and even within, the various scholarly disciplines, which must be avoided when dealing with the work of the elementary school counselors.

In 1953, Irwin D. Bross in his book, *Design for Decision*, pointed out that a twenty year lag occurs between the time ideas are first voiced by a scientist and the time they reach other scientists in intelligible form (9:3). He attributes this in part to the fact that many publications are written only for fellow specialists and that frequently even these specialists do not fully understand one another's meanings.

Intense contemporary interest in communication problems was reflected in the widespread discussion of Charles P. Snow's lecture "The Two Cultures and the Scientific Revolution" delivered in 1959 at Cambridge University. Sir Charles built his remarks around the idea that " . . . the intellectual life of the whole of western society is increasingly being split into two polar groups." (59:11) He went on to contend that many highly educated people have become virtually incapable of communicating on the planes of their intellectual concerns. In short, persons in the humanities and the sciences are in danger of losing the power to speak a common language when interchanging ideas with others not in their specialities.

By the late 1960's it has become increasingly evident that problems of encoding and decoding ideas are not only conspicuous among intellectual disciplines but that scholars in the *same* broad field of inquiry are encountering heavy static even when they make efforts to transmit ideas to their immediate colleagues. A notable recent example of communication problems within a field of study is provided by linguistics, a science which is concerned with the systematic study of language. Not only is a complex body of terminology used by linguists, but there are many divisions (dialectology, metalinguistics, phonology, and so on) of the science, and conflicting schools of opinions as to "whose linguistics is the best" (e.g., the structural, stratificational, or transformational-generative approach to grammar). No need to understand such terms to sense the confusion they have bred for the teacher of English! And it would be unfortunate to have a parallel situation develop in the rapidly expanding realm of elementary guidance.

Some Definitions of Terms

This brings us to the point that some heed should be given to certain basic terms used in this book before beginning a study of guiding human development through counseling and guidance in childhood. With what meaning should one endow the words *guidance*, *counseling*, and *counselor* in schools for young children and pre-adolescents?

GUIDANCE: *Guidance in the elementary school is a comprehensive term. It is concerned with the professionally skillful deployment of all available human and material resources at the school's command to provide a learning climate that will maximize and facilitate the development of all children as each seeks to understand, accept, and direct himself both as an individual and as a member of our society.*

COUNSELING: Counseling is one of the important functions of the whole guidance process. *Individual counseling refers to the specific one-to-one relationship designed to improve a person's understanding of himself and his transactions with some aspect(s) of his total environment. Group counseling is a one-to-many relationship in which shared interests, concerns, or problems of a cluster of people are examined and discussed.* Both individual and group counseling are concerned with helping persons clarify concepts about themselves and test those concepts against the realities of the world.

COUNSELOR: As used hereafter, *the counselor is a person whose professional background has prepared him to utilize total school-community resources to facilitate all children's wholesome psychological and intellectual progress as he interacts with them and with other significant persons in the total educative process.* With his knowledge of child growth and development and human behavior, the counselor is prepared for skillful individual and group counseling and for consulting with children, teachers, and parents. The counselor also understands the dynamics of elementary education and the elementary curriculum so that he may function as a consultant with teachers and administrators both in curriculum planning and in in-service training programs for teachers. Through his competencies in human relations, he is able to be involved effectively with teachers and other professional colleagues as well as with parents in developing learning environments that provide for the developmental needs of all children.

Guidance, if successful, helps an individual *set the course* he will follow. Counseling *helps one arrive* safely at his goals.

The Brightening Scene
in Elementary School Guidance Programs

Santayana once wrote that those who do not remember the past are condemned to relive it. Berelson and Steiner also remind us that research sometimes suffers because researchers have failed to develop greater awareness of knowledge compiled in the past (4). This generalization has implications for counseling and guidance programs now being designed to help children in the elementary schools. The counselor will be better able to plan for the present and for the future if he first "reads the minutes of the last meeting." With this premise in mind let us take a brief look at the past for the help it can give in charting a course for the future.

**Fifty Years of Significant Change
in Elementary School Guidance Programs**

Counseling and guidance programs, in the current sense of these terms, were virtually unknown at the elementary school level fifty years ago. However, the *idea* or *concept* underlying contemporary programs can be traced back at least as far as to the 1920's.

The almost complete absence of references to elementary school counseling and guidance services prior to the recent past can be demonstrated in several ways. For example, an influential and widely respected book on elementary education, written in the mid-1930's by the knowledgeable chairman of the Department of Elementary Education, Teachers College, Columbia University, mentioned neither counseling nor guidance in its index (37). Even the 1520 page *Encyclopedia of Educational Research* published in 1950 did not include a subheading on guidance in the elementary school. The 1960 edition was more generous. "Elementary School Counseling" rated a modest heading and some fourteen inches of type or 7/8 of a page. The encyclopedia included reference to a 1954 article containing the interesting information that there was an average of approximately six full-time persons per state in the U.S. who could be identified as "elementary school counselors." Quite possibly, some of these individuals' titles were euphemistic labels for persons who functioned as truant officers, remedial teachers, or social workers.

But if counseling and guidance services for elementary schools were virtually unknown fifty years ago and were barely beginning to be recognized in the late 1950's and early 1960's, many of the ideas and values implicit in modern guidance and counseling were nonetheless generally well conceived and even being practiced in our elementary schools in what might well be called "The Gaslight Era" of elementary school guidance.

The "Gaslight Era" in Elementary School Guidance

Just as the publication of Clifford Beers' book, *A Mind That Found Itself* (3), and the establishment of the Vocational Bureau by Frank Parsons in Boston in 1908 are considered two of the "firsts" in the evolvement of guidance programs for secondary schools, so are there landmarks in the historical past for elementary school programs. From these early landmarks may be traced many of the origins of counseling and guidance programs for young children. The next several pages will review some of the general developments in education which contributed to the points of view which govern contemporary guidance and counseling services for younger children.

Many of the early innovations which foreshadow elementary school "counseling" and "guidance" as we have defined them seem crude or naive when compared with some of today's practices and procedures. However, in their day and age they were significant attempts to adapt and modify school environments in terms of what was known about individual differences and human needs. The practices were relevant in their particular time.*

Before 1900. One of the early attempts to modify educational practices and to improve "guidance" at the elementary school level occurred as far back as 1862. The St. Louis schools, during that year, introduced a quarterly plan for promotions on the assumption that it would help schools more rapidly cope with changing concepts of successful pupil performance. According to a United States government report for 1890-91, 32 out of 465 cities, at the first grade level, promoted children four or more times per year (8:983). By 1894, Preston Search had worked out a multiple track plan in Pueblo, Colorado, designed to permit children to complete similar units of study at different rates of speed (52).

In addition to the St. Louis and Pueblo ventures mentioned above, Otto has described a dozen others, each of which sought to nurture, or at least to recognize, human differences and the respect for the individual with which counseling and guidance are so deeply involved (44). While some of these plans could scarcely be considered exemplary ones today, they anticipated the recent interest in continuous promotion and in a continuum of personalized educational experience. At least the seeds of change had been planted.

The Past Illuminates the Present

Historical background material is merely of academic interest unless it increases our present insights or our understandings with respect to the future. Judged by this criterion, developments that were transpiring in the preprofessional guidance period in elementary education are clearly of more than academic interest. From them, we have clear evidence that beginning in 1900 a growing number of educators stressed the importance of the individual's experiences during his early school years and also expressed ideas which eventually evolved in the form of contemporary guidance practices designed to serve young children.

*It behooves us to remember that the disciplines of psychology, sociology, and anthropology, upon which guidance and counseling draw so heavily, are relatively new sciences —in fact, barely 100 years old. While we have gained much information from them during this span of years, there is still a great deal more to be known before it can be said that a deep insight into human behavior has been achieved.

1900-1920. During the first two decades of the century, the educational influence of John Dewey began to be felt; the Francis Parker and Lincoln Schools were opened; the Binêt-Simon tests of intelligence appeared; and the early concepts of Gestalt psychology as well as the writings of Sigmund Freud began to influence educational thought in the United States. Each of these developments had a marked influence on elementary education and each foreshadowed what have become basic guidance practices in the elementary schools of the 1960's and 1970's. Dewey led the fight to abandon the school's static duty to pass on subject content and concentrate on the child as a learner, while Parker endeavored to create child-centered programs. Binêt expanded the concept of gauging intelligence, and the Gestaltists presented new theories of learning.

This was also the time of J. B. Watson and "behaviorism," of William Kilpatrick and "the project method," of the first White House Conference and the first modern-type school surveys, and of the famous *Seven Cardinal Principles of Education* that reflected newer educational thinking.* It was the beginning of a time in which education began to urge that children be studied and treated as individuals. In 1909 Frederic Burk wrote *Remedy for Lock Step Schooling* in which he contended that it was not the children who failed, but the schools (10). These were stimulating years in which new theories of learning were being explored and applied. Elementary guidance would be the poorer for it if this era were ignored.

The 1920's. As the 1920's began, a lively educational era emerged. This era was significantly affected by the testing and "new" education movement. Children were given intelligence tests and standardized tests, and textbooks presumably became more scientific as controlled vocabularies were introduced in basal readers. There even was emphasis upon the scientific method of problem solving and rational thinking, although in the early 1960's this emphasis often was described as a new one!

Along with the scientific education movement came the "progressive" movement or the "new" education. It sought 1) to improve society and strengthen democracy and 2) to introduce classroom practices tailored to an organic conception of children. Progressives stressed the uniqueness and dignity of the individual child and directed attention to his varied needs and purposes. They also anticipated later guidance theory when they emphasized the importance of a warm, humane classroom environment and, particularly, the premise that learning occurred in many ways.

*The Principles were: (1) health, (2) command of the fundamental processes, (3) worthy home membership, (4) vocational competence, (5) civic education, (6) worthy use of leisure time, and (7) ethical character.

Such an environment was one in which: 1) teachers and children planned cooperatively; 2) understanding and improving children's social environment was emphasized; 3) subject matter was organized so that it was consistent with children's developmental needs and purposes; 4) the curriculum was not adult imposed but guided by the teacher on the basis of a particular group in its own environment; and 5) the "psychological environment" of the class-room encouraged children to develop purposes and seek answers meaningful to them (54:10).

Disagreements during the 1920's between "progressives" emphasizing the teaching of children and "essentialists" emphasizing the transmission of content and cultural heritage, led to a widening schism between these two groups—each one equally anxious to serve the best interests of children.

The 1930's. The Depression Years saw the continuation of the conflict between "essentialists" and "progressives." In fact, this ideological clash continued into the 1950's and 1960's and seems fated to carry over into the 1970's. The 1930's also witnessed widespread gains in national concerns for human welfare which later influenced federal support for guidance in the 1960's. Reform plans flourished throughout the country as public and private agencies focused on reclaiming depression-eroded human beings through more relevant educational programs. Curriculum debate and reform centered on serving the needs of childhood and youth. New approaches to the appraisal of educational climates and goals by pioneers such as J. Wayne Wrightstone, Louis Raths, and Ralph Tyler helped educators assess some of the intangibles of teaching and learning. Their ideas, with modifications, later found their way into child study and appraisal tools now used by counselors.

Also during these years, the term "developmental tasks" began to be used by a few educators. Although this term is usually associated with Robert Havighurst's writings at a later date, he explains the actual historical antecedents of this concept in the preface of his pamphlet, *Developmental Tasks and Education* (26).

Havighurst also states that about this same time Erik Erikson of the Yale Institute of Human Relations developed a similar concept about the development of infants and pre-school children. This Erikson later shared with the Adolescent Study Staff while he served as consultant for the group (18). A further discussion of the importance of the work of Havighurst and Erikson appears in Chapter 7.

Leaving an imprint upon the decade of the 1930's were certain research studies on which guidance theory still draws; research done in fields related to education: anthropology, psychiatry, pediatrics, mental hygiene, sociology, biology, sociometry, semantics, and psychology. Many experimentally oriented schools were influenced by Willard Olson's concept of organismic age,* Daniel Prescott's *Emotion and the Educative Process* (48), and James Plant's *Personality and the Culture Pattern* (46) as well as by Arnold Gesell's longitudinal studies of child growth and development at the Yale Clinic.

To these one must add the writings of Robert and Helen Lynd (sociology), Ruth Benedict and Margaret Mead (anthropology), Karl Menninger (mental health), Alfred Adler and Carl Jung (psychiatry), Walter Cannon (biology), and Alfred Korzybski (general semantics). Because of their work, interest in considering the child in his total environment was sharply stimulated. Major progress was made in helping teachers to look at the child as an individual and to guide his progress toward maturity. All of these trends had a bearing on the elementary school guidance practice of today.

The 1940's. War-time problems seriously affected human activities during this decade. With large numbers of youth entering the armed forces, rumors spread that recruits were physically unfit and poorly educated. The post-war population explosion and growing conservatism also had their impact upon the schools. Many promising new educational practices that had developed from experimentation and research were derided as frills—tax-consuming, unnecessary, and perhaps even harmful. Ineffectual teaching, often labeled "progressive," was frequently blamed for the purportedly dismal state of affairs, and many erstwhile educational liberals began to speak with muted voices. Efforts to bring about educational change were also discouraged as people took sides—approving their own views—criticizing the other views—with neither side proposing any mutually acceptable solutions prior to 1947 or 1948. Educational innovations and improvements slowed down as World War II continued, and many instructional activities were redirected or suspended.

Fortunately, the later 1940's again saw greater acceptance of a child development approach and the merits of group processes began to be recognized as desirable means of helping to release human potentialities. The writing, thinking, and investigations of persons interested in the social and psychological environment and its impact upon the child also made contributions to the school program. Allison Davis did his research on the Negro child and others who were handicapped by cultural deprivation. James Bossard published his *Sociology of Child Development* (6). W. Lloyd Warner, A. B. Hollingshead, and Cecilia Stendler reported on their studies of social

---

*Olson defined organismic age as the child's central tendency of growth. Representative of factors involved: height, weight, dentition, skeletal development, muscular development, mental development, and school achievement (43).

class and the effect of caste-class upon children (62,29,60). In 1941 Carl Rogers published *Counseling and Psychotherapy* (50) and in 1948 Clyde Kluckhohn and H. A. Murphy edited *Personality in Nature, Society, and Culture*, an important presentation of the results of research in concept development upon the growth of personality (32). Also of value to elementary guidance was A. H. Maslow's identification of basic human needs* presented in a hierarchy ranging from the biological to the social (38,39).

Terms such as Robert Havighurst's "developmental tasks"† and Louis Rath's "Needs Theory"†† became part of the educator's background—or at least of his vocabulary—as did "permissive atmosphere," "life adjustment," and "persistent life situations." It almost seemed that, finally, a rapprochement could be reached—that both children and content could be recognized as important aspects of the teaching-learning experience. In keeping with these insights, today's concept of counseling and guidance broadened from a service for children having problems to a way of helping all children. Let us now look more directly at the background of guidance in elementary education.

The Historical Development of Elementary School Guidance

A number of approaches to elementary school "guidance" programs were introduced years ago. Many of these ventures involved ideas and practices in the education of children that are completely in keeping with the definitions of guidance that have appeared in recent years in books of guidance specialists. Consider the following statements from these professionals.

> *Roy DeVerl Willey:* Guidance provides an environment in which every child can grow into a socially desirable, happy, and wholesome personality (64:3).
>
> *Merle M. Ohlsen:* Guidance is a cooperative effort of the counselor and his colleagues to help a pupil improve his adjustment to school, and to help him develop skills for dealing more successfully with the problems he encounters after he leaves school (42:1).

*Needs identified ranged from basic physiological needs to higher level needs 1) physiological, 2) safety, 3) belonging and love, 4) self-esteem, and 5) self-actualization (37).

†Havighurst defines "developmental tasks" as those tasks that occur around a certain period in an individual's life. If they are successfully achieved, happiness and success with later tasks follow. If not, failure leads to unhappiness and difficulty with later tasks as well as disapproval by society (26).

††Raths identified the following human needs which, when met, should improve human development and school atmospheres: 1) belonging; 2) achievement; 3) economic security; 4) freedom from fear; 5) love and affection; 6) freedom from guilt; 7) sharing and self-respect; and 8) understanding (49:6-18).

John A. Barr: Guidance may be defined as the *process of helping individuals to assess their abilities and liabilities and to use that knowledge effectively.* (Italics in original.) (2:5).

Ralph Garry: Guidance programs at the elementary level call for skills that are suitable to the particular developmental levels of five- to fourteen-year-olds and objectives consistent with the developmental tasks of these age levels (22:10).

Bruce Shertzer and Shelley C. Stone: Guidance, as used throughout this volume, is the process of helping an individual understand himself and his world (56:31).

Donald Blocher: Developmental counseling is aimed at maximizing *human freedom* . . . (and) has as its second goal maximizing *human effectiveness* . . . that behavior that gives an individual *the greatest possible long-term control over his environment and the affective responses that are evoked by that environment.* (Italics in original.) (5:5-6).*

Anna Meeks: Guidance, then, provides a systematic approach to more effective education through the active involvement of the child in his own educational process (40:11).†

Now let us look at a sampling of plans, programs, and publications which show that major efforts were made years ago to guide young children in the same spirit as Blocher, Ohlsen, and others have more recently recommended.

Burnham's Early Insights. With good reason, Faust credits William Burhnam with pioneering in the concept that was translated into the tasks of the elementary school counselor (19:11). Burnham's first major work was *The Normal Mind* (1942), but his next publication, *Great Teachers and Mental Health* (1926) was the one that motivated Percival Symonds to speak of him as the first man of his era to perceive ". . . the role of the human behavior specialist as extending beyond a focus on crisis children, testing, and clinical diagnosis." (19:11-12) It was also Symonds who wrote that "Burnham was the first to see that mental hygiene in the school is a matter of relationship—a relationship with two poles—the teacher and the pupil." (19:13)

The Cooperative Group Plan. James F. Hosic's ideas on guiding pupil progress, as set forth in his "Cooperative Group Plan," reappeared with surprisingly few changes during the last decade under the label "team teaching." Hosic advocated cooperative planning among teachers to meet individual differences and needs over forty years ago (30).

---

*Donald H. Blocher, *Developmental Counseling.* Copyright © 1966 The Ronald Press Company, New York.

†Anna R. Meeks, *Guidance in Elementary Education.* Copyright © 1968 The Ronald Press Company, New York.

The Department of Educational Counsel in Winnetka, Illinois. One of the most outstanding programs to anticipate many current ideas in planning for pupil needs in the elementary schools was created under the leadership of Carleton W. Washburne. In the 1920's the Winnetka elementary schools established a Department of Elementary Counsel which Washburne later called ". . . a full-fledged child guidance clinic." (63:60) Eventually, a psychiatrist, pediatrician, psychometrist, psychologist, an educational counselor, a psychiatric social worker, and one or two clerk-typists were among the personnel employed.

While these resource personnel for guidance were not all invariably employed at the same time, at least two or three practitioners in the professions named formed the basic cadre during any one year. Counseling, child study, psychotherapy, psychometric services and analyses, work with parents, referrals, and numerous related functions were performed by members of the Winnetka Department thirty to forty years ago.

The Ohio State University Campus Elementary School Program. During the 1930's, particularly under the leadership of Laura Zirbes, the idea of guiding children's learning experiences began to assume a character analogous to the descriptive statements as defined by the eight writers in counseling and guidance cited above. Two of Zirbes' books describe, with anecdotes and detailed illustrations from the classroom, the way in which the guidance of learning activities was taking form as principles of the "new" education were tested and applied (65,66). These activities are very similar to those found in the better guidance programs.

The American Council Report. Nearly a quarter of a century ago the American Council on Education published a report on understanding children which serves as a concluding example of milestones in the historical development of elementary school guidance concepts. Six statements interpreting what it means to "understand" a child remain as valid today as when they were first listed by the distinguished members of the Commission on Teacher Education of the American Council.

The following excerpts might have been written in 1970 by an elementary counselor in an effort to sensitize teachers to the subtleties of guiding child development:

> We believe, in the first place, that teachers who understand children think of their behavior as being caused.
>
> A second characteristic of teachers who understand children is that they are able to accept all children emotionally, that they reject no child as hopeless or unworthy.
>
> Our third point is that teachers who understand children invariably recognize that each one is unique.

We believe, in the fourth place, that the various sciences concerned with human growth and behavior have demonstrated that young people, during several phases of their development, face a series of common "developmental tasks."

A fifth characteristic of [the] understanding teacher is that [he] knows the more important scientific facts that describe and explain the forces that regulate human growth, development, motivation, learning, and behavior.

Finally, we believe that the understanding teacher habitually uses scientific methods in making judgments about any particular boy or girl (27:8-12).

Other Programs and Developments of Merit. Many elementary school programs, other than those sampled above, operated in a guidance context even though the label was not yet used. Virtually none, however, had the extraordinary resources provided in Winnetka.

The laboratory schools at the University of Michigan were among those doing a great deal of work related to the longitudinal development of children (43). Inquiries by Ronald Lippitt and Kurt Lewin (36), made at the State University of Iowa, cast light on the importance of "classroom atmospheres"—autocratic, democratic, and laissez faire—while H. M. Skeels and his associates worked on environmental stimulation of intelligence, also at Iowa (57,58).

Elementary counseling practices remain in debt to programs and inquiries such as these. A modest number of school districts have worked diligently and effectively to create better programs at the elementary level—programs that involved principles and practices that are remarkably similar to present day guidance concepts. Innovative schools representing those of the era ranged from coast to coast and included: Newton, Massachusetts; Shaker Heights, Ohio; Glencoe, Illinois; University City, Missouri; and San Diego County, California.

In summary, it would seem that there were three ways in which elementary school guidance was interpreted—in at least a small group of innovative schools—during the first half of the 20th century:

1) In the 1920's, it was often looked upon as a *remedial* function. Children who experienced personal or academic difficulties were sent to a person especially trained and equipped with the tools needed to identify the source of the difficulty and help the child redirect or modify his behavior.

2) In the 1930's, guidance began to acquire a *preventive* function. The specially trained person attempted to anticipate difficulties and prevent them from arising. Teachers were counseled with regard to what would be desirable to keep potential problems from developing.

3) The third phase, which is currently emerging in the guidance literature is the conception of guidance as the *continuous function of the classroom teacher* working in consultation with the counselor who serves as a consultant (55).*

It was also recognized a rather long time ago that children and young adolescents welcomed certain guidance and counseling experiences. Among some of the things on which youngsters themselves said they wanted advice or information in the mid-1950's were the following:

1) How to progress in school subjects
2) How to study
3) What their particular school believes to be important to youngsters
4) How to get along with teachers
5) The values of an education
6) How to become acquainted with all of the offerings of the school
7) How to bridge the gap to the succeeding grade
8) To take part in social activities
9) To make effective use of leisure time
10) The value of earning money
11) How to grow up emotionally
12) How to speak before your own age group
13) How to get along more easily with adults
14) To know themselves and others better
15) How to keep and improve their physical and mental health (41:7).

It would seem reasonable then to conclude that the incipient stages of elementary school guidance can be traced historically and that practices and ideas from many professional fields led to the recognition of the importance of elementary guidance which occurred in the mid-1960's.

Increased Vision from the Past

The criticisms of elementary and secondary schools which began in the 1940's grew louder and more caustic in the 1950's. Parents, educators, and interested citizens often voiced their concerns about U.S. educational programs and institutions. They demanded that educators re-examine what they believed in and also determine whether what they were doing was relevant.

*From *Creative School Administration* by Harold G. Shane and Wilbur A. Yauch. Copyright © 1954 by Holt, Rinehart and Winston, Inc. Reprinted by permission of Holt, Rinehart and Winston, Inc.

As a result of these criticisms, both elementary and secondary school curricula were studied and substantial changes began to be made (23). This was done under the burden of serious handicaps as elementary enrollments in the 1940's rapidly expanded toward the 30 million mark. In the years that followed, the schools became ever more overcrowded and funds became even more inadequate for meeting building and personnel needs.

As the 1950's began, curriculum change centered around the up-dating of academic content and on better preparation of students for college. Later in the decade emphasis was placed upon new programs in physical and biological sciences, mathematics, and foreign language. While alarm over Russia's success in beating the U.S. in orbiting the first satellite was not the sole cause for subject matter receiving greater attention in the schools, it was one of the major factors. In 1957 and for some years thereafter there was the fear that faulty education had let Russia outstrip the U.S. in technology. The satellite also lent a sense of urgency to the rapid changes which began to occur in the physical sciences and mathematics programs.

Following initial movements toward curricular change in mathematics and science, social studies received attention along with the teaching of English. There was also some passing concern for improving support for the humanities, arts, and health education but not to the extent that was really needed. It was during the 1950's that vehemently written criticisms by such writers as Arthur Bestor and Hyman Rickover were widely circulated through books and magazine articles. The attacks on education were read with alarm by large numbers of people who saw education as one of the major means through which better lives could be obtained for their children. Obviously, they did not want these children's educations to be debased. As a result, many of the post-sputnik curriculum reforms stressed academic proficiency and mastery of content. Most also were aimed at assisting the middle class child and the college-bound student.

As America moved further into the 1960's, it began to be evident that tremendous changes were taking place in the American way of life. Technology not only knocked on the school house door; it moved right in. In industry, too, the impact of technology was felt by millions of people as certain types of jobs either vanished or became obsolete, and the fears of unemployment assailed many persons ill-equipped to undertake the re-training demanded in an era of rapid change.

By the middle 1960's one heard the strident urgings of the spokesmen for the poverty-stricken and the disadvantaged—a large group of people whose educational welfare had not even been considered as recently as 1958 when Conant wrote his first report on the high schools (14,15). In the late 1960's, the voices of the disadvantaged became louder and were heard more frequently as more citizens asked to participate in and benefit from the abundance that seemed to characterize life in the United States. It seems clear that the past has sharpened the school's vision of what *can* be done to improve education. It remains to be seen what actually *will* be done. In any case, human individuality and human welfare have come to be more fully respected, both for the sake of the individual and of society. With this concern and respect has come more interest in the early and middle years of childhood as both the federal government and private foundations begin to help to support programs for this age level as well as for the young high school dropout and the unemployable adult. All of these developments promise to strengthen and extend guidance programs in elementary educations.

A Preview of the Future for Guidance in Elementary Education

A thoughtful person not only reviews the history of the past, he analyzes the present, and speculates rationally about the future. Some important clues as to possible future directions of elementary guidance can be inferred—developments that are receiving great attention in both educational and popular journals or books at the present time. Among some of the more widely publicized are:

1) changes and uprootings in family life
2) the unprecedented increase in population in the U.S. and overseas
3) major developments in automatic control systems (cybernetics)
4) the problem of the exploding urban areas (megalopolitanism) and rural slums
5) the need for improved international relations; the threat of widespread war
6) increased pollution of the biosphere including massive accumulations of waste materials.

The Nature of "New Directions"

In many sections of our country people representing different professional backgrounds are carefully studying the dynamics of the recent political, economic, social, and technological revolutions of our time. Important elements in our lives, such as the six mentioned above, provide a basis for forecasting and anticipating new dimensions for elementary school guidance. Revolutionary socio-technical changes deserve the great concern and close attention of people interested in the education of young children. Since the counselor is greatly concerned with people, he must be particularly aware of the impact revolutionary changes can have on humans—in their reactions to these changes and in their ability to adjust their lives and to cope with the problems that change is bringing about. What are some of the implications for the elementary school counselor? Changes in American family life serve to illustrate both the changing fabric of society and the tasks with which the counselor is confronted because the change has taken place.

Changing Patterns of Family Life
as Illustrative of
Social Changes Influencing Elementary Guidance

In many parts of America at the turn of the century a clan-like or "tribal" family sense of responsibility for children was prevalent. Many relatives, both old and young, were immediately concerned with a child's welfare in small towns or in urban neighborhoods. As industrialization increased and transportation improved, the "tribal" family began to disappear and was replaced by what might be called the "transitional" family. During this period, although the old clan was remembered with nostalgia and occasional massive family picnics marked special occasions, the immediate family rather than an extended family cared for its young.

Ease of travel by 1930 had made the population even more fluid, and many families left their old home towns and moved into urban areas as they sought better work opportunities. As land values in city areas were high, population concentration demanded a different type of housing. With this came multiple-dwelling units and high rise apartment buildings with many, many people crowded into the smallest amount of space. The "atomistic" family emerged; a small family unit located among a large group of neighbors who remained strangers. This was the antithesis of the tribal family with its great individual acceptance of responsibility for all members of the clan.

The breakdown of the tribal clan and the intensified problems of megalopolitanism are closely related like two sides of the same coin. As many people have moved into new and strange surroundings and into closely compacted areas, so many of our cities have turned from melting pots to pressure cookers. It would seem that elementary counselors are challenged with a threefold task as a result of changes in the family's structure:

1) to help children learn and practice the skills of enforced "togetherness" in crowded areas
2) to lessen or remove threats to individuality in an almost overpowering atmosphere of conformity, sameness, mass opinion, and mass production
3) to find socially acceptable and constructive ways of letting off steam in situations that breed frustration, resentment, and seething discontent

While facing tasks or problems such as those cited, the elementary counselor will want to make certain that he does not consider that difficulties are *solved* just because they are *identified*, and that he goes deeper than accumulating a fund of sloganized half-truths that are too superficial to be of real value to classroom teachers requesting assistance for children with problems.

Some Specific Directions of Change in Guidance Services

While this entire book is concerned with new, action-directing interpretations of elementary guidance programs, six specific areas of future development which should be anticipated during the 1970's are now singled out to suggest the emerging nature of the counselor's work:

1. *The program in elementary school guidance will place much more emphasis on creating an effective and desirable environment for teaching and learning.*

At least since the last quarter of the nineteenth century, scholars have attempted to explain the phenomenon known as learning. The literature is replete with the names of persons who have contributed to the structure of our knowledge: Wundt, Kohler, Wertheimer, Cannon, Lashley, Coghill, Watson, Hilgard, Piaget, Skinner, Vygotsky, Bruner, and so on (28). Over the years, substantial and occasionally surprising insights into teaching and learning have accumulated from psychology and, increasingly, from biology and biochemistry.

In the immediate future elementary counselors will find that they will need to know a great deal more about the environment, motivation, and other factors such as the particular subculture in which a child has membership and how it influences learning if he is to contribute a full measure of leadership. Particular attention will focus on:

a) the modifiable nature of the human organism as new information pertaining to the biological, cognitive, and affective domains is examined and organized

b) human interpersonal relating and the ways its concepts can be taught to every child during the years of early and middle childhood

c) timing, pacing, and the importance of the teachable moment in terms of the individual learner and his transactions with an evocative environment

d) the unifying linkages among bodies of knowledge rather than increased fragmentation of subject matter among the divisions of content

e) the importance of communication and culture not only in terms of the meaning of written and verbal symbols but in non-verbal forms—time, space, distance, and sensory experiences and what they mean to man.

The counselor's task of informing himself in greater depth about learning is made all the more interesting by three problems facing educational psychology. *First*, every person has had some experiences with learning and as a result has opinions and "common sense" explanations that satisfy *him* as to how one learns. This creates a hard-to-convince audience for new theories and applications. As Scriven has noted:

> . . . We find, if we view the study of human behavior as an enterprise to produce systematic information, that a colossal quantity of information (a point which Skinner often has emphasized) has already long since been snapped up and incorporated in our ordinary language . . . . Psychology must begin beyond that level, and that level was founded upon fifty thousand years of close observation of human beings (51:167).

Second, learning is involved with a matrix of virtually infinite variables and complexities that come from a child's unique inner qualities and the sum of his personalized interpretations of the cumulative lifetime of experiences to which he has been exposed.

Third, as will be made more clear in Chapter 2, psychologists' efforts to interpret learning have suffered from the inroads made by "annexation." That is, the psychologists' task of explaining and describing learning and what facilitates it has been encroached upon, and in some instances annexed by, other disciplines such as genetics, pediatrics, biology, biochemistry, or anthropology which also provide research and opinion relevant to learning (51).

The counselor should be aware of significant developments within these fields, and this vital task will be well worth his best efforts. Furthermore, the counselor will want to avoid quick and easy conclusions as to how he and classroom teachers can improve teaching and learning, which are likely to be faulty conclusions.

2. *Related disciplines such as cultural anthropology will provide even more significant "leads" toward new directions in elementary school guidance.*

Fields such as cultural anthropology* offer ideas and research data which can help the counselor at the elementary school level more clearly sense and interpret for teachers the relationship between culture and behavior (33,34).

Reference is made here not so much to the cultures of people in foreign countries as it is to an understanding of the importance of intra-United States

---

*Cultural anthropology in its broadest sense includes: the study of present day cultures (ethnology); the study of dead cultures (archaeology); and the study of speech forms (comparative linguistics).

cultures. Each child is introduced by birth into some one of our subcultures which are permeated by certain guides to behavior: religious, linguistic, social, and so on. One of the counselor's especially appreciated skills, during the coming decade, might well be that of helping elementary school teachers accommodate themselves to, and work effectively with, children whose values, time sense, gesture, language, and motivation differ appreciably from those of youngsters from other socioethnic groups (24,25).

3. *The counselor will find himself moving in new directions because of the increasing application of educational media and technology in elementary school guidance and in general instruction.*

With literally billions of dollars already invested in the "learning business" or "education industry" by United States corporations and by the United States government, it seems inevitable that counseling and guidance services will be profoundly influenced. At least one major development will be in the greater use of information storage and retrieval systems to improve curricular resources, pupil personnel records, and the continuing assessment of learning programs. Quite probably, coded information about children will supplement and, to some extent, supersede anecdotal, academic, and other types of records now largely preserved through laborious hand recording.

Changes have transpired so rapidly with respect to technology that by mid-1967 a dozen school systems throughout the country from New York to California were involved in a Computer-Based Instruction (CBI) venture sponsored by one of the large learning industry combines (20,21). A single 1967 issue of the *Phi Delta Kappan* serves to illustrate the impact of technology and media. This issue of the magazine dealt with such interesting and wide-ranging topics as educational controls, educational engineering, the systems approach, the Department of Defense involvement, the copyright problem, satellites and schools, and the future of educational technology (45).

Initially there has been a tendency in education either to demonize or belittle machines, on the one hand, or to make extravagant claims that technology would solve numerous long standing problems, on the other hand. One of the elementary counselor's opportunities in the next several years may be that of assessing and introducing, as they prove feasible, those techniques or procedures that are successfully tested under his leadership. The combination of education, technology, and big business offers both promises and perils. Many questions must be raised and answered in the years ahead.

4. *There will be a number of new counselor-teacher relationships emerging in the elementary schools.*

There is no reason to doubt that the present dynamic rate of change in all aspects of our lives will lose momentum during the 1970's. At the same time there is considerable precedent for expecting the pace of change to continue to increase in all fields including education. Assuming this to be true, what is likely to develop with respect to the counselor's relationships with principals, psychometrists, classroom teachers, special teachers, psychologists, psychiatric social workers, and similar colleagues?

Insofar as classroom teachers are concerned, it seems certain that the counselor-teacher working relationship will be improved because both will be more professionally prepared. Many teachers will complete the equivalent of five years of preparation before finishing their pre-service education. It is also likely that larger numbers of teachers will develop specialties at the sixth and seventh year levels in order to qualify as leaders in team teaching, as media specialists, and as content experts in reading or science instruction, for example. Counselors will also complete an appreciably more rigorous program of professional specialization that will extend well beyond the new typical one year of study at the master's degree level. Guidance programs should be considerably strengthened as both teachers and counselors become more knowledgeable and sophisticated, each providing specialized resources for the facilitating of an individual's growth.

It is also entirely possible that roles and relationships will be even more modified later in the 1970's by such potential developments as a maximum three-hour pupil contact day for all elementary teachers. The remainder of their time presumably would be devoted to individualized instruction, personal academic preparation, assistance to children using media and following self-instructional programs, planning with clusters or teams of other teachers and specialists such as counselors, conferring with parents, and engaging in a myriad of comparable professional transactions of a sort largely limited to university faculty members in the 1960's and before.

It can be anticipated that a new amalgam of man, media, and machines will have a decided influence on both the tools and the functions of the counselor, the guidance program, and the patterns of personal-professional relationships that are emerging (31).

5. *Changes in the organization of the elementary school will have a marked influence on the guidance program.*

Trends already clearly discernible in educational literature and in emerging practices indicate that the overall organization of U.S. education will assume the form of a continuum extending from nursery to the upper reaches of a vitalized and extended adult education or "lifelong education" concept.

The guidance program at the elementary level can expect to be concerned with a ten- to twelve-year segment of early and middle childhood ranging from age two or three to age twelve or fourteen. This will be a segment of continuing education that will receive even greater attention in our culture as we look for new means for maintaining the vigor, health, and morale of society in the United States.

In this climate for life-long learning, increased attention in elementary guidance will need to be given a) to improved *continuing* guidance services, as distinct from short-term or a "one-shot" or "two-shot" crisis approaches, b) to means of maintaining and transferring information about pupils professionally and efficiently, and c) to meshing or articulating guidance services for the individual as he moves through the different educational programs that comprise the continuum.*

Important opportunities for guidance reside in increased organizational flexibility which is of particular importance where such a special service is concerned. Lifelong guidance services may well be needed in a world in which it is now considered commonplace for an individual to be equipped over a period of time to function vocationally in a sequence of different occupations dictated by the way in which technology creates new jobs while rendering others obsolete.

6. *New settings for learning will influence the directions for future planning of counseling and guidance services.*

Because of their visibility, major changes in school housing will become dramatic symbols of innovation in the next several decades. The new plants should facilitate work in elementary school guidance (17).

Generally, the unimaginative school houses built prior to World War II were replaced with more handsome, better-ventilated and acoustically superior structures during the 1950's and much of the 1960's. Such buildings as were constructed, however, were refinements of old models rather than new types of structures with significant evolutionary changes in their architecture.

Really important new ideas began to appear in scattered instances in the early 1960's. Learning laboratories foreshadowing greater use of technology began to be designed. Movable walls, carpeted floors, individual carrels for studying, programmed instruction, team teaching, and new media caused changes in school plants as educational changes were assessed. The schools were *becoming media* of instruction rather than mere sources of protection from the elements.

As the teaching profession moves further into the 1970's, information coming from urbanologists should shed more light on problems of adults and children living in over-crowded slum areas of the cities.† In the same way, data from sociologists such as James S. Coleman should inform the U.S. more fully as to the educational inequalities which limit the opportunities of Negro and rural poor white students (13). Social class research likewise will make

---

*It is likely that terms such as pre-school, elementary, junior high, senior high, and so on will be changed radically or disappear in the coming decade as a "continuum" is better understood.

†Centers for the study of urban problems are located at several universities and more are planning to establish such centers. The MIT-Harvard Joint Center for Urban Studies was founded in 1959.

teachers and general citizens cognizant of the fact that even new and improved educational settings are still inadequate for meeting today's demanding social and educational needs. City planners, architects, engineers as well as educators, sociologists, and government officials are giving serious attention to these problems.

Will large "educational parks" be the answer for the future—parks that will permit people of all kinds and all ages to live, study, and work together—parks that incorporate schools, recreational opportunities, adult and youth employment centers, museums, theaters, medical clinics, libraries, etc.? Or will they be smaller units—the non-school, preschool, and minischool structures? Will these settings be mere brick and mortar edifices? Or will they be open all year and for a longer day, serving as centers designed for people whose needs, wants, problems, and concerns cannot be conveniently classified and channeled into the traditional rigid time concept that characterizes the present school day?

Hopefully, responsive and supportive environments will be planned—environments that will appeal to all human senses, capacities, and concerns. As James Platt said in the mid-1960's, we may, if we are able to save ourselves in the years ahead, participate in an incredible evolution, the step to man. He states, ". . . we have been men. We are emerging as Man." (47) One measure of our success as "Man" will be the environments we create or re-create.

Much more might be said of the educational future which, with almost alarming speed, is becoming today's way of life and then yesterday's history. Enough has been said to indicate that guidance in the elementary school years promises to have an exciting and socially useful future in the "Great Schoolhouse" of pooled learning resources for tomorrow. Here is a summary of a few points that pertain to the elementary school counselor.

New resources and the speed with which they can be utilized will be vastly increased. Opportunities to help young children through guidance will be much enhanced, and the variety of procedures and choices will multiply. New information will be provided from many different disciplines and professions; the setting for counseling will become broader—one that is more life-centered than it is school-centered; and the means for studying and helping children will be improved as new knowledge and technological devices enable the counselor to help children attain higher and better levels of self-understanding and self-direction.

The nature of "new directions" in counseling taxes the imagination of all concerned because *virtually everything mentioned above with respect to socioeducational changes and developments already exists somewhere in some form.*

Some Implications of New Directions
for the Elementary School Counselor

For the counselor of *today*, what are some of the inferences that can be drawn from our backward glances and our future conjectures about the educational programs of tomorrow? At least two implications seem clear: it is necessary to grasp and to accept the sweep of change; it is important to seek and maintain leadership by facilitating rather than opposing what appears to be the path of reasoned educational change.

The effectiveness of the counselor is enhanced by his ability to comprehend and accept change even as he accepts his youthful clients. This is both a psychological *and* a cognitive challenge. It is also affective in that it involves emotional as well as intellectual acceptance of change and the use of the innovations it makes possible.

Facilitating Educational Change

To facilitate educational change one must first understand it as proposed above, then transfer such general understandings to his field of special competence. In elementary guidance this involves a number of considerations:

1) Determining the implications of change for the more effective performance of the particular guidance tasks related to elementary education

2) Being mindful of the definite or anticipated problems and opportunities generated by social change in and out of school and the accompanying effect on the self-concepts, attitudes, and behavior of children and their parents

3) Keeping alert to changes—or needed changes in the curriculum and how individual children are responding

4) Taking steps to insure that one's self-education is directed so as to help one serve as an agent of change, including contributing to the re-education of one's teacher-colleagues where possible

5) Bearing in mind the importance of one's colleagues as sources of help—and persons in need of help—in living with rapid change. Both the knowledge and support of the faculty of an elementary school is needed for a meaningful program. In a period of rapidly changing ideas, facilities, and events close working relationships are a prerequisite for sound changes

The basic personal equipment the elementary school counselor needs for his job clearly suggests that the field is not one for a person who lacks a strong sense of commitment. There is a great deal to be learned about people and their personal, social, and vocational needs. There is also a great deal to be learned about children of elementary school age, about educationally desirable programs, and about the services and functions most needed to help people achieve both individually and socially desirable goals. In a word, *professional* study is needed to give meaning to *commitment*, and *intelligence* is essential to give strength to both. Schiller, the German poet and dramatist, phrased it very well: *Mit der Dummheit kämpfen Götter selbst vergebens.* "With stupidity the gods themselves do battle in vain."

For the important responsibilities in the elementary school, counseling and guidance programs require the best talent available.

Summary

Chapter 1 introduces the purpose of the book: to help students understand both elementary education and how to apply counseling and guidance skills with younger children.

The historically interesting background of guidance in elementary schools reviews the contributions from years past and appraises them with respect to their application for the present. Broad social trends are presented as well as conjectures about the future. These trends—both in the very broad social sense and in the narrower educational sense—provide new directions for elementary school guidance programs. The nature of new directions and the implications of new directions for both education practice and program are presented.

References

1. Armstrong, Robert J., Terry D. Cornell, Robert E. Kraner, E. Wayne Roberson. *Development and Evaluation of Behavioral Objectives.* Worthington, Ohio: Charles A. Jones Publishing Co., 1970.

2. Barr, John A. *The Elementary Teacher and Guidance.* New York: Holt, Rinehart and Winston, Inc., 1958.

3. Beers, Clifford. *A Mind That Found Itself.* New York: Doubleday and Co., Inc., 1908.

4. Berelson, Bernard and Gary A. Steiner. *Human Behavior: An Inventory of Scientific Findings.* New York: Harcourt, Brace and World., Inc., 1964.

5. Blocher, Donald. *Developmental Counseling.* New York: The Ronald Press, 1966.

6. Bossard, James H. S. *The Sociology of Child Development*. New York: Harper and Bros., 1948.

7. Boulding, Kenneth. *The Meaning of the Twentieth Century*. New York: Harper and Row, Publishers, 1964.

8. Boykin, J. C. "Class Intervals in City Public Schools." *Report of the Commissioner of Education* 2 (1890-1891).

9. Bross, Irwin D. *Design for Decision*. New York: The Free Press, 1965.

10. Burk, Frederic. *Remedy for Lock Step Schooling*. Winnetka, Ill.: The Winnetka Education Press, 1935. (Originally published by the Department of Education, State of California in 1909.)

11. Burnham, William. *Great Teachers and Mental Health*. New York: D. Appleton and Co., 1926.

12. ____. *The Normal Mind*. New York: D. Appleton and Co., 1924.

13. Coleman, James S., et al. *Equality of Educational Opportunity*. Washington, D.C.: U.S. Department of Health, Education, and Welfare, 1966.

14. Conant, James B. *The American High School Today*. New York: McGraw-Hill Book Co., 1959.

15. ____. *Slums and Suburbs*. New York: McGraw-Hill Book Co., 1961.

16. Davis, Allison, Burleigh B. Gardner, and Mary R. Gardner. *Deep South: A Social-Anthropological Study of Caste and Class*. Chicago: University of Chicago Press, 1941.

17. *Educational Change and Architectural Consequences*. New York: Educational Facilities Laboratories, 1968.

18. Erikson, Erik. "Problems of Infancy and Early Childhood." *Encyclopedia of Medicine, Surgery, and Specialties*. Philadelphia: F. A. Davis Co., 1940.

19. Faust, Vernon. *History of Elementary School Counseling: Overview and Critique*. Boston: Houghton Mifflin Co., 1968.

20. "Flanagan: A Consultant Comments." *Phi Delta Kappan* 49 (September, 1967): 32-33.

21. Flanagan, John C. "Functional Education for the Seventies." *Phi Delta Kappan* 49 (September, 1967): 27-32.

22. Garry, Ralph. *Guidance Techniques for Elementary Teachers*. Columbus, Ohio: Charles E. Merrill Books, Inc., 1966.

23. Goodlad, John I., et al. *The Changing School Curriculum*. New York: The Fund for the Advancement of Education, 1966.

24. Hall, Edward T. *The Hidden Dimension*. New York: Doubleday and Co., Inc., 1966.

25. ____. *The Silent Language*. New York: Fawcett World Library: Premier Books, 1969.

26. Havighurst, Robert J. *Developmental Tasks and Education*. New York: Longmans, Green and Co., 1950. (First copyright 1948 by the University of Chicago Press.) (Havighurst says the first publication to give the concept a central role was 1942 North Central Association's book, *General Education in the American High School* in which he, Prescott, and Redl wrote Chapter 4.) Havighurst states that he first heard the term used by Lawrence K. Frank, who along with Caroline Zachry, probably got the kernel of the idea from the 1930 writings of Frankwood Williams which emphasized the developmental problems of adolescence. The term was

discussed at meetings of the Adolescent Study Staff of the Progressive Education Association. The term "task" was first used in print by Peter Blos—not as a concept, but as an illustration—in 1941.

27. *Helping Teachers Understand Children.* Washington, D.C.: The American Council on Education, 1945.

28. Hilgard, Ernest R. (ed.). *Theories of Learning and Instruction.* LXII *Yearbook.* National Society for the Study of Education. Chicago: University of Chicago Press, 1964. The reader seeking to refresh his memory will find an excellent résumé of teaching and learning theory.

29. Hollingshead, August B. *Elmtown's Youth: The Impact of Social Class on Adolescence.* New York: John Wiley and Sons, Inc., 1949.

30. Hosic, James F. *The Cooperative Group Plan.* New York: Teachers College Press, 1929.

31. Joyce, Bruce R. *The Teacher and His Staff: Man, Media, and Machines.* Washington, D.C.: Center for the Study of Instruction, National Education Association, 1967.

32. Kluckhohn, Clyde and H. A. Murphy. *Personality in Nature, Society, and Culture.* New York: Alfred A. Knopf, Inc., 1948.

33. Kneller, George F. *Educational Anthropology: An Introduction.* New York: John Wiley and Sons, Inc., 1965.

34. Landes, Ruth. *Culture in American Education.* New York: John Wiley and Sons, Inc., 1965.

35. Leonard, George. "A Hopeful Look at Education in 2000 A.D." *Planning for Education in Litchfield Park in 2000 A.D.* Edited by Harold E. Moore. Educational Services Bulletin No. 21. Tempe, Ariz.: Arizona State University Bureau of Publications, January, 1967.

36. Lewin, Kurt, Ronald Lippitt, and R. K. White. "The Social Climate of Children's Groups." *Child Behavior and Development.* Edited by R. Barker, J. S. Kaunin, and H. F. Wright. New York: McGraw-Hill Book Co., 1943.

37. McGaughy, J. R. *An Evaluation of the Elementary School.* Indianapolis, Ind.: The Bobbs-Merrill Co., 1937.

38. Maslow, A. H. "Preface to Motivation Theory." *Psychosomatic Medicine* 5 (1943): 85-92.

39. ____. "A Theory of Human Motivation." *Psychological Review* 50 (1943): 370-396.

40. Meeks, Anna. *Guidance in Elementary Education.* New York: The Ronald Press, 1968.

41. O'brien, Margaret. "Viewpoints in Guidance in the Elementary School." *Counseling and Guidance Services in Education Today.* Edited by Frank W. Miller. Evanston, Ill.: School of Education, Northwestern University, 1951.

42. Ohlsen, Merle M. *Guidance Services in the Modern School.* New York: Harcourt, Brace and World, Inc., 1955.

43. Olson, Willard. *Child Development.* Boston: D.C. Heath and Co., 1949.

44. Otto, Henry J. "Historical Sketches of Administrative Innovations." *Educational Administration and Supervision* 20 (March, 1943): 161-172.

45. *Phi Delta Kappan* 48 (January, 1967): 185-256.

46. Plant, James. *Personality and the Cultural Patterns*. London: H. Milford, 1937.

47. Platt, James R. "The Step to Man." *Science* 149 (August 6, 1965): 607-613.

48. Prescott, Daniel (ed.). *Emotion and the Educative Process*. Washington, D.C.: American Council on Education, 1938. See also chapter reference to the benchmark study, *Helping Teachers to Understand Children* for which Prescott was a consultant.

49. Raths, Louis. *An Application to Education of the Needs Theory*. New York: School of Education, New York University, 1949.

50. Rogers, Carl. *Counseling and Psychotherapy*. Boston: Houghton Mifflin Co., 1941.

51. Scriven, Michael. "Views of Human Nature." *Behaviorism and Phenomenology*. Edited by T. W. Wann. Chicago: University of Chicago Press, 1965. © 1965 by The University of Chicago Press. All rights reserved.

52. Search, Preston W. "Individual Teaching and The Pueblo Plan." *Educational Review* 7 (February, 1894): 154-170.

53. Shane, Harold G. "Future Shock and the Curriculum: Education's Collision with Tomorrow." *Phi Delta Kappan* 49 (October, 1967): 67-70.

54. ____ and E. T. McSwain. *Evaluation and the Elementary Curriculum*. Revised edition. New York: Henry Holt and Co., 1958.

55. ____ and W. A. Yauch. *Creative School Administration*. New York: Henry Holt and Co., 1954.

56. Shertzer, Bruce and Shelley C. Stone. *Fundamentals of Guidance*. Boston: Houghton Mifflin Co., 1966.

57. Skeels, H. M. and H. Dye. "A Study of the Effects of Differential Stimulation in Mentally Retarded Children." *Proceedings of the American Association for Mental Deficiency* 44 (1939): 114-136.

58. Skodak, Marie and H. M. Skeels. "A Final Follow-up Study of 100 Adopted Children." *Journal of Genetic Psychology* 75 (1949): 85-125.

59. Snow, Sir Charles P. *The Two Cultures and a Second Look*. New York: Mentor Books, 1964.

60. Stendler, Cecilia. *Children of Brasstown*. Urbana, Ill.: University of Illinois Press, 1949.

61. Thompson, Sir George. *The Foreseeable Future*. Cambridge, Mass.: Harvard University Press, 1960.

62. Warner, W. L. and Paul Lunt. *The Social Life of a Modern Community*. New Haven, Conn.: Yale University Press, 1941.

63. Washburne, Carleton W. *A Living Philosophy of Education*. New York: The John Day Co., 1940.

64. Willey, Roy DeVerl. *Guidance in Elementary Education*. New York: Harper and Bros., 1952.

65. Zirbes, Laura. *Focus on Values in Elementary Education*. New York: G. P. Putnam's Sons, 1960.

66. ____. *Spurs to Creative Teaching*. New York: G. P. Putnam's Sons, 1959.

2

Foundations for the Elementary School Counseling and Guidance Program

The elementary school counselor at the present time enters a field of leadership activities in which there are relatively few clearly established precedents. Certainly, working with young persons in the first six or eight years of formal schooling must not involve a wholesale or even partial downward extension of secondary school techniques and practices. Indeed, many components of the high school program such as vocational counseling, occupational information, placement, and follow-up have very different meanings and applications at the elementary school level, if they apply at all. Neither does elementary counseling and guidance involve a large-scale take-over of certain functions traditionally performed by teachers who, in most schools, have had no specialist in this area to provide professional assistance.

The Unique Value of the School Counselor

What, then, are the functions and contributions of the counselor at the elementary level? The unique value of the specialist is not just a matter of what he *does* in his field of expertise. It is also a matter of *degree*—the degree or extent to which he contributes to the successful deployment of school and community resources to direct and to improve the ongoing educational experiences for all children during their elementary school years.

To some extent, many things that a counselor does in his work with children have been undertaken in some school situations by educationally creative teachers, school psychologists, psychiatric social workers, versatile and sensitive elementary principals, remedial specialists, or special educators who work with either the "normal child" or with those having special mental, physical, or emotional problems. However, it is the greater breadth of the counselor's familiarity with the role of total available resources and his acquired ability to use them for guiding human development that make him an important agent in the attainment of individual and educational goals. The status, the acceptance, and the contribution of the elementary school counselor reside both in the *merit* of his ideas and the *depth* of his knowledge and skills in carrying them out.

We have already endeavored, in Chapter 1, to emphasize the peculiarly important need for the counselor's personal competence, and we reiterate it here for emphasis. No role in elementary education in the years immediately ahead is likely to be more demanding than that of the school counselor. In order to lead through merit, he must have a sense of commitment and the motivation to prepare himself professionally for the task. The present chapter and others which follow in Part One are designed to suggest and explain the many developments not only in guidance per se, but in other fields and specialties that have a bearing on contemporary elementary education. These the counselor will wish to explore and study, and with them he must also maintain a continuing life long acquaintance.

Lest this proposed level of competence seem unreasonably high—and demands for academic preparation potentially too arduous and expensive—one point should be made. Various stages of advanced counselor preparation should be anticipated over a period of several years; or more accurately, a continuum of study is envisioned at the graduate level. The "continuum of study" described later in Chapter 5 suggests developmental experiences for elementary counselors which are reasonable, relevant, and necessary in terms of the purposes of an effective counseling and guidance program in elementary education.

Understanding Young Children

The proposition that counselors in elementary education should "understand" the individual boys and girls who are in the pre-school and elementary school programs could not have been made a few years ago with any degree of sophistication. Persons working in the elementary schools today represent the first generation in history really to have access to a modest amount of human development information about the important young personalities whom they serve. Now and in the years ahead there will be a continued need to pursue with sustained purpose studies relating to human behavior.

Research and theory in a number of disciplines are combining to provide school counselors with some important foundations for their work with teachers and children. *Understanding* a child, however, involves appreciably more than completing a few disparate courses in, say, educational psychology, elementary education, or counseling and guidance. Changes are transpiring with such speed and in so many areas of inquiry that specialists in any one realm may be quite out of date, or completely unacquainted with what is germinating in such fields as cybernetics, neurophysiology, linguistics, urbanology, molecular genetics, pharmacology, or biochemistry. Yet developments in these fields promise to have a marked influence upon human life (45).

Much of this book deals directly with the challenges of learning to know children. The task is especially important to school counselors because it entails a considerable depth of understanding of related disciplines as well as of curriculum and school organization—in addition to understanding counseling and guidance techniques, skills, and procedures.

Counseling, Guidance, and the Understanding of Human Development

As concepts of elementary school counseling and guidance emerge, the importance of this field and of qualified counselors becomes increasingly conspicuous. At one time in U.S. history the elementary school was a place in which a few formal skills in ciphering, reading, spelling, and writing supplemented the "real" education—what a child learned from his family and neighbors on the isolated farms and small towns of 18th and 19th Century America. The teacher of the time often was more of a tradesman than a professional, and his status and salary reflected the humorous but also somewhat contemptuous dictum, "Those who can't do, teach."

Technological, social, and economic changes of the present century, and especially of the past 50 years, have virtually eliminated from the American scene the remnants of a world in which children acquired many of their life skills in the mills, kitchens, and shops of small towns.

As the home and village environment became a less comprehensive source of education for life activities, the institution we call the elementary school became of increased importance. Gradually it became one of our society's major means of introducing the child to the organized way of life we call culture. In addition, the humane implications of democracy for education began to be more fully understood. As Lawrence A. Cremin phrased it:

> In the last analysis, there is no more humane view of education than as growth in understanding, sensibility, and character, and no more noble view of democracy than as the dedication of society to the education of all its members (13:35).

It was as this educational change occurred that the concept of guiding human development in elementary education began to assume greater importance, although *practice* lagged far behind *need.*

In addition to the larger load of responsibility which society began to place on the schools in this century, rapid changes in our ways of living, as previously noted, increased the schools' responsibilities. Many of the forces or events making for increased complexity and for accompanying confusion, insecurity, and frustrating uncertainty were so well publicized from pulpit, press, radio, and television as to need no more than a mention rather than explanation to call their importance to mind. As implied in Chapter 1, they include such things as: exploding city populations, problems of the culturally different, increasing federal involvement in local government, interracial stresses, changes in family life, an increase in life-spans and in the ranks of the elderly, U.S. commitments in and to countries overseas, presumed threats to individuality, use of hallucinogenic drugs, greatly extended influence of mass media, space exploration, poverty amidst increased affluence, extension of the scope and content of education, the knowledge explosion, applications of the computer, etc. (6,9).

Some of the magnitude of these changes is made evident by Donald N. Michael in *The Unprepared Society.* He warns that the extent and the speed of certain social and technological trends are taking us toward ". . . much more extensive use of long-range planning even though we are ill-prepared institutionally, methodologically, and personally to do it well . . . [furthermore] the type of education needed to realize the opportunities and avoid the threats in this situation is not at all likely to be available as soon as we will need it or on the required scale." (34:3)

Our point is that in the face of rapid and extensive technological, social, and educational changes there is a most pressing need for guidance (and its concomitant, skilled counseling) to be concerned with a broad understanding of human development, which is important for planning the content and the experiences of the curriculum. In-depth understanding of human development is essential if one is concerned with human interactions and transactions as mediations required between content and individual children. This is the challenge to counseling and guidance that is implicit in Michael's pessimistic comment.

A recent statement from Robert H. Anderson, a Harvard University professor in the field of elementary education, suggested eight road-blocks to more progress in educating children (1). Guidance, as conceived in these pages, is not only concerned with removing such impediments as the eight listed below; it is also concerned with cultivation of the counselor's knowledge of human development.

Anderson's eight problems or barriers to be surmounted include 1) reducing the gap between what we *are* doing and *could* do in the schools, 2) overcoming the *increasing* gap between knowledge and practice, 3) increasing the rate at which children learn, 4) attaining greater teacher competence through increased command of a special field, 5) evaluating and adopting educational technologies, 6) making a break-through with respect to provision for individual needs, 7) helping teachers gain professional skill and knowledge that will further distinguish them from the well-educated nonteacher college graduate, and 8) increasing excellence, efficiency, and flexibility in education without harming the personality of teacher or child.

The years ahead already promise to be even more dramatic and more critical than those an earlier generation spanned in moving from the horse and buggy days to the space age. In moving from a technologically based society into a service oriented society, tremendous changes confront both the individual and society. Both a flexible and humane version of *men* is required if tomorrow's life is to become rich and fully satisfying for *man*.

Clearly, the judgment one must exercise in successfully approaching these years ahead involves knowing children. Counselors in the elementary school must have a substantial knowledge of human development if they are to contribute to the realization of this goal.

The Counselor's Insights into Related Disciplines

What does it mean to "know" a child? As noted previously, the present generation of teachers and school counselors is among the first to begin to find out. On the whole, our knowledge of the learner has tended to come from *without* rather than from *inside* the teaching profession—in which, of course, the field of counseling and guidance is included. As an important part of the counselor's fundamental knowledge of elementary school children, therefore, he should have some insights into how scholarly disciplines have helped shape the conclusions which currently support and direct youngsters' school experiences. An explanation of what is meant by "contributions from related disciplines" follows.

Understanding Related Disciplines

The word *discipline* once meant *education*. That is, "to discipline" was "to educate." Today the term refers to a field of specialized study. When "related to education," it is construed to be a field which directly contributes to education through its content (as in mathematics or physics) or through the light it sheds on learning and behavior (as in anthropology, biology, or psychology).

A considerable amount of direction, not always widely recognized, has been given to elementary school counseling and guidance by such fields as anthropology, psychology, psychiatry, philosophy, and sociology among others. However, the guidelines are not tightly drawn, and new information that outmodes some of the thinking we have done in the past continues to become available. The counselor should have some knowledge of what other fields such as these have and have not contributed. It is unfortunate to be ignorant of such contributions and equally unfortunate to imagine that more has been contributed than actually is the case.

Some Illustrations of Contributions

The speed with which events occur and developments transpire today makes it difficult to present examples of the most contemporary contributions from related disciplines. There is the risk of producing a list that is already becoming obsolete a few months or a year or two after it is compiled. For this reason, the writers have chosen not merely to introduce a few of the more current studies but also to provide a perspective of some long-term contributions from other fields. With some temerity, we have not resisted the temptation to include a very small sampling of significant and recent developments.

Contributions from Content Fields

One of the oldest and most familiar ways in which other fields contribute to education is in the area of substantive content. We shall mention rather than elaborate on such contributions since many books have appeared on such things as the so-called "new mathematics," the "new science," or the application of linguistics to the improvement of work in the language arts. Probably, without exception, every academic discipline has made at least a clearly discernible contribution to the substantive content children encounter during the first six to eight years in school. While it is important for counselors to have some general understanding of the content fields in which some young students may encounter problems—it is disciplines which illuminate human behavior that are most relevant to their particular professional role.

Psychology and Human Development. Traditionally, psychology has been one of the disciplines most intimately related to childhood education. Psychology along with its first cousins measurement, educational psychology, and human development studies is of especial importance to the counselor because of the nature of his concern for children and the educative process. For a clear understanding of the elementary school it is essential for the counselor to understand how psychology was weaned from its mother, meta-physics, in the 19th century and started on its way to becoming a methodical study of behavior by persons like William James, G. Stanley Hall, Wilhelm Wundt, and Joseph M. Rice. Freud, Jung, and Adler subsequently had an important role in probing man's inner being. The understanding of learning was advanced by the Gestaltists such as Kohler, Koffka, and Wertheimer; while behaviorists like Lashley and Watson proposed the connectionist theory or S→R interpretations of learning. This inherited body of information is important to have at one's command since many present practices stemmed from and are still influenced by it. These include certain basic teaching methods, certain approaches to therapy, and certain forms of programmed learning.

Related work by such "giants" in the early era of testing or assessment as Binêt, Terman, Thorndike, and Pintner is also important. Corporate or cooperative development of scales and tests, such as those by the Educational Testing Service of Princeton and Science Research Associates of Chicago, however, has largely replaced major test development by individuals in the Binêt tradition. Certainly, testing remains an important although controversial field closely tied to elementary education (24).

Elementary guidance today has been influenced by a number of ideas and concepts in the blurred borderland between psychology and human development research. Widely known contributions, some of which were mentioned in Chapter 1, are Gesell's longitudinal studies of infants' and children's growth; Olson's idea of "organismic age"; Havighurst's "developmental tasks"; and Erikson's "Eight Ages of Man." Havighurst's and Erikson's work is frequently referred to in the literature of guidance and in counseling.*

At the present time it is prudent for students of elementary school guidance to be aware of how learning theory and our knowledge of human development and its evaluation have been extended through work in psychology.

---

*So well-known to the teaching profession are Gesell, Olson, Havighurst, Erikson, and others whose names appear here that a sampling of their writings generally is not included in the chapter readings. If by chance the elementary counselor is unfamiliar with the place of such persons in the literature, he should become acquainted with their importance.

It is equally important to recognize that insights regarding both the learner and learning continue to accumulate. For example, for many years it was assumed that intelligence was fixed and unchangeable. In fact, so established was this belief that when Skeel's and Skodak's work in the thirties questioned this idea, their findings were severely criticized (2). Even today many people labor under the conception of fixed intelligence ignoring new possibilities that could be developed for educating people previously believed to be un-teachable. How important it is that professional people be aware of new developments within fields. Recognizing that opportunities for rich and varied experiences are important in the nurturing of intelligence—and that their neglect may be highly detrimental to the individual—is an important concept for a school counselor to understand. The psychology of human development specialists have had their work extended by experiments in the chemistry of learning and memory.

Cultural Anthropology. For 25 or 30 years books on education have made tantalizing, and oftentimes vague, allusions to the educational contributions and significant research bearing on the schools made by the field of anthropology. What are some examples and how do they relate to the school counselor?

First, cultural anthropology has exploded the turn-of-the-century idea that certain races of mankind were inherently (i.e., genetically) inferior—a matter of singular importance in human relations, integration, civil rights, etc. (3). Also, the way in which environment and experience influence human nature has been clarified through cultural anthropological study, a field of inquiry opened up by Franz Boas at Columbia University. In his concept of culture, according to one of his widely known students, Margaret Mead, human beings were dependent on *learned* ways of life. Their behavior was not the result of instincts of heredity (33). M. F. Ashley Montagu, the geneticist-anthropologist, was even more precise in noting, for example, that the evil in our nature is not innate but acquired. "Aggressiveness is taught, as are all forms of violence which human beings exhibit." (36:172)

Clearly, the conclusions of Boas and others in the last 40 years have affirmed the meaning, purpose, and potential influence of education—including guidance in the elementary school. Since the nature of the individual human is greatly influenced by his milieu, the importance of the work of the counselor-teacher team in improving the psychological input from the child's environment is enhanced accordingly. To put it even more succinctly, cultural anthropology tends to support the value of applying concepts of guidance in the early years of school and underscores their importance.

In the 1950's and 1960's, sophisticated thinking and research by Benjamin L. Whorf and Edward T. Hall, both linguistic anthropologists, added to our understandings of how the language of a given culture influences behavior and conceptualization (52,23). In his important book, *The Silent Language,* Dr. Hall discusses how membership in a subculture influences a person's behavior (23). He treats culture as a form of communication in explaining how our manners and behaviors often speak more loudly than words as we interact with other people both in the United States and in other countries. This book, along with his *The Hidden Dimension,* increased our understanding of how man's sense of space is molded and patterned by his culture (22). Through studies of people's different uses of their sensory apparatus, Hall points out, conflict and distorted communication may be minimized or avoided. It seems certain that education will continue to learn a great deal from activity going on in this discipline.

Sociology. The point that the sociologist and the educator share many common concerns and overlapping purposes is inherent in the scope of sociology. The sociologist is interested in human groups: their structure, development and interactions, as well as their institutions. He provides a substantial portion of the foundation on which guidance practices are based in elementary education.

Some examples of sociologically oriented research range from Robert S. and Helen M. Lynd's two classic Middletown studies which probed the anatomy of a middlewestern community, Muncie, Indiana (29,30), to social class inquiries by Lloyd Warner (49,50,51) and A. B. Hollingshead (25). Inquiries such as these have done a great deal for counselors in providing insights about the group matrices in which the individual spends his life.

The field of sociometry pioneered by J. L. Moreno in the 1930's probably can be classified under sociology (37). Moreno, following a study of interpersonal problems among female inmates of a state institution, developed theories regarding measurement of the nature and quality of relationships within a group. Sociograms and assorted sociometric devices had come into extensive use by the 1950's and are discussed elsewhere when we consider the tools of guidance in elementary education.

The wide-ranging interests of the sociologist in the 1940's, 1950's, and 1960's from Gunnar Myrdal's monumental study of the Negro in the U.S. (38), through C. Wright Mills' *White Collar* (35), to Basil Bernstein's current research in social class and its linguistic concomitants (5) are of such variety as to defy simple categorization. Suffice to say that they have added up to a lively body of data which can be of value to the counselor. Through the counselor's knowledge of sources treating the sociological pressures of race, class, language, etc., which help shape childhood, he can considerably help each individual to maximize his opportunities for living and learning.

Biology and Biochemistry. In a discussion with two of the writers in Geneva during 1965, Jean Piaget, the internationally recognized Swiss psychologist, expressed the opinion that we would discover more about learning and development in the future from biology than from psychology (43). What are past and present biological or biochemical developments that support this distinguished scholar's opinion?

Periodically, there have been studies that have given educators greater depth perception in their field because of biology. W. B. Cannon's classic *Wisdom of the Body* is, despite its age, a good example of intellectually exciting ideas (8), as is George E. Coghill's *Anatomy and the Problem of Behavior* (1929), an early venture in explaining the neurological bases of behavior, the complex interrelationships of organic development, and the way in which bio-development is influenced by environment (11).

In recent years work in genetics—including the inducement of controlled mutations, the influence of drugs on mental processes and on human development, and the study of old age as a disease and subject to substantial postponement—are ventures with conceivably important socio-educational consequences. It is particularly desirable for school counselors to be alert for other publications which cast light on behavior such as Charles H. Southwick's report on primates' intergroup behavior (46) and John B. Calhoun's longitudinal study of deliberately changed patterns of living among wild Norwegian rats (7).

Among educationally portentous biochemical contributions are those of Dr. Bernard Agranoff of the University of Michigan's medical school; particularly, his work on memory as mediated by such antibiotics as puromycin (28). Dr. James McGaugh's work at the University of California at Riverside has also been cited for his central nervous system studies of metrazol and other drugs related to memory processes (28).

In short, it seems likely that mind, mood, and memory may be modified or improved during the next decade or two by biochemistry.

> While pharmacies and surgical suites operated by boards of education seem unlikely to dominate our schools, there is reason to believe that very early school contacts with children who have personality and learning problems may permit chemical therapy to reclaim boys and girls who otherwise would become liabilities to society (44).

David Krech has coined the term *psychoneurobiochemeducation* to describe the current interdisciplinary study of chemistry and learning (27). By 1968 he and other scholars felt confident enough to state:

> It is now abundantly clear that . . . thinking and learning are vastly more complicated processes than traditional stimulus-response learning theory would suggest and the panelists seemed to agree that what has passed for "learning theory" in psychology texts is irrelevant and probably incorrect. Indeed, some members suggested that no more books called "learning theory" will be written: future texts will be titled, "Problems (or Processes) of Learning and Memory." (26)

Patently, in psychoneurobiochemeducation there are certain to be break-throughs that will be germane to elementary education. Many of these are reviewed by G. R. Taylor in his widely read book, *The Biological Time Bomb* (47). In the years ahead, counselors face a task of deciding whether they agree with B. F. Skinner's statement—it has become "... the duty of our society to attempt actively to control human behavior in such a way as to achieve the effects we consider desirable before some other group be-comes more proficient at controlling behavior and directing it into paths we consider undesirable."

Leadership in guidance, as previously pointed out, should depend on ideas of merit which may improve elementary programs. By being aware of significant developments in other fields, new ideas can be generated to improve counseling and guidance programs.

Communications: Mass Media. Although the interests of specialists in communication theory and in educational media extend backwards through time for many years, the general public has become aware of the impact of mass media and the communications speed-up only since the early 1960's. Films and slides began to be used in elementary schools during the 1920's. By the 1930's teachers had some idea of communication as an area of study and had begun to acquire a rather dim awareness of the influence of language on behavior. In the 1940's Edgar Dale's widely read *Audio-Visual Methods in Teaching* first appeared and made many persons aware of the versatility and impact of education media (14). By the mid-1950's "communication theory" was well established as the methodical study of the complex process of sharing meanings of all kinds.

The new significance of mass media communications, however, did not become apparent to most persons until the 1960's. It was then recognized that technology had reached a point where many of the world's people, at any time, soon could have contact both verbal and visually with anyone else on the globe (40). Psychologically, socially, educationally, and *certainly with respect to guidance,* we need to learn as much as we can about the implications of the new face-to-face contact among people everywhere, and the possible changes which mass media may stimulate in behavior.

Public sensitivity and perhaps some uneasiness as to the influence of television was evident in 1967 when within a few weeks the ideas and theories of Marshall McLuhan were publicized in such widely read journals as *Time, Newsweek,* and *Saturday Review,* among others (31). McLuhan, as a spokesman for media and an interpreter of their influence, is important—regardless of whether his theories prove to be lasting ones. Among his con-jectures: mass media are "retribalizing" mankind by altering his sensory life; the *medium* used in communicating is inseparable from its *meaning* and accordingly shapes the *message* (32).

School counselors will want to keep abreast of developments in mass media and communications even though some of the publicity media received proves to be overblown. After all, by the time many young adolescents have finished the secondary school, they will have spent 3 hours televiewing for every 2 hours spent in the classroom (40). Studies in communication are equally deserving of consideration as the counselor continually strives to communicate or find "common understanding" with children. Much help can also be derived from studies in the field of linguistics, particularly semantics, psycholinguistics, and sociolinguistics (42).

Cybernetics. Automatic control systems, the field of cybernetics, has been selected to round off this sampling of elements which are providing foundations for past, present, and future changes in elementary schools and in their counseling and guidance programs. Just as *television* is a major element in present-day mass media, so the computer is a central element in the cybernetic approach to the programming of instruction. By 1968, computer based instruction (CBI) and individually planned instruction based on analysis of the learner's background and purposes was moving from the experimental to the applied state. As noted in Chapter 1, a dozen well-known school systems were cooperating with the American Institutes of Research and the Westinghouse Learning Corporation during 1967 in an attempt to tailor individual learning experiences to the individual child in various academic fields (16). This is but one of a number of ventures in planning technologically individualized instruction. An examination of these developments makes immediately apparent the stake which elementary school counselors have in relation to the inexorably expanding use of computers in teaching-learning situations.

The computer, as used in certain current programs, retrieves background data, for example, for an 11-year-old. After tentative goals have been established through teacher-pupil planning, the student receives—again via computer—descriptions of several teaching-learning units in various academic fields which are deemed congruent with his background. Assessment of progress (e.g., test scoring), selection of new units, and cumulative records are all handled by computer (16).

Patently, such developments could be extended rapidly as smaller schools are linked to central control systems. These innovations plainly have implications for the guidance function as identified in Chapter 1, namely, deploying with professional knowledge and skill all available human and material resources at the school's command in order to effect socially desirable changes in children's individual and group learning environments.

The counselor needs to keep himself advised of what CBI can and cannot do at present, and what it is likely to accomplish in the future. Further, he will want to evaluate cybernetically oriented educational changes with the sort of thoughtfulness displayed by a *Phi Delta Kappan* consultant who has raised a number of relevant questions regarding computerized techniques. Among points on which information is needed: 1) the nature of suitable content; 2) the influence of CBI on children who learn slowly; 3) age levels at which CBI can be used effectively; and 4) the extent to which behavior and behavioral goals can be meshed with automechanisms (15).

The matter of certain social, individual, and group experiences, the importance of which was stressed by the Coleman Report in its treatment of equality of educational opportunity also becomes relevant as we seek to develop greater skill and wisdom using computer based instruction (12). Like the other fields singled out for attention as areas of specialized study, cybernetics has great promise as a source of contribution to education.

Drawing on related disciplines—studying and annexing relevant ideas—is particularly important in education. This is because education is primarily concerned with applied knowledge. In other words, many important innovations can be made efficiently in education only if counselors and teachers aggressively look for new developments in related disciplines as well as in their own. This knowledge must be studied by counselors and teachers to determine what implications it has for newer programs and practices.

Understanding Trends in Elementary Education

A professional knowledge of children is an obvious part of the personal foundation that the school counselors need to acquire. Indeed, the responsibility for increasing the wholesome psycho-social development and intellectual progress in children inherently requires that the counselor have a depth of insight into the inner world of childhood in which emotion, aspiration, motivation, interest, and dozens of similar qualities have their being. Lacking such insight he cannot expect to have even a peer relationship, let alone play a leadership role, with members of an elementary school faculty.

Most elementary teachers as a part of their preparation have course work and related experience in psychology, human development, backgrounds of education, teaching methods, and academic coursework in relevant fields such as mathematics and linguistics, plus student teaching. Current trends, already a reality in many teacher education programs, lead to the conclusion that five years of educational preparation including a teaching internship and greater academic preparation is becoming commonplace on a number of campuses.

Many things that the counselor can or cannot do reside in the excellence of his ideas. Classroom teachers probably are not going to have much confidence in either the school counselor or in the results of his work if he is uninformed about the children whom he is attempting to serve.

We do not attempt to write, in a dozen pages, the essence of what the elementary school counselor needs to know about the child's development and the experiences that able teachers seek to provide under the auspices of the school. The depth and breadth of the topic would make this impossible here, and Part Two of this book deals with the counselor's functions. It seems feasible, however, to provide certain guidelines as to the nature of sometimes neglected understandings that one needs in order to work contributively with elementary school children in the field of counseling and guidance.

The Pre-School and Primary Years

In addition to the usual material which can be located in authoritative writing on human development and elementary education, several points can be made by way of introduction to the understandings the counselor will need to cultivate in order to work with younger elementary school children.

First, we are almost certain to find a reversal of long-established priorities in U.S. education which have a direct bearing on childhood—and which promise to enhance the role of the school counselor. A decade or two ago, it did not occur, even to most educators, that we were investing our largest sums of money at the wrong end of the educational program. As children moved through the grades and secondary years and on into college, it was taken for granted that the financial resources provided should increase—along with per-pupil costs—and reach an apex at the advanced graduate and professional school levels.

At the college level alone we probably have spent millions of dollars since the late 1940's on *remedial instruction.* At last social psychiatrists, pediatricians, psychologists, neurobiologists, and educators are recognizing that the *sooner* we begin to provide appropriate guided learning experiences the *better* it will be. At incongruous cost we have been trying 10 to 15 years too late to modify the behavior of adolescents. What may take months to achieve at eighteen, if, indeed, achieved at all, might have been an easy goal to reach at age three or four. One phase of the counselor's foundations of knowledge, then, would be a clear, sound concept of how greatly improved elementary school services can be contributed to the greater realization of full human potential for all students.

Second, and as a natural concomitant of the first point, school counselors will need to develop a much greater understanding of what are now generally called pre-school children. If present trends continue, these boys and girls will not be in *pre-school* but in school programs that are an integral part of public education.

Certain aspects of Operation Head Start, the massive, federally supported program for early childhood education, after its strong beginning in the mid-1960's, will probably become indistinguishable parts of publicly supported schooling. As the early childhood education movement, after long delays, wins greater recognition and becomes a part of the U.S. way of life, work with quite young children and their parents may well add personnel, responsibilities, and opportunities for service for those counseling and guidance programs which are able effectively to assimilate the substantial, specialized information involved in work with the youngest age groups.

University counseling and guidance departments, if need is any index, will be called upon to prepare the well-educated men and women to provide depth study of individuals for this field of early childhood education. As programs of this nature develop, closer working relationships between counselors and teachers of young children will be established as both groups participate in cooperatively conceived courses, practicums, observation, intern service in social agencies, etc.

A third basis for obtaining a deeper understanding of broad developments in elementary education is to be extracted from newer conceptions of children's learning and development. One of the most important of these notions is that human development is modifiable. The work of Arnold Gesell in the 1940's was highly valuable but tended for a time to support the inference that at a particular age certain observable forms of behavior were "normal." (17,18) While Gesell and his associates did not rigidly prescribe the behaving to be expected at certain ages or stages, their enthusiastic readers sometimes developed large charts or used analogous means to portray what overt behavior to anticipate. Apparently unimpressed by the point that a normative description of growth or behavior was an artificial concept that drew upon a wide range of deviating qualities or characteristics, many people erroneously spoke and acted as though children should perform in certain ways at certain times. There were certain assumed stages through which children passed, and one simply waited until they occurred.

Because of what oftentimes are very close personal relationships, occasionally even involving childhood confidences, it is uniquely important for counselors to have a highly superior knowledge of emerging ideas as to how children respond to environments and seek to cope with problems. In short, counselors need to understand how widely children vary while remaining within the span of what we recognize as "normal." Counselors must also be aware of newer studies that move from the concept of "unfolding maturation" to that of "modifiable development" that are found in the literature concerned with child development. Ira Gordon presents interesting data based on both human and infra-human studies that he organizes under biological, cognitive, and social-emotional development (20,21). This, with his analogy of "Linear Causation Model Man" and his "Transactional Model

Man" help to explain changes in views about children based on insights from the behavioral sciences. This point is developed in greater detail in Chapter 7.

The child and his growing fund of knowledge provide a *fourth* factor of a fundamental nature which is important to teacher and counselor alike. The child and his knowledge involve the *amount* of subject matter that the child must learn. Because of the great increase in knowledge, it has been estimated that children are expected to learn from 50% to 100% more than their parents were called on to master a generation ago. In addition to the quantitative increase in knowledge that elementary school age children must master, a new and unpredictable element has been added in recent decades. This element, as previously intimated, is the influence of mass media on the unorganized, out-of-school learnings acquired from television programs, radio, films, etc. One might say that most U.S. children, from a very early age, are exposed to an informal but powerful "phantom curriculum" containing clusters of information dealing with past, present, and future. Children's in-school hours never do catch up with the hours they spend in contact with mass media.

The teacher and counselor alike face the task of determining what the "new knowledge," both in the amount presented in school and in the unindexed but potent phantom curriculum, imply for guiding learning as personality development.

Children During the Middle School Years

A sharp line cannot be drawn between early and middle childhood. One can, however, make a few fundamental points that tend to be more closely associated with children in the upper years of elementary education than in early childhood. Whether for good or ill, and opinions vary, it seems likely that experimentation and practice will be concerned with the presentation of more content at an earlier age. While an increase in content learning may begin at the early childhood level, it seems virtually certain that substantial pressure for added achievement will be affecting children appreciably by age 10 or 11 (4,39). The counselor—and teachers, of course—will need to be skilled in making wise decisions as to when, *for a particular child,* pressure for academic attainment becomes unreasonable and premature. The importance of developing this foundational understanding—of differentiation in terms of a particular learner—probably cannot be overemphasized.

New amalgamations of content also will confront elementary education. It is altogether possible that much of today's subject matter will not be taught with its present labels or in its present form in the future. The counselor's foundational understandings of classroom learnings will need to be constantly refreshed. The importance of the child's ability to communicate and the enhancement of his skills in human relations, for example, are certain to be recognized as equally or more important than science or mathematics learnings per se, particularly during the elementary school years.

The changing adult world toward which the elementary child is moving also demands the application of new thinking by the counselor. For example, elementary teachers, many of whom have middle class values if research is to be believed (10,49,50), have tended for years to stress the value and prestige of managerial, professional, and ownership occupations. Although only a relatively small proportion of the population *can* be executives, professionals, or proprietors, many youngsters acquire from teachers, by contagion, the idea that these are the "better" vocations into which to move. Some of the lack of reality involved is reflected in data from medicine which reveals that in proportion to the U.S. population the number of physicians has actually declined since 1900 while the number of their associates such as nurses, medical technicians, and X-ray operators, has increased eight-fold. (In part at least, this is due to the increase in medical sophistication and technicians such sophistication demands.)

We undoubtedly could make use of more physicians, especially in remote or inner city areas where facilities and medical services are often inadequate. At the same time, limited enrollments in medical schools and the high cost of a medical degree preclude the possibility of a medical career for many students whom well-meaning but uninformed teachers have urged to contemplate it.

We are not, by any stretch of the imagination, advocating elementary level occupational and vocational counseling. We are, however, taking serious note of the fact that the *climate* of the elementary school should be one in which there is a realistic, knowledgeable, and respectful position taken with regard to the changes transpiring in the world of work. Certainly, there is no point in preserving the fiction that, as an adult, one has failed to fulfill his promise if he hasn't "risen above his station" by becoming a practitioner in a "prestige" professional field: banking, pediatrics, engineering, etc.

A close corollary to reducing and then eliminating occupational snobbery, a corollary that also involves fundamental insight into the elementary school, is the development of realistic understandings of the new concepts of vocations emerging today. These have a considerable bearing on the child's understanding and acceptance of the control system-space travel-media mediated world of the final quarter of our present century. Again, we do not mean to stress vocations in isolation. We mean to reiterate the fundamental importance of an elementary curriculum and school atmosphere which looks toward tomorrow rather than yesterday. As we consider vocational prospects for the future, it is possible that children now in the elementary school have before them the prospect of re-training themselves for new types of positions three or four times between 1975 and 2025 as their careers unfold.

Individualizing the
Elementary School Guidance Program

There are many meanings for the structure of the elementary school counseling and guidance program that can be inferred from the foregoing review of the kinds of foundational knowledge which it is desirable for the counselor to have. However, most of the remainder of this volume is concerned with the nature of elementary guidance programs. At this point, therefore, we wish to stress what appear to be two preeminently important general implications: 1) The "good" counseling and guidance program at the elementary level is personalized or *individuality centered,* and 2) an individuality-centered approach has certain specific meanings for the counselor as he works with all children.

Individuality-Centered Elementary Education

For at least a century the elementary school has striven to recognize and to cope with the problem of individual differences. By the 1960's it was clear that the literally dozens of approaches that have been made to the problem of grouping were not basic solutions to the problem of dealing with human differences (41). Some of the most sophisticated current research on grouping is beginning to support the view that mechanical designs or devices for adapting school programs to suit individual differences are not effective. M. L. Goldberg, A. H. Passow, and Joseph Justman, for example, reported on a carefully designed research study in 1966, ". . . narrowing the ability range in the classroom," they concluded, ". . . is not associated with greater academic achievement for any ability level." (19:161) Herbert A. Thelen's "teachability grouping" research, a longitudinal inquiry that began in 1957 and was published on its completion in 1967, reported on the promise of a creative and personalized rather than mechanical concept of grouping (48).

Goldberg et al. rather clearly recognized the futility of arbitrary approaches to providing for so-called individualized groupings. These groupings simply do not accomplish their purpose, despite a century of effort, of finding some magic plan that significantly improved individualized instruction. Thelen, for his part, documented what we will refer to as an individuality-centered approach to elementary education. His concept of grouping is related to two queries: "What sort of student can a given teacher teach most effectively?" and "What sort of teacher can a given student learn from most effectively?" (48:190) After classroom observation-in-depth over a substantial period, Thelen concluded that the best grouping for teachability was a combination of the two—matching pupil to teacher and teacher to pupil.

The significance of this conclusion is considerable. Instead of seeking ways to individualize programs, the schools should be endeavoring to study the individuality of pupils and their teachers. This is a view that probably has been held intuitively by sensitive teachers and insightful administrators for many years!

Implications for School Counselors in the Individuality-Centered Approach

The fundamental importance of the individuality approach in elementary school guidance is that this approach requires close study of children, professional appraisal of teachers' varied abilities, and careful pairing of individual children with the teacher who is "best" for them. Counselors and teachers, beginning at the pre-school or kindergarten level, need methodically to gather relevant data as a prerequisite for determining the optimal placement or "matching" of child and teachers as soon as possible in his initial school experiences.

On a continuing basis, during the months and years to follow, the counselor will need to work closely and cooperatively with teachers in order to be sure that proper judgments have been made in the pairing of teachers and children. In the process, the mature and able counselor will continually work to orient teachers to the emerging social, cognitive, physical, and affective nature of the children in their classrooms. To accomplish this purpose, teacher and counselor need to be "tuned in" on feedback from boys and girls: data from their spoken and unspoken communications, creative writing, inter-personal successes and shortcomings, academic performance, educational morale, etc.

The counselor in his interaction with the faculty also should strive to help each teacher evaluate and modify his instructional methods in response to ongoing appraisal of pupils' social development and the assessment of progress with regard to appropriate academic skills. Program modification, understandably, calls for flexibility on the part of the teacher and the imaginative employment of instructional resources—to both of which a knowledgeable counselor should be able to make a contribution. While many elementary teachers are quite capable of flexibility in their teaching, the counselor has a substantial contribution to make in sensitizing teachers to the *kind* of flexibility which seems wisest in a particular child's program. Especially, as he develops longitudinal contact with boys and girls as they progress through school over a period of years, and through his continuing analysis of records, discussion sessions with youngsters, professional observation of their behavior, and contacts with parents, the counselor becomes an important force in an individuality-centered education.

Guidance and Counseling: An Integral Aspect of the Effective Education of Children

As education for young children has grown in complexity and importance, it has become too much of a task for many teachers to perform by themselves. As responsibilities and pressures have mounted, there has been a proportionately greater need for guidance and counseling. Although many schools have yet to introduce significant services, and a dwindling band of administrators do not yet seem to recognize or acknowledge the importance of elementary school guidance, there is no doubt of the fact that guidance has become an integral part of early and middle childhood. Developments in the schools have made this an accomplished fact.

The counselor's necessary foundation of knowledge introduced and explained in this chapter, and the counselor's work with the teacher in improving human individuality, *require that all elementary schools have persons responsible for performing the guidance functions.* The problem is no longer one of establishing the need and clarifying the meaning of guidance; the problem is to proceed with all due speed to implement programs.

Summary

The purpose of Chapter 2 is to weave together the general background knowledge and the understandings of elementary education which are prerequisite to working with children. After identifying the unique value of the counselor with both his specialized preparation and his skill in utilizing school and community resources to serve children, Chapter 2 notes the importance of his knowledge of fields other than education. Among the related areas of study identified are psychology, human development, cultural anthropology, sociology, biology and biochemistry, communications, mass media, and cybernetics. Each field is shown to be related to the counselor's tasks and examples of important research are briefly identified.

Trends in the education of the young from early childhood through the middle school years are used to illustrate how necessary it is for the counselor to understand them. In the concluding pages, attention is centered on the concept of personalized or individuality-centered education and its implications for guidance.

All parts of Chapter 2 serve to suggest the kind of broad foundation which will sustain the counselor and help insure successful performance of his functions as described in Chapters 7 through 11.

References

1. Anderson, Robert H. *Teaching in a World of Change*. New York: Harcourt, Brace, and World, Inc., 1966.
2. Asbell, Bernard, "The Case of the Wandering I.Q." *Redbook* 129 (August, 1967): 32.
3. Benedict, Ruth and Gene Weltfish. *Races of Mankind*. New York: Public Affairs Committee, 1943.
4. Bereiter, Carl and Siegfried Englemann. *Teaching Disadvantaged Children in the Pre-School*. Englewood Cliffs, N.J.: Prentice-Hall, Inc., 1966.
5. Bernstein, Basil. "Language and Social Class: Research Note." *British Journal of Sociology* 11 (1960): 271-276.
6. Brooks, John. *The Great Leap*. New York: Harper and Row, Publishers, 1966.
7. Calhoun, John B. "Population Density and Social Pathology." *Scientific American* 206 (February, 1962): 139-146.
8. Cannon, Walter B. *The Wisdom of the Body*. New York: W. W. Norton Co., 1932.
9. Chase, Stuart. *The Most Probable World*. New York: Harper and Row, Publishers, 1968.
10. Coffman, L. D. *The Social Composition of the Teaching Population*. New York: Teachers College Press, 1911. This was the first highly influential social class research report on teachers.
11. Coghill, George E. *Anatomy and the Problem of Behavior*. London: Cambridge University Press, 1929.
12. Coleman, James S. et al. *Equality of Educational Opportunity*. Washington, D.C.: U.S. Department of Health, Education and Welfare, 1966.
13. Cremin, Lawrence A. *The Genius of American Education*. New York: Alfred A. Knopf, Inc. and Random House, Inc., Vintage Books, copyright by Lawrence A. Cremin, 1965.
14. Dale, Edgar. *Audio-Visual Methods in Teaching*. Revised edition. New York: The Dryden Press, 1954.
15. "Flanagan: A Consultant Comments." *Phi Delta Kappan* 49 (September, 1967): 32-33.
16. Flanagan, John C. "Functional Education for the Seventies." *Phi Delta Kappan* 49 (September, 1967): 27-32.
17. Gesell, Arnold and Frances L. Ilg. *The Child from Five to Ten*. New York: Harper and Bros., 1946.
18. ____. *Infant and Child in the Culture of Today*. New York: Harper and Bros., 1943.
19. Goldberg, M. L., A. H. Passow, and Joseph Justman. *The Effects of Ability Grouping*. New York: Teachers College Press, 1966.
20. Gordon, Ira. "Newer Conceptions of Children's Learning and Development." *Learning and Mental Health in the School*. Washington, D.C.: The Association for Supervision and Curriculum Development, 1966.
21. ____. "The Beginnings of Self: The Problem of the Nurturing Environment." *Phi Delta Kappan* 50 (March, 1969): 375-378.

22. Hall, Edward T. *The Hidden Dimension.* New York: Doubleday and Co., Inc., 1966.

23. ____. *The Silent Language.* New York: Fawcett World Library: Premier Books, 1959.

24. Hilgard, Ernest (ed.). *Theories of Learning and Instruction. LXIII Yearbook*, Part I. National Society for the Study of Education. Chicago: The University of Chicago Press, 1964.

25. Hollingshead, August B. *Elmtown's Youth: The Impact of Social Class on Adolescence.* New York: John Wiley and Sons, Inc., 1949.

26. Hyden, Holger (Seminar Chairman). *The Chemistry of Learning.* (Report on a Kettering Foundation Seminar.) Unpaged pamphlet. /I/D/E/A/ Information Office, POB 446, Melbourne, Florida.

27. Krech, David. "Psychoneurobiochemeducation." *Phi Delta Kappan* 50 (March, 1969): 370-375.

28. ____. "The Chemistry of Learning." *Saturday Review* 51 (January 20, 1968): 48-49.

29. Lynd, Robert S. and Helen M. Lynd. *Middletown.* New York: Harcourt, Brace, and World, Inc., 1929.

30. ____. *Middletown in Transition.* New York: Harcourt, Brace, and World, Inc., 1937.

31. McCulkin, John. "A Schoolman's Guide to Marshall McLuhan." *Saturday Review* 50 (March 18, 1967): 51-53.

32. McLuhan, Marshall. *Educational Media.* New York: McGraw-Hill Book Co., 1964.

33. Mead, Margaret and Ruth L. Bunzell (eds.). *The Golden Age of American Anthropology.* New York: George Braziller, Inc., 1960.

34. Michael, Donald N. *The Unprepared Society.* New York: Basic Books, Inc., 1968.

35. Mills, C. W. *White Collar.* New York: Oxford University Press, 1951.

36. Montagu, M. F. Ashley. *The Humanization of Man.* New York: World Publishing Co., 1962.

37. Moreno, J. L. *Who Shall Survive?* Scranton, Pa.: Nervous and Medical Diseases Publishing House, 1934.

38. Myrdal, Gunnar. *An American Dilemma.* New York: Harper and Bros., 1949.

39. Pines, Maya. "A Pressure Cooker for Four-Year-Old Minds." *Harper's* 234 (January, 1967): 55-61.

40. Sarnoff, David. "Tomorrow's Communicating World." *The Exchange* 28 (May 17, 1967): 27-29.

41. Shane, Harold G. "Grouping in the Elementary School." *Phi Delta Kappan* 41 (April, 1960): 313-319. Contains a roster of nearly three dozen approaches to grouping.

42. ____. *Linguistics and the Classroom Teacher.* Washington, D.C.: The Association for Supervision and Curriculum Development, 1967.

43. ____. "Old Fabrics and New Patterns in Education Overseas." *Phi Delta Kappan* 47 (March, 1966): 352-356.

44. ____. "The Renaissance of Early Childhood Education." *Phi Delta Kappan* 50 (March, 1969): 369; 412-413.

45. Shane, June Grant. "Contemporary Thought With Implications for Counseling and Guidance: A Bibliography." *Bulletin of the School of Education*. Indiana University, Bureau of Educational Studies and Testing Vol. 43, No. 4, July, 1967.

46. Southwick, Charles H. "Patterns of Intergroup Social Behavior in Primates." *Annals of the New York Academy of Science*, 102 (1962): 436-454.

47. Taylor, Gordon R. *The Biological Time Bomb*. New York: World Publishing Co., 1968.

48. Thelen, Herbert A. *Classroom Grouping for Teachability*. New York: John Wiley and Sons, Inc., 1967.

49. Warner, W. L. and Paul S. Lunt. *The Social Life of a Modern Community*. New Haven, Conn.: Yale University Press, 1941.

50. ____and Paul S. Lunt. *The Status System of a Modern Community*. New Haven, Conn.: Yale University Press, 1942.

51. ____, M. Meeker, and K. Eels. *Social Class in America*. Chicago: Science Research Associates, 1949.

52. Whorf, Benjamin Lee. *Language, Thought, and Reality: Selected Writings of Benjamin Lee Whorf*. Cambridge, Mass.: Technology Press, 1956.

3

Research and the Elementary School Counselor

For thousands of years man has turned to various sources of authority for "answers," for security, and for new knowledge. Among these sources have been hereditary or intellectual leaders, the supernatural, familiar customs, established traditions, trial and error, etc. Beginning in the 19th century, research became a new referent, a source of answers and a means of providing a sense of direction for the educated man.

As research moved from its infancy, as typified by the early triumphs of Louis Pasteur, it became more and more respected by many men—particularly its major beneficiaries in the industrialized Western World. At present, during the declining decades of the 20th century, research, along with its technological fruits, has become almost universally respected. Sometimes, if only briefly, as during the first 1969 moon landing, the respect for research mirrored in the accomplishments it has nurtured has verged on Delphic veneration.

In Chapter 3 of *Guiding Human Development* the focus of our book shifts to research as it bears on the work of the elementary counselor. Specifically, what are examples of research studies with which the elementary counselor—already acquainted with his special field—should also be acquainted and why or how do they relate to superior practices in elementary school counseling and guidance?

Identifying and
Understanding Significant Research

The word "research," like the word "statistics," appeals to many people who like to have "facts" with which to reinforce their professional judgment. But research, like statistics, can be used to confuse, mislead, prejudice, or over-simplify issues for the naive or uninformed individual. Mention "research," follow it with "findings of the study," and at least some people are willing to accept almost any statements which follow as true now, true under any circumstances, and presumably true forever. Even greater impact can be achieved if the findings can be presented using a specialized or technical vocabulary, and if the researcher's sentences are both compound and complex. The successful utilization of research findings whether verbally or in written form usually submerges all but the most cynical or best informed audience in an "ocean of awe that surrounds a few islands of sloganized information." (84:11)

One of the skills the counselor needs to develop quickly is that of knowing what makes research *important*. Literally, thousands of research reports are published annually in the form of monographs, theses, dissertations, or articles. In a 1966 issue of the *Review of Educational Research* approximately 650 studies completed between 1963 and 1966 were cited and treated that dealt with "Guidance, Counseling, and Personnel Services." (53,54) How does one separate the intellectual gold from the trivial dross?

Certainly, it is important for us to understand the accumulated knowledge about human beings and how they behave. Without this knowledge, each of us would be individually condemned to working through the long history of study and thought about man and his actions. (This does not mean, however, that all information we encounter, whether it is labeled "research" or not, should be immediately swallowed before it has been examined and digested.) Relevant research in the behavioral sciences is a recent source of help for educators. In fact, for practical purposes it may be said that such inquiries are almost entirely a product of the twentieth century. Despite the recent arrival of the behavioral sciences on the educational scene, we have obtained from them many clues about the complicated organism that we call man. Some of the information that we received seemed relevant at a particular time. But what was an "important" finding in 1910 is not necessarily either true or useful in 1970. Counselors need to understand that the field of science changes, and that what seems enduring and important may really be of no more than a transient nature. As explanations and theories are explored and tested, some are discarded as new data are obtained and outmode them. As knowledge continues to increase, as research skills develop and become more sophisticated, findings that seem relevant and important in the 1970's also will undoubtedly change.

If a spirit if inquiry is maintained, however, important and unifying generalizations about human behavior are almost certain to emerge—generalizations which counselors and teachers with a respect for both an element of doubt and for new information will continue to put to the test of reexamination and further inquiry. For "education is not a mass of inert facts or ideas, but an attitude, a style, an appetite, an approach, a frame of mind, a continuing function of the full personality." (114)

Criteria for Selecting Research

No one can hope to keep abreast of even a substantial fraction of research bearing on counseling and guidance in elementary schools, let alone the related research under way in the behavioral sciences and in elementary education. At the same time, five guidelines or criteria can be suggested which should help counselors to make discriminating judgments and selections:

1) *The authorship, auspices, and source of a research report are sound ones.* Any one of these three elements can enhance the authenticity and probable value of a research report. The author, if a well-known educational writer, has an established reputation to preserve. So do professional groups such as APGA (American Personnel and Guidance Association), the APA (American Psychological Association), or an NEA Department such as the ASCD (Association for Supervision and Curriculum Development). What they sponsor is quite likely to be a contribution of substance.

2) *The research is original rather than a review or an interpretation.* Whenever possible, *original* rather than *cited* research should be examined. Second-hand material almost invariably is abridged and a reviewer may inadvertently misrepresent findings. Research reviews are valuable to help one find leads, but they do not replace the need for one's personal inquiry into primary sources.

3) *The research is a threat to established or accepted knowledge in the field.* Important research creates new ideas and concepts or replaces old ones as it extends knowledge. This often threatens old ideas and stimulates the intellectual controversies through which much progress is made. Valuable research also may confirm what is assumed to be true or what is partly established knowledge.

4) *The research meets acceptable standards of design.* It is objective, reliable, and valid. In other words, personal biases are
minimized; the study presumably would bring similar results
if replicated; and it fulfills its stated purpose.

5) *The research is reasonably conclusive.* Some research projects
use samples that are unduly small or that have so many similar
deficiencies that the writer somewhat lamely calls attention to
them himself in a heavily qualified conclusion which reduces
the value of the findings. It also is desirable to avoid being too
strongly influenced by research which supports one's biases
but which is suggestive or presumptive rather than conclusive.

Bernard Berelson and Gary A. Steiner present an inventory of scientific
knowledge about human behavior in their book, *Human Behavior*, that
reflects findings up to 1964 (7). The book also contains a useful chapter
entitled "Methods of Inquiry" which treats the nature of science as applied to
human behavior. The counselor interested in methods usually attributed to
the physical and behavioral sciences will profit from reading these pages.

The Counselor's Participation in Research

Because of the counselor's access to a substantial accumulation of pupil
personnel data, it is important that he both know and understand the
findings of certain major research studies, and how to apply them, as well as
how to engage in his own original research and study. Such personal research
may range from simple investigations in his own school district to substantial
contributions, perhaps made in connection with the pursuit of an advanced
degree or under the auspices of a reputable professional association.

There is a growing consensus among counselors that at least some personal
research-inquiry activity should become an integral part of the elementary
counselor's function in education. This point of view is supported by the
fact that pupil personnel problems are now so complex and are changing so
rapidly that some type of ongoing research activity is necessary in all school
districts at least part of the time.

The School Counselor's
Knowledge of Research in Related Disciplines

Fields Where Competence Is Needed

There are five general realms of research disciplines related to counseling
about which the elementary school counselor needs to be informed. These are:

1) Basic or "classic" research studies having a bearing on education in general.

2) Research in elementary education; particularly research bearing on curriculum theory, the several fields of content, teaching methods and materials, and school organization.

3) Research in related fields which has a direct bearing on the strategy and tactics of elementary program development and guidance functions; e.g., human development, learning, group processes, and so forth.

4) Professional inquiries in the field of guidance; those that are both general in nature and that are germane to the elementary school.

5) The broad realm of research theory; the projection of needed research; and the acquisition of "know-how" with regard to recent and current developments in the funding of research.

No single area of emphasis among the five cited above is "most important." Some across-the-board knowledge of all of them provides necessary balance for the counselor of young children. It should be kept in mind, too, that becoming knowledgeable is not a periodic crash program based on the rapid reading of a few studies. It is rather a process of self-renewal; a product of a *continuing*, planned self-study extending throughout one's professional lifetime.

Important Sources of Research Information for the Counselor

John Gardner has written with considerable eloquence about the self-renewing man and his importance to a healthy culture (48). Self-renewal also is an important aspect of the counselor's life. As he makes decisions, confers with children, and plans with teachers, he must have a freshening fund of knowledge and vitalizing experiences that helps to keep him alive, to stimulate his thinking, to sharpen his leadership, and to maintain at a high level his ability to counsel.

There are at least eight categories under which one may classify the sources of research information related to professional education and to some of the major developments in related disciplines.

Bibliographic Tools. All libraries that counselors are likely to use have a number of excellent tools for unearthing research data. Persons seeking reference information often can save themselves hours of time in the library files if they are aware of various research bibliographies. Among the well-known general bibliographical tools are:*

1. *Bibliographies and Summaries in Education to July, 1935.* Edited by Walter Scott Monroe and Louis Shores. New York: H. W. Wilson Co., 1936, 470 pp.

    Includes all important educational bibliographies published up to summer of 1935. Annotation indicates periods covered, number of references, degree of completeness, character of references, types of materials included, kinds of annotations, if any, and general character of summaries.

2. *Cumulative Book Index: A World List of Books in the English Language.* New York: H. W. Wilson Co., 1928-to date.

    Published monthly with semi-annual and biennial cumulations, superseded by the permanent five-year cumulation. It is a supplement to the *United States Catalogue,* but has a wider scope, including all books in the English language, no matter where published. Information includes: author, short title, edition, publisher, price, and generally, date, paging, and illustration. Each volume includes a directory of publishers.

3. *Education Index.* New York: H. W. Wilson Co., 1929-to date.

    Published ten times a year, monthly except June and August, with annual and triennial cumulations. Indexes more than 150 periodicals, varying somewhat from volume to volume, and covers all educational books in the United States, including college texts but not elementary and high school texts. In general, articles are indexed under both author and subject, except that 1) book reviews are indexed only under that heading and 2) poems are listed only under the word *poems* unless the author is very well known. Bibliographies are listed under main headings; i.e., arithmetic, education, international relations, etc.

4. *Monthly Catalogue of United States Government Publications.* Washington, D.C.: United States Superintendent of Documents, 1895-to date.

    A monthly listing of publications issued by all branches of the federal government. Each issue contains instructions for ordering documents, and a list of the documents published during the month, arranged by department or bureau. There is an annual index for each volume.

5. *Publishers' Weekly.* New York: R. R. Bowker Co., 1872-to date, vol. 1.

    Contains a list of new publications of the week, as well as books announced for publication. There is little need to use any but the latest issues, which include publications too recent to be listed in the latest *Cumulative Book Index.* The bibliographic list of new titles published during the week is located in the back of each issue. It is an author list with full title, imprint, collation, and descriptive notes. Lists only books published in the United States.

6. *Textbooks in Print.* New York: R. R. Bowker Co., 1872-to date.

---

*The writers are indebted to Ernest Weyrauch, director in 1967 of the Reading Room, School of Education, Indiana University, for the descriptions of reference materials used in this chapter.

Formerly knows as the *American Educational Catalog.* This is an alphabetical list of textbooks produced by leading publishers, arranged by author, except for those better known by title or editor. This list is compiled from information supplied by the publisher, giving price and series, if any. Published annually.

7. *United States Catalogue: Books in Print.* January 1, 1928. Edited by Mary Burnham. New York: H. W. Wilson Co., 1928, 3164 pp.

The most complete listing of American books in print at the beginning of 1928. This includes Canadian books in English, not published in the United States. The preface lists early book catalogs compiled in the nineteenth century.

Researches in Education. There are numerous other standard tools that the counselor may use in searching for research data that apply particularly to studies completed in education. These include:

1. *Bibliography of Research Studies in Education.* Washington, D.C.: U.S. Office of Education, 1929-42, 14 vols.

Lists doctoral dissertations, masters' theses, and other research studies. A classified list with institution, author, and subject indexes.

Discontinued during World War II, the work was eventually resumed by Mary Louise Lyda and Stanley B. Brown in their compilations entitled *Research Studies in Education,* published by Phi Delta Kappa.

2. *Dissertation Abstracts: A Guide to Dissertations and Monographs.* Available on Microfilm. Ann Arbor, Michigan: University Microfilms, 1938-to date.

Volumes one to eleven, 1938-51, were called *Microfilm Abstracts.* This is a subject arrangement of 300 word abstracts of dissertations from leading U.S. universities. Full bibliographic information plus the price of a microfilm copy is included. In 1957, this publication absorbed *Doctoral Dissertations Accepted* (listed below) thereafter including listings of dissertations by subject and author with no abstract.

3. *Doctoral Dissertations Accepted by American Universities.* Complied for the Association of Research Libraries. New York: H. W. Wilson Co., 1934-56, 22 vols.

Contents: alphabetical subject index; publication and preservation of American doctoral dissertations; list of periodic university publications abstracting dissertations; statistical tables; list of dissertations arranged by subject and then by university, giving for each dissertation its author, title, and in the case of those printed, bibliographical data as to separate publication, or inclusion in some periodical or collection; alphabetical author index.

The section, "Publication and Preservation," gives important reference information about the practice of different universities as to requirements of printing, number of copies deposited in the Home library, and library regulations about interlibrary loan of dissertations.

4. *Encyclopedia of Educational Research.* Various editors. New York: Macmillan Co., editions in 1950, 1960, and 1970.

Not an encyclopedia in the usual sense, this summarizes the outstanding research on a wide range of educational topics, problems studied, the findings, and issues under investigation or awaiting further research.

A long selective bibliography of references mentioned in the text follows each article.

The Third Edition (1970) is a completely rewritten volume that puts into perspective the findings of research. Articles are signed. A detailed subject index on tinted paper is inserted in the middle of the volume.

5. *Handbook of Research on Teaching.* Edited by Nathaniel L. Gage. Chicago: Rand McNally and Co., 1963, 1218 pp.

Under the sponsorship of the American Educational Research Association, this presents an evaluative and documented summary of the current status of educational research in many fields. The four parts include theoretical orientations, methodologies in research in teaching, major variables and areas of research on teaching, and research on teaching various grade levels and subject matters. This volume is of special value to advanced students in education.

6. *Index to American Doctoral Dissertations.* Ann Arbor, Michigan: University Microfilms, 1957-to date.

A complete indexed listing of dissertations by all students who were granted doctoral degrees during the previous academic year, including those abstracted in *Dissertation Abstracts.* Arranged by degree-granting institutions under the appropriate subject headings. An alphabetical author index is included.

7. *Master's Theses in Education.* Edited by Tom Arthur Lamke and Herbert M. Silvey. Bureau of Research, Cedar Falls, Iowa: Iowa State Teachers College, 1953-to date.

A subject listing of theses in education on the master's level. Published annually.

8. *Research Studies in Education.* Compiled by Mary Louise Lyda, Stanley B. Brown, and Carter V. Good. Bloomington, Indiana: Phi Delta Kappa, 1953-to date.

A subject index to doctoral dissertations, reports, and field studies, and a research methods bibliography. Beginning when the U.S. Office of Education's *Bibliography of Research Studies in Education* was discontinued in 1940, this series, scheduled to appear annually under the sponsorship of Phi Delta Kappa, provides a subject listing of doctoral studies completed, as well as a listing of doctoral research under way.

Miscellaneous Publications Dealing with Research. Over the years, various individuals and groups have prepared scholarly resources that deal with research on a broad basis. An annotated sample of these "research tool" publications follows:

1. *American Foundations and Their Fields.* Edited by Wilmer Shields Rich. New York: American Foundations Information Service, 1955.

Supplemented by *American Foundation News Service,* which is published approximately eight times a year. Lists foundations which give financial support to studies in the field of education. Such information as officers and trustees, purpose, year established, capital assets, expenditures, grants, and methods of operation included. Supplements give information on new foundations, foundation policies, reports, etc.

2. *Cyclopedia of Education.* Edited by Paul Monroe. New York: Macmillan Co., 1911–13, 5 vols. in 3.

A very good work when published. Still valuable for historical and biographical information prior to the date of publications.

3. *How to Locate Educational Information and Data.* Carter Alexander and Arvid J. Burke. New York: Columbia University, 1958.

An excellent guide for persons doing educational research. Periodically revised (1958 edition is the 4th edition) covers potentiality of libraries, techniques for using libraries, procedures in library searching, locating periodicals and serials, using educational indexes, making bibliographies, how to use and find government periodicals—especially USOE materials, statistics, legal aspects, and a host of other areas of concern and technique, a knowledge of which is necessary for successful educational research.

4. *Mental Measurement Yearbook.* Edited by Oscar K. Buros. Highland Park, N.J.: Gryphon Press, 1959, vol 5.

Vol. 1, 1938; vol. 2, 1940; vol. 3, 1949; vol. 4, 1953; vol. 5, 1959. Title and publisher varies; covers educational, psychological, and vocational tests available commercially. Buros provides reviews of the tests by authorities with divergent viewpoints.

5. *Psychological Abstracts.* American Psychological Association. 1927-to date, vol. 1.

Complete monthly bibliography listing new books and articles by subject with full abstracts of each item. Captures many items of interest to educators. Gives English abstracts of foreign language articles.

6. *Public Affairs Information Service Bulletin.* Publication of the Public Affairs Information Service which is a cooperative clearing house of public affairs information. 1951-to date, vol. 1.

Publication consists of weekly bulletins, accumulative and permanent annual volumes. Excellent for ephemera, i.e., documents, pamphlets, or mimeographed materials published by a variety of institutions and corporate bodies. Includes selective indexing of more than 1,000 periodicals.

Useful for political science, government, economics, and sociology.

7. *Sociological Abstracts,* 1953-to date, vol. 1. Nine times per year.

Abstracts, English and foreign journals. All abstracts are in English and are of moderate length—usually from 500 to 700 words. This tool embraces some 21 areas of sociology and human behavior. The abstracts are of high quality and will be of interest to students in business and education, as well as those working specifically in sociology.

8. *Tests in Print.* Edited by Oscar K. Buros. Highland Park, N.J.: Gryphon Press, 1961, 479 pp.

A list of published tests as of June 1, 1961, compiled by the editor of the *Mental Measurements Yearbooks.* It serves as a comprehensive bibliography of tests—achievement, aptitude, intelligence, personality, and certain sensory-motor skills—published as separates and currently available in Enslígh-speaking countries; to serve as a classified index and supplement to the published volumes of *The Mental Measurements Yearbook;* and to give wider distribution to the excellent recommendations for improving test manuals by reprinting those made by the American Psychological Association, the American Educational Research Association and the National Council on Measurements Used in Education.

9. *U.S. Library of Congress Catalog of Books Represented by Library of Congress Printed Cards*
   Main set published in 1942. This is a retrospective compilation of cards arranged by author of titles in Library of Congress. It is inclusive, represents books also in cooperative libraries and gives full bibliographical citations. This has been kept up to date with supplements since the issuance of the set.
10. *U.S. Library of Congress Subject Catalog,* 1950-to date.
    This is retrospective to approximately 1945 and is methodically kept up to date. It has materials arranged under subject headings and is useful in keeping educators, among others, abreast of new publications in their areas. Tends to rely upon entries appearing in the Library of Congress author catalogs cited above, but arranges these entries under subjects.
11. *ERIC Clearinghouses.* Washington, D.C.: Superintendent of Documents, U.S. Government Printing Offices.
    Journal articles listed in *Current Index to Journals in Education* are reviewed and indexed by the Clearinghouses. Bibliographic citations and abstracts of research documents are announced in *Research in Education* and disseminated through the ERIC Document Reproduction Service.*

Continuing Publications. For an understanding of current research developments, elementary school counselors will want to be aware of publications appearing at regular intervals which present, summarize, interpret, or list research. A classic example of this type of material is the *Review of Educational Research.* Five issues appear each year and 15 topics are reviewed during a three-year cycle. Some topics of particular interest to counselors and elementary teachers bear the following titles:

1) *Education for Socially Disadvantaged Children,* December, 1965.
2) *Educational Programs: Early and Middle Childhood,* April, 1965.
3) *Guidance, Counseling, and Personnel Services,* April, 1966.
4) *Curriculum Planning and Development,* June, 1969.
5) *Education of Exceptional Children,* February, 1966.
6) *Growth, Development and Learning,* December, 1967.
7) *Counseling and Guidance,* April, 1969.

The American Educational Research Association, besides publishing *The Review of Educational Research,* has a journal that is printed five times a year. In *The American Research Journal* are original reports of both theoretical

---

*The 19 Clearinghouses are concerned with: 1) Adult Education, 2) Applied Linguistics, 3) Counseling and Personnel Services, 4) Educational Administration, 5) Exceptional Children, 6) Educational Facilities, 7) Educational Media and Technology, 8) Teaching of Foreign Languages, 9) Higher Education, 10) Junior Colleges, 11) Library and Information Services, 12) Early Childhood Education, 13) Reading, 14) Rural Education and Small Schools, 15) Science Education, 16) Teacher Education, 17) Teaching of English, 18) Disadvantaged, and 19) Vocational and Technical Information.

and experimental studies in education. Included as well are reviews of newer books that might be of interest to counselors.

Continuing publications designed to disseminate research in guidance include those published by the national professional organization The American Personnel and Guidance Association and its divisions.* A subscription to the *Personnel and Guidance Journal* is included with one's membership in APGA. The eight divisions of APGA and their publications are:

(NECA)   National Employment Counselor's Association-*Journal of Employment Counseling*

(ARCA)   The American Rehabilitation Counseling Association-*Rehabilitation Counseling Journal*

(ASCA)   The American School Counselor Association - *The Counselor* and the *Elementary School Guidance and Counseling*.†

(ACPA)   The American College Personnel Association-*Journal of College Student Personnel*

(ACES)   The Association for Counselor Education and Supervision-*Counselor Education and Supervision*

(NVGA)   The National Vocational Guidance Association-*Vocational Guidance Quarterly*

(AMEG)   The Association for Measurement and Evaluation of Guidance-*Measurement and Evaluation in Guidance* (First published January, 1968).

(SPATE) The Student Personnel Association for Teacher Education-*Student Personnel Association for Teacher Education.*

Many journals produced at regular intervals provide research data on some aspects of elementary education. Often these focus on certain fields, as in the case of *Elementary English*, which frequently includes research commentaries of reports on studies. *The Elementary School Journal* is an example of a general publication in the field. Of general research interest in both the elementary field and guidance are such periodicals as the *Journal of Educational Research*, *Journal of Experimental Education*, and *Journal of Educational Psychology*. Of course, any continuing publication in education may have valuable research findings presented or preserved between its covers, but the following ones are representative ones that tend most often to contain articles that are helpful to counselors.††

*Included in the appendix is a list of articles appearing in these journals in recent years that pertain to elementary school counseling and guidance.

†The elementary journal was first published by APGA in 1967 with Don Dinkmeyer as the editor. Dr. Dinkmeyer has also been instrumental in distributing the mimeographed newsletter *Elementary School Guidance News and Views* in the fall of 1965.

††The ERIC publication, *Current Index to Journals in Education*, indexes articles for over 200 education and education-related journals on a monthly basis. The first issue covered journals published in January and February of 1969 and included winter

American Anthropologist
American Behavioral Scientist
American Education
American Educational Research Journal
American Psychologist
American Sociological Review
Behavioral Scientist
Childhood Education
Contemporary Psychology
Counseling Psychologist
Education
Education Digest
Educational Administration and Supervision
Educational Forum
Educational Horizons
Educational Leadership
Educational and Psychological Measurement
Educational Record
Educational Technology
Educational Theory
Elementary School Journal
Handbook for Counselors of College Bound Youth
Harvard Education Review
Journal of Abnormal and Social Psychology
Journal of Applied Psychology
Journal of Clinical Psychology
Journal of Consulting Psychology
Journal of Counseling Psychology
Journal of Developmental Sociology
Journal of Educational Psychology
Journal of Educational Research
Journal of Experimental Education
Journal of Personality Psychology
Journal of Psychology
Journal of Secondary Education
Journal of Teacher Education
Nation's Schools
Phi Delta Kappan
Psychological Bulletin
Psychological Review

quarterlies. In January, 1969 the Institute for Scientific Information, 325 Chestnut Street, Philadelphia, Pennsylvania, produced *Current Contents Education*. This weekly publication contains the table of contents of over 700 foreign and domestic journals many in advance of publication.

Research Quarterly
Review of Educational Research
School and Society
Scientific Monthly
Social Education
Sociology of Education
Sociometry
Today's Education
Understanding the Child
Urban Education
Urban Review

Numerous university bulletins appear throughout the country and throughout the years, and many contain valuable bibliographies, reports, critiques, and summaries related to research. Typical of this genre are:

Teachers College Record — Columbia University
Harvard Educational Review — Harvard University
The Bulletin of the School of Education — Harvard University
Theory into Practice — Ohio State University
Education Perspectives — University of Hawaii
Michigan College Personnel Association Journal Wayne State
        University

Information on Statistics and Research Format. Another type of research resource deserves to be included here—those publications treating statistical procedures and matters of form and style in presenting findings or preparing articles based on research inquiries. Among current and useful books concerned with concepts, procedures, and terminology used in statistics are:

1. Chase, Clinton. *Elementary Statistical Procedures.* New York: McGraw-Hill Book Co., 1967. 245 pp.
2. Dixon, Wilfred J. and Frank J. Massey. *Introduction to Statistical Analysis.* New York: McGraw-Hill Book Co., 1957. 488 pp.
3. Edwards, A. L. *Statistical Methods.* New York: Holt, Rinehart, and Winston, 1967. 420 pp.
4. Garrett, Henry. *Statistics in Psychology and Education.* New York: David McKay Co. , 1966. 491 pp.
5. Guilford, J. P. *Fundamental Statistics in Psychology and Education.* New York: McGraw-Hill Book Co., 1966. 451 pp.
6. McNemar, Quinn. *Psychological Statistics.* New York: John Wiley and Sons, Inc., 1966. 451 pp.

Among long-recognized treatments of form and style are volumes by Dugdale, Turabian, Campbell, and Perrin.

1. *American Psychological Association Publications Manual.* Washington, D.C., 1967.

2. Campbell, William G. *Form and Style in Thesis Writing.* Boston: Houghton Mifflin Co., 1954

3. Dugdale, Kathleen. *Manual of Form for Thesis and Term Reports.* Bloomington, Ind.: Indiana University Press, 1962.

4. Perrin, Porter G. *Writer's Guide and Index to English.* Chicago: Scott, Foresman, 1965.

5. Turabian, Kate L. *Student's Guide for Writing College Papers.* Chicago: University of Chicago Press, 1963.

These books help to insure that footnotes, bibliographic entries, and general format are appropriate and clear regardless of whether one is writing for publication or preparing a crisp and attractive bulletin for one's colleagues in the elementary school.

A Basic List of Tests. The following is a list of representative tests that are widely used to collect data about students (135). (Cf. Appendix) Additional information about tests of this kind will be found in Chapter 9 (18,19).

General Intelligence Tests

California Short Form Test of Mental Maturity, 1957 Revision
Chicago Non-Verbal Examination
College Qualification Test
Cooperative School and College Ability Test (SCAT)
Davis-Eels Test of General Intelligence of Problem Solving Ability
Henmon-Nelson Test of Mental Ability, Revised Edition
Kuhlmann-Anderson Intelligence Test, Sixth Edition
Kuhlmann-Anderson Intelligence Tests, Seventh Edition
The Lorge-Thorndike Intelligence Tests
Ohio State University Psychological Test, Form 21
Otis Quick-Scoring Mental Ability Tests
Pintner General Ability Tests, Non-Language Series
Pintner General Ability Tests: Verbal Series
SRA Tests of Educational Ability
Terman-McNemar Test of Mental Ability

Aptitude Test Batteries

Chicago Tests of Primary Mental Abilities
Differential Aptitude Test Battery
Flanagan Aptitude Classification Test (FACT)
General Aptitude Test Battery
Guilford-Zimmerman Aptitude Survey
Holzinger-Crowder Uni-Factor Tests
Multiple Aptitude Tests (MAT)

Reading Tests

Davis Reading Test
Diagnostic Reading Tests: Survey Section
Durrell-Sullivan Reading Capacity and Achievement Tests
Gates Advanced Primary Reading Tests
Gates Basic Reading Tests
Gates Primary Reading Tests
Gates Reading Survey-Form 1
Iowa Silent Reading Test: New Edition, Revised
Kelley-Greene Reading Comprehension Test
Lee-Clark Reading Test, 1958 Edition
Nelson-Denny Reading Test, Revised Edition
Reading Comprehension: Cooperative English Test
Traxler High School Reading Test
Traxler Silent Reading Test

Elementary School Achievement Batteries

California Achievement Tests, 1957 Edition
Iowa Tests of Basic Skills
Metropolitan Achievement Tests, 1959 Edition
Sequential Tests of Educational Progress (STEP)
SRA Achievement Tests
Stanford Achievement Tests

High School Achievement Batteries

California Achievement Tests
Cooperative General Achievement Tests, Revised Series
Essential High School Content Battery
The Iowa Tests of Educational Development
Sequential Tests of Educational Progress (STEP)

Interest Inventories

Brainard Occupational Preference Inventory
Kuder Preference Record-Occupational
Kuder Preference Record-Vocational
Kuder Preference Record-Personal
Occupational Interest Inventory-1956 Revision
Strong Vocational Interest Blank for Men, Revised
Strong Vocational Interest Blank for Women, Revised
Study of Values, Revised
Thurstone Interest Schedule

Adjustment and Temperament Inventories

Adjustment Inventory (Bell)
California Psychological Inventory (CPI)
California Test of Personality, 1953 revision
Edwards Personal Preference Schedule (EPPS)
Gordon Personal Profile
Guilford-Zimmerman Temperament Survey
Heston Personal Adjustment Inventory
Minnesota Counseling Inventory
Minnesota Multiphasic Personality Inventory (MMPI)
Mooney Problem Check List
Personality Inventory (Bernreuter)
SRA Junior Inventory
SRA Youth Inventory
Thurstone Temperament Schedule

Fugitive Materials. The tremendous numbers of pamphlets, reports, monographs, and brochures now being poured out by state and federal government agencies, foundations, universities, and professional groups are a formidable challenge even to the information storage and retrieval equipment used in modern libraries. Such materials are designated as "fugitive" because they can so quickly and easily elude capture and sometimes are not precisely catalogued.

While difficult to locate, the large variety of available fugitive materials often contain monographs or comparable material worth patient search through indexes, catalogs, and files. It is recommended that the elementary counselor set up a personal file of fugitive material, recognizing that it can become of increasing value over the years if he is careful to organize it in such a way that he can retrieve items easily from folders and file boxes.

Leads from Outside Usual Professional Education Sources. One of the problems facing any professional worker in education revolves around the question, "How can I keep myself informed with respect to developments in disciplines and fields other than education?" In this regard, selected articles appearing in many stimulating periodicals of a general nature offer many good possibilities. Either consistently or periodically, the following journals tend to publish articles with a bearing on guidance and elementary education.

The Atlantic
Saturday Review
Fortune
New Republic
Harper's Magazine

The Scientific American
Daedalus
American Scholar
Trans-action
Psychology Today
Public Opinion Quarterly
Human Relations
The Public Interest
New York Times Sunday Magazine
Annals

The articles relevant to counseling and guidance that are published in such a magazine as *Harper's* are not always labeled in such a way as to suggest the implication they have for education. Among them may be articles on urban renewal, minority groups, cybernetics, or developments in biochemistry or molecular physics. The reader must make his own inferences and applications—growing more adequate both in professional education and in general background during the process. The sources listed are especially good "leads" or keys to work of interest which is developing in related disciplines such as psychiatry, pediatrics, or physics.

Finally, one must remember that the librarian, the most valuable resource tool of all, can be helpful in advising the counselor on publications such as those we have listed and other types of educational media. Recent developments in technology such as computers, video communications systems, and facsimile printing systems are significantly affecting the educational scene. We are only beginning to appreciate the potential of these new tools of communication and how new library systems can facilitate new interactions, disseminate research, pool ideas, and stimulate teaching and learning.

Research and Professional Writing with Implications for Elementary School Counselors: 1900-1970

The material below concerns studies and research which have influenced elementary education and which have a direct or indirect relationship to the work of the elementary school counselor. The authors have selected a representative *sample* of studies, the findings of which, with intelligent interpretation and adaptation, should enable the counselor to perform his duties with increasing skills and with greater maturity as he makes professional decisions. To include all references would be a most difficult, if not impossible, task and could easily fill more pages than are in this book.

Fifty Years of Educational Studies in Retrospect

During the first five decades of this century the place of the school in American society has significantly changed just as its teaching methods and materials have altered. Many of these changes are as dramatic as the broad social and technological forces that have transformed the face of our country. Let us review briefly some of these changes to obtain a perspective for understanding today's practices as well as for planning our long range futures for educational tomorrows.

From the Turn of the Century to 1920. During the first two decades of the 20th century many ideas and innovations were introduced into education—a new world was being born. This world saw a need to recognize the demands of mass education as millions of children entered the schools and it became evident that many of them would be going on to high school. Initial efforts were made to study children and treat them as human beings; there was a beginning recognition for a curriculum adjusted to the realities of life; and the "Seven Cardinal Principles of Education" were advanced. The voice of John Dewey was heard; testing was begun; Gestalt psychology, Watson's behaviorism, and experimental schools opened their doors fired by the educational imaginations of Parker, Meriam, Wirt, Parkhurst, and others. John Dewey had published *My Pedagogic Creed* (1897) and had established his experimental school at the University of Chicago in 1896. His books, *The School and Society* (1900), *How We Think* (1910), *Democracy and Education* (1916), and *Education and Experience* (1938) among others had tremendous influence on educational thought and practice throughout the centry (36-40).

1897   J. M. Rice's "The Futility of the Spelling Grind," is conceded to be the first modern-type research report done in the field of education (119).

1901   The Francis Parker School opened in Chicago and emphasized the importance of motivation, needs, and growth of children. The project method was used before it had a name.

1905   Alfred Binêt published the first of his scales for the measurement of intelligence. This became an important part of the scientific movement in education.
         1905 – The first series of Binêt-Simon Tests
         1907 – The Pinter-Patterson Performance Scale

1906   William Graham Sumner, considered by some to be the first American Sociologist, published *Folkways* (131).

1907   *Pragmatism* by William James was quickly recognized as an important treatment of a concept influential in shaping twentieth century thinking (71).

1909   The first White House Conference on Children and Youth was held and led to the formation of the Children's Bureau in the Department of Labor.

1909   The National Committee on Mental Health was established in 1909 to help conserve mental health and prevent mental and nervous disorders. Clifford Beers (*A Mind That Found Itself*, 1908) was instrumental in its organization (5).

1909   L. P. Ayres published *Laggards in Our Schools* which emphasized the tremendous non-promotion or failure rate in the schools during the early part of the century (4).

1910   E. L. Thorndike devised a handwriting scale.

1911   L. D. Coffman completed his teacher status study, *The Social Composition of the Teaching Population* (23).

1912   The Binêt-Simon test was revised by Louis Terman and the American testing movement was inaugurated.

1913   The United States Office of Education established a Kindergarten division reflecting an interest in early childhood education.

1913   Edward L. Thorndike in his *Educational Psychology* postulated his stimulus-response connectionist psychology (134).

1914   Educational and child-care practices were influenced by James B. Watson's books and articles on behaviorism, the school of psychology generally attributed to him (139).

1914   Sigmund Freud's principles of personality development and behavior motivation influenced the social sciences. His book *The Interpretation of Dreams* had been published in 1900, and his *Psychotherapy of Everyday Life* in 1914 (45,46).

1915   Leonard P. Ayres distributed an influential spelling scale.

1917   The Lincoln School of Columbia University was founded and served as a prototype for other experimental centers.

1917   *Collected Papers on Analytic Psychology* typified the influential publications of Carl Jung (76).

1918   *The Commission on Reorganization of Secondary Education* proposed the famous seven "Cardinal Principles of Secondary Education" marking a shift in emphasis from subject matter to concern for the individual student (27).

1918   The philosophical bases of progressive education were further clarified by William H. Kilpatrick in his *The Project Method* (1918) and later in his *Foundations of Method* (1925) and *Source Book of Philosophy* (1923) (80,81,82).

1919   The Progressive Education Association was founded emphasizing respect for the uniqueness and dignity of the individual, recognition of varied needs and purposes, and the importance of a warm, humane classroom.

1919   Carleton W. Washburne began work on individual instructional materials associated with the "Winnetka Plan" in Winnetka, Illinois.

1920-1940. In the 1920's along with unprecedented prosperity, rising hemlines for women, the Bryan and Darrow joust at the Scopes Trial, and the marvel of Lindbergh crossing the ocean in the *Spirit of St. Louis*, education entered a lively era. The Progressive Education Association (1919) stepped onto the scene; the testing movement gained momentum; and the scientific method of problem solving was applied to school organization and curriculum practice.

The 1920's drew to their economically disastrous close to be succeeded by the Great Depression of the 1930's and the chill of poverty which accompanied it. Education became embroiled over social reforms, and many teachers felt the need to build attitudes reflecting greater social and economic responsibility. The curriculum was examined; ways of best serving children and youth were debated; and child and human development research began to leave an imprint upon the decade.

1920   Helen Parkhurst opened the Dalton School in Massachusetts and began producing "contract" plan materials.

1923   The first so-called modern application of Kilpatrick's ideas as to classroom changes suggested by John Dewey's philosophy was reported in Ellsworth Collings', *An Experiment With a Project Curriculum* (26).

1923–   W. W. Charters applied his job-analysis technique to edu-
1924   cational problems and published his *Curriculum Construction* (21).

1924   Wolfgang Kohler completed *The Mentality of Apes* (1924), a Gestaltist milestone. His later work *Gestalt Psychology* (1929) and Koffka's *The Growth of the Mind* (1924) further disseminated Gestalt concepts (85,87,88).

1924   *How to Make a Curriculum* was published by Frank Bobbitt stressing the importance of scientific curriculum building (11).

1925   A. N. Whitehead's *The Aims of Education and Other Essays* presented his views on rhythm in education, his insistence on vital content, and his protest against the inert ideas of dead knowledge (141).

1926   The writing of the book *Great Teachers and Mental Health* by William Burnham helped to establish him, according to some writers, as the father of modern elementary school counseling (17).

1926   One of the first writings to suggest how socio-economic change required concomitant changes in American education was William H. Kilpatrick's *Education for a Changing Civilization* (79).

1926   A pioneer in inquiry into the development of children's concepts and reasoning was Jean Piaget. His work *The Language and Thought of the Child* was a classic in the field (115).

1927   Pitirim Sorokim, a Russian psycho-neurologist, found a place in American sociology with his *Social Mobility* (129).

1927-   Boyd Bode described the reorganization of experience as
1929   the basis of purposive learning and published *Modern Educational Theories* (1927), and *Conflicting Psychologies of Learning* (1929) (12,13).

1928   Margaret Mead's book *Coming of Age in Samoa* (1928) helped to explain the influence of cultural developments upon personality. *Growing Up in New Guinea* (1930) and *And Keep Your Powder Dry* (1942) further clarified her points (102,103,104).

1928   Although different procedures were used in interrogating teachers and mental hygienists and the research design was criticized, Wickman's study, *Children's Behavior and Teachers' Attitudes,* was widely cited as "evidence" that teachers lacked understanding of mental health (144).

1929   Robert and Helen Lynd described the complexities of cultural patterns and mores in an American community in *Middletown* (1929) and *Middletown in Transition* (1937) (97,98).

1929   The physiological bases of development and the unity of the growing organism were stressed in George E. Coghill's *Anatomy and the Problem of Behavior* (24).

1929   K. S. Lashley, one of the early experimenters in regard to relationships between abnormalities in the nervous system and behavioral deviations published *Brain Mechanisms and Intelligence* (91).

1929   *Problems of Neurosis* by Alfred Adler stressed how important the drive to achieve superiority is in mediating human behavior (1).

1930   Herbert S. Jennings, interested in genetics and the influences of the environment on both organic structure and behavior, published *Biological Bases of Human Nature* (72).

1932   Walter B. Cannon in his *Wisdom of the Body* developed the concept of homeostasis and described the organism's quest for a balanced environment (20).

1932   George S. Counts wrote *Dare the Schools Build a New Social Order?* a provocative book asserting that schools have an obligation to exert leadership in social change rather than merely to carry out a passive role (30).

1933   Arthur Jersild made several studies on children's interests and motivation and his book, *Child Psychology,* provided leadership in interpreting the psychological bases of elementary education (73).

1934   Ruth Benedict's *Patterns of Culture* contributed to knowledge about the impact of cultural expectations upon child growth and development (6).

1934   *Who Shall Survive: A New Approach to the Problems of Human Interrelations,* a monograph by J. L. Moreno, added to mental health interpretations and introduced many concepts of sociometry (110).

1935   J. Wayne Wrightstone's *Appraisal of Newer Elementary School Practices* was the first significant application of evaluative processes in a school situation (145).

1935   Field psychology and the dynamics of interaction and development were presented by Kurt Lewin in *A Dynamic Theory of Personality*. He also gave leadership to the group dynamics movement (92).

1935–   The Eight Year Study was undertaken by the Progressive
1942   Education Association to assess the effects of progressive practices. W. M. Aikin reported the results in *The Story of the Eight Year Study*. The Association's work also led to gains in the development of evaluative instruments and new appraisal techniques (2).

1936   Paul Hanna documented how "socially useful work" by children functioned in community improvement in his *Youth Serves the Community* (58).

1937   Talcott Parsons, a sociological theorist interested in systematized sociology, published *The Structure of Social Action* (113).

1937   James Plant's *Personality and the Cultural Pattern* served as an important document encouraging viewing the total individual within his total environment (116).

1937   Gordon Allport stressed the wholeness of the child and emphasized the importance of environmental forces upon the individual in his *Personality, A Psychological Interpretation* (3).

1938   *Emotion and the Educative Process* by Daniel Prescott typified the mental hygiene movement that is still a chief area of concern for educators (117).

1938   The Educational Policies Commission published its widely cited objectives of education in general in *The Purposes of Education in American Democracy* (42).

1938   The Iowa Studies (Skeels and Dye, 1939; Skodak and Skeels, 1942) championed the view that intelligence was not static but a phenomenon of development with growth due to human learnings (124,125,126,128). (Adult follow-up studies were done in 1966.)

1938   Furthering our understanding of behavior were Karl Menninger's *Man Against Himself* (1938) and *Love Against Hate* (1942) (105,106).

1939   F. J. Roethlisberger and W. J. Dickson published their report on the Hawthorne Study in *Management and the Worker*. This was one of the early studies concerned with worker's behavior and had implications for group morale and effective group action (121).

1940–1960. The realities of World War II governed most activities during the first part of the decade. Many liberal voices of the 1930's were hushed or changed as efforts in the schools were redirected. The late 1940's, however, saw the child development approach widely accepted, the concept of guidance was broadened from a service for children with problems to a service for all children, and the split between the progressives and the essentialists seemed to be lessening.

In the 1950's some of the bitterest criticisms of the schools in the United States since the time of Horace Mann arose. They found a large audience particularly after the Russians launched their satellite *Sputnik* in 1957. Crowding, lack of funds, and increase in elementary enrollments to the 30 million mark conspired to hamper progress. Emphasis was again placed on content and "academic success" as academic excellence became a catchword.

1940   Ronald Lippitt and Kurt Lewin, in Iowa, began a series of research publications dealing with authoritarian, democratic, and laissez-faire classroom atmosphere which supported the value of the democratic classroom (95).

1940–   Allison Davis and John Dollard's *Children of Bondage*
1948   (1940), James H. S. Bossard's *The Sociology of Child Development* (1948), and Allison Davis' research on cultural bias as it works to the detriment of the Negro child made contributions to child socialization sduties (33,14).

1941   Carl Rogers' *Counseling and Psychotherapy* emphasized the unity of personality and fostered the development of nondirective or client-centered therapy (122).

1941–   A number of "social class" studies were published during
1949   this period: Allison Davis, Burleigh B. Gardner, and Mary A. Gardner—*Deep South: A Social Anthropological Study of Caste & Class* (1941); W. Lloyd Warner, Robert Havighurst, and M. B. Loeb—*Who Shall be Educated?* (1944); Allison Davis and Robert Havighurst—*Father of the Man* (1947); A. B. Hollingshead's *Elmtown's Youth* (1949); and W. Lloyd Warner and Paul S. Lunt—*The Status System of a Modern Community* (1942) (32,137,34,64,138).

1942   Karen Horney added a socioanthropological dimension to understanding neuroses in her *Self-Analysis* (68).

1943   William F. Whyte's famous study of groups, *Street Corner Society*, was published (143).

1943   Contributions to the field of child development were made by Arnold Gesell, Frances Ilg, and their associates. *Infant and Child in the Culture of Today* (1943) and *The Child from Five to Ten* (1946) were influential parts of a series of reports made by Gesell and his co-workers (49,50).

1944 Gunnar Myrdal made a comprehensive examination of the status of the Negro in America in his *An American Dilemma* (111).

1945 *Helping Teachers Understand Children,* an American Council on Education publication, represented the general interest and concern of educators in a child-study approach to educational planning and practices (61).

1945 Ralph Linton's *Cultural Backgrounds of Personality* became one of the major definitive statements on the implication of culture for education (94).

1947 Florence Stratemeyer in her *Developing a Curriculum for Modern Living* proposed the concept of curriculum based on persistent life situations and an analysis of the needs and nature of the child in his social environment (130).

1948 Ernest R. Hilgard's *Theories of Learning* became a widely accepted text presenting summaries of learning and instructional theory at midcentury (63).

1948 Clyde Kluckhohn and Henry Murray edited *Personality in Nature, Society, and Culture* bringing together research and concept development related to the growth of personality (83).

1949 *Child Development* by Willard Olson centered on the concept of organismic age which indicated that varying rates of growth within and among individuals should mediate curriculum and encourage methodological changes in instruction (112).

1949 *Social Theory and Social Structure* was published by Robert K. Merton, the sociological theorist (107).

1950 David Riesman's *The Lonely Crowd* described the changing American character. William F. Whyte's *The Organization Man* (1956) dealt with the life of men in large organizations. These books were widely read and cited (120,142).

1950 The pamphlet *Developmental Tasks and Education* by Robert Havighurst stressed both cultural pressures and expectations and individual needs and adjustments (60).

1950 Erik Erikson in his *Childhood and Society* presented his "Eight Ages of Man" using the developmental task concept and the incorporation of both inner forces and society's forces on the individual (43).

1951 *White Collar* by C. W. Mills and his *The Power Elite* (1956) looked at the salaried segment and the power structure of society, respectively (108,109).

1952 Arthur T. Jersild's *In Search of Self* provided insights into children's self-concepts while his publication with Ruth Tasch, *Children's Interests and What They Suggest for Education* (1949), was concerned with the implications of 25 findings related to children's lives and self-concepts (74,75).

1952   Earl Kelley and Marie Rasey provided information pertaining to the contribution of research in fields other than education in their *Education and the Nature of Man* (78).

1953   Arthur E. Bestor's *Educational Wastelands* was a critical appraisal of the schools bringing him national recognition as an oppoent of "the educationists" (8).

1953   Robert M. Hutchin's well-written analysis of educational practices in *Conflict in Education* was especially effective in identifying educational errors (69).

1953   Hans Selye's work *The Stress of Life* led to the "stress theory of disease" and further research relating stress to various body ailments (123).

1953   B. F. Skinner's *Science and Human Behavior* established the author as a leader in conjecture about the analysis and control of behavior (127).

1954   In *Motivation and Personality* Abraham Maslow conceptualizes about human development, seeing human behavior growing from within the individual rather than shaped from without (101).

1954   A supreme court decision legally terminated school segregation.

1955   Rudolph Flesch's *Why Johnny Can't Read* was a conversation piece for years. It attacked reading practices and triggered numerous articles of rebuttal from reading specialists (44).

1955   Congress authorized *The Joint Committee on Mental Health and Illness* to conduct studies on these topics. Marie Jahoda began the first aspect and reported it in her *Current Concepts of Positive Mental Health* in 1958 (70).

1956   *Taxonomy of Educational Objectives* by Benjamin S. Bloom presented a scheme to clarify the meaning of meaning with respect to educational objectives (10).

1957   Noam Chomsky's *Syntactic Structures* was published and the horizons of linguistics in education were extended (22).

1957   Calvin S. Hall and Gardner Lindzey's *Theories of Personality* presented a review of the personality theories of Sigmund Freud, Carl Jung, Alfred Adler, Eric Fromm, Karen Horney, Harry Stack Sullivan, Henry A. Murray, Kurt Lewin, Gordon Allport, Carl Rogers, William H. Sheldon, Gardner Murphy, among others (55).

1958   John K. Galbraith's book *The Affluent Society* advanced the thesis that our society can conduct an effective war on poverty (47).

1959   *The American High School Today* assessed education more than criticized it and problems and needs were implicit in James Conant's proposals for change (28).

1959   Thirty-five scientists, scholars, and educators met at Woods Hole on Cape Cod to examine the fundamental processes involved in having students understand the substance and method of science.

The 1960's: Portents of Change

Since entering the 1960's, man has been confronted with a tremendous increase of knowledge. So vast has this increase been, particularly in technology, that many individuals find it difficult to understand cause and effect relationships with any clarity, especially where mechanisms, tools, and social, political, and economic conditions in his environment are concerned. Although the new age of science had released men from the performance of many menial tasks, the "age of experts" also exploded in many ways his feelings that individual human beings were important and could be masters of their own private lives and worlds.

Man's technological capacities seemed to improve more rapidly than his skill in understanding his fellow man. Also, it became evident that we had entered a period in which the governments of technological societies threatened to become inadequate to cope with the affairs of 20th century man. After a look at important federal legislation, the chapter concludes with an overview of the current educational scene.

Significant Legislation. A brief review of some of the more recent federal legislation indicates some of the growing and widespread concern for the general welfare of the country.

1958 *National Defense Education Act.* Provided assistance for four years for science, mathematics, foreign language, counseling and guidance, graduate fellowships, research and experimentation in instructional tools such as TV, and improvement in informational and statistical services. Extended in 1961 for two years.

1958 *Fogarty-McGovern Act.* Provided federal funds for the training of teachers for the mentally retarded.

1961 *Peace Corps Act.* Provided for the establishment of a permanent Peace Corps for supplying American technicians and teachers for underdeveloped countries.

1961 *Exceptional Children.* Authorized funds for the training of teachers for deaf children and for the use of speech pathologists and audiologists.

1962 *Manpower and Development Training Act.* Occupational training and retraining of the nation's labor force were provided for under the joint responsibility of The Department of Health, Education and Welfare and The Department of Labor.

1962 *Educational TV Act; All Channel TV Act.* Federal grants were authorized to educational institutions or non-profit groups to help build educational television stations.

1963 *Vocational Education Act.* Strengthened and improved the quality of vocational education and expanded vocational educational opportunities in the nation; extended for 3 years the NDEA Act of 1958, and Public Laws 815 and 874 of the 81st Congress—federally affected areas.

1964   *Civil Rights Act.* Provided for technical and financial aid to local public school districts going through or planning to go through the process of desegregation. Discrimination was also barred under federally assisted programs.

1964   *Economic Opportunity Act* (Anti-Poverty Law). Stimulated the cooperation of local, state, and federal governments in establishing programs to aid public schools. Youth programs, work experience programs, volunteer services in America, urban and rural community actions programs, special programs for poverty in rural areas, and employment and investment incentives were included.

1964   *NDEA and Impacted Areas Program Extended.* Federally "impacted" school areas aid was extended to 1966 and the NDEA was extended until 1968.

1965   *Elementary and Secondary Education Act.* Strengthened secondary and elementary education programs for educationally deprived children in low income areas and provided for additional school library resources, textbooks, and other instructional materials, supplementary educational centers and services, and the improvement of educational research and state departments of education. Nonpublic school students were also included as beneficiaries of the Act. The educational centers could include special counseling and guidance services.

1965   *Higher Education Act.* Undergraduate scholarships and fellowships for experienced or prospective teachers were provided. A Teacher Corps was authorized to serve in urban and rural poverty areas.

1967   *Education Professional Development Act.* Designed to help school systems, state education agencies, and colleges and universities develop more effective ways to recruit, train, and utilize educational personnel.

Education in the Last Decade. The closing years of the 1960's are too close to us to permit us to view the research and publications of this period in any sharp perspective. However, the following materials are illustrative of those the reader should find most interesting.

1960   Jerome Bruner published his "sense of the meeting" report on the Woods Hole Conference under the title, *The Process of Education.* In 1962, his *On Knowing* presented ten essays which stimulated thought on new approaches to teaching and learning (15,16).

1961   An authoritative resume of progressivism in American culture was written by Lawrence Cremin in his *The Transformation of the School* (31).

1963   Ethologists, scientists interested in *inherited* behavior, created interest in territoriality and related concepts. A leading exponent was Karl Lorenz, the author of *On Aggression* (96).

1964　Possibilities for mediating the future were suggested by T. J. Gordon and Olaf Helmer in their *Report on a Long-Range Forecasting Study* made for RAND. Interesting books devoted to the future were: Bertrand de Jouvenel's *The Art of Conjecture* (1967); Herman Kahn and Anthony Wiener's *The Year 2000* (1967); and American Academy of Arts and Science Journal, "Toward the Year 2000: Work in Progress" (1967) (52,35,77,136).

1964　Benjamin Bloom's summaries focused attention on mental development and early childhood in his book, *Stability and Change in Human Characteristics* (9).

1964　A new wave of educational literature speculating about improving in-school and out-of-school learning experiences for children began to appear. Among them were John Holt's *How Children Fail* (1964); *How Children Learn* (1967), and *The Underachieving School* (1969) (65,66,67).

1965　*The Other America: Poverty in the United States* by Michael Harrington reflected the attention given to the need for improving human welfare. Head Start programs designed to diminish inequalities in education were started (59).

1965　Marshall McLuhan, widely recognized for his "global village" concept created by mass media, wrote *Understanding Media: The Extensions of Man* (99).

1966　Jean Piaget was re-discovered as a result of fresh interest in cognitive development in early childhood.

1966　The Education Policies Commission stated that public education should be available to all children beginning at age four.

1966　James Coleman developed a strong place for compensatory education for the culturally deprived as a result of his studies published under the title, *Equality of Educational Opportunity* (25).

1966　Anthropologist Edward T. Hall emphasized the influence of membership in a subculture group in the *The Hidden Dimension*. His *The Silent Language* (1959) is also of relevance (56,57).

1967　The results of big business discovering the education market began to become evident. The January, 1967 edition of the *Phi Delta Kappan* was devoted to this topic.

1967　The black American became an object of widespread educational attention along with smaller minority groups.

1968　David Krech's article, "The Chemistry of Learning," reviewed environmental mediation and the use of bio-chemistry in education (90).

1968　The Educational Facilities Laboratories captured the implication of educational change for school house construction in their *Educational Change and Architectural Consequences* (41).

1968   Eighteen essays on urgent issues confronting the new administration and the Congress in 1969 were presented in the Brookings Institute report, *Agenda for the Nation* (51).

1967–   A renewed interest in humanizing education was reflected
1970   in books critical of educational conditions and practices. Among those widely read: James Herndon, *The Way It 'Spozed to Be*; Jonathan Kozol, *Death at an Early Age*; and Herbert Kohl, *36 Children* (62,89,86).

1969–   Student unrest became endemic and the cause of major
1970   education changes in both secondary and higher education.

In order to catch the educational spirit of the times, a dozen trends of the past decade are summarized.

A new scrutiny of educational goals began as Americans discussed the role of the school, what should be taught, who should be taught, and how children and youth should be taught.

Changes in the curriculum brought the professional teacher and the academic scholar closer to a partnership in decision making.

The impact of "change agencies" became formidable as the government and private foundations sponsored basic research, experimentation, demonstration, and the dissemination of educational information and activities.

The application of technology to education introduced the computer as a versatile tool and the use of various media became of increased importance.

The expansion of the learning industry increased rapidly as business began to see the financial possibilities in applying technology to education.

An expanded role for the school was reflected in educational programs for learners of all ages which extended downward toward the nursery, upward toward older adults, outward into the community, and inward in the form of more varied offerings.

The concept of a more responsible society led to renewed attacks on poverty and the problems of the disadvantaged. "Compensatory" and "intervening" programs were initiated by public schools, foundations, industry, and government agencies in Appalachian-type and inner city areas.

Megolopolitanism and automation increased together as millions of people continued to crowd into urban areas and as technical changes created greater demands for skilled workers. The uprooted family and the unskilled transient became the object of educational and welfare activities.

Integration began to change from a concept to a reality despite opposition, delays, and confusion. Greater efforts also were made to decrease more rapidly the social and economic disparities between black and white Americans which perpetuated educational inequalities.

Emphasis on the learner and his behavior increased without diminishing interest in the scope and quality of what he learned. Knowledge about the child increased through studies of infants, creativity, intelligence, the gifted, ethnicity, social class influences, etc.

Innovations in education took many forms. Among them were flexible scheduling, nongrading, team teaching, continuous progress concepts, modern elementary guidance practices, greater use of educational technology including computer assisted instruction and programmed learning, and personalized programs.

Broader cross-cultural perspectives accompanied the international involvements and commitments of the U.S. Greater interest was shown in the educational strivings and social accomplishments of people overseas. Increased teacher exchange programs, such as the Peace Corps and foreign aid programs, accompanied a greater acceptance of international responsibility by the U.S.

Educators began to see the need for curriculum change in order to protect the human environment from the consequences of overbreeding, pollution, diminishing resources, accumulating waste products, and the danger of warfare.

These examples suffice to illustrate more fully how educators have been thrust from yesterday into tomorrow during the 1960's. Probably at no time in history has more money, time, or effort been invested in education and the extending of its frontiers. Yet this represents only a small part of what must be done as we move into the latter part of the 20th century. Unprecedented technological and human resources will be available to us. Using these resources wisely in adapting to the challenging demands of society is one that will test the mettle of all persons concerned with public education. It will be a time for *solving* problems not *labeling* them, and for *actions* not *words*.

Summary

The chapter discusses the importance of identifying and understanding significant research. Several guidelines are suggested which should help the counselor make discriminating judgments and careful choices among research studies.

General areas of research in which the counselor needs to be informed are mentioned. To provide sources of research information, examples of representative tools are reviewed under eight headings: bibliographic tools, researches in education, miscellaneous publications, continuing publications, information on statistics and research format, a basic list of tests, fugitive materials, and leads to research data from publications that are outside the usual professional listings.

In presenting a sampling of research and writing from the beginning of the century, the third part of the chapter is concerned with studies between 1900-1920, 1920-1940, and 1940-1960. The concluding section discusses the years since 1960 and significant developments occurring during this time.

The references which follow are unusually extensive. They are included, nonetheless, as a basic list of publications of enduring importance with which elementary counselors and teachers gradually may wish to become acquainted.

References

1. Adler, Alfred. *Problems of Neurosis.* London: Kegan Paul, 1929.
2. Aikin, Wilford. *The Story of the Eight Year Study.* New York: Harper and Bros., 1942.
3. Allport, Gordon. *Personality, A Psychological Interpretation.* New York: Henry Holt and Co., 1937.
4. Ayres, L. P. *Laggards in Our Schools.* Troy, New York: The Russell Sage Foundation, 1909.
5. Beers, Clifford. *A Mind That Found Itself.* New York: Doubleday and Co., Inc., 1908.
6. Benedict, Ruth. *Patterns of Culture.* Boston: Houghton Mifflin Co., 1934.
7. Berelson, Bernard and Gary A. Steiner. *Human Behavior: An Inventory of Scientific Findings.* New York: Harcourt, Brace, and World, Inc., 1964.
8. Bestor, Arthur E. *Educational Wastelands.* Urbana, Ill.: University of Illinois Press, 1953.
9. Bloom, Benjamin S. *Stability and Change in Human Characteristics.* New York: John Wiley and Sons, Inc., 1964.
10. ____. *Taxonomy of Educational Objectives.* New York: David McKay Co., Inc., 1956.
11. Bobbitt, Franklin. *How to Make a Curriculum.* Boston: Houghton Mifflin Co., 1924.
12. Bode, Boyd. *Conflicting Psychologies of Learning.* Boston: D. C. Heath and Co., 1929.
13. ____. *Modern Educational Theories.* New York: The Macmillan Co., 1927.
14. Bossard, James H. S. *The Sociology of Child Development.* New York: Harper and Bros., 1948.

15. Bruner, Jerome. *The Process of Education*. Cambridge, Mass.: Harvard University Press, 1960.

16. ____. *On Knowing*. Cambridge, Mass.: Harvard University Press, 1962.

17. Burnham, William. *Great Teachers and Mental Health*. New York: D. Appleton and Co., 1926.

18. Buros, Oscar K. (ed.). *The Sixth Mental Measurements Yearbook*. Highland Park, N.J.: The Gryphon Press, 1965.

19. ____. *Tests in Print*. Highland Park, N.J.: The Gryphon Press, 1961.

20. Cannon, Walter B. *Wisdom of the Body*. New York: W. W. Norton Co., 1932.

21. Charters, W. W. *Curriculum Construction*. New York: The Macmillan Co., 1924.

22. Chomsky, Noam. *Syntactic Structures*. New York: Humanities Press, Inc., 1957.

23. Coffman, L. D. *The Social Composition of the Teaching Population*. New York: Teachers College Press, 1911.

24. Coghill, George E. *Anatomy and the Problem of Behavior*. London: Cambridge University Press, 1929.

25. Coleman, James S., et al. *Equality of Educational Opportunity*. Washington, D.C.: U.S. Department of Health, Education, and Welfare, 1966.

26. Collings, Ellsworth. *An Experiment With a Project Curriculum*. New York: The Macmillan Co., 1923.

27. Commission on the Reorganization of Secondary Education. *Cardinal Principles of Secondary Education*. Washington, D.C.: U.S. Government Printing Office, 1918.

28. Conant, James B. *The American High School Today*. New York: McGraw-Hill Book Co., 1959.

29. ____. *Slums and Suburbs*. New York: McGraw-Hill Book Co., 1961.

30. Counts, George S. *Dare the Schools Build a New Social Order?* New York: The John Day Co., 1932.

31. Cremin, Lawrence A. *The Transformation of the School: Progressivism in American Education*. New York: Alfred A. Knopf, Inc., 1961.

32. Davis, Allison, Burleigh B. Gardner, and Mary R. Gardner. *Deep South: A Social Anthropological Study of Caste and Class*. Chicago: University of Chicago Press, 1941.

33. ____ and J. Dollard. *Children of Bondage*. Washington, D.C.: American Council on Education, 1940.

34. ____ and R. J. Havighurst. *Father of the Man*. Boston: Houghton Mifflin Co., 1947.

35. deJouvenel, Bertrand. *The Art of Conjecture*. New York: Basic Books Inc., 1967.

36. Dewey, John. *Democracy and Education*. New York: The Macmillan Co., 1916.

37. ____. *Education and Experience*. New York: The Macmillan Co., 1938.

38. ____. *How We Think*. Boston: D. C. Heath and Co., 1910.

39. ____. *My Pedagogic Creed*. New York: E. L. Kellogg and Co., 1897.

40. ____. *The School and Society*. Chicago: University of Chicago Press, 1900.

41. *Educational Change and Architectural Consequences*. New York: The Educational Facilities Laboratories, 1968.

42. The Educational Policies Commission. *The Purposes of Education in American Democracy*. Washington, D.C.: National Education Association, 1938.

43. Erikson, Erik. *Childhood and Society*. New York: W. W. Norton and Co., 1950.

44. Flesch, Rudolph. *Why Johnny Can't Read*. New York: Harper and Bros., 1955.

45. Freud, Sigmund. *The Interpretation of Dreams*. London: Hogarth Press, 1953. (First German edition, 1900).

46. ____. *The Psychopathology of Everyday Life*. New York: The Macmillan Co., 1914.

47. Galbraith, John K. *The Affluent Society*. Boston: Houghton Mifflin Co., 1958.

48. Gardner, John. *Self-Renewal*. New York: Harper and Row, Publishers, 1964.

49. Gesell, Arnold and Frances Ilg. *The Child from Five to Ten*. New York: Harper and Bros., 1946.

50. ____. *The Infant and Child in the Culture of Today*. New York: Harper and Bros., 1943.

51. Gordon, Kermit (ed.). *Agenda for a Nation*. Washington, D.C., The Brookings Institute, 1968.

52. Gordon, T. J. and Olaf Helmer. *Report on a Long-Range Forecasting Study*, RAND Collection, 1964.

53. "Guidance and Counseling." *Review of Educational Research* 30 (April, 1969): 127-281.

54. "Guidance, Counseling, and Personnel Services." *Review of Educational Research* 36 (April, 1966): 203-337.

55. Hall, Calvin S. and Gardner Lindzey. *Theories of Personality*. New York: John Wiley and Sons, Inc., 1957.

56. Hall, Edward T. *The Hidden Dimension*. New York: Doubleday and Co., Inc., 1966.

57. ____. *The Silent Language*. New York: Fawcett World Library: Premier Books, 1969.

58. Hanna, Paul. *Youth Serves the Community*. New York: John Wiley and Sons, Inc., 1936.

59. Harrington, Michael. *The Other America: Poverty in the United States*. Baltimore: Penguin Books, Inc., 1965.

60. Havighurst, Robert. *Developmental Tasks and Education*. New York: Longmans, Green, and Co., 1950.

61. *Helping Teachers Understand Children*. Washington, D.C.: The American Council on Education, 1945.

62. Herndon, James. *The Way It 'Spozed to Be*. New York: Bantam Books, 1968.

63. Hilgard, Ernest R. *Theories of Learning*. New York: Appleton-Century-Crofts, Inc., 1948.

64. Hollingshead, A. B. *Elmtown's Youth: The Impact of Social Class on Adolescence*. New York: John Wiley and Sons, Inc., 1949.

65. Holt, John. *How Children Fail*. New York: Pitman Publishing Co., 1964.

66. ____. *How Children Learn*. New York: Pitman Publishing Co., 1967.

67. ____. *The Underachieving School*. New York: Pitman Publishing Co., 1969.

68. Horney, Karen. *Self-Analysis*. New York: W. W. Norton Co., 1942.

69. Hutchins, Robert M. *The Conflict in Education*. New York: Harper and Bros, 1953.

70. Jahoda, Marie. *Current Concepts of Positive Mental Health*. New York: Basic Books, Inc., 1958.

71. James, William. *Pragmatism*. Boston: Longmans, Green, and Co., 1907.

72. Jennings, Herbert S. *Biological Bases of Human Nature*. New York: W. W. Norton Co., 1930.

73. Jersild, Arthur T. *Child Psychology*. New York: Prentice-Hall, Inc., 1933.

74. ____. *In Search of Self*. New York: Teachers College Press, 1952.

75. ____ and Ruth Tasch. *Children's Interests and What They Suggest for Education*. New York: Teachers College Press, 1949.

76. Jung, Carl. *Collected Papers on Analytic Psychology*. New York: Moffat, Yard, 1917.

77. Kahn, Herman and Anthony Wiener. *The Year 2000*. New York: The Macmillan Co., 1967.

78. Kelley, Earl and Marie I. Rasey, *Education and the Nature of Man*. New York: Harper and Bros., 1952.

79. Kilpatrick, William H. *Education for a Changing Civilization*. New York: The Macmillan Co., 1926.

80. ____. *Foundations of Method*. New York: The Macmillan Co., 1925.

81. ____. *The Project Method: The Use of the Purposeful Act in the Educative Process*. New York: Teachers College Press, Teachers College Bulletin, No. 1918.

82. ____. *Source Book of Philosophy*. New York: The Macmillan Co., 1923.

83. Kluckhohn, Clyde and Henry A. Murray. *Personality in Nature, Society, and Culture*. New York: Alfred A. Knopf, Inc., 1948.

84. Koch, Sigmund. "Psychology and Emerging Concepts of Knowledge." *Behaviorism and Phenomenology*. Edited by T. W. Wann. Chicago: University of Chicago Press, 1964.

85. Koffka, Kurt. *The Growth of the Mind*. Translated by Odgen. New York: Harcourt, Brace, and World, Inc., 1924.

86. Kohl, Herbert. *36 Children*. New York: New American Library, 1967.

87. Kohler, Wolfgang. *Gestalt Psychology*. New York: Liveright, 1929.

88. ____. *The Mentality of Apes*. Translated by E. Winter. London: Kegan, Paul, 1924.

89. Kozol, Jonathan. *Death at an Early Age*. New York: Bantam Books, 1967.

90. Krech, David. "The Chemistry of Learning." *Saturday Review* 51 (January 20, 1968): 48-49.

91. Lashley, K. S. *Brain Mechanisms and Intelligence*. Chicago: University of Chicago Press, 1929.

92. Lewin, Kurt. *A Dynamic Theory of Personality*. New York: McGraw-Hill Book Co., 1935.

93. Lieberman, Myron. *The Future of Public Education*. Chicago: University of Chicago Press, 1960.

94. Linton, Ralph. *Cultural Backgrounds of Personality*. New York: D. Appleton-Century Co., 1945.

95. Lippitt, Ronald. "An Experimental Study of Democratic and Authoritarian Group Atmospheres." *University of Iowa Studies in Child Welfare* 16 (1940): 43-195.

96. Lorenz, Karl. *On Aggression*. New York: Harcourt, Brace, and World, Inc., 1963.

97. Lynd, Robert and Helen Lynd. *Middletown*. New York: Harcourt, Brace, and Co., 1929.

98. ____. *Middletown in Transition*. New York: Harcourt, Brace, and Co., 1937.

99. McLuhan, Marshall. *Understanding Media: The Extensions of Man*. New York: McGraw-Hill Book Co., 1965.

100. Martensen, Donald G. and Allen M. Schmuller. *Guidance in Today's Schools*, 2nd ed. New York: John Wiley and Sons, Inc., 1966.

101. Maslow, Abraham. *Motivation and Personality*. New York: Harper and Bros., 1954.

102. Mead, Margaret. *Coming of Age in Samoa*. New York: William Morrow and Co., Inc., 1928.

103. ____. *Growing Up in New Guinea*. New York: William Morrow and Co., 1930.

104. ____. *And Keep Your Powder Dry*. New York: William Morrow and Co., Inc., 1942.

105. Menninger, Karl. *Love Against Hate*. New York: Harcourt, Brace, and Co., 1942.

106. ____. *Man Against Himself*. New York: Harcourt, Brace, and Co., 1938.

107. Merton, Robert K. *Social Theory and Social Structure*. Glencoe, Ill.: The Free Press, 1949.

108. Mills, C. Wright. *The Power Elite*. New York: Oxford University Press, 1956.

109. ____. *White Collar*. New York: Oxford University Press, 1951.

110. Moreno, J. L. *Who Shall Survive: A New Approach to the Problems of Human Interrelations*. Scranton, Pa.: Nervous and Mental Disease Publishing Co., 1934.

111. Myrdal, Gunnar. *An American Dilemma*. New York: Harper and Bros. 1944.

112. Olson, Willard. *Child Development*. Boston: D.C. Heath and Co., 1949.

113. Parsons, Talcott. *The Structure of Social Action*. New York: McGraw-Hill Book Co., 1937.

114. Peterson, Peter G. "The Class of 1984 . . . Where Is It Going?" an address before the National Conference of State Legislators, December 4, 1966.

115. Piaget, Jean. *The Language and Thought of the Child*. New York: Harcourt, Brace, and Co.

116. Plant, James. *Personality and the Culture Pattern*. London: H. Milford, 1937.

117. Prescott, Daniel (ed.). *Emotion and the Educative Process*. Washington, D.C.: American Council on Education, 1938.

118. *Questions and Answers on the California Achievement Tests,* Monterey, Calif.: California Test Bureau, 1961.

119. Rice, J. M. "The Futility of the Spelling Grind," *Forum Magazine* 23 (April-June, 1897): 163-172; 409-419.

120. Riesman, David, Nathan Glazer, and Revel Denny. *The Lonely Crowd*. New Haven, Conn.: Yale University Press, 1950.

121. Roethlisberger, F. J. and W. J. Dickson. *Management and the Worker*. Cambridge, Mass.: Harvard University Press, 1939.

122. Rogers, Carl. *Counseling and Psychotherapy*. Boston: Houghton Mifflin Co., 1941.

123. Selye, Hans. *The Stress of Life*. New York: McGraw-Hill Book Co., 1953.

124. Skeels, Harold M. "A Study of the Effects of Differential Stimulation on Mentally Retarded Children: A Follow-Up Report," *American Journal of Mental Deficiency* 46 (January, 1942): 340-350.

125. ____. "Adult Status of Children with Contrasting Early Life Experiences: A Follow-Up Study," *Child Development Monographs* 31: No. 3, Serial No. 105, 1966.

126. ____ and H. B. Dye. "A Study of the Effects of Differential Stimulation on Mentally Retarded Children," *Proceedings and Addresses of the American Association on Mental Deficiency* 44 (1939): 114-136.

127. Skinner, B. F., *Science and Human Behavior*. New York: The Macmillan Co., 1953.

128. Skodak, Marie and H. M. Skeels. "A Final Follow-Up Study of 100 Adopted Children," *Journal of Genetic Psychology* 75 (1949): 85-125.

129. Sorokim, Pitirim. *Social Mobility*. New York: Harper and Bros., 1927.

130. Stratemeyer, Florence. *Developing a Curriculum for Modern Living*. New York: Teachers College Press, 1947.

131. Sumner, William G. *Folkways*. Boston: Ginn and Company, 1906.

132. Taba, Hilda. *Intergroup Education in Public Schools*. Washington, D.C.: American Council on Education, 1952.

133. *Test Interpretation at the Elementary School Level*. Los Angeies City Schools Evaluation and Research Section, No. 259, 1964.

134. Thorndike, Edward L. *Educational Psychology.* 3 vols. New York: Teachers College Press, 1913.

135. Thorndike, Robert and Elizabeth Hagen. *Measurement and Evaluation in Psychology and Education.* New York: John Wiley and Sons, Inc., 1964.

136. "Toward the Year 2000: Work in Progress." *Daedalus.* Cambridge, Mass.: American Academy of Arts and Sciences, Summer, 1967.

137. Warner, W. L., Robert Havighurst, and M. B. Loeb. *Who Shall Be Educated? The Challenge of Unequal Opportunities.* New York: Harper and Bros., 1944.

138. ____ and Paul S. Lunt. *The Status System of a Modern Community.* Vol. 2, The Yankee City Series. New Haven, Conn.: Yale University Press, 1942.

139. Watson, James B. *Behavior: An Introduction to Comparative Psychology.* New York: Henry Holt and Co., 1914.

140. Webster, Staten W., ed. *The Disadvantaged Learner: Knowing, Understanding, Educating.* San Francisco, Calif.: Chandler Publishing Co., 1966.

141. Whitehead, A. N. *The Aims of Education and Other Essays.* New York: The Macmillan Co., 1925.

142. Whyte, William F. *The Organization Man.* New York: Simon and Schuster, 1956.

143. ____. *Street Corner Society.* Chicago: University of Chicago Press, 1943.

144. Wickman, E. K. *Children's Behavior and Teachers' Attitudes.* New York: The Commonwealth Fund, Division of Education, 1928.

145. Wrightstone, J. Wayne. *Appraisal of Newer Elementary School Practices.* New York: Teachers College Press, 1935.

4

Issues Related to Counseling and Guidance in the Elementary School

When one probes the fund of knowledge upon which a counselor draws when working with children, it quickly becomes apparent that a good background of understanding in elementary education, counseling and guidance, and research is not, in itself, enough to insure a first-rate program. The counselor also needs to acquire a stock of intellectually examined values which serve as a guide to thought and action in his work, particularly in his interpersonal relationships with teachers and children. Furthermore, the counselor needs to be governed by a set of beliefs which his professional activity, reading, and other sources of experience have helped him to accumulate, and which determine what he believes to be "good" elementary counseling and guidance practice. Plainly he needs to stand for *something*, or by default, he stands for *nothing*. It follows, therefore, that he must be equipped with the body of examined values which serve as guides to conduct.

Chapter 4 discusses issues in counseling and guidance at the elementary school level *to which counselors need to apply their values.* The reader is introduced first to ten general issues which deal with the counselor's role in the field of elementary education. Then, certain issues are probed because they are directly associated with guidance practices in early and middle childhood. The values expressed here as viewpoints on issues are especially important because they serve as an underpinning for the *functions* of the counselor which are developed in Part Two of the book and as a foundation for a discussion of the human and physical environment for guidance as presented in Part Three.

The beginning of wisdom is calling things by their correct names. It seems fitting, therefore, to turn first to the meaning of the abstract noun "issue" as it is used here.

What Is an Issue?

The College Edition of the Webster New World Dictionary defines "issue" as a matter of debate or controversy or a point that is in dispute between two or more people. In education, at least, much more can be said about what creates an "issue," about the question of how one *interprets* the term, and about some of the elements that often help to *resolve* issues in the area of guidance services.

What Creates an Issue?

In view of the widespread and frequent use that educators make of the term *issue*, it is remarkable how few of them make an attempt—except by implication—to suggest what they mean.

Actually, at least five "levels of difference" can be identified in educational disagreements or disputes. These levels have a response-range that extends from mild to vehement, and may be categorized as follows:

I. *The Level of Preference.* Here the educator believes that one procedure, method, idea, etc., may be better than another but does not feel involved or threatened. He may think that one primary school reading program is better than another, for instance, but as an art teacher he does not feel very concerned.

II. *The Level of Opinion.* Here definite choices are made and may be defended quite vigorously, but more for the joy of discussion than to persuade or force others to accept a given person's views. There is little if any basic affective involvement.

III. *The Level of Debate.* Discussions become heated and there may be overtones of dispute at Level III. Basically, at this level, the parties concerned are motivated to gather information to support their contentions and want to bring others to accept their persuasions in grouping or promoting children, for example, or in educational evaluation practices.

IV. *The Level of Controversy.* This differs from the *Preference*, *Debate*, or *Opinion* Levels in that there is sharp dispute, and often a desire to employ any arguments that seem likely to work regardless of whether or not they are reasoned ones. Furthermore, there is substantial resistance here to changing one's educational posture because of personal involvement, a loss of face, or the suspicion that an individual or group will be weakened or inconvenienced in some professional endeavor. Introduction of the "New Mathematics" by administrative directive without teacher participation or adequate in-service education is an example of a move that could trigger *Controversy*.

V. *The Level of Issues.* Just when a *Controversy* is escalated to the "issue" level is difficult to determine because some participants in disputes have lower boiling points than others. However, the elements that characterize an issue can, with some clarity, be identified. An issue in education is created as the result of a threat, *either genuine or imaginary*, to one's professional reputation, welfare, or security. There is a strong sense of identification and involvement, usually accompanied by the powerful emotional impact of the ingredients involved. Salary discussions, proposals involving major changes in one's instructional or administrative assignment, and basic changes in the content of instruction are representative of elements that can affect, respectively, the welfare, reputation, and professional security of teachers, guidance personnel, administrators, supervisory consultants, or even custodians.

Educators sometimes behave as though they had solved a problem in education simply because they have labeled and explained it. To avoid this trap, it is necessary to look more carefully at the matter of how it is sometimes possible to *resolve* issues in education.

How Can Issues Be Resolved?

Because of his highly visible position with respect to human and instructional problems of many varieties, it is unusually important for the counselor to have certain insights where problem-issues are concerned. One cluster of these insights should pertain to the matter of how conflict-situations can be eased through knowing something about how certain kinds of issues, at least, can be resolved. At the outset, one must realize, because of their inherent "threat" to some people involved, that issues are extremely difficult to resolve. Anything so infused with emotional content is quite likely to have an unthinking or irrational element in it.

Nonetheless, there are at least four sources of assistance; four allies that offer help to the counselor in resolving issues:

1) *Time:* A glance backward reveals that many problems which generated heat in the 1950's or 1960's have lost their controversial qualities during the intervening years. There is little current debate, for instance, as to whether manuscript or cursive writing is better for the beginner to use. This was a matter of controversy if not a full-fledged issue in the 1930's and 1940's.

2) *Data*: Factual information or research findings can help to dispel an issue. If he is open-minded, even a very stubborn opponent will retreat or concede when confronted with substantial and well-compiled evidence.

3) *Education*: Sound education, whether "formal" in the sense of schooling or "informal" in the sense of a planned program for informing a population, can open the mind by providing both knowledge and developmental experiences.

4) *Improved communication*: We are becoming more and more aware of the semantic and linguistic barriers which not only can blur communication but actually cause trouble because faulty meanings are transmitted from speaker to listener. Current study in sociolinguistics (the relation to and the influence of language on personal relationships) and in psycholinguistics (concerned with the acquisition of language and concept development through language) holds considerable promise for reducing the unintelligibility on which issues feed.

The pressure that can sometimes be brought to bear through power or influence may, of course, also be used in an attempt to resolve issues. Pressure of this kind should be used sparingly if at all, however. Too often, pressure begets counter-pressure, and, when this happens, an issue may become more rather than less difficult to cope with.

Effective counseling and guidance programs *in themselves* also should be an important force in arresting the development of some issues by creating an atmosphere of mutual trust and good will that is conducive to the reasoned solution of problems.

Some Issues Are Insoluble

Before turning to some actual issues, it is a matter of simple honesty to recognize that certain situations are likely to have within them problems that are insoluble in the immediate future. Why? Because at least two groups with which it is difficult, if not impossible, to work exist in most populations: 1) those whose emotional immaturity limits their capacity for reaching a reasoned consensus with others, and 2) those who do not wish to see a problem-issue resolved because they believe that it is to their personal profit to keep a particular controversy alive or to postpone a decision.

The emotionally immature person may be literally incapable of ridding himself of a fancied threat, hence, cannot be expected to share effectively in the quest for rational solutions. Unless the counselor can persuade such persons to seek help in improving their mental health, there is little to do except to "quarantine" them as kindly and as deftly as possible in the sense of limiting their participation in situations which they only worsen by their presence.

Also, great patience and compassion are needed in working with the unreasonably threatened and fearful so that they do not feel by-passed and, as a result, become chronic trouble-makers in an effort to retaliate for being ignored.

Those persons motivated by self-interest who endeavor to keep us wandering in a wilderness of unresolved issues merit less consideration than the immature persons above. Here we have persons who seem to thrive on demagoguery, the ax-grinders, and those who exploit either or both sides of a group divided by a controversy. This self-seeking minority often does not wish an issue or conflict to terminate because such issues bring them attention, psychological or financial benefits, a misguided following—or a combination of all three. Remember that data are often good weapons to use in the arena in which demagogues put up their fight. Here they also are most visible—and here their spurious arguments can sometimes be swept away with factual information presented in full public view.

So much for the nature and theory of educational issues. Let us now look at ten general issues related to the counselor's work in elementary education.

Issues Related to the
Counselor's Role in Elementary Education

For purposes of presentation in this section a distinction is made between certain problem issues pertaining to the role, status, or function of the *counselor* and other issues having more of a bearing on the elementary school guidance *program*. Naturally, the school counselor and his goals or tasks are inseparable; there are, however, separate issues related to each.

Rather than use the traditional form for stating the issues we have phrased them as questions to increase clarity and to simplify. Since most of the potential sources of problems are closely related, we first list all ten, then discuss them in relationship to one another.

1) How shall the role of the school counselor in the elementary school be developed so that he becomes the teammate and peer of other faculty members rather than either the "boss" or servile to the teachers and administrators?

2) What are the counselor's functions in curriculum planning, counseling, consulting, and developmental planning that inevitably exercise an influence on the intellectual and psychological climate of the child's learning environment?

3) How does the counselor create a sound leadership role that is authoritative rather than authoritarian in the image it creates for the faculty?

4) How can the counselor cope with the rapid increase in knowledge and information which presently is complicating nearly every realm of education?

5) What is the correct balance, in a given elementary school, between the creative role of the counselor and the time that must be given to establishing and maintaining the storage and retrieval system which preserves pupil personnel data?

6) What is the counselor's role with respect to the current emphasis on cultivating "excellence," beginning in the early and middle childhood years?

7) How shall the work of the counselor be developed so that it utilizes but is not dominated by educational media?

8) In the elementary school, what necessary distinctions need to be made between technology in guidance services as a *means* and as an *end*?

9) What insights should the school counselor in the elementary school help teachers to develop as increased stress is placed on the international dimensions of education and its concomitant, human rights?

10) As an elementary counseling and guidance program becomes established, what can the counselor do to avoid the dry-rot of set routines and practices that become institutionalized and "traditional" in a few years?

At first glance the reader may have at least two reactions to the 10 issues: 1) What "threat quality" makes these *genuine* issues, and 2) What is a sound position for the school counselor to take? *As we examine these two queries we are, in effect, discussing a philosophy of counseling and guidance with respect to the counselor's role in elementary education.*

A Viewpoint on the Counselor's Role

The first four issues are closely related and call for a great deal of tact and skill in human relations. The matter of being a teammate rather than a "boss," for instance, involves skill in avoiding a two-way threat. Teachers are alarmed and threatened if they feel that they have a new "director" or "supervisor" to please, and when this occurs the relationships among teachers, children, and the counselor are jeopardized. Conversely, the professional stature of the counselor is threatened if the impression is somehow created that he is little more than a disciplinarian, a test administrator, or an errand boy performing menial or clerical tasks. This situation is roughly paralleled in curriculum planning where teachers welcome help from a specialist who understands children's needs and problems but become alarmed if they feel that their prerogatives in the curriculum realm or in their classrooms are being usurped. The same thing is true in reverse if the counselor's contributions to curriculum planning and coordination are ignored.

Issue 3 challenges the counselor to be authori*tative* rather than authori*tarian*, and issue 4 confronts him with the task of playing his role well when the so-called knowledge explosion, as pointed out in Chapter 2, confronts children with perhaps 50 to 100 per cent more subject matter than was taught a generation ago. Here, the teacher and counselor alike must pool their separate skills and talents so that each helps rather than threatens the other through his expertise. In the process each person—be he teacher or counselor—becomes a source of authoritative help for the other in creating effective learning programs for children.

Implicit in the preceding paragraphs is a theme encountered repeatedly throughout this book: the knowledge of the school counselor is his "touchstone," for example, in reaching a reasoned solution to problems before they arise, if possible, or for their successful resolution if they become problem issues (22). It is this know-how on the part of the counselor which also holds the brightest promise for resolving or alleviating the other six problem issues which were identified.

Balancing creative contributions and service functions (issue 5 above) is no problem as long as the counselor does not become threatened by his colleagues on the faculty as to the meaning of "balance" in his role. The counselor can contribute to finding creative solutions for problem situations which interfere with children's learning and also function as an effective professional person in helping to maintain the myriad of professional services, such as testing, which a sound program requires.

The same general approach holds for issues 6, 7, and 8. Exposing children to premature and unreasonable academic pressure in the name of "excellence" on the one hand and having a disdain for standards and achievement on the other are equally undesirable. Nor need the use of either educational media or technology become a threat. The well-informed counselor welcomes technology as a means of facilitating guidance services and keeps his work "people-centered" rather than "machine-centered" so that in a well-handled situation no issues arise with respect to mass media nor to the tools of the "education industry."

To a casual reader issue 9, pertaining to the international dimension of education, may seem a remote and even a contrived item to include in a selected sampling of issues. However, the significance of education for international understanding is so great as to require that it be phased methodically into the counselor's role. This viewpoint seems justifiable because the acquisition of a sound international posture by the many millions of children in elementary schools today, one that will stand them in good stead during the years ahead, is a matter of top priority.

Furthermore, desirable attitudes are not built merely by helping children acquire factual information about foreign lands and peoples. International attitudes of outreaching friendliness, compassion, and a willingness to cooperate with other men of good will are not "taught" but are "caught," or absorbed, from a school climate which *itself* reflects respect for human personality. This suggests that suitable guidance policies aimed at the creation of the most effective boys and girls and young adolescents provide the best foundation for enlightened participation at a level of international effectiveness in later life.

"International" education, then, begins in the home and the school and, to a large degree, reflects the development of wholesome attitudes toward others, a sense of security, and acceptance rather than rejection of one's classmates.*

Issue 10, concerned with how the counselor may avoid living only with the satisfaction of past successes and the outmoded traditions of practice it frequently supports, can be kept from becoming a problem issue *if the other nine issues are adeptly and intelligently handled.* Elementary schools throughout the U.S., and in a growing number of instances in schools overseas, are looking to guidance programs for substantial help. The opportunities and obligations this implies leave no excuse for complacent elementary school counselors.

Guidance Program Practices and Policies in the Early and Middle Childhood Years

Because effective elementary school guidance programs are relatively new and hence not yet well developed in the majority of school systems, there is still a great deal of discussion and comment concerning the matter of what constitute sound practices. While the nature of many general goals for children's development, e.g., developing the ability to think clearly, cultivating physical well-being, acquiring useful skills and knowledge, and functioning in a desirable learning environment, are generally accepted, many specific issues

---

*The 1969 *Yearbook* of the National Society for the Study of Education, *The United States and International Education*, p. 273, defines international education as pertaining to ". . . the accumulating body of accurate information and mind-opening experience, selected and directed by the school, which determines the attitudes and the actions of the student in matters related to peoples and the policies of nations beyond the borders of his own country."

remain. Educational goals to be sought through curriculum content and organization are discussed in Chapter 5.

A Roster of Issues, Practices, and Policies of Concern to Counselors

As in the previous section treating the role of the counselor, a selection of controversial items on programs and policies, phrased as problem-questions, are presented.

1. *Should there be a guidance and counseling program in the elementary school?* There are a number of persons who, in the past, have contended that guidance is a function of the classroom teacher in the elementary school; therefore, there is no place for a guidance counselor.

Actually, guidance in early and middle childhood involves cooperatively performed functions on the part of both the teacher and the counselor. Each of whom, if competent and motivated, has a unique contribution to make to a child's successful adjustment, performance, and progress in school. What, in particular, is the counselor's contribution? A number of advantages suggest themselves, and also substantiate the need for specialized persons in the elementary program. Eight assets the counselor should bring to the elementary school are:

A broad knowledge—in excess of the teacher's knowledge—and of the dynamics of human behavior.

A strong elementary school background based on courses both in elementary education and counseling and guidance together with a practicum and field experiences having a broad orientation to elementary school children and their educational programs.

An understanding of cultures and subcultures comprising American society and their implications for communicating effectively with polyethnic children and in planning their learning experiences.

A depth understanding of the counseling process and the ability to use both individual and group counseling techniques in working with children and adults.

The ability to interact with skill and finesse as a consultant with parents, teachers, administrators, and other school personnel in curriculum planning and program development designed to create an optimum learning environment for all children.

Skill in sensitizing teachers both to the subtleties and the importance of their interactions with children, in increasing their awareness of developmental changes in boys and girls and in alerting them to the importance of the total environmental situation.

A knowledge of channels of referral for children having specialized needs: school psychologists, social workers, psychometrists, nurses, special education teachers, remedial teachers, etc.

A high respect for all people; the ability to work cooperatively with others; and the maturity to accept one's strengths and weaknesses, realizing that the counselor through his interactions with others should continue to grow both personally and professionally in the process.

Counselors, if they have the right type of preparation for fulfilling the role in the elementary schools that these eight assets imply, are in an excellent position to contribute appreciably to children's development. For one thing, their time is not structured, as is the teacher's, by full-time teaching responsibilities. They are able to obtain a broad overview of children in several settings through: 1) the home (visitations and parent conferences as needed), 2) the school (observation and consultation with teachers), 3) personal contact (individual and group counseling sessions). In addition, 4) counselors have opportunities for sustained and extensive study, when required, of individual children from problem situations. Finally, 5) the counselor is able to engage in the longitudinal study of children during their entire period of enrollment in the elementary school as distinct from most teachers' one-year to three-year contacts.

While classroom teachers also have analogous personal assets in the form of *their* specialized talents, preparation, and experience, such assets neither replace nor duplicate the counselor's work. Teachers and counselors complement and supplement one another. Hence, there seems little reason to doubt that there is a distinct place for the professionally directed elementary school guidance program.

2. *How large should an elementary school be in order to justify the introduction of a counseling and guidance program?* In view of the great range and variety of children's educational and personal needs, there is no school (not even of the all-but-vanished one-room variety) that is "too small" for counseling and guidance services. At the same time, in the interests of economy, it is unrealistic to propose that a full-time counselor be hired in the tiniest of districts. It is recommended, therefore, that if necessary in launching a program, one counselor might initially serve as many as three or four small elementary schools. However, the emerging elementary school guidance program, as portrayed in subsequent chapters, merits the employment of a full-time counselor in a primary and middle school (i.e., a N-6 or N-8 elementary school) with 25 children in each of 12 rooms and with 100 four- and

five-year-old preschool enrollees. In other words, for modest services a ratio of approximately 250-300 children per counselor is the maximum that should be contemplated.*

3. *Should the guidance counselor also be a qualified elementary classroom teacher?* There are several reasons, both professional and psychological, as to why counselors in elementary schools should be qualified teachers. A person who is a graduate of a reputable undergraduate program in elementary education usually has completed course work in child growth and development, psychology, sociology, and anthropology. He has thus begun to establish the broadly based, multidisciplinary background that is essential for both teaching and counseling with young children. In addition, he becomes familiar with the purposes, content, and methods of elementary education and in ways of working with children of this age. During his student teaching or teaching internship experience, he continues not only to broaden his base for understanding the developmental needs of children, but also to increase his awareness of the importance of the learning environment.

Other subtle insights can be gained during these preparatory years. He begins to understand the mixture of aspirations and competence, of gripes and insecurities one nearly always encounters in any organizational structure whether a corporation, an Army division, or a school. He begins to become part of a professional "in-group." The opportunity for empathy and insight thus created can be of lifelong value when he subsequently becomes a specialist in counseling and guidance.

Psychologically, the counselor who has some experience in the elementary school before or during his graduate study in counseling and guidance is likely to be more quickly accepted, and not be viewed with veiled uneasiness or even unveiled hostility until elementary teachers recognize that he knows something of what goes on in the classroom. Very few persons are willing to accept a person as a leader or consultant if they feel he has not the background that qualifies him for the role he purports or desires to fill.

Personal qualities such as integrity and intelligence are important in any educational position, including a leadership role in guidance and counseling. These are as important as the academic requirements regarding preparation for teaching and counseling. Nonetheless, while some teaching experience does not guarantee subsequent success, it can provide a foundation which is of unquestionable value when one begins work in guidance leading to one of several possible advanced degrees. Issue 5 below provides further relevant comments regarding preparation for a position in elementary school guidance and counseling.

*This assumes that the counselor is backstopped by a clerk-secretary. When the counselor-child ratio exceeds 300, the services of a paraprofessional may be needed.

4. *Is a man or a woman more likely to work effectively in the elementary school guidance services program?* Despite the fact that it is an "unanswerable" question, some people contend that one or the other—a male or a female—is "better" with children. One person may be superior to another as a counselor or teacher, but effectiveness is related to *individual qualities* rather than to gender. A sensitive, creative man may be excellent even with three or four year olds; a young woman can be "just right" for a high-risk delinquency group in a deprived urban or rural slum. Any discrimination because of sex *per se* in counseling is not merely an issue, it is an irresponsible expression of prejudice.

5. *What should be the nature of the counselor's preparation?* No one is ever completely or permanently qualified for a professional position today no matter what their field may be because of the continuing flow of new developments and research. The best generalization to make about the counselor's preparation is that it is continuous and life-long—as is that of the superior elementary teacher who also diligently avoids reliving one year of classroom experience twenty times in two decades.

In general, the matter of what is the "best" preparation for the elementary counselor depends on what he has done—on where he stands, educationally speaking—when he first contemplates a career in elementary guidance. Early in the process of planning his graduate study the tyro in counseling needs 1) to assess his background and 2) to make a rough estimate of the level of leadership competence that he wishes to reach. Self-assessment suggests *where* one begins his advanced preparation; general career planning should indicate *how* he approaches his self-selected goals.

In preparing for elementary school counseling there are three levels of contribution for one to contemplate. Each involves approximately the following *cumulative* study and experience:

Level I: The Level of Service. Here the beginning counselor (unless he already has a baccalaureate or a master's degree in elementary education) begins his preparation with a study of young children and the elementary school—its purposes, programs, and procedures. Presumably, the fledgling counselor already has a modest background in psychology and educational measurement, and in such fields as sociology, anthropology, and communication skills. Lacking such a background, he will methodically plan to obtain it.

In addition, he will complete work in counseling and guidance, taking those courses designed to develop his sophistication in elementary school counseling. These would include studies in the behavioral sciences, human growth and development, communication theory, and human relations as well as a practicum and supervised field experience. At the end of a one- to two-year program of study (depending upon the background with which he began), the beginning counselor should have a good orientation toward the elementary school and be able to operate at *Level I* as an elementary school counselor.

The elementary school counselor is concerned with all the children in the school, not just with those who have problems. Working closely with classroom teachers, he helps them focus their attention upon developmental changes in children and the uniqueness of each individual child's nature and needs. Rather than concentrating on "curing" problems or on "preventing" problems, the counselor is concerned with the total developmental process of all pupils and what can be done to enhance their learning opportunities.

Level II: The Level of Direction. Often associated with the pursuit of a 6-year diploma, certificate, or post-master's degree such as the Ed.S., *Level II* studies introduce the advanced student to opportunities for greater leadership in the elementary school.

During this additional period of study, the counselor completes advanced work in the field of counseling and guidance along with field experiences and an internship in an elementary school. His course work has included work in personality theory, group dynamics, and group processes. He also has continued work in the behavioral sciences focusing on human behavior and the learning process. Equally important, he has continued his study of elementary education as new developments and insights are gathered about curriculum, and the methods and materials of instruction.

At the close of this period of study, and presumably after performing successfully for several years at *Level I*, the counselor in the elementary school is capable of lending mature direction to guidance and pupil personnel activities.

Hopefully, many persons in elementary school counseling and guidance will begin to function at *Level II* during the next decade or two and will continue to enhance their professional role through in-service and self-improvement activities. As they closely consult with teachers and parents, their opportunities for guiding children's learning more effectively should certainly increase.

Level III: The Level of Leadership. Some practitioners in elementary school guidance will undoubtedly elect to go on to *Level III*, the doctoral level or its equivalent, in preparing for leadership responsibilities. The leadership role as envisioned here should permit the person to work effectively in university teaching or in serving as the director of pupil personnel services. This individual would have completed the broad outline of experiences suggested in the programs for *Level I* and *Level II*. In addition, however, this person will have examined the broad proposal of studies encompassing further study in the behavioral sciences. As specialists at this level will be operating on a high professional plane, they will also have completed internships which will provide them experiences in program administration, in school and community affairs, and in interprofessional relations.

Counselors at *Level III* will also be concerned with facilitating, initiating, implementing, demonstrating, or disseminating research findings. For this reason it becomes essential that they understand research design and the applications of the computer as well as other technological devices available to improve educational practices.

The counselor at the *Level III* order of competency should feel comfortable and capable of functioning as do his comparably advanced professional colleagues: specialists in the area of elementary education, psychologists, psychometrists, psychiatrists, physicians, pediatricians, social workers, and so forth, whose educational backgrounds have included preparation for the doctoral degree in their particular area of proficiency.

Only in the very broadest of terms, can a program of study and experience be designed for the three levels of counselor preparation as described above. The following chart illustrates some interesting possibilities that might be considered.

Hypothetical Model of Program for Preparing Elementary School Counselors and Directors of Pupil Personnel Services

Level I. M.S. Elementary School Counselor

Possesses well developed repertoire of professional skills and knowledges that enables him to be a competent generalist in school guidance programs and a competent specialist in these programs designed for the pre-school and elementary school child.

Foundations: Human Development
Social and Cultural Foundations
Elementary Curriculum and Teaching Techniques
The Computer in Education

Specialization: Counseling and Guidance Practicum
School and Community Resources
Individual and Group Appraisal
Counseling and Guidance Programs for Children
Group Counseling

Electives: *Studies in the liberal arts:* Sociology, Anthropology, Psychology, Biology, Social Work, etc., to be determined by the individual student's need to support, extend, or compensate for his particular professional capabilities.

Level II. Ed.S. Pupil Personnel Specialist or Elementary School Counselor

Possesses the skills of the elementary school counselor but, in addition, understands in greater depth than the Level I counselor the impact of personal, social, and cultural factors that influence him, the students, and the school. Demonstrates the professional competencies required of a counselor working with children, teachers, parents, colleagues, and other professional persons found in referral agencies.

General: Analysis of Interpersonal Behavior

Social Relations, Urban Community and Ethnic Considerations

The Sociology and Biology of Childhood

Theories of Personality

Individual Testing

Specialization: *Seminar:* Planning for Schools in New Towns and Urban Renewal Areas

Internship: Elementary School Children

Seminar: Advanced Counseling Theories

Research: Seminar in Counseling and Guidance

Statistics in the Social Sciences

Research and Writing Seminar

Level III. Ed.D. or Ph.D. Director of Pupil Personnel Services or Counselor Educator

Possesses the skills and competencies of the pupil personnel specialist and the counselor, but in addition, is aware of and sensitive to the relevant process and product cues of the broad school and community situation which enable him to make independent and rational decisions on the basis of relevant evidence in coordinating and administering pupil personnel services.

Seminars: *Interprofessional Seminar:* Behavioral Sciences and the Health Professions

Interprofessional Seminar: School and Community

Specialization: *Internship:* Phase I-Administration of Pupil Personnel Services

Phase II-School and Community Resources

Phase III-Interprofessional Relations

Seminar: Advanced Study of Educational and Social Change

Research: *Computer Programming for Educational Research Dissertation*

Seminar: Research Design

Minor Area: Requirements determined by Ed.D. or Ph.D. programs of the University

Certainly, one can no longer afford to ignore cultural and social relationships. Nor can one afford to dismiss lightly the needs, expressed desires, and dreams of a community as plans are generated for educational programs and for children's futures. Like the children they serve, counselors are unique, and their advanced study programs, too, must be personalized, continuously examined and revised as we begin to cope with man's first entrance into a highly advanced technological society. In this society where our institutions are in a constant state of flux, the preparation of counselors also should be one in which necessary changes are given an opportunity to evolve and emerge.

6. *What should be the nature of the "power relationships" between the principal and the counselor?* The web of administrative relationships among superintendents, principals, supervisors, consultants, and so on, while highly important in accomplishing tasks is also difficult to describe. Not only are power relationships subtle; they vary from time to time, from place to place, from situation to situation; and from person to person. Age, experience, personality, seniority, academic status and stature all may enter into and complicate patterns of interaction. Under such variable circumstances, it is difficult to generalize with respect to the question-issue of the "right" or "sound" answer as to a counselor's proper role in influencing or even re-directing administrative policies.

As a rule, the counselor in a *Level I* guidance position would expect to operate under administrative direction, either the principal's or preferably that of a *Level II* or *Level III* counselor. A *Level II* counselor would work more nearly in a peer relationship with principals, and/or elementary consultants or supervisors. Presumably, they would *coordinate* their activities rather than *control* one another.

In a top or *Level III* position it may not be unusual to find the Elementary Pupil Personnel Director or head of a Department of Developmental Guidance in an appreciably more important role than that of individual elementary principals in the administrative structure. This would be particularly true when he is attached to the central administrative offices of a large school district, or when he heads services provided for a cluster of elementary schools. Because of the range of relationships mentioned above it seems clear that the counselor needs to assess his position from time to time, using his professional preparation, his discernment, and his accumulated skill in human relations to maintain an equitable and effective balance between his program and the principal's responsibility for the school on a whole.*

7. *Should the guidance worker be responsible for disciplinary problems?* The literature of guidance in the *secondary* school reflects the strong opinion that the counselor's relationship with his adolescent clients is impaired when he engages in teaching, administrative, or clerical assignments. This is particularly true if the counselor is asked to function as a disciplinarian. This point is

---

*Useful books dealing with elementary administration are listed in the chapter bibliography.

well-taken and we do not choose to dispute it. However, in elementary schools there are child/teacher/counselor relationships which surround discipline problems which *involve* counselors even though they do not *participate* in the process of disciplining youngsters. The elementary school counselor is inescapably linked to matters of problem behavior through such acitivities as:

> Consulting with faculty members to improve their understanding of theory and practice in discipline,
>
> Drawing on information extracted from previous conferences with parents and/or with a child who is having problems,
>
> Offering appropriate interpretative information obtained through longitudinal study of individual children and from pupil personnel records in view of the fact that few if any teachers have a sustained contact with comparably comprehensive data, and
>
> Insuring that discipline cases are not handled in such ways as might be psychologically harmful to a boy or girl because faculty members have a faulty or incomplete basis for interpreting the cause of a discipline problem.

It should be understood that the elementary school counselor does not "administer discipline" personally. On the other hand, he has a moral responsibility as a specially prepared professional person to see that children are protected from unwise procedures or practices. He has the further responsibility of helping teachers understand the cause of unacceptable behavior (insofar as it can be identified) in the case of each individual's departure from expected conduct.

While the premise of confidentiality with respect to the counseling of clients is widely respected, the concept of confidentiality is not violated or demeaned when a counselor uses his knowledge of a child to help teachers cope with a problem. Indeed, "standing by" while a child is being ineptly disciplined debases the counselor's commitment to serve children.

8. *What should be the role of the counselor in the development of elementary school pupil personnel policies?* Broadly conceived, pupil personnel policies include those which bear on grouping, reporting, admissions, promoting, assessing progress, attendance and health policies, discipline, records, and record-keeping.

Because of his direct or indirect involvement in most of the aspects of school life noted above as well as in matters pertaining to instruction, curriculum, and school plant, the role of the counselor is closely associated with pupil personnel policies, especially considering the responsibilities of *Level II* and *Level III* specialists. The counselor has a contribution to make to almost every aspect of pupil personnel policy development because these policies directly relate to the counselor's functions as described and treated in Part Two.

9. *Should special housing for a counseling and guidance center be provided at the elementary level?* Some specialized setting for counseling and guidance services is desirable in all elementary schools large enough to support a full or even a part time employee (see also Chapter 14). While it may seem self-evident that a counselor requires some type of quarters, it is less well-accepted that there is a need for such quarters to be carefully planned and constructed so as to coincide with and support the qualities of a good program.

10. *In an N-12 school system, how should the elementary and secondary school counseling and guidance programs be coordinated and administered?* Whenever possible, the elementary and secondary school guidance program should have complete continuity and coordination throughout its 12 to 17 years.* This viewpoint is developed further in Chapter 6 which deals with the concept of elementary school guidance services in a continuum beginning with early childhood.

Unless all guidance programs in a school district are under a central-office director of elementary pupil personnel services, it is proposed that there be an independently administered program at the elementary level but one that is carefully articulated with the high school program. The alternative—a program operating under the direction of the secondary school— might tend to provide a downward extension of secondary school services or adaptations of such services or lead to neglect of elementary school guidance functions. With respect to administration, two coordinate programs, one for the elementary schools and one for the secondary schools, are preferable.

Several additional reasons can be given to support this position. *First,* by the very nature of their preparation secondary school counselors usually have a limited understanding of young children and of the operation and nature of the schools they attend. *Second,* high school counseling and guidance services have been distinctly different in practice from those suitable for children in early childhood and elementary school programs. *Third,* in most elementary schools, one or two full-time counselors would not be seeking activities; their time would be completely occupied. Hence, there would be no need to employ a person at a high school level to give a little "spare" time to the younger school population while working under the supervision of a high school counselor. *Finally,* a competent elementary school counselor is

---

*A 17-year span would include nursery and kindergarten groups and two years of community college or junior college under the same general administration. Downward extension of elementary education to encompass the threes, and perhaps the two-year-olds, will increase the span accordingly.

likely to work more effectively when he has direct administrative responsibility for the development of programs for young children.

Presumably, then, in the absence of a central-office coordinator of elementary guidance, elementary and secondary specialists should be deemed of coordinate importance. That is they should be similar in rank and in importance to the work of the schools, but independent and self-directive in performing their different functions. At the same time, the most meticulous care is needed to insure that the elementary-secondary programs are articulated so that they *operate* as a continuum despite their autonomy.

11. *In the elementary school, who should coordinate and administer the services of such specialized faculty members as the school psychologist, teachers of the physically handicapped, the disadvantaged, and slow learning, the psychometrist, etc.?* The matter of devising a workable administrative control structure for the variety of non-classroom faculty members now being employed at the elementary school level in increasing numbers is one of the more important issues of the present day. In past years there were so few schools with human resources (such as the psychometrist or remedial teacher) that the need for someone to lend direction to their work and to coordinate their pupil personnel services was an academic question. The growing demand for elementary counselors, school psychologists, social workers, and so forth, now is creating the opportunity for counselors to contribute their leadership skills and increase the effectiveness of pupil personnel services. Chapter 13 reviews in considerable detail the administration of guidance and counseling services and proposed responsibilities for the counselor-leader of a department of educational counsel.

It is suggested that as rapidly as possible counseling and guidance centers or departments of developmental guidance be established for elementary school children. Such centers would serve either a large elementary school or a cluster of small schools and would function as a hub for the broadly conceived pupil personnel services radiating from it. A variety of strong arguments support this stance:

> The number of services provided under the auspices of the school has greatly increased and some coordinating agency should insure that the major focus of all activities remains on the child; that services related to pupil personnel are administered, coordinated, and supervised; and that information about children remains confidential and used only in ways helpful to them.

> The professional preparation of the counselor and the role he plays in the elementary school reflects his concern and responsibility for the development of all children, the total learning environment, and his close consulting function with classroom

teachers. He is concerned with *all* children, not just those having emotional or adjustment problems.

Persons in special education who deal with the handicapped (e.g., the hard of hearing or partially sighted) are not directly concerned with total pupil populations. Neither are the academic clinicians ("remedial teachers") nor the school psychologists. None has the breadth of concerns and continuing contact with most pupils' lives that is an integral part of the counselor's function. Their preparation is likely to be more specialized than that of the guidance person, hence, they would not be suited to a leadership role in a center for pupil personnel services.

Presumably, the existence of a guidance and counseling center that would include space for machine installations for the storage and retrieval of information relating to pupil records is in itself an argument for housing pupil personnel services in one central location. In the interest of economy, and because all services are concerned with the broad component aspects of the total guidance function, it seems very sensible to have located within the same cluster of offices and conference rooms these facilities for housing health services, psychological, remedial, special education, and counseling and guidance services as well as similar fields involving physical therapy.

Unlike many specialists at the sixth and seventh year level who become more and more *specialized*, the counselor will have acquired greater *breadth* in his overall understanding of elementary school children as well as greater *depth* in counseling and guidance as he moves toward the *Level III* stage of preparation. From an administrative point of view this should enhance his contributions as a coordinator of pupil personnel services.

The proposed responsibilities of the counselor as coordinator of pupil personnel services should not present a threat to the elementary school principal, school psychologist, or anyone else who already has a full-time position prior to the proliferation and extension of pupil personnel services. As their important role and preparation as specialists in particular areas was cast some time ago, it cannot reasonably be expected that they assume a double role.

Implicit in this recommendation are two points. The coordinating and administrative role suggested above should be reserved for the counselor who has been prepared at the advanced *Level III* stage. This person presumably should be able to direct the work of *Level I* and *Level II* guidance specialists;

consult with classroom teachers in planning wholesome learning atmospheres for children; and work with specialists as particular children's problems indicate that certain types of help are required.

Also, pupil personnel leadership cannot operate smoothly without due attention being given to the role of the elementary school principal. Within the individual school building, he has long-standing responsibilities both in organization and in management (as in planning for nongrading or for team teaching) and in program development (as in curriculum change and the supervision of instruction) which must be recognized and respected by the counselor who serves as the director of the pupil personnel center as explained under issue 6.

12. *What is the content and scope of an effective elementary school guidance program?* Guidance is concerned with "the professionally skillful deployment of all available human and material resources at the school's command" as was noted in Chapter 1. Since it is concerned in many ways with *already* existing resources, the content and scope of guidance services seem self-evident; they are of the same dimensions as the elementary program itself. Such being the case, an inevitable question arises: "Is guidance merely absorbing or 'cannibalizing' the already established field of elementary education—or does it have a unique content, scope, and contribution?"

Since the realm of elementary guidance by definition already lies within the same boundaries as the elementary school, it patently does not invade or usurp its program. Rather, it makes a unique contribution of great merit. This can best be explained by turning to a point of Gestalt psychology which is that *the whole is greater than the sum of its parts.* Guidance services, while drawing upon extant human and material resources in elementary education, *blend them into a new and creative synthesis* that is of greater significance and use than were the original scattered parts. The concept of the whole being greater than the sum of its parts is sometimes referred to as synergism. Throughout the following chapters the synergistic outcomes of guidance in the elementary program will become evident (13).

As the separate instruments in a symphony orchestra are brought into harmonious relationship under the direction of the conductor, sounds that are vastly different from the uncoordinated noise of each individual instrument are produced. Similarly, the guidance worker in elementary schools "orchestrates" and directs the disparate elements already present but uncoordinated with respect to the guidance function. This is his unique contribution. An important related element is the longitudinal, personal relationship a counselor develops over a period of years with children, classroom teachers, and parents. This development is a continuum of human interaction through which the wise and insightful counselor is able to protect children from being misunderstood, to anticipate and interpret to teachers the nature and onset of developmental changes (e.g., early onset of puberty) and environmental changes (e.g., the arrival of a younger child in the family) with a bearing on his in-school behavior, and to interpret the ongoing learning experience of children in a broader context than assessment instruments by themselves provide.

The reader will note that the preceding roster of issues pertaining to the counselor's role and to practices in guidance provide a foundation, both explicit and implicit, for the brief following section which is a résumé of the characteristics of a sound program.

Characteristics of a Good
Counseling and Guidance Program

As an added means of understanding the characteristics of a good counseling and guidance program, it is worth the reader's time to examine the following "Joint Statement Prepared by the ACES-ASCA Committee on the Elementary School Counselor".(20) This document helps to explain how two of the major professional organizations of the APGA have sought to influence the model of the modern elementary school counselor.

Joint Statement Prepared by
the ACES–ASCA Committee on the Elementary School Counselor,
Association for Counselor Education and
American School Counselor Association,
Divisions of the American Personnel and Guidance Association

We believe that guidance for all children is an essential component of the total educational experience in the elementary school. We recognize the teacher's many responsibilities in the guidance process but we recognize also the significant complementary role of personnel in addition to the teacher. We believe such additional personnel are essential if the elementary school is to provide the maximum opportunity for learning, enabling each child to learn effectively in terms of his own particular abilities and his own developmental process.

We envision a counselor as a member of the staff of each elementary school. The counselor would have three major responsibilities: counseling, consultation, and coordination. He would counsel and consult with individual pupils and groups of pupils, with individual teachers and groups of teachers, and with individual parents and groups of parents. He would assist in coordinating the resources of the school and community in meeting the needs of the individual pupil. The counselor would work as a member of the local school staff and as a member of the team providing pupil personnel services.

We believe that guidance for all children is an essential component of the total educational experience in the elementary school.

By *guidance* we mean a continuing process concerned with determining and providing for the developmental needs of all pupils. This process is carried out through a systematically planned program of guidance functions. These guidance functions are a vital part of the elementary school's organized effort to provide meaningful educational experiences appropriate to each child's needs and level of development.

We envision a counselor as a member of the staff of each elementary school.

By *counselor* we mean a professional person, educationally oriented, highly knowledgeable in the area of child growth and development, with a broadly based multi-disciplinary background in the behavioral sciences and a high degree of competence in human relations.

By *educationally oriented* we mean having a knowledge of the elementary school program including curriculum, the learning process, and school organization. We recognize the value of teaching experience in the elementary school but believe that knowledge of the school program and processes can also be gained through a planned program of experiences in the school as a part of the counselor's preparation.

By *broadly based multi-disciplinary background* we mean a program of preparation carefully planned to include the contributions of several disciplines—anthropology, economics, education, philosophy, psychology, sociology. The graduate program would, of course, be determined by the undergraduate program, but we would like to see the graduate program take a multi-disciplinary approach from the very beginning. There would be a need for cooperative effort by all university and college departments concerned in order to provide appropriate programs designed specifically for elementary school counselors. In the attainment of such a multi-disciplinary program we are not thinking of combining the traditional programs of preparation for secondary school counselors, social workers, or clinical psychologists.

We recognize the value of different types of experiences in the counselor's background regardless of his professional preparation. To broaden his understanding of human nature and to develop skill in human relations we would encourage for the counselor a variety of experiences in addition to those directly related to education.

We realize that for many individual schools this long-range goal of a counselor in each elementary school will not be immediately possible. The size of the school, the community resources, and the nature of pupil needs will determine the number of professional personnel and the organizational pattern required to provide a continuous, systematic approach in meeting the developmental needs of all pupils.

We also recognize that there will be varying levels of responsibility in such a program and that contributions to the total guidance process may be made by persons less highly prepared in counseling than the counselor we have described. We definitely need to explore the specific functions that may be performed by such personnel.

We would emphasize, however, our belief in the importance of first having a counselor such as we have described as a member of each elementary school staff.

The counselor would have three major responsibilities: counseling, consultation, and coordination.

The counselor would perform a counseling function with pupils as well as with parents and teachers.

The counselor would perform a consultative function with parents and with other school and community personnel. One significant area of consultation in the school would be as a participant in the development of curriculum and in making decisions about the use of curriculum. The counselor's point of emphasis would be to include in the curriculum experiences that would be meaningful to the child and appropriate to his needs and level of development. The more closely the counselor can be identified with a particular school the more effective he can become in this phase of the consultant's role.

The counselor would perform a coordinating function in helping to integrate the resources of the school and community—ideas, things, and people—to meet the developmental needs of the individual. Many persons through many different programs are working in separate ways to affect the child's concept of himself. The counselor in the school can help to bring into a meaningful pattern the effort of these many individuals. As elementary schools change their organization and teaching procedures this integrated support for the individual pupil will become increasingly important.

In addition to integrating the resources of the school and community, the counselor must also see himself and the school as an integral part of a total community effort. He will need to perceive relationships clearly and to define functions in working with community personnel. He will need to recognize the strength of community resources and to relate the efforts of the community to those of the school. We see the counselor and other personnel in the school and community as colleagues willing to explore together new ways of achieving mutual goals.

As one reflects upon these statements, it is also important to review certain distinguishing characteristics that guidance programs in elementary schools possess. These are summarized under twelve headings. The dozen points also suggest the tasks and functions of the able counselor as he interacts with teachers and children and with other elements of the total school milieu.

In the good counseling and guidance program the counselor:

1) sensitizes the teacher to developmental changes in children and their significance in determining how to individualize his school experiences

2) acquaints the teacher with—or increases his sophistication in— using the tools or techniques involved in study and analysis of behavioral change

3) increases the teacher's awareness of the subtleties and significance of human interaction in solving social, academic, and the more simple of emotional problems

4) quickens the teacher's insight with respect to the fact that he works with a child who is influenced by a myriad of factors and forces in a *total* home-school-neighborhood environment, each component of which mediates or governs his behaving

5) introduces or clarifies goals that teachers study and will accept as desirable guides for directing children's individual and group experiences

6) provides bases for assessing the growth or progress of pupils without emphasizing academic achievement per se

7) promotes individualized instruction by increasing teacher's sensitivity to the needs, nature, and previous nurturing of children which influences his present classroom performance

8) increases teacher-teacher cooperation, as in team teaching, by highlighting the point that guiding pupil growth calls forth the combined efforts of a faculty including specialized personnel such as the counselor

9) improves school-community public relations by increasing parental participation in home-school conferences and cooperation and by deepening community appreciation for genuinely professional educational and guidance services

10) provides a high type of in-service education with particular regard for what it means to "understand" a child

11) involves a continuous process of longitudinal study of individual pupils, constant curriculum change as children's behavior and group interaction are scrutinized, and flexible planning based on individual pupil needs as the total educative process is evaluated

12) strengthens democratic skills because the guidance function is inherently democratic due to its commitments to

interaction in decision making and to the improvement of human welfare through the educative process

The chapters which follow introduce, explain, and document some of the ways in which the good program operates in order to reflect the wholesome characteristics suggested.

Summary

Although Chapter 4 deals with issues, phrased as problem questions, in guidance at the elementary school level, it is not a mere listing of conflicts. First an effort is made to explain the nature of issues and to suggest possible ways of easing or resolving them. Then divergent opinions regarding the work of the counselor and the components of a desirable program are explored.

In addition, Chapter 4 serves as a viewpoint chapter, presenting the statements of the ACES-ASCA Joint Committee on the Elementary School Counselor. The chapter concludes with a succinct statement of "Characteristics of a Good Counseling and Guidance Program."

References

1. Anderson, Robert H. *Teaching in a World of Change.* New York: Harcourt, Brace, and World, Inc., 1966.
2. Burr, James B., William Coffield, Theodore Jenson, and Ross Neagley. *Elementary School Administration.* Boston: Allyn and Bacon, 1963.
3. Campbell, Roald F., John E. Corbally, and John A. Ramseyer. *Introduction to Educational Administration.* Boston: Allyn and Bacon, 1964.
4. Carlsen, Evelyn F. (chairman). *Role of Supervisor and Curriculum Director.* Washington, D.C.: Association for Supervision and Curriculum Development, 1965.
5. Castettler, William B. *Administering the School Personnel Program.* New York: The Macmillan Co., 1962.
6. Cooper, John. *Elementary School Principalship.* Columbus, Ohio: Chalres E. Merrill Books, 1967.
7. Dell, Ronald C. (chairman). *Individualizing Instruction.* Washington, D.C.: Association for Supervision and Curriculum Development, 1963.
8. Elsbree, Willard S., Harold McNally, and Richard Wynn. *Elementary School Administration and Supervision.* New York: American Book Co., 1967.
9. Flanagan, John. "Functional Education for the Seventies," *Phi Delta Kappan* 49 (September, 1967): 27-32.

10. Griffiths, Daniel, David L. Clark, Richard Wynn, and Laurence Iannaccone. *Organizing Schools for Effective Education.* Danville, Ill.: Interstate Printers and Publishers, 1962.

11. Jackson, Phillip. *Life in Classrooms.* New York: Holt, Rinehart and Winston, Inc., 1968.

12. Jacobson, Paul B., William C. Reavis, and James D. Logsdon. *The Effective School Principal.* Englewood Cliffs, N.J.: Prentice-Hall, Inc., 1963.

13. Kahn, Herman and Anthony J. Wiener. *The Year 2000.* New York: The Macmillan Co., 1967.

14. Keith, Lowell S., Robert Infelise, and George Perazzo. *Guide for Elementary School Administration.* Belmont, Calif.: Wadsworth Publishing Co., 1965.

15. Manolakes, George. *The Elementary School We Need.* Washington, D.C.: Association for Supervision and Curriculum Development, 1965.

16. Michaelis, John V., Ruth H. Grossman, and Lloyd F. Scott. *New Design for the Elementary Curriculum.* New York: McGraw-Hill Book Co., 1967.

17. Misner, Paul J., Frederick W. Schneider, and Lowell G. Keith. *Elementary School Administration.* Columbus, Ohio: Charles E. Merrill Books, 1963.

18. Morphet, Edgar L., Roe L. Johns, and Theodore L. Reller. *Educational Organization and Administration.* Englewood Cliffs, N.J.: Prentice-Hall, Inc., 1967.

19. Otto, Henry J. and David C. Sanders. *Elementary School Organization and Administration.* New York: Appleton-Century-Crofts, 1964.

20. "Joint Statement Prepared by the ACES-ASCA Committee on the Elementary School Counselor." Association for Counselor Education and American School Counselor Association, Divisions of the American Personnel and Guidance Association.

21. *The Right Principal for the Right School.* Washington, D.C.: American Association of School Administrators, 1966.

22. Thompson, James D. *Organizations in Action.* New York: McGraw-Hill Book Co., 1967.

23. *The United States and International Education.* LXVIII *Yearbook* of the National Society for the Study of Education. Chicago: University of Chicago Press, 1969.

5

The Counselor
and the Curriculum

In assisting children to make optimum progress toward the goals of affective and cognitive maturity, the counselor needs to understand many of the concepts and practices related to the term *curriculum*. This is especially important if the counseling and guidance program for the elementary school is going to be concerned with a continuum of services for all boys and girls rather than with specialized functions for a few. In common usage, *curriculum* refers to a written statement of the educational experiences which the school proposes to provide or to create for children. Curriculum guides or outlines often specify the aims, procedures, and materials of instruction that presumably help teachers develop desirable experiences for young learners.

The counselor's qualifications and functions as described in earlier chapters make him a potentially important figure in elementary school curriculum planning and in the designing of educative experiences for guiding the development of children. One reason for the counselor's increased importance is that the educational scene has changed a great deal as previously indicated. The scope and responsibilities of the elementary school have increased; instructional technology has become more sophisticated; physical facilities have expanded; pupil personnel services have increased; transportation problems have multiplied; and teachers with increasing frequency have become specialists in content fields. There is no doubt that under these circumstances the counselor can help the school to ease the impact which the many and rapid changes of the past have had upon the individual child.

One of the responsibilities the counselor can assume is that of working cooperatively with other members of the staff in helping plan a "good" curriculum—one which enables each child to acquire efficiently both knowledge and the personal values which help him to move toward maturity. Both knowledge and values are important if boys and girls are to acquire a positive self-concept; one that permits them to engage in socially acceptable behavior with their peers and with adults.

Chapter 5 provides the elementary counselor and teacher with a digest of current and useful curriculum information. This condensed content provides only an introduction or an overview. However, the list of readings at the end of the chapter has been selected because the works provide a substantial background including information as to the philosophy, content, method, and organization of the curriculum of the elementary school.

Educational Goals and the Curriculum

Any curriculum developed for an elementary school today reflects certain educational goals, either stated or understood. These goals serve as criteria for selecting subject matter and various other educative experiences for which the school takes responsibility. While a counselor must eventually create within himself those objectives which have meaning for him, some examples of the kinds of goals which are congruent with good guidance practices can be suggested. Here are ten of the goals that should lend direction to soundly designed experiences for children.*

Curriculum Practices Should Strengthen Many Qualities in the Child:

1) *Skill in human relations.* The curriculum encourages a classroom climate of acceptance and respect; of co-operation and sharing.

2) *Improvement of emotional and mental health.* Heed is given to a child's psychological health, to his sense of security, and to dispelling his fears, in addition to maintaining and improving his physical condition.

3) *Equality of opportunity.* Experiences planned for children are personalized so as to permit individuals to succeed at different rates of speed and at different levels of ability.

*Educators have a profound liking for carefully formulated statements of purposes or goals or objectives. Three of the most widely and frequently quoted in the past 50 years are cited among the Chapter 5 references. Cf. 4, 7, and 8.

4) *Critical and clear thinking.* From an early age, an inquiry and *discovery*-centered rather than *drill*-centered approach is made to learning; active answer seeking replaces passive receptivity of content.

5) *Recognition of learner's subcultures.* Even with relatively similar school populations the curriculum recognizes that no two children have exactly the same sensory input when exposed to the same experience. The subculture or ethnicity of each affects what he sees and hears and is a factor influencing his learning and attitudes.

6) *Command of content.* Good education has never downgraded the importance of skills and knowledge. It does require, however, that learning have meaning for the learner, and that it have a purpose that he understands and accepts as relevant for *him*.

7) *Insight into the social and economic realities of the present.* Within the broad limits of accepted good taste, the content of instruction is honest and has no falsifications or omissions deliberately intended to "protect" children from information that certain political, ecclesiastical, or social groups might seek to include or to censor in ways favorable to their values.

8) *Methodically developed awareness of democracy.* As they move through school, children are helped to understand that the democratic way of life practiced in school is not haphazard but a deliberate process which has been tested and found good.

9) *Loyalty to democracy.* Children are encouraged to *support* democracy as a form of associated living which is the best we have yet devised for the individual's and for the group's well-being.

10) *Skill in the exercise of democracy.* The school itself serves as a "teaching aid" by personifying democracy and demonstrating democratic practices as children, parents, and faculty interact among themselves and with the broad community.

A well-conceived program in guidance, the principles under which the school is organized, the curricular experiences which are selected, and the teaching-learning procedures that are used should be designed to attain goals similar to the ten listed above. As these four aspects of the school combine their influence, an atmosphere should prevail that will make children actively aware of the values which give purpose and worthy direction to American life.

From the general statement of ten representative objectives of the teaching-learning process, attention now turns to some of the specialized information pertaining to the curriculum that will help the elementary school counselor to exercise his responsibilities and to function as an educational leader. First let us look briefly at curriculum backgrounds at the elementary level. Then we will examine several definitions of curriculum, and subsequently look closely at conflicting philosophies as to the purpose of the curriculum. Concluding portions of the chapter will increase the counselor's familiarity with trends in *content*, in *methods* of instruction, and in the *organization* of the school for instruction.

Curriculum Backgrounds

Textbooks and the Curriculum

In historical perspective, the textbook was one of the important forces which influenced the design of children's in-school experiences. In many ways, at least until late in the 19th century, the books used often *were* the curriculum in the sense that they determined much of *what* was taught and *when*. For example, the *New England Primer*, a small book first published in the late years of the 17th century, was used for generations in the United States and much work at the elementary level centered around its small, religiously oriented pages.

The various editions of Webster's spellers and of McGuffey's readers also had a great influence on what was taught. Originally published in 1782 with the formidable title, *The First Part of a Grammatical Institute of the English Language*, Webster's spelling book sold a million or more copies each year between 1840 and 1880. By 1920, a total of 122,000,000 of McGuffey's seven titles had been sold. Even after World War II a 70,000 copy edition of the McGuffey readers was sold to antiquarians, to the nostalgic, and to the dwindling group of schools that continued to use the books more than 100 years after their debut (31).

During the present century, including the present decade, textbook materials have continued to exert a powerful influence on what went on in the classroom. Even in the late 1960's and early 1970's when programmed lessons and computer assisted and computer based instruction were introduced into some schools, the repackaged content performed a function that was an extension of the text. Computer based instruction also continued to depend upon the use of books.

The Authority

For the past 60 to 80 years authoritative figures, both in content fields and in pedagogy, have had a great deal to say about what was taught to children (3,20). William Gray, whose basal readers made Dick and Jane familiar to millions of children, and William Kilpatrick, who was noted for his lectures on teaching methods, are examples of personages whose ideas and writings influence the content and nature of the curriculum.

Research

Especially after 1920, research in education began to have a substantial effect on the U.S. classroom. For a decade or two thereafter, many leaders in education were convinced that scientific investigations of educational problems would lead the teaching profession to superior practices much as research in medicine had led to improved public health. Such endeavors or projects as patiently compiled word lists, grade placement studies in mathematics, and investigations of speed and legibility in manuscript writing were widely discussed and led to many changes in both content and in the methods and materials of instruction.

Group Processes in Curriculum Change

Textbooks, authorities' viewpoints, and research workers' reports all represented ideas, concepts, and information that were produced *for* rather than *by* teachers. By the mid-1940's a new element had begun to influence curriculum development and to modify guides or teachers' handbooks that subsequently appeared. This was the idea that teachers through "group processes" should share in the act of curriculum change and in various other forms of decision making. The idea of this type of cooperative planning was not an entirely new one. Teacher-teacher and teacher-pupil planning, for instance, had been advocated, at least since the 1920's, by the group of educational theorists and practitioners labeled progressive educators. But in the years immediately following World War II, the idea of deliberate *procedures* for group action and of "action research" for finding cooperatively derived answers to classroom problems caught on and a genuinely novel approach to designing learning experiences was added to the familiar ones: the textbook, the authority, and research (12).

Several meritorious qualities recommended the use of group processes which, by the way, also began to have an enduring influence on guidance and counseling practices during the 1950's. Among the virtues were the following:

1) The concept that "Everybody is smarter than anybody" (Carl Sandburg's phrase), and that group interaction, therefore, led to superior decisions.

2) The "It's ours" reaction. When an entire faculty participates in a curriculum decision, it is likely that the group will accept and abide by new ideas and innovations they themselves have generated.

3) The self-study of an educational problem by a group of teachers is a valuable form of in-service education.

4) When many teachers participate in a curriculum study or decision, they more fully understand it and acquire an insight into proposed changes that will help them to introduce such innovations successfully in the classroom.

5) There are certain cathartic and sensitizing experiences for the individual participating in group processes (which in this sense seems to have anticipated group encounter or T-group developments of the 1960's).

The passing years have served to substantiate the values of faculty participation in curriculum planning. They also have revealed certain problems of which the elementary school counselor should be aware if he is to help his colleagues interact efficiently and in desirable ways. In the first place, it is necessary to bring *knowledge* and *data* to group sessions lest they become mere "gripe sessions" through lack of reliable information on which sound decisions can be based. It is also important to know how to protect a group from "minority tyranny," the bitter-end struggle of a few who may seek to abuse group processes by using them largely to obfuscate and to delay an action in which they think they see a personal threat. There is the ever present danger that group "decisions" will end up as lowest common demoninator compromises that actually leave no one satisfied. Other problems include finding time in which a group can think at leisure; learning how a group can assume authority for a curriculum decision for which the principal has the responsibility (and for which he probably would bear the burden of blame if a group of teachers reached an immature decision); and the fact that some faculties are inexperienced in group processes and, hence, perform ineptly when first seeking to reach cooperative decisions.

Emerging Contemporary Influences

In addition to the four elements which have had a long-standing influence on the curriculum: the textbook, the authority, research, and group processes—it is desirable to remind the school counselor of two recent influences having a bearing on any curriculum planning in which he may engage with classroom colleagues. These include the "discipline-centered" curriculum changes of the late 1950's and 1960's which have been described concisely by Goodlad (11). In mathematics, science, language arts, and in some measure in the social studies both new content and new methods are having an impact.

Also important is rapidity of change and the advancement of new knowledge, noted in Chapter 1, which makes it mandatory for one to verify the latest developments and trends in curriculum innovations with much greater frequency than was necessary prior to 1950. One might say that the validity of an idea today has only a "half-life" in many instances! We must now check and recheck our curriculum thinking, our goals and our procedures, at shorter intervals today than we did 15 or 20 years ago. Interdisciplinary contributions (e.g., from linguistics) and technical developments (as in Computer Based Instruction) leave no other choice.

The Meaning of Curriculum

Some years ago, Robert M. Hutchins, who was then Chancellor of the University of Chicago, commented on a paradox of our age. As the *means* of communication have improved, he noted, the *intelligibility* of the messages we exchange has declined. His generalization also seems to apply to the meaning of *curriculum*! Despite the efforts of educators who have attempted to explain it, the definition of "curriculum" has remained rather murky. What the counselor needs at the outset is not so much a *definition* of curriculum as *an interpretation* of the several concepts that are current. Below is a sampling of the viewpoints of authors writing during the past 35 years.

The Curriculum as Content

The idea that the curriculum designates what children should learn in school and what teachers should teach is probably the oldest interpretation— and one which continued to be accepted in many school districts in the 1970's. Henry C. Morrison, writing in 1940, referred to the curriculum as ". . . the content of instruction without reference to instructional ways or means." (21:58) This is the concept of the curriculum as an index to what is to be learned. The idea of the curriculum as an academic prescription for the teacher to administer could be found lingering on some 26 years later (1966) in a book by King and Brownell who characterized the curriculum as ". . . a planned series of encounters between a neophyte and the communities of symbolic discourse." (17:213) ("Communities of symbolic discourse" as used here refers to the various academic disciplines.)

The Curriculum as
Experiences Sponsored by the School

During the 1930's a number of curriculum theorists began to make the point that schools were responsible for the child's overall *education* rather than his academic *schooling*. The curriculum, therefore, was construed by Dorris and Murray Lee to include "... those experiences of the child which the school in any way utilizes or attempts to influence." (19:165). This interpretation was a popular one and later was rephrased as "... all the learning experiences that children have under the direction of the school" by Krug in 1950 (18:1). Spears at about the same time wrote that the curriculum consisted of "... all the activities of the children which the school in any way utilizes or attempts to influence." (29:9) The last two definitions clearly mirror the Lees' early phrasing.

The Curriculum as Derived from the Needs of Society

As the concept of a child-centered school lost popularity, more attention focused on the school as an instrument of society which was designed to influence children and youth in ways determined by the culture of which they were members. An influential book by B. Othanel Smith, W. O. Stanley, and J. Harlan Shores identified the curriculum as "a sequence of potential experiences ... set up in school for the purpose of disciplining children and youth in group ways of thinking and acting." (28:4) In the same general vein, Roland B. Faunce and Nelson L. Bossing refer to the curriculum as being composed of "... those learning experiences that are fundamental for all learners because they derive from 1) our common, individual drives and needs, and 2) our civic and social needs as participating members of a democratic society." (9:4)

Society's interest in (and contributions to) the curriculum was also pointed out by George A. Beauchamp who spoke of it as "... the design of a social group for the educational experiences of their children in school." (2:41) The Beauchamp statement also suggests the influence of group processes and cooperative planning during the 1950's.

While the three definitions cited do not de-emphasize the breadth of the school's responsibility as noted by the Lees, much heavier stress is placed on the school as a social agent. The curriculum is clearly recognized as a means of strengthening and perpetuating democratic values.

The Psychological Curriculum

Because of the nature of his preparation, duties, and responsibilities, the elementary school counselor is likely to be especially interested in the idea of the "psychological curriculum" as identified by L. T. Hopkins (14) and P. E. Harris (13). These writers make the point—and it is a provocative one—that the true curriculum consists of the experiences the child has had in school that have added to or modified his ways of behaving. Harris comments that ". . . there will be as many curriculums as there are teachers and separate groups of children." What is more, he contended, ". . . there will be a curriculum for each child . . . " (14:443)

The inner or psychological curriculum is not a design for a planned series of encounters with the disciplines at the child's level; it is the product of the transactions he has with his school environment.

Criticisms of Contemporary Definitions

Naturally, with several divergent conceptions of the curriculum now current, there are bound to be criticisms of each point of view. For years, for example, many curriculum writers have contended that Morrison's idea of the curriculum as the content of instruction is too narrow an interpretation. However, the point that the curriculum consists of all of a child's in-school experiences is not very useful either. It is preferable, W. B. Featherstone once noted, to speak of it as only ". . . the limited and selected body of experiences which a school deliberately . . . uses for educational purposes." (10)

Hilda Taba summarized the basic areas of disagreement as follows:

> Some definitions seem too all-encompassing and vague to help precision in thinking. When curriculum is defined as "the total effort of the school to bring about desired outcomes in school and out-of-school situations" or "a sequence of potential experiences set up in school for the purpose of disciplining children and youth in group ways of thinking and acting," the very breadth may make the definition nonfunctional. On the other hand, excluding from the definition . . . everything except . . . objectives and content outlines and relegating anything that has to do with learning . . . to "method" might be too confining (30:9).

A Proposed Interpretation of Curriculum

Despite the critical comments made about practically all attempts to set down the meaning of curriculum, one is led to conclude that each of the several concepts described has some merit. If this be the case, then a composite and compromise description is the most feasible one for the school counselor. We suggest that the various definitions of curriculum can be synthesized as in the following descriptive statement:

> *The curriculum is a written document* (a necessity if it is to be consulted, planned, or revised) . . . *suggesting the educational experiences of students* (it is meaningless without significant content) *and often proposing aims, materials, and procedures* (lest each teacher, without reference to what his colleagues are doing and at incongruous effort, be obliged to determine and select them for himself).

In some form the curriculum indicates a faculty consensus as to the breadth and often the general sequence of what is to be learned (to diminish overlapping and the problem of professional anarchy) . . . *and it includes, directly or indirectly, ventures that instruct the learner in those values of his culture which schooling can communicate* (since the curriculum is inevitably shaped by the cultural values of the adults who support it).

The success of a particular curriculum design is determined by the nature of changes in the behavior desired of the learner (hence, the teachers' and counselor's evaluative functions, as they gauge the intellectual, social, and psychological changes in children, and the effectiveness of the curriculum).

A Comment on Curriculum Theory and Terminology

The problem of finding an acceptable definition of the curriculum is but one of the communication problems which confront the counselor as he interacts with his classroom colleagues who teach in elementary schools. There is also the matter of curriculum terminology which frequently is used in a confusing fashion. Terms such as *fused, core, broad fields, emergent, problem-centered, transactional,* and so on, have flourished and declined for several decades. The philosophical and psychological bases of curriculum theory, more often in conflict than in agreement, also have created communication problems between teacher and teacher and between counselor and teacher. In order to bring this body of theory and of terminology into focus the writers will attempt, as simply as possible, to do three things.

FIRST: to interpret the terminology which has been used to describe various approaches to curriculum organization.

SECOND: to explain how differing viewpoints as to the purposes of the elementary school have led to conflicting interpretations of the content of the curriculum.

THIRD: to explain the nature of the two major opposing viewpoints with regard to the *organization* of the curriculum.

We begin with a very brief look at the pernicious problem of slogans and terminology.

The Problem of Terminology

Confusion arising from the several interpretations or definitions of *curriculum* is equalled if not surpassed by the alarming quantity of terms and slogans that have grown up in the recent years to explain various ways in which the curriculum can be interpreted. Not only is the jargon voluminous, it is often used so loosely that its meaning diminishes. One is reminded of a comment by G. Donald Adams made some years ago in the *Saturday Review* (1). Words, he said, are like money. They are subject to evaluation and deflation; they are hoarded and squandered; their sharp edges become dulled with use, and some are even counterfeit!

A Glossary

In an attempt to ease the problem of communication it is well to keep in mind that there are two fundamentally basic concepts of the curriculum: the *subject*-centered and the *learner*-centered. Various types of approaches or organizations of the curriculum can be grouped below each of these as follows:

Subject-Centered Curriculum*	Learner-Centered Curriculum
1. *Correlated*: subject-centered	1. *Correlated*: learner-centered
2. *Fused*: subject-centered	2. *Experience* curriculum
a. subject core	a. emergent core
b. "integrated"	b. problem-centered
c. unified studies	c. social functions
d. broad fields	d. activity
e. subject-centered activity curriculum	e. self-selected
	f. human relations curriculum
	g. culture-centric
	h. transactional curriculum

In order to provide the counselor with a map through the verbal maze of terminology the following somewhat oversimplified definitions/explanations are offered:

Types of Curriculum Organization	Proposed Definitions
1. *Correlated*: subject-centered:	Pertains to the teaching of two subjects in *relationship*.
2. *Fused*: subject-centered:	Refers to a situation in which three or more subjects are brought together and taught in combination. (See variations below.)
a. *Subject core*:	Involves scheduling two or more class periods sequentially and assigning them to the same teacher

*Adapted and expanded from Harold G. Shane and Wilbur A. Yauch (27).

Types of Curriculum Organization	Proposed Definitions (cont.)
	for the same time block. Used particularly at the middle school or junior high school level.
b. *"Integrated"*:	Teaching in such a way that subject matter lines are erased, thus using subject matter as a resource in developing a unit or project. (Quotation marks reflect the writer's feeling that this is a misleading assumption. *Children* integrate or internalize learning. There can be an integrat*ing* but not an integrat*ed* curriculum.)
c. *Unified studies*:	Similar enough to the fused curriculum to be considered as a synonym.
d. *Broad fields*:	Refers to a combined or survey-type of organization such as combining civics, history, and geography as "social studies." A variation of fusion.
e. *Subject-centered activity curriculum:*	Whether planned by the teacher or determined by the course of study, this approach to learning is made more meaningful by the use of project activities, which often involves utilizing arts and crafts skills as a form of creative activity in, say, the area of social studies.
3. *Correlated*: learner-centered:	An approach in which the learner's nature, needs, and motives are used as a basis for teaching two subjects such as mathematics and science in relationship.
4. *Experience curriculum*:	A flexible plan or organization planned so the experiences of children serve their needs and purposes in ways congruent with principles of human development. It pertains to the total life space of the child not merely events occurring within the school.*
a. *Emergent core:*	A form of organization which acquires structure and substance

*This is congruent with John Dewey's definition of experience as the continuous interaction of the living organism with its environment. Cf. his *Art as Experience*, New York: Minton, Balch, and Co., 1934, p. 35.

Types of Curriculum Organization	Proposed Definitions (cont.)
	through the process of teacher-pupil planning.
b. *Problem-centered*:	Centered around problems which suggest projects that promise to meet children's purposes and needs. Lacking in clarity as to basic concepts.
c. *Social functions*:	Children's experiences organized so as to acquaint them cumulatively and functionally with such human activities as earning a living, maintaining health, choosing leaders, and so forth. There is some question as to whether this is a *type* of organization or a *source* of experiences.
d. *Activity*:	Direct, first-hand participatory approaches are emphasized. It assumes that learning experiences are meaningful to the extent that children plan cooperatively with teachers and learn by doing.
e. *Self-selected*:	Related to emergent planning but with special emphasis on the uniqueness of each child. Involves the inherent assumption that the school provides a rich environment challenging all children (22).
f. *Human relations curriculum:*	An emergent approach influenced by its aim to build better intergroup–intercultural understandings and adjustments.
g. *Culture-centric*:	Based upon methodical use of the discipline of anthropology to create an educational "map" of the terrain of culture, and then selecting and planning instructional materials which will provide content that is both accurate and relevant to improved cultural insights (32).
h. *Transactional curriculum*:	Assumes that the child is engaged in a chain sequence of formative transactions with his milieu. Thus the curriculum is based on the guidance of a unique learner

Types of Curriculum Organization

Proposed Definitions (cont.)

through experiences based on optimally paced interaction with personalities, sequenced learnings, and materials that are relevant to his progress towards maturity.

Conflicting Ideas as to the Nature and Purposes of the Curriculum

Throughout their lives human beings are exposed to experiences which help shape their values. What a person prizes or rejects, how he sees things, how he attempts to identify with certain subcultures or social groups—in fact all of his behavior—is conditioned by the chain of experiences that link his lifetime together.

The attitudes that are current today with respect to the nature and purposes of the elementary school and its curriculum can, for purposes of presentation, be said to reflect educational values that range from the *reactionary* through the *conservative* and *liberal* position to an *experimental* viewpoint.

The educational *reactionary* maintains that methods of instruction should return to practices now generally discarded: "training the mind" through memorization and by introducing "hard" or "solid" subjects. The content of the curriculum, furthermore, should be selected by authorities in the various disciplines and should be classical or traditional in nature. Curriculum documents ought to prescribe what is to be studied at each of a series of distinct grade levels. In effect, the reactionary viewpoint would have the schools turn back to what was deemed a sound formal education 40 or 50 years ago.

Educational *conservatives* may be characterized as being loath to try anything for the first time and, as the name suggests, tend to preserve the *status quo* in the schools. Established educational methods are commonly used by the conservative, and curriculum guides are looked on as statements of essential or fundamental content for schools to pass along to children and youth. While a genuine reactionary curriculum is rare, many elementary schools today reflect a conservative attitude toward curriculum change.

The *liberal* school generally has a policy of deliberately seeking exciting or promising new ideas both with respect to what shall be in the curriculum and how it can be taught most effectively. A liberal curriculum frequently will include at least some untested ideas, or ones which are new enough to be in the process of being verified and accepted. Often the curriculum guides or handbooks will offer only broad or general procedural suggestions and leave to the teacher's professional judgment a substantial number of decisions as to the breadth and order of what is taught.

The *experimentally* oriented curriculum is found in those schools that seek to be the agents of change and innovation. Here are reflected both novel educational experiences and new ways of improving learning through better instructional procedures.

The elementary counselor will recognize that the four viewpoints—from reactionary to experimental—are somewhat oversimplified and arbitrary. He should also sense that no school curriculum, methodology, or faculty is entirely retrogressive or completely change-oriented. Not only are individuals of many persuasions found in a single school; many diverse practices are found in adjacent classrooms and even in a given teacher's room. He may, for instance, be conservative in interpreting the scope and sequence of children's experiences in the social studies while being innovative in the use of original materials of his own devising to improve pupil performance in mathematics.

It is not our purpose to stereotype the nature or purposes of the curriculum. It *is* our intent to make clear to the counselor that the educational values of parents and other school patrons, as well as those of teachers, include at least four divergent positions and the various shades or gradations that lie between any two of them. It is through such insights into the curriculum that the counselor can clarify his perspective of what *he* deems good and begin to exert the wholesome functions that he has the opportunity and responsibility for filling in the elementary school setting for learning.

Trends in Curriculum Organization in the Elementary School

The *organization* of the elementary school refers to the structure that the faculty judges to be the best for effective teaching and learning. More precisely, organization is the sum of the means or devices employed in an elementary school to use space, resources, and teachers efficiently to promote the education of children.

Past Developments

In many schools during the past century there was very little organization (5,16,23). Indeed, many schools in rural areas were of the one-room variety and the same teacher worked with children at all grade levels in a truly ungraded situation. In one sense, such teachers were also an early form of "counselor" to the extent that they successfully helped six- to sixteen-year-olds discover ways of improving their transactions with the environment.

As urban centers during the first half of the 19th century brought large groups of children in together in small areas, the *graded* school evolved in U.S. cities. Boston's Quincy Grammar School, beginning around 1848, was one of the first to organize for instruction by using "grade-level grouping." This is the same as "chronological" or "heterogeneous" grouping and simply involves assigning a group of entering six-year-olds to the first grade teacher. At the end of the school year those boys and girls who had completed their work were moved to grade two and so on. Originally, no attempt was made to work out any groupings based on intelligence, achievement, or social relationships with other children.

Since 1860, many efforts have been made to allow for human individuality. The various viewpoints as to the nature and purpose of the curriculum—the reactionary, conservative, liberal, and experimental positions—discussed above have a distinct bearing on how the proponents of each position tend to prefer to see the elementary school organized to carry out the curriculum design of their choice. It is of utmost importance for the counselor to have thought about the relationships between the performance of the functions associated with his field and the way in which the school is organized for learning.

During the past several decades there has been a distinct trend away from the more rigid of the graded plans used in the past. Only "reactionary" schools retain them. The organizational patterns, even of some conservative schools, have begun to be marked by modest changes such as team teaching, flexible scheduling of large and small groups, and non-grading. On the whole, however, elementary school organization up to the early 1970's had not been fully successful in accomplishing one of its main purposes—that of coping with the myriad of ways in which human individuality expresses itself in a school environment. Improving the elementary teacher's ability to meet the personalized needs of a particular child remains one of the major contributions that a counselor at this level can make.

The Shape of the Future

While it is difficult in the extreme to project possible trends in school organization, it seems more than likely that major changes in elementary school organization will occur during the next ten years. A joint publication of the Center for the Study of Instruction and the National Commission on Teacher Education and Professional Standards which appeared in 1967 serves to illustrate a trend in the deployment of human and material resources (15). In this booklet the teacher is conceived of as a part of a direct-instruction team consisting of perhaps eight members. This includes four professionals and four "paraprofessionals."* Their relationship may be diagrammed as follows:

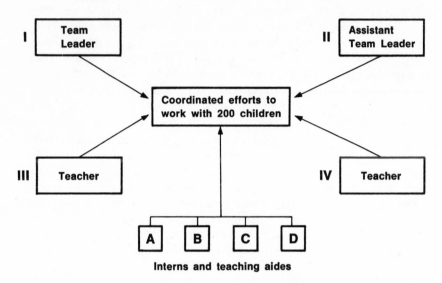

Figure 1. The Direct-Instruction Team

Each of the professionals (such as number "I" who may be a language arts/linguistics specialist) contributes to the total on-going experiences of approximately 200 children in a "planning situation"—one in which meaningful learning is emergent rather than prefabricated.

The direct instruction team is backstopped, as envisioned here, by "support centers." (15)   These include:

1) A *computer center* concerned with, e.g., simulation, programmed instruction, or automated test scoring.
2) A *self-instruction center* containing programmed learning material and concomitant resources.
3) An *inquiry center* combining the functions of educational media and library materials.
4) A *materials creation center* with professional audiovisual personnel, writers, and artists producing material for a cluster of schools.
5) A *human relations center* dedicated to improving social climates.

---

*A convenient term, paraprofessional is explained by its prefix. "Para-" (as in parallel) means "by the side of" or "beside" or "alongside of."

6) A *guidance and evaluation center* concerned with the analysis and channeling of individual progress.

It seems evident especially in view of the two last-mentioned innovations—a human relations center and a guidance and evaluation center—that a large number of new and important avenues will become open to the counselor during the next ten years. The likelihood of even greater opportunities for counselors in the late 1970's and early 1980's seems probable. In fact, possibilities in the field of guidance seem certain to arise as a far more refined type of learning center appears on the horizon. Such a center may be conceived of ". . . as a unified educational complex providing learning services for an entire population." More specifically:

> What was, in the 1960's labeled "elementary," "secondary," and "higher" education doubtless will be handled on a unitary or coordinated basis in such a complex. Such elements in our social infrastructure as recreation and health services, museums, conservatories, planetaria, and aquaria might also be administered and operated in the educative center—at least until such a time as their functions are superseded by multi-dimensional simulation (24:69).

Taking a long view of things curricular, it seems likely that the school of the 1980's may not be built around or served by media—the school plant will itself become media from which all persons from early childhood to advanced age can profit. Chapter 14 elaborates on the school as media.

Content and Method

Content and method—*what* is taught and *how* it is presented to children—undoubtedly will change greatly in the next several decades.

A Changing Focus

In past years, that is, prior to the 1920's, the focus of elementary education was on content rather than on the learner. In the 1920's there began to be greater interest and the small beginnings of a sharper focus on the child rather than the subject. As far back as 1935 one could review professional books treating elementary education of the era and identify the following trends:

General Curriculum Changes

From:	To:
Subject-matter curriculum	The school—children's experiment station—projects, life situations, work units, activity units

General Curriculum Changes (cont.)

From:	To:
Single learnings	Multiple learnings
Emphasis upon textbooks	Other ways of study besides books: excursions, experimentation, investigations, pictures, moving pictures
Mass teaching	Developing creative, dynamic, integrated personalities; development of individuality
Saving time and securing certainty of results by acquiring ideas formulated by others	Supplying experiences and activities that take child where he is and extend his development at rate determined by his capacity; providing an environment in which children continually propose and act in situations of meaning to them—where they live richly, fully, happily
Scheduled daily program	Programs planned on weekly basis
Definite class divisions	Flexible groupings
Training in habits, skills and factual knowledge	Building desirable social attitudes, appreciations and understandings
Question-answer recitation	Children taking initiative, making and carrying out plans; group discussions, conferences, conversation on common interests
Isolated subjects	Correlation of curriculum and child's growing stream of life experiences
Definite direction	Sympathetic guidance
Content values of curriculum	Process values of curriculum
Delivery of formulated truth	Development of methods and means of truth discovery
Ready answers to stated problems	Cultivation of a problem-consciousness challenging independent solutions
Subject matter and skills	Growth in behavior and conduct
Formalized recitation	Socialized recitation
Learning in order to use	Using in order to learn
Storing up facts	Learning in order to think
Group precision and straight line marching	More individual movement
Curriculum based on tradition	Curriculum based on experiences that are educationally worthwhile and socially significant
Educating a passive child	Further initiative, self-reliance, cooperativeness, purposes in life,

General Curriculum Changes (cont.)

From:	To:
	interest in the world and developing intellectual and moral honesty
Restrictive repression to satisfy traditional standards	Freedom with rich opportunity for varied social activities
Preparation for later adulthood	Meeting problems and conducting enterprises calling for present efforts
Rigid, permanent scheme of pigeon-holed subject matter	Longer intervals of related activities; a more flexible program
Complete mastery of subject matter	Opportunities for boys and girls to recognize their own purposes
A series of short recitation periods	Long periods conducive to related activities; free time for individual activities of a creative nature
Definite lesson assignments in a textbook	Guiding children in selection of purposes in real life
Passive mastery of finished products of thought	Exercising true intelligence in making wise adaptations to changing environments (33:16-17)

Worthy of note is the "modern" tone of this report from so many years past. However, although they were forecast in the 1930's and identified as "trends," many of the ideas above were not rapidly adopted. In fact, in numerous elementary schools during the 1950's and 1960's, attention continued to be placed on content rather than on the learner. The "new" science, mathematics, language arts/linguistics, and social studies programs introduced on a wide scale during the 1960's testify to the subject-matter orientation of recent practices.

After a considerable period of time spent in learning new content, for instance from specialists in linguistics, teachers in the middle and later 1960's began to show signs of once again becoming more concerned with the learner and more aware of the need to humanize education. In summary, an interest in the elementary school's child was advocated and made some headway in the 1930's, began to tincture practice to some extent in the late 1930's and 1940's, then tended to lose ground in the 1950's and early 1960's. The curriculum in the 1970's has reached what may prove to be the most suitable balance between "teaching subjects" and "teaching children" that has existed in the U.S. to date.

Granting that the curriculum *has* recently displayed better balance between stress on content and concern for the learner, what does this "better balance" mean?

Content and the Learner "In Balance"

During the past decades when a sharp division or schism existed between the proponents of content as the school's main focus and the proponents of the total development of the learner, each group advanced one of two bipolar or antithetic views. Before indicating how the conflict has been reduced (if not resolved), let us look at some of the arguments for supporting the subject curriculum versus the case made for the learner-centered curriculum as they were stated from about 1935 to around 1960.

The Human Development or LEARNER-Centered Curriculum	The Content or SUBJECT-Centered Curriculum
1) Reassures the parent that his child will be considered as an individual with varied needs, purposes, and abilities.	1) Reflects the existence of a presumably logical design for insuring that children will be introduced to the cultural heritage.
2) Removes from the teacher the need to follow a more or less prescribed order of scope and sequence.	2) Gives the teacher a sense of security by indicating the nature and extent of his responsibilities for transmitting a given segment of knowledge.
3) Frees the teacher to draw on a wide range of content for any age group.	3) Clearly indicates a given teacher's responsibility.
4) Increases the likelihood that content has meaning for a particular group of children.	4) Increases the likelihood that children will be exposed to an orderly overview of the cultural heritage.
5) Provides data regarding evidence of behavioral change in children: ability to plan, acceptance of others, and so on.	5) Encourages methodical assessment of pupil progress through standardized tests.
6) Encourages the teacher to plan appropriate learning experiences on the basis of his professional judgment.	6) Creates a basis for planning the scope or breadth and the sequence (or order) of the subject matter selected for each age level.

Even a passing glance at each of the two columns above suggests that there is some value in each of the viewpoints. The "balance" which has begun to characterize the curriculum actually reflects a rapprochement, in the late 1960's, between emphasis on the learner and emphasis on content. The pointless argument over whether one teaches children OR subjects may be said to have boiled down at present to an acceptance of the point that one begins to teach children effectively only when he has developed insights into the transactional relationships which exist among these children, their environments, and the learning experiences toward which a balance curriculum directs our efforts.

While the timing and pacing of a particular learning experience remain open to considerable dispute, a general consensus has been reached among most elementary school workers that content, methods, and the learner are best conceived of in an interactive or complementary relationship. An effort is made to depict this in Figures 2, 3, 4, and 5 which follow.

In Figure 2 the curriculum is seen as a continuum, one which might begin with the enrollment of two-year-olds and which begins *no later* than with four-year-olds, and extending throughout the years of schooling provided by society. As he moves through the continuum on his personalized "progress route," the child's learning experiences in the continuum are shaped or mediated by the use the astute, insightful counselor and teacher make of:

1) Individual *child development data* which provide a practical basis for estimating expected socio-intellectual performance.

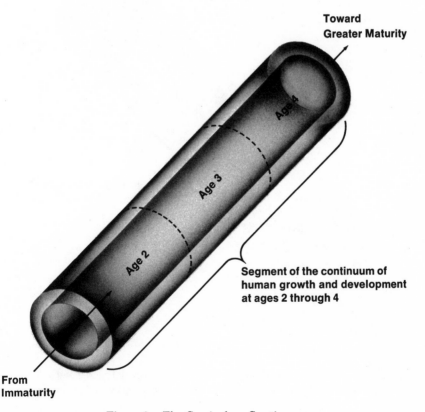

Figure 2. The Curriculum Continuum

2) Implications of the *culture*, including subcultures in an expanding environment, which have a bearing on the child's understanding and, hopefully, his acceptance of other human beings.

3) The *curriculum* which we have described is a *written document suggesting the educational experiences of students* and often proposing aims, materials, and procedures. The reader should also bear in mind our statement that: *in some form the curriculum indicates a faculty consensus as to the breadth and often the general sequence of what is to be learned; and it includes, directly or indirectly, ventures that instruct the learner in those values of his culture which schooling can communicate.*

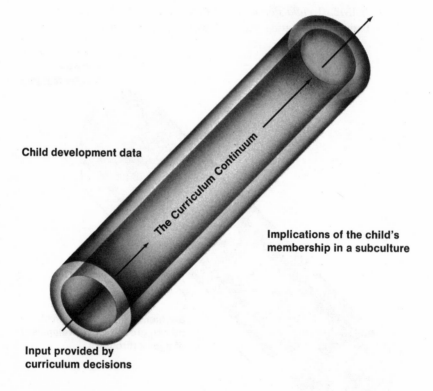

Child development data

The Curriculum Continuum

Implications of the child's membership in a subculture

Input provided by curriculum decisions

Figure 3.   Sources of Reference for the Counselor and Teacher in Guiding Individual Human Development Through an Educational Continuum

Figure 3 indicates how these three important elements in guiding human development serve as sources of reference and input for a personalized curriculum continuum.

Now examine Figure 4. This presents a model designed to explain more clearly how children progress individually through the seamless curriculum which is depicted here as analogous to a tube. The shaded upper portion of the tube represents the route or portion of the school's program through which particularly capable children presumably would progress. The upper line represents the hypothetical route followed by an "above average" child. The broad center section symbolizes the wide range of "normal" or "average" academic, social, and physical performance, a route which most boys and girls follow. The lower stippled section represents the path of the slower learner: the immature, the deprived, and in some cases, the culturally different. The route one of these youngsters might follow also is portrayed by the lower line.

In general, in many if not most U.S. schools, the child who performs academically in a superior way has more emphasis placed on *interpretative* aspects of knowledge in a milieu which supplements his cognitive experiences. Rather than moving through the general sequence of what is to be learned at high speed, he usually learns more about a given topic if he has an able teacher who seeks to broaden him intellectually. This widening of the scope of his learning keeps the fast learner from moving so far ahead of his agemates in the continuum that his social relations are thrown askew.

The "below average" route which is followed by the slow or disadvantaged in common practice often places greater emphasis on *replicative* learning. This is not to be confused with rote drill work. Replicative work, if properly developed with the slow learner, involves the replication of a *meaningful* input of enriching experiences which is carried on in diverse ways until the child has mastered whatever task or skill that had given him difficulty. As Figure 4 indicates, the slow-learner is helped by a *compensatory* or *supportive* environment for learning. Compensatory experiences are designed to make up for past deprivations. *Supportive* learnings are planned to increase opportunities for the culturally different to succeed and to excel. They are designed to build on particular talents and on the cultural background which a child has acquired by virtue of his membership in a given subculture: Oriental American, Black American, Jewish American, Puerto Rican American, American Indian, and so on.

It must be kept in mind that Figure 4 is not a picture of reality; it is only an attempt to present a model that helps to symbolize and to explain reality. Actually, there can be no really "average" child for at least three reasons:

1) Human individuality is unique—and, by definition, "unique" refers to the fact that it has no duplicate.

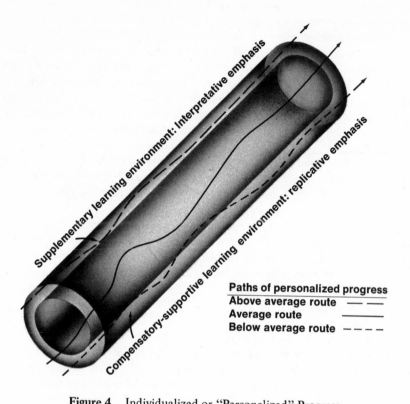

Figure 4.   Individualized or "Personalized" Progress
in a Curriculum Continuum*

*One of the writers has elaborated on *individualized* and *personalized* experience in a curriculum continuum as follows:

The *personalized* curriculum differs from *individualized* instruction in at least one major respect. Individualized instruction, which has been attempted for many years, was intended to help a child meet group norms or standards, but at his own rate of progress. (In the "Winnetka Plan" as begun by Carleton W. Washburne, for instance, the curriculum was basically the same for all children in a given grade, but the rate of progress varied. The rapid learner was kept from moving beyond the company of his agemates by providing him with enrichment activities and similar paracurricular experiences.) The meaning of a personalized continuum-type of curriculum can be clarified further by means of literary allusion. The curriculum of the 1930-vintage graded school was one in which the child was forced to fit the program. That is, it was analogous to the mythological bed of Procrustes. This was an iron bedstead on which the ancient, unfriendly Greek giant bound the unwary traveller, then cut off his victim's legs or stretched them to fit.

The individualized, and sometimes nongraded, approach to instruction was a distinct improvement since it endeavored to shorten or lengthen the Procrustian bed to fit the child. The personalized curriculum continuum, on the other hand, is one in which the child, with teacher guidance, figuratively speaking, is encouraged—and indeed expected—*to build his own bed* (25).

2) Children cannot actually be grouped homogeneously or compared with their fellows because each child is constantly changing product of a unique endowment and of the personalized input that began with his birth and his concomitant entry into a subculture.

3) Norms cannot be transferred from child to child or from group to group. Each child or cluster of children has its own norms. In other words, all norms are artificial and arbitrary. They can not be used to appraise any one particular child.

With these limitations in mind, let us look at another model, Figure 5, and determine what it seeks to convey. First, let us for purposes of discussion make the assumption that "Phase III" represents one academic year of *grade* 3 in a conventional graded school program. Now note the arrows which are labeled Child "A," "B," "C," and "D." Each arrow represents the hypothetical

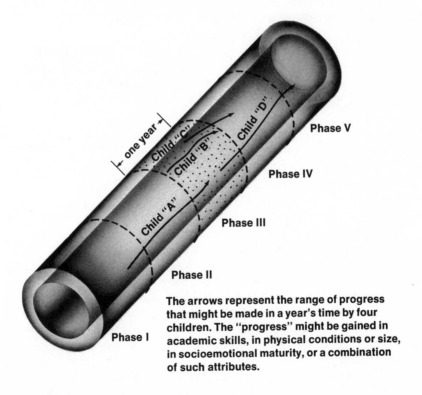

The arrows represent the range of progress that might be made in a year's time by four children. The "progress" might be gained in academic skills, in physical conditions or size, in socioemotional maturity, or a combination of such attributes.

Figure 5. *The Curriculum Continuum* Drawn so as to Show the Actual Variation to Be Expected in Children's Progress During a Given Year

overall academic progress made by each one of these four children. Observe that Child "A" has spurted ahead but is still behind his peers in performance. Child "B" has made "average" progress moving through the grade with little deviation in performance during the year. Child "C," while he started the year in a more advanced position than either "A" or "B," relatively speaking, has lost ground. Child "D" has maintained his comfortable academic level.

One more point must be made here. At some time and in some way, all children to some extent need experiences that are interpretative and supplementary as well as replicative and compensatory-supportive. The subtle nuances of this statement provide the counselor with some of his greatest opportunities and challenges. These points are developed and explained with models in Chapter 6.

Considerable information is contained in the four figures if the reader studies the interpretative statements and makes extrapolations in the light of his experience. True "balance" in the curriculum—a sound relationship between learner and subject matter—is of course obtained as teachers and counselors in the elementary school develop the depth of insight needed to bring reality-in-practice to the ideas in the diagrammatic illustrations.

As suggested by our model, one of the important contributions that the counselor can make is to help teachers become aware of how they best can intervene in each child's school environment to influence his academic performance, social development, and total self-concept in desirable ways.

A Comment on Methods

Since entire books have dealt with human development, with general methods, and with teaching procedures in such fields as language arts, science, mathematics, or social studies in elementary schools, it is impossible to do much more here than to draw to the counselor's attention the close relationship existing between what is to be taught—the *content*—and what can be done to facilitate learning it—that is, the *methods* of teaching.

For the counselor to begin to develop expertise in gauging or recognizing an effective teaching-learning situation, he must rely in part on the background he has already created for himself through experience and advanced preparation. On the basis provided by this background, several suggestions can be made to help the counselor. His knowledge of good learning situations can assist teachers in their efforts to evaluate and refine the methods they are using to help children learn.

When evaluating the methods that one observes a teacher using, it is desirable to bear in mind that such an evaluation should be "three-dimensional." That is, it should consider how teaching and learning proceed with respect to 1) the individual child, 2) the total group in which he has membership, and

3) the immediate social-psychological setting of the school within which the learning experiences take place. Let us examine the nature of sound teaching methods which are essential in bringing meaning to the curriculum designs in a given school. For purposes of convenient and concise sequencing a sampling of the qualities which characterize desirable elementary school methods are presented in the form of a question checklist which a counselor might use as he observes children in the classroom. The points that follow should be especially useful when they are checked prior to a counselor's conference with a teacher regarding some of the ways in which the values sought through elementary school guidance are sustained by skillful selection of teaching procedures.

With respect to the *individual* child, do classroom methods:

		Yes	No
1)	allow for differences in intellectual endowment?	___	___
2)	as appropriate, allow for problems related to physical deprivations such as faulty vision?	___	___
3)	reflect awareness of cultural differences; of the deprivations or the culturally derived advantages of a given child?	___	___
4)	indicate the teacher's active awareness of divers levels of each child's achievement?	___	___
5)	provide individualized readiness experiences?	___	___
6)	show the teacher's awareness of the various configurations of social relations in the classroom?	___	___
7)	reveal that the teacher recognizes that the *physical*, *mental*, *social*, and *emotional* components of the individual child's personality add up to a total *Gestalt* which is greater than the sum of the parts?	___	___

With regard to the *group* of children, do instructional procedures:

8) allow for the range of spectrum of differences among the children without stigmatizing the slower learners?   ___   ___

9) suggest that a continuing effort is made to verify, insofar as possible, that the total

Yes   No

group's interest is cultivated and that the children see meaning and purpose *which they accept* in the work they are doing?   _____ _____

10) indicate that new work undertaken builds on and is strengthened by *past* experience?   _____ _____

11) promise to carry the group forward to suitable *new* experiences?   _____ _____

12) allow for multiple learnings which increase the rate at which information and concepts are acquired?   _____ _____

13) permit and encourage group planning and respect and use group processes at the children's level?   _____ _____

Finally, with respect to the *socio-psychological setting* in which the teacher and children are working, do the methods which are used:

14) indicate that the teacher is aware of concomitant learnings and how the intangibles of personality, of situations, and of group and personal relationships affect the learning environment?   _____ _____

15) reflect the teacher's concern not only for the information that children are acquiring but with their attitudes toward this information, toward other children, teachers, adults, and the total configuration that comprises their milieu?   _____ _____

16) show that the timing and pacing of learning experiences are appropriate to the level of children's development?   _____ _____

17) prove suitable with regard to the teaching materials and instructional methodology that are needed?   _____ _____

18) suggest that the teacher has used good judgment with regard to the availability of community resources (such as places to visit) which can add pleasure and bring increased significance to what is in the curriculum?   _____ _____

With reasonable practice the elementary counselor can learn to apply the preceding "three-dimensional view" of good teaching in his contacts with teachers and do so in ways consistent with contemporary concepts of sound elementary school practices. His knowledge of counseling, for instance, should enable him to be especially valuable in increasing a teacher's sensitivities to the kinds of methods or procedures that help serve both the individual and the group in the chain of experiences that each day moves the learner a step closer to contributive living and to self-realization.

The Counselor and Curriculum Concepts

A "Find-Yourself" Diagram

If one accepts the view that the curriculum is the sum of the educational experiences that the school proposes to provide or create, then the counselor is automatically and deeply involved in its planning because of his professional concern for the total development of *all* children. Such being the case the counselor should clarify his thinking as to where he stands in connection with the various curriculum viewpoints identified in this chapter. Here, in concentrated form, is a "find-yourself" diagram prepared so that the counselor can begin to think even more seriously about the curriculum outcomes, the learning theory, the curriculum guides, and the structure of the curriculum he finds most viable and defensible.

In some instances the reader may discover that his views vary, that he is "conservative" in certain respects and "experimental" in others. Such inconsistency should not be construed to be a sign of professional ambivalence or of the indecisiveness which psychologists sometimes describe as *abulia*. Each of us, in certain ways, is a bundle of value conflicts. Furthermore, growth in one's field is characterized by the slow process of finding one's way through a series of uncertainties, position shifts, and new perspectives of what is "right" or "good." The important thing is that thought be given, through methodical introspective study, to where one is in his concept of the "good" curriculum. Further, It is the direction of one's mental processes that matters rather than the place one occupies during a given moment as he progresses toward professional maturity.

In the process of reviewing beliefs, Figure 6 should be of more than passing value.

Summary

Some of the factors and forces which have influenced the curriculum in recent decades are reviewed for the elementary school counselor in Chapter 5.

	Curriculum Goals	Nature of Learning	The Curriculum Guide	Curriculum Organization
The Reactionary position	To develop a "meritocracy"; to provide a classical background for an élite.	An abstract process of mental discipline; intellectual training.	Formal course of study. Directive.	Subject-centered; compartmentalized content.
The Conservative position	To teach the "fundamentals" (3 R's); to develop mastery of content.	Instilling the "proper" response to the "right" stimulus. Behavioristic.	Specific study guides. Prescriptive.	Some correlation between or among subjects.
The Liberal position	To help all children develop their potentialities. To emphasize human development, and social competence.	Gestaltist and field theory oriented. Meaning, purpose, interest, and motivation stressed.	Flexible; often suggestive and permissive within limits agreed on by cooperative planning.	Emphasis on flexible structure governed by professional judgment.
The Experimental position	Exploratory. Methodically concerned with experimentation to bring about changes and improvements in child and society.	Continuing probes into the nature of learning; no fixed commitment to a given theory.	Usually in a state of process or emergent development; also may be highly structured for experimental purposes.	Varied. Seeks to be functional in a given situation rather than set or preformed.

Figure 6. Representative Choices Open to the Counselor with Respect to Curriculum Goals, the Nature of the Learning Process, the Form for Curriculum Guides, and the Type of Curriculum Organization to Be Developed

The confusion which has sometimes prevailed when an attempt is made to define "curriculum" is discussed—and in considerable depth—because the meanings accepted have an important bearing on the counselor's perception of the experiences that a school endeavors methodically to provide for children.

Curriculum trends going back to the 1930's are examined following a scrutiny of conflicting ideas as to the goals of the curriculum and the practices to which they point. Both the past and general emergent possibilities in curriculum are suggested.

The next section deals with content or subject matter during the elementary years. While space limitations preclude comment on each individual area of study (such as science or the language arts), the general status of contemporary curriculum theory is presented.

Models are used to convey the idea of a curriculum continuum and to illustrate concepts related to the learner, his environment, and the process of learning. Particular attention is given to individual differences and the influence of membership in a given subculture. Instructional methods, which are described as closely related to the curriculum, constitute the last main segment of the chapter.

References

1. Adams, G. Donald. "The Magic and Mystery of Words," *Saturday Review* 46 (August 31, 1963):8.

2. Beauchamp, George A. *Planning the Elementary Curriculum.* Boston: Allyn and Bacon, 1956.

3. Beck, Robert H. "Educational Leadership, 1906-1956," *Phi Delta Kappan* 37 (January, 1956): 159-165.

4. Commission on the Reorganization of Secondary Education. *Cardinal Principles of Education.* Washington, D.C.: U.S. Government Printing Office, 1937.

5. Cubberley, Ellwood P. *Public Education in the United States.* Boston: Houghton Mifflin Co., 1919.

6. Dewey, John. *Art as Experience.* New York: Minton, Balch, and Co., 1934.

7. Educational Policies Commission. *The Purposes of Education in American Democracy.* Washington, D.C.: National Education Association, 1938.

8. _____. *The Central Purpose of American Education.* Washington, D.C.: National Education Association, 1961.

9. Faunce, Roland B. and Nelson L. Bossing. *Developing the Core Curriculum.* New York: Prentice-Hall, Inc., 1951.

10. Featherstone, W. B. *A Functional Curriculum for Youth.* New York: American Book Co., 1950.

11. Goodlad, John, et al. *The Changing School Curriculum.* New York: The Fund for the Advancement of Education, 1966.

12. *Group Processes in Supervision.* Washington, D.C.: The Association for Supervision and Curriculum Development, NEA, 1948.

13. Harris, P. E. *The Curriculum and Cultural Change.* New York: D. Appleton Co., 1937.

14. Hopkins, L. T. *Interaction: The Democratic Process.* Boston: D.C. Heath and Co., 1941.

15. Joyce, Bruce R. *The Teacher and His Staff: Man, Media, and Machines.* Washington, D.C.: National Education Association, 1967.

16. Kandel, I. L. (ed.). *Twenty-Five Years of American Education.* New York: The Macmillan Co., 1924.

17. King, Arthur R., Jr. and John A. Brownell. *The Curriculum and the Disciplines of Knowledge.* New York: John Wiley and Sons, Inc., 1966.

18. Krug, Edward A. *Curriculum Planning.* New York: Harper and Bros, 1950.

19. Lee, Dorris and Murray Lee. *The Child and His Curriculum.* New York: D. Appleton Co., 1940.

20. Moehlman, Arthur. "Fifty Years of Educational Thought," *Phi Delta Kappan* 37 (January, 1956): 131-140.

21. Morrison, Henry C. *The Curriculum of the Common School.* Chicago: University of Chicago Press, 1940.

22. Olson, Willard. *Child Development.* Boston: D.C. Heath and Co., 1949.

23. Parker, S. C. *History of Modern Elementary Education.* Boston: Ginn and Co., 1912.

24. Shane, Harold G. "Future Shock and the Curriculum," *Phi Delta Kappan* 49 (October, 1967): 67-70.

25. ____. "Secondary Education As Part of a Curriculum Continuum: Possible Trends in the '70's." *Phi Delta Kappan* 51 (March, 1970).

26. ____. *The United States and International Education.* LXVIII *Yearbook,* Part I. National Society for the Study of Education. Chicago: University of Chicago Press, 1969.

27. ____ and Wilbur A. Yauch. *Creative School Administration.* New York: Henry Holt and Co., 1954.

28. Smith, B. Othanel, W. O. Stanley, and J. Harlan Shores. *Fundamentals of Curriculum Development.* New York: World Book Co., 1950.

29. Spears, Harold. *The Teacher and Curriculum Planning.* Englewood Cliffs, N.J.: Prentice-Hall, Inc., 1951.

30. Taba, Hilda. *Curriculum Development: Theory and Practice.* New York: Harcourt, Brace and World, Inc., 1962.

31. *The Textbook in American Education.* XXX *Yearbook,* Part II. National Society for the Study of Education. Bloomington, Ill.: Public School Publishing Co., 1931.

32. The United States and International Education. LXVIII *Yearbook.* National Society for the Study of Education. Chicago: University of Chicago Press, 1969. Chapter XI contains a detailed discussion of "culture-centric curriculum change."

33. Zirbes, Laura. *Curriculum Trends.* Washington, D.C.: Association for Childhood Education, 1935.

Part
TWO

6

The Guidance
Continuum
in Elementary Education

The physical, social, emotional, and intellectual development of a child is continuous, somewhat like the smooth flow of a small river. He is "fed" and broadened by experiences just as the river is fed and widened by the input of tributary streamlets. Also, the channel the child follows is governed by the changing terrain of the environment in which he moves, even as the river's course is influenced by its variations in depth and by the strengths and flaws in the rocky or earthen banks between which it makes its way. The uneven continuity of human growth, like the gliding continuity of the river, suggests that guidance services and functions provided in elementary education also should be continuous. An apt name that suggests itself for this uninterrupted flow is *the guidance continuum*.

The human continuity described above also implies that the elementary school's organization and its program should provide a continuum of wholesome experiences which support and facilitate the counselor's work.

The Counselor and the Culture

In order to guide a child skillfully, it is essential to have certain insights into the topography of the environment from which he comes. That is, the

155

elementary counselor needs to understand the subculture into which a particular child was born. Lacking such an understanding, the counselor may have a great deal of difficulty, and perhaps even fail in some respects, as he and the teachers attempt to help each boy and girl make individualized progress toward the goal of desirable maturity.

The Terrain of Culture

Culture may be simply defined as the ". . . way of life of a people . . . the sum of their learned behavior patterns, attitudes, and material things." (14:11) In view of this interpretation it seems clear that counselors need to have a reasonably accurate "map" of the terrain of the subcultures—the differing socio-ethnic environments—from which come the children of the school in which he is working (12,17).

Every child lives in a milieu created or at least appreciably influenced by the subculture in which he has membership, and by his contacts with other subcultures with which his own has interfaces or interrelationships. How this child sees and hears and even his modes of listening are influenced by his acquired culture patterns (13). He "sees and hears and listens" by means of his physical equipment, but his *interpretations*—the *meanings* he ascribes to his sensory input—are the result of his culture-derived understandings.

Some Important Cultural Insights

In order to bring continuity to guidance and to smooth the flow of the elementary school child's life, there are a half-dozen essential insights related to subculture group membership which can serve as a foundation for the counselor's work. These points are particularly important when one realizes that within a decade many schools probably will assume at least some responsibility for children as early as at age two or three (23).

In order to bring sound, culturally oriented professional judgment to the guidance of boys and girls from the time of their very earliest transactions with the school, the following points should influence the counselor's thinking:

1) A child's membership in a given subculture helps to determine his values, to influence his sensory input, to shape his responses, and to govern his communication with others.
2) Human relations can best be improved in a school milieu which makes intelligent use of "school living" (i.e., the non-academic school experiences of children). The language arts and the social studies are particularly useful among the academic areas for developing inter- and intracultural insights.

Other areas of experience such as the fine arts and physical education also can be helpful.

3) Reduced interpersonal friction among children and increased evidence of their mutual trust best can be brought about through helping children to understand their own and other subcultures.

4) Children can be made aware that they have membership in a given subculture and begin to develop pride in this culture as well as sense that much of their behavior is culturally derived.

5) Children can be helped methodically to begin to evaluate their own feelings, to distinguish between feelings and actions, and to analyze and understand their own behavior and the behavior of others in the context of membership in a given subculture.

6) The best way for children to understand the cultures of others in the world as a whole is for them first to understand their own subculture and its related subcultures (25:291).

Particularly if a counselor is to work deftly with the inner city child, the six points above are useful referents. They become invaluable as he endeavors to synchronize social class and ethnocultural factors, substantive learnings, and human relations skills to help insure a child's smooth flow through the continuum. *One must understand the child in his subculture in order to mediate his school experience wisely.*

Working with Teachers to Create Continuity of Experience for Children

The elementary counselor who brings a sense of commitment to his work with boys and girls assumes a continuum of responsibility for safeguarding the quality of each child's input of experience. Since the counselor cannot be in every classroom five days a week or work with each of several teaching teams at the same time, he can only meet his responsibility through advising or otherwise helping others.

The Counselor's Role as Exercised Through the Teacher

It is a subtle and demanding task to learn the skills of working with other professional colleagues. Several forthright suggestions may prove helpful at this point for counselors who will be working closely with teachers.

Many counselors have learned that teachers are not always clear as to what guidance services involve. If the counselor is to exercise part of his role through the teacher—and this is literally unavoidable—then time for in-service preparation for both teacher and counselor must be found. This is necessary in order to help the uninformed teacher understand the goals, scope, and practices of guidance. It also helps the counselor to understand the strengths that are a part of each teacher's professional profile.

In addition, the counselor, with genuine humility and with an open mind, must inform himself of the teachers' self-concepts, of their academic prowess or lack of it, of their understanding, empathy, and overall rapport with children. He also needs gradually to learn more about each individual teaching team and their composite know-how. "What are the teaching and learning goals?" he must ask. "Why are these procedures being used?" "Will these methods help or impair what we are trying to achieve with Myron and Will and Kathy in this situation?"

While the counselor ostensibly is employed to work with young girls and boys, he will find that teachers and his other colleagues also need sympathy and understanding. Rare, indeed, is the institution, whether school or corporation, that does not have on its roster certain human beings with unmet personal needs. Often such persons consciously or unconsciously seek to satisfy their needs in various ways: stubborn spells, sublimation, exploitation of children, both idle and malicious gossip, displacement, pointless feuds, by showing favoritism, and so on. A school psychologist once said off the record, "I can't do a thing about this group [of children] until I can do something to help Miss B___." Such "problem teachers" are by no means rare.

It might as well be acknowledged at once that the counselor's role, as he develops it in a particular school or small cluster of schools, takes form and functions smoothly and soundly depending on the accuracy of his assessment of his classroom colleagues and on his strategy and tactics in working with them.

Below are seven principles or points to observe that may be useful when working with teachers:

1) Remember that the "best" procedure is a variable which depends, among other things, on maturity, experience, values, age, and personality of both the teacher and the counselor.

2) Avoid becoming a real or fancied threat to teachers who may feel that the counselor's work with "their" children may reveal weaknesses in discipline, methods, or pupil achievement.

3) Help teachers develop a confident, professional approach and demeanor when discussing children among themselves, with parents, and with non-certified staff members.

4) Recognize that local districts vary a great deal in their readiness for innovation. In some, teachers are genuinely eager to accept better procedures in guidance. In others they *say* so, but one discovers that they do not really want major changes, or that they simply assume a skeptical or negative stance. Such variations demand on-site study *before* a guidance program is launched and suitable changes, as dictated by the counselor's experiences, *after* the program is in operation.

5) See that teachers quickly understand that a counselor is not a specialist to "take over" or relieve them of work or responsibility, but someone to work *with* them in a shared endeavor to do a superior job with children.

6) Beware of the way in which the teachers' cultural and class backgrounds—and the counselor's—may color thinking and the values placed on elementary school guidance services.

7) Classroom colleagues should be helped to understand *what* the counselor hopes to accomplish; *how* he would like to go about it; and *why* his objectives and guidance procedures are desirable.

Many common-sense (or *un*common good sense) points probably could be added to the seven that are listed. However, it is not intended to be an exhaustive list. The points are made to stress the idea that effective relationships with the faculty are imperative if the counselor is to exercise guidance functions with a good prospect for early success in developing a continuum of good experiences for children.

One must learn to work with his colleagues lest, through lack of cooperation and understanding, they impede rather than help the child to progress along his personal development continuum.

Grouping Children
for Continuity Through Guidance

One hundred and fifty years ago one-room schoolhouses dotted the landscape of large sections of a predominantly rural America. Often in these schools a teacher taught fifteen or twenty children ranging from five- or six-year-olds to young adolescents who were 14 or 15 years of age. Here, indeed, was an ungraded group—one in which some forms of individualized work were inescapable. Although guidance was unheard of, methods were sometimes primitive, and materials were scarce and poor, children of a century ago did move through an individualized continuum of a kind because there was no other way to teach them.

The Graded School

As the U.S. population (at one time over 90 per cent rural) began to grow, cities expanded and elementary schools increased in size even more rapidly. This shift in population became pronounced as northern European immigrants began to flood in after 1840 and as the early movement from American farms to urban centers began. When a class became too large for one teacher to handle during this era, a two-room school often was built. Then one teacher would teach grades 1-4 while the second instructor taught in grades 5-8. Particularly after 1840 a number of arbitrary administrative and organizational devices were introduced to cope with the problems of climbing enrollments.

Among these innovations was the *graded school* where children of around six years of age were labeled "first graders" and assigned to the same teacher. Youngsters of about seven were designated "second graders," and so on. Since grading children did not reduce differences in their learning ability, the concepts of annual promotion or failure were devised in the hope that boys and girls of roughly comparable academic performance could be kept together to simplify instruction. Individual differences were looked upon not as a human resource but as a classroom nuisance and little was known about them. This is understandable, since neither anthropology, sociology, nor psychology existed to explain human individuality. It was the 20th century that marked "the coming of age of the behavioral sciences" according to Bernard Berelson and Gary A. Steiner (3:11).

In retrospect, it must be acknowledged that, in a *mechanical* sense, the 19th century practice of grouping children heterogeneously in age-grade clusters was a success. It helped the schools deal with the transitional problems of moving from one-teacher to multiple-teacher schools. In all fairness, *and especially in view of what was then known about teaching and learning*, the graded school proved to be a workable and valuable organizational scheme well into the present century.

Despite their widespread use, age-grade practices began to be criticized by teachers in the 1920's. It was generally agreed that when young learners were grouped on the basis of age, the resulting range in their behavior and academic performance was enormous. Often, five years or more separated the high and low scores made on standardized tests by children in the middle grades. But aside from a handful of ingenious approaches such as the Winnetka and Dalton Plans, few attempts were made to break the lockstep of the graded school or to individualize teaching (21).

The Transitional Nongraded School

By the 1950's, interest had begun to develop in the idea of the *nongraded* school. Interpretations of the meaning of "nongraded" have varied to some extent among such writers as John I. Goodlad and Robert H. Anderson (11), John L. Tewksbury (26), and David W. Beggs and Edward G. Buffie (2). William P. McLoughlin has even argued that true nongradedness seldom has been tried, although by 1965 from 5.5 percent up to 30 percent of U.S. school districts reported using some kind of a nongraded approach to grouping (19).

Regardless of conflicting data, diverse definitions, and disagreements, by the late 1960's it was reasonable to state that the nongraded school had made a firm place for itself as "... a school which denies the limitations of grade structure and is organized so that the individual student may develop his academic and creative talents as rapidly or as slowly as his abilities permit." (2:21)

The nongraded school of the 1960's was unquestionably a desirable innovation; a sound intermediate step in the direction of a true continuum. As Anderson said in his thoughtfully written book, *Teaching in a World of Change*, nongradedness "... is a concept of the proper way to provide for children's educational needs and a plan for implementing that concept." (1:54) However, nongradedness is more of a transitional step rather than it is a basic innovation. The name itself, as Anderson notes, is in certain ways "... a rather unfortunate term since it refers primarily to what is not, rather than to what is." (1:53-54) Important as its concepts are, nongrading in practice has reduced rather than eliminated the problem of helping children make fluid progress at their own rate—with a breadth and depth of learning suited to their personal growth channel.

Grouping for Continuity:
The Contribution of Guidance

The nongraded school and the continuum school are similar in certain respects. First let us look at eight beliefs that guide or at least influence both the nongraded *and* the continuum concepts of a good school. Then let us look at certain ways—both developmental and organizational—in which the guidance continuum approach to education promises to carry elementary programs to even higher levels of excellence.

The eight beliefs shared by proponents of the nongraded and continuum school are as follows:

1) Children are unique and the differences among them should be developed or enhanced by personalized school experience.

2) Children should be respected and treated fairly despite any variations in their social, ethnic, or economic status.

3) A comprehensive policy of child study and evaluation is essential to provide data governing pupil progress.

4) Teacher planning for purposes of guiding children's development is cooperative, imaginative, and flexible.

5) A team relationship, often including paraprofessional personnel, is desirable.

6) Insofar as possible, old school buildings are modified and new
plants constructed to reduce or eliminate such physical barriers of the graded school as row on row of identical classrooms.

7) Educational technology, whenever possible, is used extensively to permit individualized programs, the use of self-
instructional materials, and richer, more meaningful group
experiences.

8) Overall study and constructive direction of the individual
child's progress in the continuum needs to be the specific
responsibility of the faculty during a given interim. However,

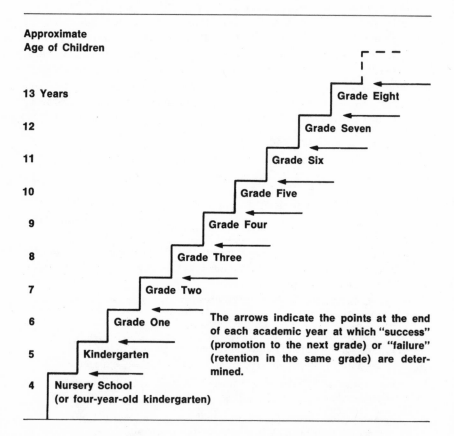

**Approximate
Age of Children**

13 Years   Grade Eight

12   Grade Seven

11   Grade Six

10   Grade Five

9   Grade Four

8   Grade Three

7   Grade Two

6   Grade One   The arrows indicate the points at the end
                        of each academic year at which "success"
5   Kindergarten   (promotion to the next grade) or "failure"
                        (retention in the same grade) are deter-
                        mined.
4 Nursery School
(or four-year-old kindergarten)

Figure 7. Sequence of Traditional or Graded School Progress

a child's progress over a period of years should be the concern of an agent or agents of the school charged with the *continuing* coordination of the child's experience.

Developmental Perspectives

From a developmental perspective, the guidance continuum is a way of conceptualizing, assessing, and guiding the growth and development of the individual child. Important concepts which underlie it include:

1) that life and learning are continuous and emergent,
2) that growth and learning are ordered, sequential, and personal,
3) that the child's inherited endowment and his environment are interactive and of coordinate importance, and
4) that changes in behavior are made by creating changes in the environment rather than by commands and admonitions.

Developmentally, the guidance continuum is inherently based on these four concepts. It is a way of looking at, thinking about, and rationally assisting in the child's development. Nongraded practices, especially as identified by Tewksbury, are attempts to minimize problems caused by grade-level barriers.* They refine the grading but do not erase, at certain points, the promotional rituals which they involve.

Organizational Orientations

How the organization of the guidance continuum departs from the graded and nongraded approaches is more easily illustrated by a series of three models. Figure 7 illustrates that if children show some mastery of content and skill in the graded school, they move in an arbitrary one-step-a-year progression from kindergarten through grade eight.

Figure 8 presents a model of progress in the nongraded school, illustrating that many nongraded practices improve but do not fully provide a setting that is thoroughly helpful in meeting the challenge of individual differences.

---

*Tewksbury's three major types of nongraded programs are achieved:
1) by means of multi-level instruction in self-contained, heterogeneous classes. (Intra-room groups.)
2) by using the performance levels of children as a basis for assignment to self-contained classrooms among which there is instruction of increasing difficulty. (Inter-classroom homogeneous grouping.)
3) by regrouping a large cluster of children periodically during the day or week for work with different teachers at different levels of difficulty and/or on differing topics. (A form of multi-level team teaching.)

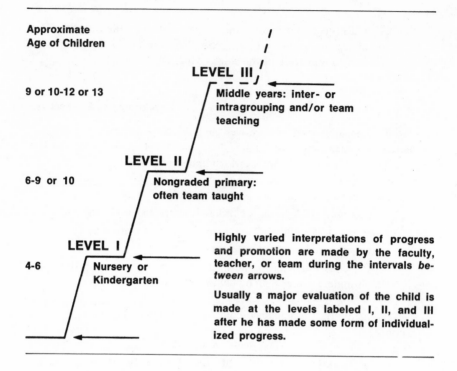

Approximate Age of Children

9 or 10-12 or 13

LEVEL III
Middle years: inter- or intragrouping and/or team teaching

LEVEL II

6-9 or 10
Nongraded primary: often team taught

LEVEL I

4-6
Nursery or Kindergarten

Highly varied interpretations of progress and promotion are made by the faculty, teacher, or team during the intervals *between* arrows.

Usually a major evaluation of the child is made at the levels labeled I, II, and III after he has made some form of individualized progress.

Figure 8.   Sequence of Progress Commonly Followed in Schools with Variations of Ungraded Plans

Now turn to Figure 9. At first glance it appears similar to Figure 4 in the preceding chapter. However, the *curriculum* continuum shown in Figure 4 is a seamless sequence of individualized experiences through which *all* children move. The *guidance* continuum depicts a seamless human development channel (HDC) that is unique to *each* child. While the curriculum and guidance continuums coincide and their models may be construed to have coterminal boundaries, the HDC is shown here to illustrate the way in which a school's human and material resources can be marshalled to maximize a child's progress by *personalizing* his experiences.

The learner moves from immaturity toward greater maturity as illustrated. Because he is unique, however, his route in the HDC is patterned in such ways as will best suit his nature and needs at a given time. The counselor and the teacher share the task of 1) designing the route as correctly as they can and then 2) using their skill to help the child maintain or redirect his course at an optimal rate of progress. Patently, rich human *and* material resources are essential to insure the inputs portrayed in Figure 9.

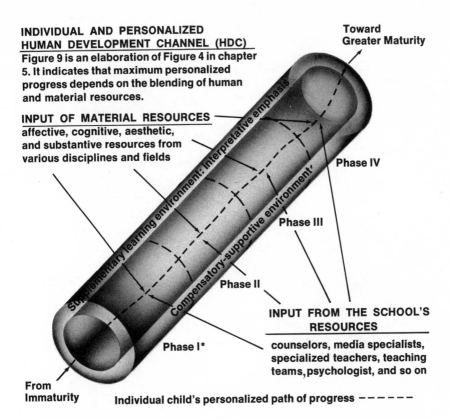

INDIVIDUAL AND PERSONALIZED
HUMAN DEVELOPMENT CHANNEL (HDC)
Figure 9 is an elaboration of Figure 4 in chapter
5. It indicates that maximum personalized
progress depends on the blending of human
and material resources.

INPUT OF MATERIAL RESOURCES
affective, cognitive, aesthetic,
and substantive resources from
various disciplines and fields

Toward
Greater Maturity

Phase IV

Phase III

Phase II

INPUT FROM THE SCHOOL'S
RESOURCES

Phase I*

counselors, media specialists,
specialized teachers, teaching
teams, psychologist, and so on

From
Immaturity   Individual child's personalized path of progress – – – – – –

*The term *phase* refers to a stage in the child's progress toward greater maturity,
hence differs from chronological age units and does not coincide with a grouping
or grade.

Figure 9. Model Illustrating the Deployment of the School's Resources
to Facilitate a Child's Personalized Progress in
His Human Development Channel

We cannot emphasize too strongly that *every* child in some measure requires all varieties of personalized learning experiences—supplementary,
supportive, compensatory, and replicative—in addition to those he shares
with others in his group. This is because no individual is ever uniformly
"clever" or "dull" or "informed" or "uninformed" in *every* way.

Therefore, the insightful counselor and elementary teacher see the so-
called "slow" learner not as a child to be fed a starvation diet of dull, un-
interesting drill, but as someone who requires an enriched, motivational diet
of many varied and satisfying experiences. *The nature of these experiences*

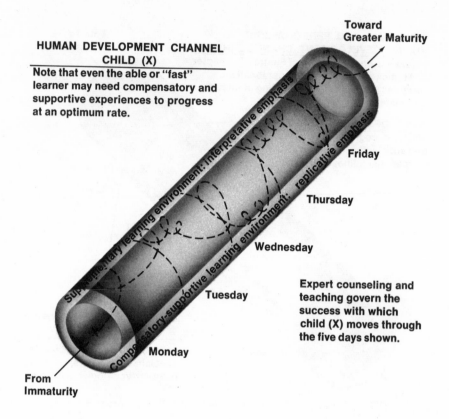

Figure 10. Hypothetical Path of an Advanced Child (X)
in a Guidance Continuum

depends on the particular transactional situation in which the triad of the teacher-learner-counselor is involved at a precise moment in time. The same generalization applies to the "fast" learner. In mathematics, for example, he may be having guided experiences that carry him well ahead of the performance level of many of his classmates. In his social relationships, conversely, he may need much compensatory-supportive experience or replicative, practice experience, perhaps, on the playground or in other group endeavors.

It is this point of view which led in Figure 10 to the portrayal of the progress model of Child (X) and in Figure 11 that of Child (Y) not as an undulating line but as a modified epicycloidal curve. This curved path appearing in each of the two models is intended to show how both fast and slow learners may be expected to move unevenly along the route from "immaturity" toward "greater maturity" in their respective growth channels.

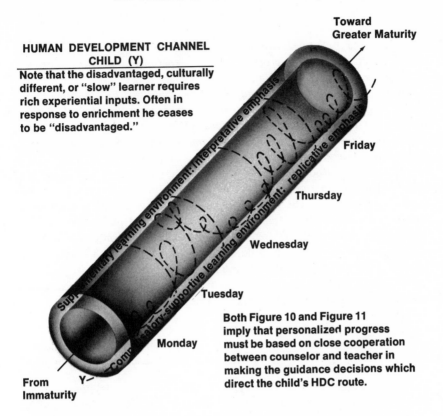

HUMAN DEVELOPMENT CHANNEL
CHILD (Y)

Note that the disadvantaged, culturally different, or "slow" learner requires rich experiential inputs. Often in response to enrichment he ceases to be "disadvantaged."

Both Figure 10 and Figure 11 imply that personalized progress must be based on close cooperation between counselor and teacher in making the guidance decisions which direct the child's HDC route.

Figure 11. Hypothetical Path of a Culturally Different or Disadvantaged Child (Y) on a Guidance Continuum

The route of child (X) tends toward cognitive, supplementary, and interpretative learnings, yet his experiences each day also carry him into the compensatory-supportive categories. Child (Y) during some part of the day likewise has a variety of enriching supplementary and cognitive learnings based on professional judgment as to his progress and personal-social needs.

While emphasis has been placed on the highly personal and unique nature of learning as experienced by each elementary school child, it also must be recognized that many children of comparable ages and similar cultural backgrounds move through a given phase of their lives at approximately the same time. The developmental tasks of learning to walk, to talk, learning an appropriate sex role, and developing fundamental skills follow a central tendency. This being the case, the teacher can readily find many ways of short-term grouping boys and girls during a given day. Common examples of such *ad hoc* groups include reading groups, shared responsibility in arranging a bulletin board or similar display, playground teams, and shared work on an art project, science experiment, or in a creative, extemporized dramatic presentation.

But in the guidance continuum children would not be grouped in the traditional sense. Rather, the counselor and the teacher would work closely together in order to place the individual child in many successive groups which were deemed most likely to maximize progress through his human development channel toward maturity.

The graded school, after a long, useful life, has become inadequate because within its structure there is no really workable way to provide for the pupils' individualities. The nongraded school reshapes the old graded structure and remains a sound transitional organization and philosophy for implementing a concept of children's educational needs. But only as counselors and teachers learn to group children for continuity through guidance, as illustrated by our models, does it seem likely that we will be acting on the knowledge of children and of learning that insightful persons in education and in related disciplines have provided for us in recent decades.

Organizing a Guidance Continuum for the Elementary School

When one understands and accepts the flow of human development and the uniquely personal education toward which it points, it becomes possible to turn to the stimulating question of how best to establish a guidance continuum, a matter which brings us to the discussion of organizing the schools in ways that permit a seamless and uninterrupted flow of wholesome growth toward maturity.

The continuum as interpreted here quite naturally concentrates on guidance functions and services. At the same time, since guidance and counseling are viewed as an integral part of the total school situation, the functions of the counselor are interlaced with those activities performed by related educational agents and agencies. This interrelatedness is not only desirable; it is essential. A cooperative counselor-teacher approach to elementary education is likely to increase rather than to diminish in the years ahead.

The Non-School Preschool Period

Guidance services and functions, when funding and other circumstances permit, should begin to take definite form no later than as the child approaches two years of age. This is the non-school preschool age and is in the process of becoming a part of the school's direct responsibility. Research which is accumulating strongly indicates that five- and even four-year-olds are being enrolled in school too late to remedy the permanent damage that is often done by impoverished, non-responsive environments (22,15).

The non-school preschool period, as the name implies, is one in which organized educational agencies (in most instances the public schools) make a first contact with children, hopefully when they are somewhere between 20 and 24 months of age. The purpose of the contact is to begin an inventory of children's needs to determine how they can be satisfied in ways which seem likely to enhance each boy's and girl's chances for success in school and in the lifetime that continues beyond the school years.

The evaluation might include: 1) medical and dental diagnoses in school-supported clinics; 2) family situation visitation and analyses by psychiatric social workers; 3) initial testing, appropriate to early childhood, to permit the development of early guidance plans for children in the three- to five- or six-year-old range; 4) initiation of early school records; 5) decisions as to what steps might best be taken to help create (at least for the under-privileged) the responsive environments that now seem responsible for *creating* what is measured as intelligence. A final important element is 6) parent education and counseling as suggested by the parents' age, education, social class, and so on. Work with parents is important both to explain the nature and value of the school's early childhood program and to enlist family support in reinforcing the school guidance program when the family is one which is capable of such cooperation.

The role of the guidance specialist with the non-school preschool level naturally should be governed by his degree of competence. If he is well-prepared (*Level II* or *III*), it would be both desirable and important for a guidance specialist to coordinate not only this period of initial school-and-pupil contact, but also the ones mentioned below beginning with the mini-school.

One of the challenges to the field of guidance today is to prepare persons with not only conventional guidance skills but with concomitant ability and experience in early childhood and elementary education. A strong case un-doubtedly can be made for the further education of persons who already have a thorough grasp of elementary school programs and practices in the substantive content of guidance.

The Minischool

As interpreted here, and viewpoints do vary somewhat, the minischool is designed to serve neighborhood clusters of children of about three years of age. Groups of approximately a half-dozen youngsters each are brought to-gether under the direction of both professionals and paraprofessionals. Usually, one early childhood professional supervises every five or six mini-units staffed by carefully instructed paraprofessionals. Associated with the early childhood specialist is an elementary school counselor who serves as a resource, or consultant, or service person, or coordinator depending on his power to contribute early-age guidance services.

The minischool combines many desirable attributes, especially in metropolitan areas with their dense clots of population. In the inner cities and ghettos they are indispensable *when adequately operated.* Some of their attributes include:

a) performing the functions of a good play group in fostering social development

b) compiling "behavior journal" data on each child for ongoing guidance purposes

c) studying nutritional needs of children and providing dietary supplementation as needed

d) keeping health records and making requisite medical and dental referrals

e) serving to identify and to combat conditions that might develop into delinquent behavior in later years

f) beginning to provide supplementary educational input experiences, such as language development, which probably serve to "create" what we measure as intelligence

g) providing a natural and relaxed contact with parents for purposes of counseling and discussion

h) creating a safe environment that encourages the child to develop a sense of security, improved coping behavior, and a resultant superior self-concept

At present the minischool is a relatively new element both as a downward extension of public education and as a challenge to elementary school counselors. Its potential contribution is great enough to merit widespread use in the 1970's and 1980's. One possibility, as "urban sprawl" continues, is the incorporation of minischools for children of three or four in housing projects as a permanent feature of the metropolitan scene and as important advanced bases in society's attacks on deprivation.

Preparatory Pre-Primary Experiences in the Elementary School

By the late 1960's the idea of programs for four- and five-year-old children had become generally accepted, and programs for both age groups had been introduced in a few schools. At present, these children often attend school for one-half day periods and teachers work with a different morning and afternoon group, each enrolling 12 to 15 youngsters.

As a significantly more useful and guidance-oriented approach to working with the four- and five-year-olds, consideration should be given to a fluid, one, two, three, or even four year period of experience including the two year interval that many schools now call the four- and five-year-old kindergarten. The pre-primary continuum is a suitable name for this one to four year span of time.

Upon leaving the minischool (or upon his fourth birthday if he has not been enrolled in a minischool), the program proposed here places the young learner in a rich, responsive environment for preparatory experiences which, as noted above, may extend anywhere from one to four years. The time spans, cooperatively determined by the counselor and by the teacher's evaluations, would determine preparatory experiences for the primary school years somewhat as follows:

> The rare, mature, and richly experienced child would spend about one year in the preparatory period.
>
> Most children would spend two years as four- and five-year-olds before entering primary school at age 6.
>
> The culturally different or intellectually disadvantaged, as study and evidence suggests, might spend three years (in rare cases, even four years) in this pre-primary time block.

The purpose of this flexible time interval, then, is to help insure that each child, within the limits of his sociocultural endowment, begins his primary school experience with an optimum opportunity for success. He does not "flunk kindergarten" if he spends more than two years here; instead, he strengthens his likelihood of moving more effectively through the next segment of his personalized educational continuum.

The importance of the preparatory pre-primary years for both teacher and counselor, and for both child and parent, are tremendous. Here for the first time there is a real opportunity to help children begin their more *structured* cognitive experiences* at age 6, 7, or 8 with a reasonable opportunity to perform successfully. Here parents are likely to be freed from the fancied taint of having a child who is a source of embarrassment because he seems to be "slow for his group." Here teachers can create the flow of experience that helps children grow socially and intellectually with *time* to do the job. And here the elementary school counselor who is insightful and knowledgeable can follow up on the non-school preschool and minischool beginnings and preclude many of the problems which heretofore have harassed

*"Structured cognitive experience" refers to beginning reading programs, methodical teaching of handwriting, organized work in mathematics, and so on.

counselors because priority help was too long postponed for those who needed it in early childhood.*

The opportunity for self-realization begins at birth and can be blighted in early childhood; hence, effective work by the counselor also should begin as soon as possible and while time remains in which to help the young learner to become what he is capable of being.

Early childhood has been stressed in this section because it is often neglected in counseling and guidance programs which historically have been largely confined to the secondary school. Because of this neglect, the years before six remain one of the large *terrae incognitae* on our "maps" of the realm of elementary guidance in which counselors so much need to work.

The Primary Phase of the Guidance Continuum

The details of the counselor's functions and responsibilities in elementary schools are evaluated and discussed in the next six chapters. This section, therefore, discusses but briefly the counselor's activities with the six- to nine-year-old child. Here are some problems which he can anticipate and some accomplishments to seek with this primary school age group.

First let us call attention to a trend in our ways of looking at human development in the years extending from birth through middle childhood. In the 1930's and 1940's there was a tendency to think of children primarily in terms of "ages and stages." The distinguished student of childhood, Dr. Arnold Gesell,† and his associates made important contributions to the study of child development in work undertaken prior to World War II (8,9). Typical Gesell generalizations read as follows:

> The 24 week old infant can pick up an object on sight. At 36 weeks he can pick up the aforementioned candy pellet, opposing thumb and index finger. At 40 weeks he can poke it with his extended index finger. At 15 months he can pluck it with precise pincher prehension . . . (8:19).

Such observed behavior records were of great value, but they often were naively interpreted by educators and viewed with alarm by parents who found that their child's baby teeth were not "erupting when Dr. Gesell's book said they should."

Gesell was careful to note that *norms* do not correspond to *normal,* and that the "typical" behavior described was simply the most frequent or modal in a wide range. Nevertheless, many persons read Gesell and other longitudinal studies superficially and thus fortified their misconceptions

*See also (16).

†A physician and former director of the Clinic of Child Development, School of Medicine, Yale University.

rather than improved their insights. As Michel de Montaigne once said, "nothing is so firmly believed as what we least understand."

Today most of what we thought we knew about the early years of human life has been seriously shaken. The old norms do not correspond with new information about children, the ways in which they learn, and the ways in which their physical growth and intellectual development is mediated during childhood by environmental influences, particularly those provided through their membership in a given ethnocultural configuration.

Although they vary because each child is unique, certain developmental problems of a general nature can be anticipated by counselors as they interact with six- to nine-year-olds.

The Intermediate Phase
of the Guidance Continuum

Strong emphasis previously has been placed on the continuity and on the uninterrupted nature of the developmental continuum of teaching and learning, of experiencing and becoming. It should be evident, therefore, that the distinction made here between primary and intermediate segments or modules is for purposes of discussion. Actually, children are not "primary" enrollees one day and "intermediate" students the next. From a developmental point of view, children may change in social and intellectual development at rates that are even more dramatic in their differences than physical growth spurts. The period of time labeled as the "primary" phase is made up of modules which may run from two or three years to four or more *depending on the amount of time a child needs to ready himself for success in the intermediate phase.*

Professionally sound and insightful decisions in which teachers and counselors share should be the basis for contemplating progress from the primary to the intermediate phase. The wisdom of these decisions should significantly reduce problems which the counselor might otherwise meet when working with the 9- to 12-year-olds, and do so without decreasing the number and variety of opportunities for fostering individual progress.*

In general, as children in the eight to ten year age range move from the primary to the intermediate phase of their schooling, the counselor encounters problem constellations that vary from those of the primary years. His opportunities also differ, requiring that he possess several types of knowledge if

*References to "levels" or "grades" have been avoided in order to write in a manner consistent with the contention that grade levels are artificial and impair one's ability to think in terms of an uninterrupted continuum. At the same time the reader must not lose sight of the point that in most schools (graded and nongraded) the "primary phase" is still identified as grades 1-3 and the "intermediate" or "middle school phase" as grades 4-6, or grades 6-8 or even 7-9.

he is to understand, enhance, and modify forces under his control which may influence the child's development.

A General Résumé of Guidance Components and Services in the Continuum

By this time it should have been made clear both directly and by implication that the effective elementary school counselor is basically a new breed of professional worker. Much current literautre strongly supports this point (4,5,6,20) *The counselor who provides leadership based on the merit of expertise is one who combines within himself a number of professional attributes which make him able to contribute in ways teachers, principals, and other personnel cannot contribute in the same measure to the elementary school.* This concluding section of Chapter 6, as it provides an overview of guidance services in the elementary continuum, once again illustrates the interrelationship of knowledge and human qualities upon which the expertise of the elementary counselor should be based (25).

Counseling Services

1) Individual counseling through which the counselor seeks to develop insights that help him better to understand a child over a period of time; insights that the counselor shares with the teacher or team to further the learner's progress toward maturity.

2) Small-group counseling, often designed to find ways of improving or alleviating interpersonal problems that may involve from two to five children.

3) Group counseling to help children learn the art of decision making, the meaning of leadership as a group function, and the sensitivities and skills involved in interpersonal relationships.

Consulting Functions

4) Learner-information service to help children develop better self-insights.

5) Consulting service for parents that involves more than skillful discussion of problem situations. Even before the school's first contact with the entering child, the counselor has the opportunity to accumulate information and impressions about the child through initial interviews. Later on, this "reverse flow" of information from parents is often useful in individual and group sessions in which the counselor hopes to help parents realize the importance of a home environment that is responsive to and stimulating for their child.

6) Consulting with individual teachers, team members, or supporting staff members about the underlying causes of certain types of behavior.

7) In-service education sessions in which the well-prepared guidance counselor, as appropriate, presents data and viewpoints that faculty members need for a deeper understanding of childhood.

8) Input for teaching teams and consultants to keep such persons advised about pupil progress in educational areas with which they may be out of touch. (The information gap, a problem for consultants—say in reading or science—can also trouble team teachers, who rarely work with all children in a variety of school situations.)

9) Advice about the therapeutic use of content. Under certain circumstances, subject matter can be used to help "heal" or lessen the problems of particular children.

Educational Biography Services

10) Assessment, a guidance function involving the use of multiple means to study pupils' progress profiles. Conventional testing is only one component of many indices of expected performance.

11) Evaluation, a continuous process of inquiry designed to lead to reliable conclusions as to how well the school is attaining the changes it is endeavoring to make in the children's behavior. Many evaluative instruments in addition to tests are used in the process.

12) Progress reports, which, as they begin to replace traditional grading, are bringing about an improved psychological effect on the elementary school learner.

13) Record keeping, data accumulation, and decisions about how records and data are to be used.

Experience-Sequencing Services

14) Grouping of teachers and children for teachability, including short-term, common-purpose grouping that cuts across age levels in nongraded primary and middle schools.

15) Sequencing the child's experiences in such a way as to keep his social, physical, and academic characteristics in balance.

School Resource Utilization

16) Intraschool referrals that help the child make optimum progress through methodical contacts with the human and material resources of such special personnel as the physical education instructor, educational media

specialist, school nurse, remedial clinicians, school psychologist, psychometrist, school dentist and physician.

17) Interagency referrals that pertain to social agencies or such personnel outside the school as psychiatric social workers.

Longitudinal Studies

18) Function-related or task-related research undertaken to obtain, through study and experimentation, the data needed for his work.

19) Original professional inquiries designed to add to current knowledge regarding the improvement of new guidance practices.

20) Follow-up studies to determine the success of decisions made in regard to grouping, experience sequencing, and similar teacher and counselor decisions.

Coordination and Leadership Contributions

21) General management of pupil records (provided the counselor has suitable clerical assistance).

22) Supervision of various special-service personnel (psychometrists, personnel in special education, school psychologists, remedial specialists) and coordination of their services.

23) Phasing in of new students, scheduling of testing programs, and development of new record forms as needed.

24) Curriculum liaison work in which the counselor conducts a continuing study of the use made of current curriculum materials and of the projected development of new materials. As one of the few faculty members presumably in contact with children from their early years in school until they depart—and as a student of childhood—the counselor is in a unique position to think clearly about the curriculum as a series of guided transactions that increase the learner's value to himself and to the culture of which he is a part.

Man or Superman?

If current writings are any index, the 24 potential contributions listed above are a reasonably accurate inventory of what the new guidance can do to freshen and enliven elementary education and to make its practices more humane and meaningful.

But making childhood education better takes more than an accumulation of long needed services and functions designed to improve the educational climate for three- to twelve-year-olds. The heart of the matter is whether higher education is capable of producing a new breed of guidance specialists quickly enough in these crucial times to perform the tasks that beg to be done.

Teachers seeking escape from abrasive day-long classroom contacts with boys and girls will not do the job. Neither will unsuccessful secondary school counselors hoping to retread themselves and make a fresh start with younger clients.

To make guidance in the elementary school become the great force it can become, we need in-depth study by persons who already know how to work with children and pre-adolescents. They must be persons who are willing to make the vigorous effort that is required in the effective performance of a reasonable number of the important services and functions of elementary school guidance. They must be willing also to exert leadership in helping schools move closer to expert guidance in early, middle, and later childhood.

Summary

Building on Chapter 5 with its discussion of the seamless curriculum, Chapter 6 develops the concept of a continuum of guidance services which, like human growth, proceeds without regard for arbitrary or lockstep devices such as a graded school organization or unrealistic grouping plans.

Stress is placed on the fact that the presence of a number of distinctly different subcultures in the United States should strongly influence both the school curriculum and the guidance curriculum. This point of view is linked to a series of premises regarding the scope and sequence of elementary education beginning with the guidance influenced services at the two- and three-year-old age levels. Pre-primary, primary, and intermediate phases of developmental learning and guidance are suggested in lieu of traditional graded or more recent nongraded practices.

Chapter 6 concludes with the identification of 24 components of a total guidance and counseling program which are examined and discussed further in Chapters 7 - 14.

References

1. Anderson, Robert H. *Teaching in a World of Change*. New York: Harcourt, Brace and World, Inc., 1966.
2. Beggs, David W., III and Edward G. Buffie. *Nongraded Schools in Action*. Bloomington, Ind.: Indiana University Press, 1967.
3. Berelson, Bernard and Gary A. Steiner. *Human Behavior: An Inventory of Scientific Findings*. New York: Harcourt, Brace and World, Inc., 1964.
4. Byrne, R. H. "For Elementary Schools: A Human Development Specialist?" *Educational Leadership* 24 (January, 1967): 349-355.

5. Faust, Verne. *The Counselor-Consultant in the Elementary School.* Boston: Houghton Mifflin Co., 1968.

6. ____. *Elementary School Counseling.* Boston: Houghton Mifflin Co., 1968.

7. Frost, Joe L., ed. *Early Childhood Rediscovered.* New York: Holt, Rinehart and Winston, Inc., 1968.

8. Gesell, Arnold, Frances Ilg, et al. *The Child From Five to Ten.* New York: Harper and Bros., 1946.

9. ____. *Infant and Child in the Culture Today.* New York: Harper and Bros., 1943.

10. Gibson, Robert L. and Robert E. Higgins. *Techniques of Guidance: An Approach to Pupil Analysis.* Chicago: Science Research Associates, 1966.

11. Goodlad, John I. and Robert H. Anderson. *The Nongraded Elementary School.* New York: Harcourt, Brace and World, Inc., 1959.

12. Hall, Edward T. *The Hidden Dimension.* New York: Doubleday and Co., Inc., 1966.

13. ____. "Listening Behavior: Some Cultural Differences." *Phi Delta Kappan* 50 (March, 1969): 379-380.

14. ____. *The Silent Language.* New York: Fawcett World Library: Premier Books, 1969.

15. Hunt, J. McVicker. "The Psychological Basis for Using Pre-School Enrichment as an Antidote for Cultural Deprivation." *Merrill-Palmer Quarterly of Behavior and Development* 10 (1964): 209-248.

16. Kimball, Solon T. "Culture, Class, and Educational Congruity," *Educational Requirements for the 1970's.* Edited by Stanley Elam and William P. McLure. New York: F. A. Praeger, 1967.

17. Kneller, George F. *Educational Anthropology.* New York: John Wiley and Sons, Inc., 1965.

18. Leonard, George. *Education and Ecstasy.* New York: Delacorte Press, 1968.

19. McLoughlin, William P. "The Phantom Nongraded School." *Phi Delta Kappan* 49 (January, 1968): 248-250.

20. Mayer, G. R. "An Approach for the Elementary School Counselor: Consultant or Counselor?" The School Counselor 14 (March, 1967): 210-215.

21. Otto, Henry J. "Historical Sketches of Administrative Innovations." Educational Administration and Supervision 20 (March, 1934): 161-172.

22. Passow, Harry A. *Education of the Disadvantaged: A Book of Readings,* New York: Holt, Rinehart, and Winston, Inc., 1967.

23. *Phi Delta Kappan* 50 (March, 1969):369-433.

24. Shane, Harold G. "International Education in the Elementary and Secondary School." *The United States and International Education.* LXVIII *Yearbook.* Edited by Herman G. Richey, National Society for the Study of Education. Chicago: University of Chicago Press, 1969. An adaptation.

25. ____and June Grant Shane. "Guidance at an Early Age: Twenty-four Contributions of the New Guidance to Elementary Education." *Today's Education* 58 (November, 1969): 36-38.

26. Tewksbury, John L. *Nongrading in the Elementary School.* Columbus, Ohio: Charles E. Merrill Books, 1967.
27. Thelen, Herbert A. *Classroom Grouping for Teachability.* New York: John Wiley and Sons, Inc., 1967.

7

Philosophy
and the Role
of the Counselor
in Elementary Education

In ancient and medieval times, money changers and jewelers used a type of black stone to determine the purity of gold or silver. In old French it was called a *touchepierre;* literally a "touchstone." When precious metal was rubbed across it, the type of streak left on the touchstone determined the purity of the metal.

The guidance counselor has as one of his central developmental tasks, as Donald Blocher once noted, the responsibility for building a personal philosophy of counseling (4:16). He needs to create *his* inner touchstone, a cluster of examined and tested values, that serve as criteria for determining the value of his work and the practices that support it. Such a body of values is of particularly great importance at the elementary school level, both because of the malleability and because of the psychosocial vulnerability of children.

The philosophical choices and insights of the elementary school counselor are also of importance because the specialists who work at this level generally did not begin to be prepared in most universities until the mid-1960's. As a result, the present is still a time when many precedents are being established. Wise choices—or their absence—seem certain to influence future practices for years to come.

The Elementary Counselor's Philosophic Choices

There is no way in which educational philosophies can be placed in neat categories. Viewpoints overlap and flow together; new terms are constantly being created and old ones acquire new meanings. Anna R. Meeks, drawing upon the literature, listed *determinism, phenomenology,* and *existentialism* as sources of concepts (26). Blocher, also turning to standard philosophical sources, selected *essentialism, progressivism,* and *existentialism* as sources of counseling philosophy (4).

What seems to be needed at this point is not so much another résumé of labels, or of the several schools of philosophy, but a more thorough examination of two markedly different positions or viewpoints governing how the counselor looks at the nature of the child; his assumptions as to the role and meaning of the environment in human development, and the conception he has of how learning takes place.

Two Contrasting Philosophical Positions

Basically there is a "closed universe" and an "open universe" approach to the way a counselor looks at his young client. The positions they represent are diametrically opposed.

The person who accepts a "closed universe" is governed by such premises as:

1) There are fixed and unchanging answers to human problems that can be found through reason; reflective thinking can interpret and explain the universe. Classical writings contain most of our heritage of ideas and rational thought.

2) Man is controlled by certain established forms of authority— ecclesiastical, political, and ideological.

3) Man should accept and conform to the tested practices which passing time has established.

4) Since there are rational, "right" answers, education is concerned with mental cultivation; proper beliefs and skills are made habitual through indoctrination.

In the "closed universe" the individual's actions are determined by forces greater than himself; the human mind is something that is *not* to be trusted.

The "open universe" is of a totally different polarity:

1) There are many and variable answers to problems. The truth of an idea is determined by its worth as an instrument of

action; thinking is a process for guiding action. Truth is modified by new discoveries.

2) Man is free of the control of supernatural restraints; his life is governed by a world of reason, and science has given us a dynamic rather than a static concept of the universe.

3) Man is in a state of *becoming* rather than in a state of *being*. As a multipotential biological being, man can become any one of many things through intelligent self-direction. Behavior—indeed, life itself—is a process.

4) In an "open universe," one in which there are no fixed answers, answer-*giving* is replaced by the idea that the learner is a dynamic answer-*seeker;* education's task is to raise human potentiality by helping each child actually *create and operate himself* through meaningful, reasoned transactions.

As the tone of earlier chapters has implied, the second of the two broad philosophical positions sketched above seems to be the more reasonable and carefully reasoned in view of contemporary knowledge in the physical, biological, and behavioral sciences. The practices presented and discussed hereinafter are of the "open universe" type—proposals to help a child create and direct himself and make socially desirable progress toward the behavior of the mature adult by being mature for *his* level at any given time.

The Counselor's Knowledge of Contemporary Philosophy

A convenient way to initiate the counselor's acquaintance with a philosophy which he finds compatible in his transactions with children can be built upon the four positions delineated by Theodore Brameld around 1950 (5,6). Brameld describes two paired "closed universe" philosophies and two related "open universe" philosophies with direct relevance for the elementary counselor.

The terms that are frequently applied to these major views are 1) *essentialism,* which is the educational philosophy concerned chiefly with the conservation of culture; 2) *perennialism,* which centers its attention on the kind of educational guidance provided by the classical thought of Greece and medieval Europe; 3) *progressivism*, which is the philosophy of liberal, experimental education; and 4) *reconstructionism,* which believes that the contemporary crises can be effectively attacked only by a radical educational policy and program of action (5:25).

Brameld goes on to point out that there are essentially two *pairs* of philosophies of education: 1) the essentialist-perennialist and 2) the progressive-reconstructionist. The essentialist-perennialist camp contains educators, including elementary counselors, who are concerned with the *transmittal* of the cultural heritage and the *giving* of predetermined answers. The progressivist-reconstructionist group is concerned with innovation that leads to educational change and to the discovering of answers during the processes of change.

As we turn to the triple role of the counselor, it should become increasingly evident that the active, answer-finding approaches implied are based on an "open universe" concept and on a faith in innovation which Brameld ascribes to persons of a progressive-reconstructionist philosophical persuasion.

It is, of course, impossible to present here a detailed résumé of the "philosophy an elementary counselor should accept." To do so would be to assume the incongruous position of dictating "closed universe" answers for him to swallow. Nor is there space in which to delineate a detailed contemporary philosophy for the elementary counselor. In view of these restrictions it is possible only to provide a paragraph or two on each of several influential philosophical viewpoints which are having an impact on guidance both at the elementary and secondary levels.

A Résumé of Five Philosophical Positions

The following discussion of the dimensions of the elementary school guidance program really is aimed at the question, "What makes a good program?" The goals of such programs and the procedures for achieving these goals usually reflect the values and resultant philosophies of those directly responsible for program development. As Edward J. Shoben points out, "Theory is inevitable and inescapable in the counseling process and in the counselor's personal behavior." (31:617)

While the most effective elementary counselor, as already was pointed out, will develop a theory of counseling that is uniquely his, he nonetheless will need to build on a foundation of established theory or theories. Since many of the currently popular theories of counseling have their origins in the philosophies of phenomenology, progressivism, existentialism, determinism, and essentialism, these will be briefly discussed in the paragraphs which follow.

Phenomenology. The phenomenological viewpoint, as described by two of its most noted spokesmen, Arthur W. Combs and Donald Snygg, seeks "to understand the behavior of the individual from his own point of view. It attempts to observe people, not as they seem to outsiders, but as they seem to themselves." (9:17)

Carlton E. Beck presents a "minimal framework of presuppositions for phenomenology" as follows:

1) A real world exists independent of the knower. Its existence can be inferred, but not experienced directly.

2) Reason exists and is the tool whereby inferences can be made on the basis of past experiences.

3) Inferences from past experiences in one's own phenomenal field are the only source of knowledge, other than certain "raw sensations" obtained by sensory experiences. "New" knowledge is just the restructuring of knowns and the incorporation of what we might call nouvelles ("raw sensations" which becomes another force in one's field of forces).

4) The pre-existent world of objects and the existent world of situations follow certain predictable "laws" and can be known by reason via inference.

5) One's phenomenal field at any given instant wholly determines his behavior.

6) Naturalism is the ontological concomitant of phenomenology, and supernaturalism is excluded as nonparsimonious.

7) The individual has "needs" which represent the actions necessary to maintain or enhance his phenomenal self (3:73).

From the perspective presented by this viewpoint, the counselor must note that behavior is determined by the phenomenological "field" and only the individual child can know his "field." Since this field is created by the individual boy or girl, it can only be changed by created changes in the inner or "under-the-skin" world of the young learner.

The counselor must understand that whatever a given child does may be rational when examined in the context of his internal perceptual field. *Reality is that which the perceiver perceives it to be.* Effective elementary school counseling, then, from a phenomenological viewpoint, would include the counselor's awareness of 1) a child's field as he (the child) perceives it, and 2) how fields may change in the private inner world of each child.

Progressivism.   Progressivism emphasizes the concept that the object and the observer are part of a single continuity and that there also is continuity between the unknown and the known (36). Progressivistic systems are interested in specific and particular experiences and empirical results. As viewed by Blocher, progressivistic theories are exemplified by *experimentalism, pragmatism,* and *instrumentalism,* terms often associated with the distinguished philosopher John Dewey (4:17-18).

The "progressivist" (not to be confused with participants in the progressive education movement) does not begin with established values, but, from an experimentalist approach, he seeks the truth.* Values are determined by results or consensus: i.e., the truth of an idea resides in its consequences as verified by experimentation. Tested propositions, if valid, lead to "warranted assertibility." Behavior, too, is judged in terms of consequences.

Such systems may place the counselor in the role of an instrument of society for ascertaining and categorizing the individual child and his behavior. For the counselor, seeking to maintain the freedom and individuality of his young counselee, however, home and school pressure for conformity and "good" academic results may pose some philosophical problems.

Existentialism. Existentialism, as discussed by Ben Strickland, "is a school of thought that is concerned with the individual and his attempt to retain his identity, make his own choices, and provide his own self-direction." (34:471) It is a "humanistic" or man-centered theory which stresses individuality.

The attainment of individuality is viewed as a desirable accomplishment and one which is encouraged through the counseling relationship. Counseling for individuality is most effective in an environment established through the following counselor approaches:

1) The counselor adopts the role of the young learner rather than that of the teacher.
2) He tries to understand what the child understands.
3) He utilizes any techniques available which seem appropriate, always remembering that the truth that the client seeks, or the choice that he must make, comes from within his own frame of reference if individuality is to be fostered.
4) He uses objective information discreetly. (Increased knowledge without increased self-knowledge might be useless or even obstructive.)
5) He helps the child find truth for himself.
6) He assists the client in developing an inward frame of reference.
7) He encourages boys and girls in articulating all the areas of their experience (34:472-473).

A popular spokesman for an existential theory of counseling, Adrian Van Kaam, defines this approach as a "process of making free, a humanizing of the person who has lost his freedom in sectors of his existence to transcend his life-situation." (35:403)

*Truth, as Charles S. Pierce once defined it, is "The opinion which is fated ultimately to be agreed upon by all who investigate . . . ."

While existential counseling may be viewed as a process for "freeing man" through insights that give meanings to life situations, it is a point of view that must be studied with care and caution rather than swallowed whole. There continues to be considerable disagreement as to what the term means and Walter Kaufman, in a scholarly essay, flatly states that "Existentialism is not a philosophy but a label for several widely different revolts against traditional philosophy. Most of the living 'existentialists' have repudiated this label . . . ." (23:11)

Determinism. At the opposite end from existential theory is the deterministic viewpoint in which the world exists and operates as a result of certain basic "laws" of nature or "facts of life." A cause-and-effect explanation of all phenomena is considered possible. To the determinist, man is viewed as developing in accordance with certain determined scientific principles. His behavior can be understood in view of the drives, needs, and wants which control or direct his actions. B. F. Skinner is explicit on this point when he argues that behavior is caused or determined. This assumption is a corollary of one's use of the methods of science (32).

Nicholas Hobbs, in a discussion of ethical considerations involved, predicted that ". . . increasingly, man will be able to employ the results of psychological science to manipulate his fellow man, often without his victim knowing that he is being controlled." (19)

The deterministic viewpoint of man is a scientific one. Therefore, since science makes manipulation possible, the counselor, in this theoretical framework presumably will tend to function as a "manipulative scientist."

Essentialism. Blocher uses the "essentialism" category loosely for grouping such subtypes as rationalism, idealism, and realism. He contends that these philosophies are based on the assumptions that, "man is the only creature endowed with reason and that his chief function is to use this reason in order to know the world in which he lives." (4:17) He further points out that these philosophies have in common a belief in the existence of fixed and unchanging absolutes "of the good, the true, and the beautiful."

Martin H. Astor suggests that idealism and realism go hand in hand, and that counselors must be the kind of idealists who are willing and able to face the facts of life. He states:

> . . . effective guidance counselors are dreamers with shovels . . . .
> The counselor always strives to assist others to achieve their ideals. But, implicit in the idealistic guidance process, we are always helping the client to focus upon the realities of life (1:1031).

The foregoing summary of assorted viewpoints should indicate why, for purposes of clarity and simplicity, the reader first was introduced to the basic ideas of but *two* opposed or polar concepts: the *open* universe and that of the *closed* universe in elementary school counseling. These two "umbrellas" cover all other more finely shaded philosophical postures.

The Role of the Elementary Counselor

One of the important opportunities which lies ahead for guidance in elementary schools is that of clearly establishing the roles—the nature of the varieties of expertise—to be exercised by the counselor as an agent who guides human development in the process of behavioral change. While 24 distinct functions of guidance were previously identified in Chapter 6, it remains to be asked, "What are the specific roles to which they point as one applies the 'open universe' philosophy?"

The well-prepared elementary school counselor—one at *Level II* or *III*—is obviously the agent for individual counseling in the elementary setting. But in this capacity he must also assume several relevant roles. These include functioning as a *developmental specialist,* as a *consultant,* and as a *catalyst.* Let us briefly characterize these roles before considering each one at length.

The Counselor as a Developmental Specialist

The elementary school is an agency of society which is designed to transmit moral and intellectual values and also to promote human development. Working within this social matrix, the counselor functions as an agent in the processes of behavioral change who guides human development. In this role, the counselor should be aware of the psychosocial processes through which the elementary school child acquires and modifies patterns of behavior for effective functioning. He also needs to be cognizant of the social forces with which the developing child interacts. These developmental and social insights are what enable the counselor to make an effective contribution to the child's progress in his personal growth continuum.

The evolving developmental relationship between counselor and child involves two fundamental purposes: *support* and *stimulation.* As one writer describes them:

> . . . the supporting function is aimed at restoring a sufficient level of security or homeostasis to an individual to free sufficient energy for differentiation or growth processes to move forward. The relationship also serves to stimulate the client toward new growth experiences and toward alternative ways of behaving that will facilitate further growth in desired directions. The function

of the relationship is to change levels of *security* and *motivation* in order for optimum development to occur (4:153).*

The Counselor as a Consultant

A major area of responsibility of the elementary school counselor, one clearly recognized by the joint ACES-ASCA Committee, is the consultation function. In his role as a consultant, the counselor works with teachers, with other professional colleagues, with parents, and with community personnel. The objectives of this role are to help these persons better understand a given child or group relationship, to gain additional insights for the counselor himself, and to share in creating meaningful experiences for children.

The counselors' *primary* consulting activities are usually undertaken with the classroom teacher. He may, for example, seek to communicate to the teacher how children perceive their environments, as well as information concerning children's interests, frustrations, abilities, and self-image. The classroom teacher can also be provided .with clues for individual or group motivation, for instruction, and for setting the tone or climate of the classroom. As the teacher becomes more and more sensitive to the individual needs of children, he also may utilize the counselor as a resource person as he seeks better to understand the various forms of deviant behavior encountered in his classroom.

As he grows in understanding the general characteristics of a given elementary school population, the counselor also increases in importance as an effective consultant to the administration and total faculty when they study and discuss changes in the pre-school, primary, or middle school curriculum, activity planning, or program evaluation.

The school counselor can also be an effective consultant to parents, 1) by helping them see their child as the elementary school views him, 2) by interpreting his educational development, and 3) by working with those parents seeking a better understanding of their child and the ways in which they may assist in his development. From time to time, the counselor also is likely 4) to serve as a consultant to others in the community interested in the development of a particular child or group of children. These may be interested parties such as clergymen, recreational personnel, community government representatives, and civic groups.

Through these and other consulting activities, the counselor not only assists others to understand and help the child but also increases his own understanding of the child and his environment. This does not in any way minimize the importance of the child himself as the most important single source for information.

*Donald H. Blocher, *Developmental Counseling.* Copyright © 1966 The Ronald Press Co., New York.

The Counselor as a Catalyst

The counselor frequently functions in the important role of a catalyst. In this capacity he seeks to assist a child in discovering and integrating the elements of a problem or a problem-cluster through his own conscious efforts. He also is a catalyst in the sense that he can bring together or pool human resources such as a school psychologist, classroom teachers, the school nurse, and teachers in special fields to assist in a boy or girl's identification and exploration of a problem situation.

To make the developmental specialist/consultant/catalyst roles of the counselor more explicit, and meaningful, it is now necessary to examine in turn the significance and deeper meaning of each.

The Counselor as a Developmental Specialist

Just what does it mean for a counselor to be a developmental specialist? It implies that he has acquired a substantial grasp of learning theory, of the developmental needs of children, including concepts as those involved in developmental tasks and self-perception, and an awareness of the importance of group interaction. A sampling of appropriate source materials which have contributed to current knowledge illustrates some of the kinds of information that help one to operate effectively as a specialist.

Assumptions about Human Development

Man has made assumptions about growth and development from earliest times. From Biblical injunctions such as "Spare the rod . . ." to the writings of 18th, 19th, or early 20th century educators such as Bernard Basedow, Henry Pestalozzi, G. Stanley Hall, William James, and Sigmund Freud, theories and propositions with a bearing on the learner's development have been advanced and defended, have influenced education, or have slipped quietly into the swampy limbo of forgotten ideas.

At present, some views regarding human development that have commanded widespread attention and respect are those advanced by Erik H. Erikson, Robert J. Havighurst, and Abraham H. Maslow. Below is a succinct summary of certain ideas and concepts associated with these men—ideas with which the elementary counselor profitably can acquaint himself.

Erikson's "Eight Ages of Man." The eight ages through which one passes present an interesting series of concepts regarding stages of personality development. These stages, the "Eight Ages," are analogous to a timetable—

a sequence of developmental levels through which the human being passes as he matures. The eight stages include:

    I. Oral sensory
    II. Muscular anal
    III. Locomotor genital
    IV. Latency
    V. Puberty and adolescence
    VI. Young adulthood
    VII. Adulthood
    VIII. Maturity

At each age, according to Erikson, there are problems which the child and the adult must solve as life unfolds. Successful coping with these problems provides the ego-strength needed if he is to mesh with his social institutions. The problems that respectively accompany the Eight Ages are: 1) developing basic trust, 2) overcoming shame and doubt and attaining autonomy, 3) mastering feelings of guilt and developing the initiative that extends autonomy, 4) overcoming feelings of inferiority and attaining skills that make one useful to himself and to society, 5) clarifying one's role in life and dropping childish behavior in favor of new, more maturing, and consistent role-interpretation, 6) learning to give of one's self in intimate personal relations without ego-loss fears, 7) avoiding stagnation and acquiring the ability to give love that exceeds the desire to be loved, and 8) recognizing and accepting the meaningfulness of one's life cycle and the ideals that endow it with meaning.

Psychoanalyst Erikson's ideas provide an excellent and important list of insights pertaining to the subtleties and the psychosocial significance of childhood. His views also suggest how problems, *as they are successfully solved,* can enhance one's long-range satisfactions in life. These insights epitomize the sensitivity toward children—the ability to empathize and to understand them—that the effective counselor continues to acquire and extend throughout his lifetime.

Havighurst's "Developmental Tasks." In a procedure analogous to that used by Erikson in his Eight Ages, Havighurst has evolved the concept of Developmental Tasks. The material which follows summarizes the bio-social and psychological adjustments and accomplishments which confront us from birth to our later years.

Havighurst, a sociologist as well as an educator, was more explicit in enumerating his tasks than Erikson. The reader will find that the task-inventory below and the Erikson model or chart are complementary.

Developmental Tasks of Infancy and Early Childhood

    Learning to walk
    Learning to take solid foods
    Learning to talk
    Learning to control the elimination of body wastes
    Learning sex differences and sexual modesty
    Achieving physiological stability
    Forming simple concepts of social and physical reality
    Learning to relate oneself emotionally to parents, siblings, and other
    people
    Learning to distinguish right and wrong and developing a conscience

Developmental Tasks of Middle Childhood

    Learning physical skills necessary for ordinary games
    Building wholesome attitudes toward oneself as a growing organism
    Learning to get along with age-mates
    Learning an appropriate sex role
    Developing fundamental skills in reading, writing, and calculating
    Developing concepts necessary for everyday living
    Developing conscience, morality, and a scale of values
    Developing attitudes toward social groups and institutions

Developmental Tasks of Adolescence

    Accepting one's physique and accepting a masculine or feminine role
    New relations with age-mates of both sexes
    Emotional independence of parents and other adults
    Achieving assurance of economic independence
    Selecting and preparing for an occupation
    Developing intellectual skills and concepts necessary for civic competence
    Desiring and achieving socially responsible behavior
    Preparing for marriage and family life
    Building conscious values in harmony with an adequate scientific world-
    picture

Developmental Tasks of Early Adulthood

    Selecting a mate
    Learning to live with a marriage partner
    Starting a family
    Rearing children
    Managing a home
    Getting started in an occupation
    Taking on civic responsibility

Figure 12.   Havighurst's Developmental Tasks (17) (cont. on p. 192)

Developmental Tasks of Middle Age

Achieving adult civic and social responsibility
Establishing and maintaining an economic standard of living
Assisting teen-age children to become responsible and happy adults
Developing adult leisure-time activities
Relating oneself to one's spouse as a person
To accept and adjust to the physiological changes in middle age
Adjusting to aging parents

Developmental Tasks of Later Maturity

Adjusting to decreasing physical strength and health
Adjusting to retirement and reduced income
Adjusting to death of spouse
Establishing an explicit affiliation with one's age group
Meeting social and civic obligations
Establishing satisfactory physical living arrangements

Figure 12. Havighurst's Developmental Tasks (17) (*cont.*)

A knowledge of the way in which the developmental tasks of early childhood blend with those of middle childhood and pre-adolescence is of especial importance to elementary counselors, although they must be seen in the *total* context of Havighurst's list of emerging tasks. The challenge to the counselor, naturally, is not to memorize the tasks *per se* but to absorb the sense of their meaning and then to interpret and to apply them as a part of his growing fund of developmental knowledge.

Maslow and "Self-Actualization." Beginning with the advent of his book *Motivation and Personality* (1954) (24), Abraham H. Maslow has become increasingly well-known for his research, pilot studies, and self-admitted conjectures as to what creates psychologically healthy persons. These healthy people, he writes in *Toward A Psychology of Being*, ". . . have sufficiently gratified their basic needs for safety, belongingness, love, respect, and self-esteem so that they are motivated primarily by trends to self-actualization." (25:23)

In this statement Maslow seeks to capture and characterize our increasing "intimations of man's capacity for enlarging his growth and expression of personal resources . . ." (2:1) which have stemmed from the so-called "Third Force" school of psychophilosophical writers.*

---

*A few comments on developments in psychology help to clarify the meaning of "Third Force." Until the 1950's there were two basic and competitive theories of human development. On the one hand were the Freudians, and on the other the experimental-positivistic-behavioristic group. During the past two decades in particular a

Although one should read Maslow, and in so doing carefully thread his way through this provocative psychologist's viewpoints, it is possible to cite a few of his key excerpts. For example, Maslow characterizes self-actualization as:

> ... an episode, or a spurt in which the powers of the person come together in a particularly efficient and intensely enjoyable way, and in which he is more integrated and less split, more open for experience, more idiosyncratic, more perfectly expressive or spontaneous, or fully functioning, more creative, more humorous, more ego-transcending, more independent of his lower needs, etc. He becomes in these episodes more truly himself, more perfectly actuating his potentialities, closer to the core of his being (25:91).

Patently, a counselor of elementary school age children can profit from acquiring the sensitivity and the insights one must build in order to extract full meaning from the Maslow definition. Of equal interest is his inventory of nine assumptions with a bearing on psychological health or illness.

1) We have, each of us, an essentially biologically based inner nature, which is to some degree "natural," intrinsic, given, and, in a certain limited sense, unchangeable, or at least, unchanging.

2) Each person's inner nature is in part unique to him and in part species-wide.

3) It is possible to study this inner nature scientifically and to discover what it is like—(not invent—discover).

4) This inner nature, as much as we know of it so far, seems not to be intrinsically evil, but rather either neutral or positively "good." What we call evil behavior appears most often to be a secondary reaction to frustration of this intrinsic nature.

5) Since this inner nature is good or neutral rather than bad, it is best to bring it out and to encourage it rather than to suppress it. If it is permitted to guide our lives, we grow healthy, fruitful, and happy.

6) If this essential core of the person is denied or suppressed, he gets sick, sometimes in obvious ways, sometimes in subtle ways, sometimes immediately, sometimes later.

7) This inner nature is not strong and overpowering and unmistakable like the instinct of animals. It is weak and delicate and subtle and easily overcome by habit, cultural pressure, and wrong attitudes toward it.

third group has taken form. This includes such interesting quasi-bedfellows as Jungians, Neo-Freudians, Adlerians, Kurt Goldstein (representing organismic psychology), Carl Rogers, Snygg, Combs, Eric Fromm, and, of course, Maslow. The Lewinian and Gestaltist groups also belong in these Third Force ranks as do certain psychologists interested in personality: Gardner Murphy, J. L. Moreno, Gordon Allport, and Ronald Lippitt.

8) Even though weak, it rarely disappears in the normal person—perhaps not even in the sick person. Even though denied, it persists underground forever pressing for actualization.

9) Somehow, these conclusions must all be articulated with the necessity of discipline, deprivation, frustration, pain, and tragedy. To the extent that these experiences reveal and foster and fulfill our inner nature, to that extent they are desirable experiences (25:3-4).

Clinical observations of healthy people, as recorded by Maslow, provide an index to qualities counselors and teachers should seek to foster in their relationships with children and youth of all ages. These 13 qualities are especially important ones to seek with primary and middle school (age 2-3 to 12-14) children because of the extent to which behavior can be guided to good effect with younger clients.

Clinically Observed Characteristics of Psychologically Healthy Persons

1) Superior perception of reality
2) Increased acceptance of self, of others, and of nature
3) Increased spontaneity
4) Increase in problem-centering
5) Increased detachment and desire for privacy
6) Increased autonomy, and resistance to enculturation
7) Greater freshness of appreciation, and richness of emotional reaction
8) Higher frequency of peak experiences
9) Increased identification with the human species
10) Changed (the clinician would say, improved) interpersonal relations
11) More democratic character structure
12) Greatly increased creativeness
13) Certain changes in the value system (25:23-24)

The reader seeking more information on self-actualization will find Elizabeth M. Drews' statement (1966) an excellent one (11).

Understanding the Elementary School Child

The views of Erikson, Havighurst, and Maslow strongly suggest that the counselor who becomes an informed developmental specialist can bring real stature to his role at the elementary level. The task of "understanding" a child, however, is one of substantial dimensions. It encompasses a considerable knowledge of what the child brings to school—his psychological field—as well as a clear picture of his social and bio-being.

The well-informed counselor sees the child as a product of *interactive* genetic and environmental factors that are constantly contributing to the emerging pattern of personality that he has the power to achieve.

Considerable help is available in the literature to aid the counselor in his continuing study of girls and boys. Examples of writings of considerable, if not enduring, significance include such milestones as the work of Daniel Prescott and Louis Raths (27), and more contemporary hypotheses and research by writers such as Jerome Kagan, Howard A. Moss, Gerald Lesser, Susan B. Stodolsky, and M. P. Deutsch (22,33,10).

Prescott in the 1930's and 1940's called attention to the germinating idea that there are emotional or affective factors in childhood and that their influence on learning and behavior is an important one. Fritz Redl's statement, "What Should We Know About a Child?" also written during the 1940's remains a basic document which, despite its age, the counselor should study and understand (28).

Raths gave much prescient, pioneering thought to what has become preserved in the literature as his "Needs Theory." A 1966 publication provides a concise and representative statement of some of his views (27). When properly understood, Raths increases the insights needed by the counselor in his contacts with children and teachers.

Contemporary understanding of children has been deepened and widened by numerous studies undertaken during the 1960's. Some of these which promise to retain their influence are listed in the references at the end of the chapter. Specific examples of contributions—a very small sampling—are given below:

Kagan and Moss reported that the established behaviors of six- to ten-year-olds foreshadowed young adult behavior (22).

Deutsch, as well as R. A. Cloward and J. A. Jones (7), identified factors which debase or impair education in childhood due to problems related to social class and to poverty (10).

James S. Coleman's widely cited article on educational inequalities made the term "compensatory education" more widely known (8).

Susan B. Stodolsky and Gerald Lesser's (33) inquiries along with Arthur R. Jensen's controversial reports (21) created much discussion as to the influence of membership in subcultures and of genetics on learning ability.

Kinsey's previously unpublished findings regarding sexuality in childhood (reported by Paul Gebhard and James Elias) (12).

There seems little virtue in extending the list of current writings since it is in reading the original studies that the elementary counselor enhances his value to children. However, mention should be made of the counselor's role with respect to children having special needs and problems associated with mental retardation, physical handicaps, or emotional disturbances.

Perhaps a most important initial point to make is one that assumes the form of a caution. The counselor should make every effort to escape the *unwitting* charlatanism that can result when he *thinks* he has acquired the skills of psychotherapy or an understanding of the problems of the emotionally disturbed. Here a little knowledge can, indeed, be a dangerous thing! Special education, in its many forms, generally it not the counselor's preserve so much as it is an area for consultation with specialists and for referrals.

The Counselor as a Consultant

Fresh, more perceptive ideas of the nature of man as a learner have emerged rapidly in recent decades. These emergent concepts have a vital relationship to the counselor's responsibilities as a *consultant*. If, as Ira J. Gordon proposes, it is one of the teachers' major tasks "... to bring about readiness and enhance intelligence". (15:3), then the counselor's value presumably will increase in proportion to his conceptualization of the meaning of learning potential and how he can help the elementary teacher to maximize this potential for the individual child.

Gordon's classic "Newtonian" and "Einsteinian" Models of Man are of relevance at this point. The Newtonian model is based on the *closed* universe; while the Einsteinian man reflects transactional and *open* universe qualities. Gordon differentiates between the two as follows:

NEWTONIAN Model Man	EINSTEINIAN Model Man
A mechanistic, fixed, closed system, characterized by:	An open-energy, self-organizing system, characterized by:
1) fixed intelligence	1) modifiable intelligence
2) development as an orderly unfolding	2) development as modifiable in both rate and sequence
3) potential as fixed, although indeterminable	3) potential as creatable through transaction with environment
4) a telephone-switchboard brain	4) a computer brain
5) a steam-engine driven motor	5) a nuclear power-plant energy system
6) homeostatic regulator (drive-reduction)	6) inertial guidance and self-regulatory feedback-motivation system
7) inactive until engine is stoked	7) continuously active (15:2)

Implications for the elementary counselor's concept of how learning occurs are elaborated in this fashion by Gordon:

> A transactional model differs from an interactional one in that interaction implies the operation of two or more independent entities. A transactional view takes into consideration the idea that, at any given moment in time, when a child or person is engaged with another person or event, both exist only in terms of each other, and *behavior cannot be understood apart from the situation in which it occurs.* In a family, for example, the child shapes his parents as much as they shape him. In the classroom, a teacher's behavior is modified by his moment-to-moment dealings with his pupils just as much as their behavior is only understandable in relation to his (15:3). (Italics added.)

The Counselor's Need for Commitment

The counselor, if he is to be an insightful consultant, needs to develop a commitment to not only the values of an *open universe* philosophy but to the *transactional* interpretation of man, and the approach to learning experiences in what we have previously described as a transactional curriculum.

Consultant services have little meaning and can even be harmful unless the elementary guidance worker has the genuine ability to ". . . provide the teacher with some of the operational tools and underlying concepts that will help him in analyzing and diagnosing where children are with respect to their development and intelligence." (15:5) More specific applications of this interpretation of consultation functions are presented in the chapters which follow.

The Counselor as Catalyst

The third role of the elementary counselor—that of a catalyst—assumes that he will bring to his work: first, the skills of the change agent; second, some grasp of the meaning of environmental mediation; and third, the personal resources of skill in communication including a talent for generating the good human relations which lubricate communication.

Skills of the Change Agent

The term "change agent" came into use during the 1960's as a means of describing a new service-person in business, in education, and in other comparable fields in which the planning of change was recognized as a necessity—as an integral part of the social and economic life emerging in the

U.S. In Dennis Gabor's nicely tooled phrase, we needed to begin to "invent the future," and the change agent has become a key person in the process (14).

Edgar H. Schein has developed a generalized model of stages in change and in the work of the change agent which has a direct bearing on the work of the counselor (30). The model developed by Schein does not, in itself, suggest exact procedures for the elementary counselor engaged in the processes of educational change. However, Carl Rogers' widely cited "characteristics of a helping relationship," when they are considered in conjunction with the Schein model, lend a meaningful interpretation (29). That is, the *viewpoints,* expressed in question form by Rogers, give the needed value-orientation to the *mechanics* of change captured in the Schein model.

The Process of Influence and the Mechanisms Underlying Each Stage

Stage 1.   Unfreezing: creating motivation to change
            Mechanisms:
> a) Lack of confirmation or disconfirmation
> b) Induction of guilt-anxiety
> c) Creation of psychological safety by reduction of threat or removal of barriers

Stage 2.   Changing: developing new responses based on new information
            Mechanisms:
> a) Cognitive redefinition through
>   (1)   Identification: information from a single source
>   (2)   Scanning: information from multiple sources

Stage 3.   Refreezing: stabilizing and integrating the changes
            Mechanisms:
> a) Integrating new responses into personality
> b) Integrating new responses into significant ongoing relationships through reconfirmation (30:98)

Figure 13. Stages in Change

Rogers has listed some of the subtle procedures of developing a catalytic helping relationship in the ten queries which follow. The elementary counselor should be able to answer each question in the affirmative:

1) Can I *be* in some way which will be perceived by the other person as trustworthy, as dependable or consistent in some deep sense?
2) Can I be expressive enough as a person that what I am will be communicated unambiguously?

3) Can I let myself experience positive attitudes toward this other person—attitudes of warmth, caring, liking, interest, respect?

4) Can I be strong enough as a person to be separate from the other?

5) Am I secure enough within myself to permit him his separateness?

6) Can I let myself enter fully into the world of his feelings and personal meanings and see these as he does?

7) Can I receive him as he is? Can I communicate this attitude? Or can I only receive him conditionally, acceptant of some aspects of his feelings and silently or openly disapproving of other aspects?

8) Can I act with sufficient sensitivity in the relationship that my behavior will not be perceived as a threat?

9) Can I free him from the threat of external evaluation?

10) Can I meet this other individual as a person who is in process of becoming, or will I be bound by his past and by my past? (29:50-56)

It should be clear that the counselor's helping relationship is the kind which is created only by a person who is himself psychologically mature.

Environmental Mediation

A second important contribution which the elementary counselor can make as a catalyst is in the practice of "environmental mediation." First, however, an explanation of the concept is needed.

Fifty or more years ago, most educators felt it was the right and the responsibility of the teacher to give personal and, if need be, *forceful* direction to instruction. Most elementary school programs predominantly were committed to transmitting the cultural heritage and to developing skill in, say, spelling or mathematics. There was little hesitancy about "intervening" in the lives of children in the classroom. The learner either "shaped up" as he was directed or "dropped out" of grade seven or eight—not infrequently, in some urban and rural areas, until after a continued series of contacts with such forms of corporal punishment as was administered by means of birch rods, straps, or paddles. (The last named were, in an execrable pun, sometimes spoken of as the "boards of education.") Also, teachers thought nothing of intervening in a child's homelife by *telling* his parents how to handle his behavior, his homework, or his educational future (if any) beyond grade six or eight.

By the 1930's a growing number of teachers were becoming reluctant to follow rigid and prescribed educational doctrines which largely reflected the views and aspirations of a so-called middle-class America. Some schools tried to become more "child-centered" and more permissive. Behavior was "guided" rather than "directed"; corporal punishment was stopped; teacher-pupil planning, or a reasonable facsimile thereof, become popular; and in some few instances children actually were bored, misled, and miseducated by fuzzy-thinking teachers who felt it desirable to try to build programs on the educational quicksand of children's whims or curiosity rather than on a sturdier foundation of motivation and the purposeful self-direction which more able teachers had learned to distinguish.

While respect for the learner continued to increase during the 1940's and 1950's, it was accompanied by a return to the practice of showing greater respect for subject matter as well. The climate of the schools, in the 1960's, also began to be permeated by the idea of *intervention in* or *mediation of* the learning milieu.

Not only did more emphasis on the structure of knowledge appear; more educators began to hold the view that learning could only be advanced effectively if the school saw its responsibility to the learner as something extending beyond the confines of the school and into the wider psychological environment or "field" in which his total life was spent. By 1970, the term "intervention" and its more gentle-sounding sibling, "mediation," were frankly accepted by educators who would have been reluctant if not down-right uncomfortable in pronouncing them in 1960.

The current acceptance of intervention concepts has increased the importance of the elementary counselor in proportion to the increased scope of his role in environmental mediation. As schools endeavor to cooperate with other agencies in the improvement of the child's total milieu and psychological field, the counselor's responsibilities, the influence of his advice on decisions, and his material and human resources for counseling and interacting with children, parents, and school employees all seem certain to increase. An awareness of the implications of the child's membership in a given ethnocultural group and in a particular social class, for instance, becomes even more vital as counselors begin to be called on to offer professional advice as to what extent and as to what sort of intervention may be needed to keep a child from falling short of his potential.

Reference has been made in an earlier chapter to the theories of George L. Trager and Edward T. Hall who established three criteria by means of which cultural systems could be identified. They also identified ten basic human activities or "cultural universals" which Edward T. Hall has discussed and for which he has developed descriptive models (16:92). He refers to these cultural universals as the Primary Message Systems (PMS) of a given culture.

It is through a knowledge of such developments in anthropology and other disciplines bearing on guidance that the counselor will establish his authoritativeness in mediation strategies increasing his value as a catalyst to both teacher and child.

Ability in Human Relations and in Communication

Present efforts to prepare counselors at the graduate level already are sharply focused on human relations skills. In fact, many aspects of elementary guidance are no more than applications of the counselor's insights in this realm. Greater stress also is being placed on the ability to communicate in counselor education. This is due to growing recognition of the fact that the accurate transmission and interpretation of messages is one important way of diminishing certain types of human problems.

The ability of a counselor to serve as an effective catalyst can be badly eroded by faulty human relations, by inept encoding or phrasing of what he says or writes, or by incorrect decoding of what he *thinks* he hears teachers and children say. Not only should a counselor understand human relations and communication skills; he should discipline himself to practice them. Perhaps of all persons on a faculty, the elementary counselor can least afford the luxury of sharp replies or sarcasm which may give him a chance to blow off steam, but which also damages a teacher's or a child's self-concept.

Good intentions in both human relations and communications are not enough to insure the success of a counselor as a catalyst. As a rule, counselors become reasonably well informed in the art of good human interactions as a part of their preparation. A real effort at self-education is usually necessary, however, if he is to grasp the subtleties that link the various spoken and unspoken language forms to culture. Communication, as Harry Hoijer notes, involves understanding the complex whole of culture—knowledge, beliefs, art, morals, law, custom, and many comparable habits and capacities that are an integral part of his membership in the human race (20:455).

Summary

The elementary counselor's need to have a guiding philosophy and his alternative choices among various philosophies are presented at some length in Chapter 7 in order to emphasize that there are basic intellectualized reasons for his role—touchstones to guide his interaction with children. It is strongly urged that the elementary guidance program be based on an "open" rather than on a "closed" philosophical viewpoint. Several philosophies with possible relevance for guidance are examined. These encompass phenomenology, progressivism, existentialism, determinism, and essentialism.

On this foundation, the various roles of the counselor are constructed and examined. Material is presented under three headings: 1) his understandings about human development, 2) his abilities as a consultant, and 3) his skill as a catalyst or change agent. Again it is emphasized that the counselor's contributions are at their best when based on broad knowledge of the myriad factors which bear on the environment of child, teacher, parent, and school.

References

1. Astor, Martin H. "Counselors Seek to Understand Themselves," *Personnel and Guidance Journal* 43 (June, 1965): 1029-1033.
2. Banmen, John. *Maslow's Self-Actualization Theory and Its Implication for Counselors*. Winnipeg, Canada: Department of Education, 1965.
3. Beck, Carlton E. *Philosophical Foundations of Guidance*. Englewood Cliffs, N.J.: Prentice-Hall, Inc., © 1963. By permission.
4. Blocher, Donald H. *Developmental Counseling*. New York: The Ronald Press, 1966.
5. Brameld, Theodore. *Education as Power*. New York: Holt, Rinehart and Winston, Inc., 1966.
6. ———. *Patterns of Educational Philosophy*. New York: World Book Co., 1950.
7. Cloward, R. R. and J. A. Jones. "Social Class: Educational Attitudes and Participation." Edited by A. H. Passow. *Education in Depressed Areas*. New York: Teachers College Press, 1963.
8. Coleman, James S., et al. *Equality of Educational Opportunity*. Washington, D.C.: U.S. Office of Education, 1966.
9. Combs, Arthur W. and Donald Snygg. *Individual Behavior*. New York: Harper and Row, Publishers, 1959.
10. Deutsch, M. P. "The Role of Social Class in Language Development and Cognition." *American Journal of Orthopsychiatry* 35 (1965): 78-88.
11. Drews, Elizabeth M. "Self-Actualization: A New Focus for Education." *Learning and Mental Health in the School*. Washington, D.C.: The ASCD, 1966.
12. Elias, James and Paul Gebhard. "Sexuality and Sexual Learning in Childhood," *Phi Delta Kappan* 50 (March, 1969): 401-405.
13. Erikson, Erik H. *Childhood and Society*. 2nd edition. New York: W. W. Norton and Co., 1963.
14. Gabor, Dennis. *Inventing the Future*. New York: Alfred P. Knopf, Inc., 1964.
15. Gordon, Ira J. *Studying the Child in School*. New York: John Wiley and Sons, Inc., 1966.
16. Hall, Edward T. *The Silent Language*. New York: Fawcett World Library: Premier Books, 1969.
17. Havighurst, Robert J. *Developmental Tasks and Education*. New York: Longmans, Green, and Co., 1950. Used by permission of David McKay Company, Inc.
18. *Helping Teachers Understand Children*. Washington, D.C.: American Council on Education, 1945.

19. Hobbs, Nicholas. "Science and Ethical Behavior." *The American Psychologist* 14 (May, 1969):217-225.
20. Hoijer, Harry. "Linguistic and Cultural Change." Edited by Dell Hymes. *Language in Society and Culture.* New York: Harper and Row, Publishers, 1964.
21. Jensen, Arthur R. "How Much Can We Boost IQ and Scholastic Achievement?" *Harvard Educational Review* 39 (Winter, 1969):1-123.
22. Kagan, Jerome and Howard A. Moss. *Birth to Maturity.* New York: John Wiley and Sons, Inc., 1962.
23. Kaufman, Walter. *Existentialism from Dostoevsky to Sartre.* New York: World Publishing Co. (Meridian Books), 1968.
24. Maslow, Abraham H. *Motivation and Personality.* New York: Harper and Bros, 1954.
25. From *Toward a Psychology of Being* by Abraham H. Maslow, Copyright ©1962, by Litton Educational Publishing, Inc., by permission of Van Nostrand Reinhold Company.
26. Meeks, Anna R. *Guidance in Elementary Education.* New York: The Ronald Press, 1968.
27. Raths, Louis E., Merrill Harmin, and Sidney B. Simon. *Values and Teaching.* Columbus, Ohio: Charles E. Merrill Books, 1966.
28. Redl, Fritz. "What Should We Know About a Child?" Chicago: Commission on Teacher Education, American Council on Education; 1940. (Mimeographed)
29. Rogers, Carl R. *On Becoming a Person.* Boston: Houghton Mifflin Co., 1961.
30. Schein, Edgar H., in Bennis, Schien, Steete, and Berlew (eds.). *Interpersonal Dynamics.* Homewood, Ill.: The Dorsey Press, 1964.
31. Shoben, Edward J. "The Counselor's Theory as Personal Trait." *Personnel and Guidance Journal* 40 (March, 1962):617-621.
32. Skinner, B. F. *Science and Human Behavior.* New York: The Macmillan Co., 1953.
33. Stodolsky, Susan B. and Gerald Lesser. "Learning Patterns in the Disadvantaged," *Harvard Education Review* 37 (Fall, 1967): 546-593.
34. Strickland, Ben. "Kierkegaard and Counseling for Individuality," *Personnel and Guidance Journal* 40 (January, 1966): 470-474.
35. Van Kaam, Adrian. "Counseling from the Viewpoint of Existential Psychology." *Harvard Educational Review* 32 (Fall, 1962): 403-415.
36. Wrenn, Gilbert, "Philosophical and Psychological Bases of Personnel Services in Education." *Personnel Services in Education.* LVIII *Yearbook,* Part II. National Society for the Study of Education. Chicago: University of Chicago Press, 1959.

8

Counseling in
the Elementary School

The school long has been accepted by many adult Americans as the most effective tool that has been fashioned by the culture for shaping the behaving or the "character" of children and youth. Developments of the past twenty years, and particularly those changes of the past decade, suggest that the United States may have been too sanguine, too confident, and too optimistic about the extent of the presumably desirable kindergarten to college level programs as they existed at the outset of the 1970's.

By 1970 there were many omens that suggested the need for continued educational reform, for large increases in educational expenditures, and for a more meaningful impact of public education on the culture. Some of these omens included:

> The worsening of a "value crisis" based on a lack of consensus as to what adults wanted their children and youth to become in an era when biochemistry, mass media, and similar resources were beginning to generate almost unlimited means of mediating personality.

> A school climate of unrest, dissatisfaction, frequent alienation, and pupil failure which has bred the dropout problem and, among older students, the campus confrontation (37).

> The point that non-school forces and factors had begun to contribute as much or more than school programs to the child's emerging self (7).

Little convincing evidence that educational programs had begun to understand the role of mass media and instructional systems as a force permeating young learners with a large but unorganized infusion of the culture—an infusion that ranged from excellence to alarming intellectual pollution (23).

Negligible evidence that young or old U.S. citizens had learned how to deal with the potential confrontation, between the economically favored "haves" and a world full of "have nots". (9)

The fact that academic success *per se* and the increasing national level of education apparently has little correlation with the characteristics of mature behavior.

It is omens such as the six above that throw into bold relief the increasing importance of counseling as a valuable, frequently neglected developmental resource for making schooling more rewarding, more relevant, and more of an intellectual challenge to learners of widely varied ability.

The Importance of Elementary Counseling in a New Culture

Much of U.S. education was created to serve a different culture than the one that now exists in our country today. Many educational practices also tend to be based on a body of learning theory that is out of date. Finally, the purposes of education and the backgrounds of the students have changed greatly since education assumed its present form. Guidance, therefore, at the elementary level, if wisely used, can do a great deal to *promote* change rather than to *avoid* it in a period during which change is a necessity. A substantial portion of the contribution of elementary guidance seems likely to be made in the context of the counseling act.

The Nature of Counseling in Elementary Schools

At all educational levels, counseling is an important dimension of the total school program. This generalization is as true when applied to eight- or ten-year-olds as it is with 14-, 16-, or 20-year-olds. It is one of the major activities through which the elementary school counselor makes his unique contribution to the total educational program (22). Here, as much or more than in any other aspects of his role, the counselor requires special competencies including insights into the child and the curriculum as well as guidance expertise.

Perspectives and Viewpoints for the Counselor

Elementary school counseling is a process by means of which the counselor helps children—both individually and in large and small groups—to gain useful self-understanding and a greater depth of vision into group relationships. Each boy and girl is helped to discover how to participate in personal and group decision-making and to sense the individual adjustments they imply.

Essentially, good child counseling is based on and reflects a warm, understanding interpersonal relationship. In Carl R. Rogers' phrase, it is a *helping* relationship. "The optimal helping relationship is the kind of relationship created by a person who is psychologically mature." Rogers continues, ". . . the degree to which I can create relationships which facilitate the growth of [a child] is a measure of the growth I have achieved in myself." (30:15)

A detailed statement of a helping relationship is found in Rogers' book, *On Becoming a Person*, which he published in 1961 (32). One of his early, classical interpretations first appeared in 1942 when Rogers wrote of counseling as "a definitely structured, permissive relationship which allows [a child] to gain an understanding of himself to the degree which enables him to take positive steps in the light of his new orientation."

As elementary counseling moves further ahead in the 1970's, it is also becoming clear that the "helping relationship" developed with younger children is one in which it is vital for the counselor "to encourage an openminded approach in himself and in the [child] . . . ." (18:18f)

Some Specific Tasks
in Elementary School Counseling

Turning from the broad, warm relationships described above to more specific viewpoints, what are some of the actual tasks of the elementary counselor that have a bearing on his work with girls and boys?*

A comprehensive or inclusive roster of the many possible counseling opportunities in elementary education and the tasks to which they point is literally impossible to compile. The individuality among children, already described and emphasized in earlier chapters, is based on varied environments,

*For an interesting, informative article see, Patricia McClure and Keith D. Barnes, "Elementary Guidance—A Critical Look from the Field," *Elementary School Guidance and Counseling* 4:2 (December, 1969) 104-111.

diverse experiential input, rapidly changing times, culture-group membership influences, physical and psychological differences, intrafamily relationships, and many comparable influences. As a result, each counseling experience is uniquely personal—in contacts with a single child as well as with many different children.

Nonetheless, many rather specific tasks and activities for the able counselor can be identified or associated with those aspects of his role which are germane to counseling (8,10,11,14,15,24,28).

Counseling, to be effective with any age group, must be based on *developmental insights and the approaches to which they point*. Since the nature of developmental strategies has been presented and interpreted elsewhere, particularly in Chapter 7, we can turn directly to some of the work in which they involve the counselor. His counseling tasks are:

1) to develop close mutual respect which supports interactive relationships with teachers. Lacking either rapport or a knowledge of counselor strategy, the teacher may undo the counselor's efforts.

2) to participate methodically in those aspects of teacher inservice education which help to develop deeper understanding of childhood. This includes the added counselor task of constantly being aware of developing his own self-concept and that of teachers as they relate to the guidance of human development.

3) to recognize—since all counseling is basically individual even when done in a group situation—that any approach to counseling must respect both individuality and pattern itself in diverse ways because each child is unique.

4) to insure that counseling of boys and girls avoids becoming remedial in nature: that it is inclusive rather than "problem child" centered. The counselor's time must be budgeted accordingly.

5) to exercise care to see that counseling is a systematic process rather than a haphazard series of responses to "crisis" situations identified by teachers, administrators, and parents.

6) to emphasize that the counseling process is concerned with an "open universe" approach to the mediation of children's experiences and consequent behavioral change, rather than testing or assessment.

7) to follow the practice of quick consultation and prompt referral whenever there is reason to believe that one has identified a genuinely disturbed child (as distinct from a merely *disturbing* child). The temptation to engage in psychotherapy without extensive preparation is one that must be resisted with vigor.

8) to create a "consultant and friend" image which will be inviting to teachers and children both within and without the structure of a systematic program of counseling.

9) to make certain that the child is seen as an organic unity functioning in a "field" and involved in a chain series of transactions.

10) to be aware and to work with others in the school constantly to improve the individual child's emerging self-concepts.

11) to remain mindful of the significance of membership in a culture group, and to be aware of the apparent influence of ethnicity on the ways in which one learns and performs most ably.

12) to keep in mind that children are socially and emotionally linked to a family or nonfamily situation and that counseling is diminished greatly in effectiveness when the out-of-school *Lebensart* or life-mode is unheeded.

13) to be motivated by understanding the importance of love in the child's life and his need for the acceptance which it brings as he becomes respected for what he *is* rather than for what he *does*.*

The résumé of the counselor's tasks underscores the point that he needs to be governed by the examined philosophy, the touchstone, proposed in the previous chapter.

At present the 13 points above have "surface meaning" rather than "deeper meaning" in the parlance of linguists such as Noam Chomsky (6). Let us now deepen their meaning by proposing certain values which have some promise as guidelines in counseling young children.

Goal Identification in Elementary School Counseling

Even the more optimistic citizen was willing to concede by the 1970's that rapid social changes and the proliferation of problems in the U.S.—

*Unlike English, Greek has two words for love, *agapé* and *eros*. *Agapé* is the kind of love, platonic and Biblical, that is our referrent here.

ranging from pollution to pornography, and from racism to riots—were signs of appreciable moral and ethical confusion. Alarmists, in the face of rapid change, even recalled Alfred North Whitehead's gloomy thought, "The major advances in civilization are processes which all but wreck the societies in which they occur." Under such circumstances, goal identification by the elementary counselor becomes of almost supreme importance as a day-to-day guide. It is with a sense of urgency that certain guiding values for elementary school counseling during a troubled era are proposed for careful consideration. The reader will note that these statements once again are extensions of an "open universe" philosophy described in Chapter 7.

Some Goals That Promise to Be Useful in the Process of Counseling

While many contemporary writers deplore the breakdown of certain long-accepted modes of conduct and mores that have a respected history, it seems reasonable to assert that there remain with us both long-established and more recently emergent objectives that can continue to give meaning to education in the remaining years of the 20th century. The concepts below are presented in the belief that they are reliable—in the sense that the multiplication table is reliable—rather than bases for ideological conflict such as the prospect of genetic manipulation of higher life forms (12,43).

Cognitive Goals. Most schools, perhaps all schools, recognize that certain intellectual academic outcomes, such as developing the ability of children to think, must be sought. While this value goal is widely acclaimed, there is much less agreement as to what it means. The process of counseling should be based on the concept that "thinking" is involvement in answer finding. The counselor does not admonish, direct, or advise in a fashion that creates greater dependence on an adult figure. Rather, through sensitive, appropriate transactions he helps children discover or create individual and group solutions to problems suitable to their level.

Approaches to cognitive goals, as is true of all of the counseling objectives introduced below, are likely to be of limited value or ineffectual without a close, cooperative, continuing interchange between counselor and teachers. The deeper meanings of thinking, for example, must be the object of a shared counselor-teacher understanding. Many school workers continue to confuse *answers* with *education* or to assume that test scores, *per se*, are sufficient evidence of progress toward the ability to "think." Counseling, particularly as it brings counselor and teacher into a series of cooperative relationships, should reflect the premise that intelligence and the ability to do clear, creative thinking is nurtured by changes in the quality of the input provided in the learning environment rather than by directions or admonitions.

Psychoemotional Health Goals. Children have shown remarkable resilience in the face of many forces in the culture that can threaten their psychological and their emotional health. Membership in given social classes (17), in certain culture groups,* and in certain language communities are circumstances representative of those which can pose serious threats to the young learner's affective domain (2,16). The counselor, in both individual and group situations, not only should seek to improve children's general psychological and emotional health, he should recognize the sources of mental health problems and the fact that his approaches to their improvement should vary with the child's ethnicity, with his social class membership, sex, age, and so forth.

Physical Health Goals. Good physical health possibly is the least controversial of any counseling objectives cited here. Even so, it is not without its complexities as an element in the counseling relationship. A basic value decision for the counselor to make for himself in the child's physical domain is that of the *extent* of society's responsibility for child health. How broad should the counselor's role be construed to be in dealing with disabilities; what is his obligation once a child's physical problems have been referred to a nurse, physician, or other health agent? Considering the alternative, it seems reasonable to say that every reasonable health need of a child should be met by society to assure his place as a contributer rather than a burden to himself and to society.

Egalitarian Goals. What is "equal" opportunity? When is a child "deprived," and when is he "culturally different"? When is supportive or compensatory education a defensible prerequisite to a child's successful participation in society in both the present and future? If premises in the previous chapters are viable ones, then equality of opportunity means that counseling processes will be infinitely varied. Instead of treating children "fairly" by treating them the *same*, counseling will endeavor to insure that creative educational opportunities are devised by treating each learner *differently*.

Utilitarian Goals. Children's experiences should be useful. "Utility" in the counseling process pertains to the significance of the relationship established and the worth of the outcomes to which it leads. A "warm, helping relationship" is not sought merely for its own sake, but for the desirable changes it makes in the private self or inner world of the child—the self-concepts which are *his* interpretations of the experiential input by which he is programmed and through which he attains his psychological selfhood at a given moment in his personalized continuum of progress.

*Culture group membership has been identified by many anthropological and psycholinguistic specialists as an important mediating factor in the intellectual and psychoemotional development of young learners.

The utilitarian goal of counseling presumably helps a child to become more useful to himself and more contributive to his culture. If it is to have optimum value in what Carl Rogers called "an understanding of himself . . . which enables him to take positive steps in the light of his new orientation," then the utilitarian goal also includes whatever guidance and support is necessary so that the learner acquires useful skills and knowledge (30). Lacking basic substantive input, no child can take the "positive steps" to which Rogers referred.

The Goal of Broader Literacy. In addition to assisting the child's progress toward utilitarian goals, counselors should encourage teachers to help the child attain a broader kind of literacy than mere acquaintance with information. This is the economic and social literacy which enables the learner to understand how the general welfare is served by the arts of mediation and conciliation, by the mutual respect necessary to social consensus, and by an understanding of social and economic forces that affect his life. The goal of "broader literacy" can be made more clear by means of a description of practices in a middle school (in this instance enrolling 11- to 14-year-olds) which through teacher-counselor cooperation ". . . found over 20 ways in which . . . children could be helped to learn many of the social and economic facts of life."

> The school store is organized as a cooperative in keeping with Rochdale principles; a student loan office permits 11- and 12-year-olds to borrow 50 cents on personal signatures (and up to $3 with a teacher as co-signer); children who do the dishes are unionized and have a bargaining contract with the "management"; insurance is issued to protect the individual from losses due to dish breakage in the cafeteria (11 cents for three years); and many more miniature replicas of adult organizations are in operation. A nursery that grows plants from seedlings, apiaries from which honey is harvested, a research company making products useful in school, a projectionists' group operating school film equipment, a livestock corporation, and a printing company are among other enterprises combining useful work and service (38:41).

Such an approach to literacy cannot be made without departing somewhat from counseling and conventional teaching procedure roles. Such departures also create a "new educational literacy" for teacher and counselor!

The Goal of Decision-making Skill. The national problems, including educational unrest and protests, which carried over from the 1960's to the 1970's, have made us aware of communication problems among individuals and groups. It also has become apparent that despite their long tradition of democracy, U.S. citizens had great difficulty in exercising decision-making skills. Under such circumstances, counselors should accept some measure of responsibility for helping children, at a very early age, to begin to learn what is involved in thinking and in reaching reasoned decisions with others. The ability to reach cooperative decisions is an acquired skill. It involves ability in human relations, skill in receptive and expressive communication, an understanding of forces at work in a culture, and many similar elements which children can first begin to sense and then more fully to understand as the mature counselors and teachers methodically exemplify and interpret the skill of reaching a community of opinion in a supportive school environment.

The goals toward which the counselors' and teachers' efforts are aimed all share one quality. *They seek a variety of ways to serve the general welfare.* This is accomplished when human dignity is enhanced in each young child, as he begins to understand that all human beings are valuable, and as his self-concept begins to mature to a point at which he sees how each *mature* person's inner being develops a "reach" which helps him to respect and to support the self-concept of others.

The wisely guided boy and girl are individuals 1) who are learning to think, 2) who are beginning to understand that thinking is a deliberate, reasoned, value-oriented process, and 3) who are beginning to recognize that they are "creating themselves" *now*, and are, thus, earning the privileges, responsibilities, and satisfactions of the mature human.

The Protection of Childhood. Much that occurs in a child's life conspires against the goals presented above. As counselors work to help boys and girls attain useful goals it is necessary to protect them from manifestations of faulty adult judgment.

Some homes are troubled by internal value conflicts which imprint upon the child's mind a picture of confusion as to how he should govern his behavior. H. A. Overstreet has made a particularly apt statement regarding the confusion that can occur as a result of a confusing atmosphere in the home:

> With the natural hazards of life vastly multiplied by the confusion of his culture, he [the child] faces an abnormal temptation to remain dependent and irresponsible. It is never easy, even at best, for the individual to build sound knowledge linkages with his world; but it becomes infinitely difficult for him to do so in a cultural atmosphere where education is both exalted and despised; where the same two parents send him to school, want him to bring home grades they can view with pride, talk about the impracticality of what is learned in school, admire people less for what they know than for what they own, and make it clear that teachers are nobodies compared with businessmen and movie stars (26:140-141).

Overstreet's illustration refers only to education. Religion, race, politics, and many other environmental influences will continue to complicate home life in the 1970's.

Premature exposure to adult problems is another out-of-school difficulty that may occur in the home setting. In Norman Cameron's words:

> Parents frequently make the mistake of trying to foster social maturity in their child by parading adult problems, adult uncertainties, and adult disillusionments continually before him—doubts concerning food and shelter, financial worries, adult social strivings, and parental discords that divide his loyalties and threaten the fundamental security of his home (4:268).

Even quite young children today may find themselves placed under considerable pressure for premature social or academic achievement because of parents or teachers who are ambitious—too ambitious, that is—to have them succeed. Under such circumstances the counselor needs to move firmly, and at the same time with tact and with understanding, to prevent serious personality damage. The prevention of undesirable guilt feelings which often result when children are expected to conform to adult moral or conduct standards when they are too young to understand such standards is another occasional development for an elementary counselor to face with both teachers and parents.

One last illustration of circumstances requiring psychological protection of children is, somewhat paradoxically, that of guarding a child from overprotection. The overprotective adult unwittingly may foster feelings of timidity and insecurity in the young by stressing dark prospects as to what might happen to him on the streets, near bodies of water, and so on. Controlled, safe experiences need to be devised for such children so that vague, groundless terrors can be overcome and dispelled.

Goals and Roles for the Counselor

The broad matrix in which counseling goals are discussed here is analogous to what Danskin, Kennedy, and Friesen have called "the ecology of the student."* They note how important it is for counselors to understand and to be a part of the milieu of each child in school and to develop an understanding of certain influences that permit the counselor to vitalize "and, if possible, to engineer" the climate for learning (7).

*Also cf. Ronald C. Winkler and others. "The Effects of Selected Counseling and Remedial Techniques of Underachieving Elementary School Students." *Journal of Counseling Psychology* 12 (Winter, 1965): 384-387 (49).

The three writers conclude that a counselor who commits himself to the broad, ecological approach will find it necessary to redefine his activities. Such a guidance person is likely to:

1) Need [to free himself] from thinking about his work in terms of the five or six traditional guidance functions. He is going to have to bargain, we think, for an open system in which he often travels in uncharted directions.

2) Vastly decrease the amount of time spent in person-to-person counseling interviews.

3) Decrease considerably the investment in traditional . . . testing. (But become a more creative user of test data.)

4) Spend much less time in planning future . . . programs for [children] while spending much more time in exploring and probing current educational experiences of students. Planning for the future will flow from being alive to the present experiences.

5) Invest a much larger part of his total resources in observation of and systematic research into the learning climate of the school. For this he will need time to reflect, discuss, and write, *without* the pressure of having to do the highly visible guidance functions.

6) Greatly enlarge the scope of his contacts with teachers and administrators. He would become the important "human development" consultant in issues concerning curriculums, activities, policies, etc. (7).*

The six points are an excellent statement of certain ways in which one may expect to find changes in traditional counseling concepts develop as the role of the elementary counselor becomes more stabilized in the near future.

Some Specific Approaches to the Counseling of Younger Clients

The Counselor's Choices Among Approaches to His Work

In the previous chapter it was established that a good guidance program is derived from a sound, examined philosophical foundation. Such a program reflects the values and beliefs of individuals who are responsible for guidance program goals and the attainment of their objectives.

Theoretical models of counseling can be evolved from one's philosophy which, in turn, influences the practices adopted in the counseling act itself. In this process, research also should play an important role in bridging the gap

---

*Cf. also William L. Cash and Paul F. Munger. "Counselors and Their Preparation." *Review of Educational Research* 33 (April, 1966): 256-263, for a review of the research for the three-year period, April, 1963 to April, 1966 (5).

between theory and practice by verifying or "proving" theoretical premises. This progress from values to practice can be charted as indicated below:

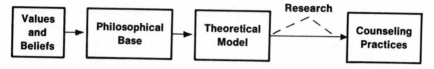

Figure 14. Bridging the Gap from Theory to Practice

A simplified model such as this one helps to provide the counselor with his own unique counseling model as he brings his personal meanings (values and beliefs) to bear on the creation of a strongly based theoretical model to support practice.

Several popular models of counseling theory are discussed below.

Psychoanalytic. A psychoanalytic approach to counseling assumes the separation of the mind into three major systems, the *id*, the *ego*, and the *superego*. The *id* represents hereditary factors. It functions in the "inner world" of one's personality and is largely unconscious. The *id* seeks gratification and avoidance of pain and is conceived of as potentially non-logical and amoral. The *ego* is seen as partly functioning in the conscious and partly in the unconscious. In maturity, it becomes the rational element of the personality. The *superego* is the "conscience of the mind." It is a repository for the individual's grasp of the moralities and the taboos of society. In this triangle, the *superego*, since it also resides largely in the subconscious, is more aware of the *id's* impulses and seeks to direct the *ego* to control the *id*. Conflict, tension, and anxiety are thus viewed as inevitable in man, and his behavior is seen as directed toward tension reduction.

In this context, the reduction of tension becomes a major goal of psychoanalytic counseling. In this process, the counselor assumes: 1) that the causes of the counselee's tensions must be identified, and 2) that these causes may exist in either or both the conscious and the unconscious (3,13).

It should be pointed out that the psychoanalytic approach requires qualifications beyond those of most elementary school counselors and may be generally more relevant in long-term therapy treating personality disorders. The application of psychoanalytic techniques to counseling practice is particularly limited in the elementary school setting. Paul R. King suggests that:

> One may consider the application of psychoanalytic theory from two points of view. The first view would be that of therapeutic intervention, or the modification of the life adjustment of the individual by psychotherapy . . . .
>
> If one considers psychoanalytic theory from a second point of view, that of providing a frame of reference for evaluating the behavior and personality structure of clients, then, even in educational settings, psychoanalytic theory can be useful (42:109).

Client-Centered. The client-centered counseling model, especially as it has been described and interpreted by Carl Rogers, remains an extremely popular one. This model represents basically a phenomenological point of view. This approach suggests that a counselee's behavior can be understood only as the counselor begins successfully to perceive a client's viewpoint. This model is "optimistic" or "positive" in its orientation towards man. Man is viewed as good and effective; as possessing capacities for self-understanding, insight, problem solving, change and growth; and as engaging in purposeful and goal directed behaviors which are based on how things seem to the client at a particular time (31,34).

The counselor's role is viewed as that of a "facilitator" and "reflector." He facilitates a counselee's self-understanding and clarifies and reflects back to the child his own expressed feelings and attitudes. Information giving for problem solving in a client-centered context are not usually considered as counselor responsibilities. The client-centered counselor would not seek to "direct" the mediation of the child's "inner world" but rather would seek to provide a climate in which the counselee could bring about change in himself.

Teacher-Learner Model. The teacher-learner counseling model, in effect, places the counselor in the role of the teacher helping the counselee to learn more about himself and his environment. In this context, while he in no way usurps the teacher's role, the counselor deals with both the emotions and cognitive processes in a highly personalized way. The counselor actually backstops, reinforces, and supports the teacher as they join forces to help the counselee function more effectively in problem solving and living as a productive being in his school and out-of-school environment. To increase his effectiveness as a temporary or surrogate teacher the counselor may use diagnostic data and instruments such as psychological tests; he may give the counselee useful information and also point out possible courses of action and the probable consequences of each (47,48).

This model assumes that learning is nurtured and flourishes best when there is sensitive insightful teaching. That is, the effective teacher-learner setting and warm relationship enhances this phase of individual development. It also presupposes a child's development in self-understanding, self-control, and progress towards the achievement of his potential.

Behavioral. Behavioral counseling models have been derived by theorists and practitioners in counseling and guidance from experimental research in learning theory, most directly from Pavlov's 19th century discoveries in classical conditioning and B. F. Skinner's contemporary work with operant conditioning (40). The behaviorist views behavior as a set of learned responses to events, experiences, or stimuli in the individual's life history. And he feels that behavior can be modified by providing appropriate learning conditions and experiences. The experimental origins of the behaviorist's approach explain his indifference to concepts which can not be empirically observed or measured. Thus, rather than concern himself with the emotional dynamics of behavior characteristic of the insight approaches of either Freudians or Rogerians, the behaviorist focuses on specific behavioral goals emphasizing precise and repeatable methods (1,21).

For the behaviorist, counseling involves the systematic use of a variety of procedures that are used specifically to change behavior in terms of mutually established goals between a client and a counselor (19,45). The procedures employed encompass a wide variety of techniques drawn from knowledge of learning processes. John D. Krumboltz places these procedures into four categories. They are:

1) *Operant Learning*—this approach is based on the usefulness of reinforcers and the timing of their presentation in producing change. Reinforcers may be concrete rewards or expressed as approval or attention.

2) *Imitative Learning*—this approach facilitates acquisition of new responses by exposure to models performing the desired behaviors.

3) *Cognitive Learning*—this technique fosters learning of appropriate responses by simply instructing the client how he may better adapt.

4) *Emotional Learning*—involves substitution of acceptable emotional responses for unpleasant emotional reactions using techniques derived from classical conditioning (20:13-20).*

So much for some of the theoretical bases for possible approaches to elementary counseling that carried over into the 1970's. Attention now turns from theory to practice.

Individual and Group
Counseling in Elementary Schools

The pay-off for the counselor's long preparation and careful, rational examination of values and procedures occurs when he begins his actual contacts and interactions with boys and girls. Many times at this juncture, he will be reminded of the importance of carefully developed contacts with classroom teachers. Without a good foundation of interpersonal rapport with

---

*The book presents very readable discussions of behaviorism by Krumboltz, Bijou, Shoben, McDaniel, and Wrenn.

teachers, both individual and group counseling are likely to lose much, if not most, of their effectiveness.

Eighteen Questions
Regarding Individual and Group Counseling

Since they are intimately related—indeed, almost two phases of a single process in elementary schools—individual and group counseling are best considered together. As one contemplates individual and group counseling processes, a number of professional questions arise:

1) When should individual or group counseling begin?
2) Does age have a bearing on group size and on individual counseling?
3) Is the counselor (age, sex, race, personality, etc.) a factor?
4) How do counseling objectives influence people?
5) Does the nature of the problems involved influence counseling procedures?
6) How long should a child be in an individual counseling session?
7) Does sex or the boy-girl ratio have a bearing on the composition of a counselee group?
8) What bearing, if any, do such factors as a child's psychological makeup and his cultural membership have on counseling procedures?
9) How should transfers among small groups, individual counseling experiences, and large group counseling be handled?
10) What is a "small" group?
11) How big can a "large" group be?
12) When is it best to arrange a counseling session with an individual child?
13) When is it desirable to work with a group of children?
14) What criteria serve to determine whether small group, large group, or individual counseling is best for a given boy or girl?
15) Is there an optimum length of time for large or small group sessions to run?
16) Is there a "mix" that is best in small or large groups?
17) What is the role of the teacher in determining how decisions regarding various counseling practices are to be made?
18) How shall the elementary counselor develop parental understanding, support, input, and feedback?

Each of these eighteen queries will be considered briefly in turn.

When should individual or group counseling begin? There may be dramatic differences in the development of children, therefore, age *per se* is not a criterion for beginning counseling. Some six-year-olds may be as intellectually or physically mature as seven-year-olds. Again children with a chronological age of eight may sometimes have the physical and psychological characteristics of the so-called average seven-year-old or be as immature as some six-year-olds. Professional study and judgment rather than dogmatic policies must determine when either individual or group work is introduced. In general, however, it is possible that some children can begin to develop rewarding relationships with counselors as early as age four.

Does age have a bearing on group size and on individual counseling? Indeed, it does. As a rule, the younger the counselees the smaller a group should be, although it does not follow that the very young (4- to 5-year-old) child should be counseled only individually. Children learn social behavior through interaction—through transactions, involving peer groups and children of varied age levels—as well as through counselor contacts.

Is the counselor's age, sex, race, or personality a factor in group and individual contacts? The image a counselor projects from within is of great importance. In this sense, personality rather than either age or sex is of paramount importance. Yet there is no precisely "right" personality for the elementary counselor. It is the *relationship* between the *counselor* and a *given individual child* that is important—and some boys and girls "match" one counselor or teacher better than they do another as research reported by Herbert A. Thelen suggests (44: 191-194).

How do counseling objectives influence priorities and procedures? Comments on objectives made earlier in Chapter 8 were intended to anticipate and point out that a counselor's success in goal identification has a great deal to do with both his immediate and long-range success. With few exceptions, preliminary inquiry about a given child (based upon teacher conferences, school records, parent conferences, personal interviews, and observation techniques) should clarify priorities with regard to procedures based on an emergent, uniquely personal goals for each young counselee. Decisions regarding group and/or individualized approaches often are determined early in this inquiry process.

How does the nature of a child's problems influence counseling procedures? As the previous paragraph proposes, counseling processes are based on *information* which accumulates until it becomes an organized body of *knowledge* out of which *wisdom* is extracted. During the progression from information to knowledge, one "sorts out" problems among young clients and the sorting profoundly influences who is counseled, under what circumstances, and in what ways. None of these decisions can be prescribed ahead of time, but accumulating wisdom quietly and quickly shapes practices.

How long should a child be in an individual counseling session? A child's motivation, his maturity, the purpose of a given counseling session, the child's age, the status of his needs, and the nature and number of previous meetings with the counselor are among the elements to be considered when deciding how long an individual counseling session shall run. A physiologist was once asked, "How long should the average ten-year-old's legs be?" The scientist replied, "Long enough to reach the ground." In determining the duration of a counseling session, one can only base his decision on the length of time required to satisfy the purpose for which the meeting was arranged.

Does sex or the boy-girl ratio have a bearing on the composition of a counselee group? Once again, a firm policy cannot be recommended. Especially in early childhood (age five or below), sex-group membership seems to make relatively little difference. With young children—those between six and eight—there is greater awareness of the sex role in which a given subculture casts the male and female. This must be kept in mind by the counselor. Conferences with middle school children are distinctly influenced by what Lionel Tiger, the Canadian anthropologist, calls the "male bond," a tendency on the part of *Homo sapiens* to form male groups that methodically exclude females (46). Young adolescents often are extremely aware of sex differences in certain kinds of counseling situations. But, again, no precise prescription can be written for the course of action to be followed since subculture group membership, topics for discussion, and similar circumstances and conditions need to be assessed in the context of each group session.

What bearing, if any, do such factors as a child's psychological makeup and his culture group membership have on counseling procedures? Here a definite response can be made. Every possible consideration should be given to the psychological, private "inner world" of the child. Faulty judgment by the counselor can lead to harmful outcomes from the sensitive counseling relationships if he is misinformed, uninformed, or errs in his premises. Culture group membership is of equal importance. As repeatedly emphasized in earlier chapters, a child literally sees and hears differently from other children who do not share the experiences which have imprinted him with the invisible, "psychological tattoo" of his socioethnic group.

How should transfers among small groups, individual counseling experiences, and large group counseling be handled? Who goes into which type of group, and when? Here the importance of the counselor's grasp of his objectives and the clarity of his insights are of prime consideration. The individual child's group memberships invariably reflect counselor-teacher judgments of a professional nature. These are "on-site" decisions and cannot be described in a textbook except in the form of the general suggestions presented in previous sections of Chapter 8.

What is a "small" group? and *How big can a "large" group be?* One can be more specific about the size of "small" and "large" groups than about the membership in these human clusters. In general, small groups range from three to five children. Large groups may include an entire class—as many as 12 or 15 to 20 or 25. Although very large groups (25 or more) are rare, there are occasions when a large cluster of boys and girls have a shared interest or problem and can profit from this type of group experience. Also, the distinction is often made that *group counseling* can take place only in small groups and that *group guidance* is the province of large groups.

When is it best to arrange counseling sessions with an individual child? and *When does it become desirable to work with a group of children?* The timing of individual counseling usually should be based on a cooperative decision reached by the counselor and one or more teachers who are well acquainted with the young prospective client. Among factors to be considered in the process of arriving at such a decision are: 1) the child's age, 2) his inner psychological climate, 3) available personal background data, 4) urgency—the extent to which an opportunity is available or a particular problem is threatening the child, 5) previous high priority commitments made by the counselor, 6) home milieu conditions, and 7) the child's history, including past counseling records, if any. Other variables (ethnicity, previous experience in school, etc.) can easily be listed depending upon the child under discussion.

Group work, like individual counseling, is also influenced by the total field or configuration in which it transpires. Particular considerations include such questions and items as: 1) the extent to which a topic or problem has relevance for a group, 2) previous group experiences, 3) whether group interaction might prove harmful to one or more individuals within it, 4) the emotional tone of the topic(s) or problem(s) that might emerge, and 5) whether or not something can be done about any conclusions or decisions that might be reached. A number of similar or comparable points will occur to the reader.

What criteria serve to determine whether small group, large group, or individual counseling is best for a given boy or girl? Points previously made above suggest the flexibility of any criteria that might be evolved to determine the "best" combination of personalities in the human environment involved in counseling. In fact, one might use the term "process criteria" to describe the situation. Counselors and teachers in the *process* of deciding on desirable procedures need constantly to refer to criteria emerging from their judgmental discussions. A child's age, available data, his emotional climate, personality traits, and many similar elements such as are listed above have relevance.

Is there an optimum length of time for large or small group sessions to run? Any specific answer to this query would violate the "open universe" approach. What is "optimal" is determined by professional judgment, not by dogma or by directives. The same answer applies to the query, *Is there a "mix" that is best in large or small groups?* When one recognizes the transactional nature of learning, he also recognizes that the right "mix" of personalities is determined in light of the unique combination of past events, present realities, and future possibilities which surround the child's guided progress toward mature interactions with his world.

What is the role of the teacher in determining how decisions regarding various counseling practices are to be made? A competent teacher's insights are indispensable to the elementary counselor, and in most ways the background of one complements the knowledge of the other. Furthermore, the counselor very much needs the follow-up help, the observations, and the follow-through of classroom teachers if he is to reach his goals.

The belligerent, insecure, uninformed, negative, or disinterested teacher can seriously impair the work of even the most skilled and dedicated counselor. Such a teacher, for example, has much more hourly contact with children and often has the opportunity for numerous formal and informal parent contacts. As a result, a supportive teacher can be an invaluable colleague on the one hand or an almost insurmountable roadblock if he is persuaded that the counseling program is unsound or "too much bother," or if he is threatened by the counselor.

The policy here seems clear. The counselor must make sure that the teacher is "in" on decision-making. Only when common understanding is built through shared decisions will the teacher 1) feel that the counseling program is *ours* rather than *his* (the counselor's), 2) have a clear understanding of *why* certain procedures are desirable, and 3) be likely to be supportive because he has become identified with the child's and the counselor's goals.

Guiding Behavior Through Individual Counseling

The questions pertaining to factors and decisions which have been reviewed above begin to coalesce into a meaningful configuration as one turns to the actual challenge of modifying children's behavior in desirable ways. Here, as Ronald A. Peterson has suggested, one must work to improve the child's self-concept (his interpretations of *who* and *what* he is, and his *place* in his milieu), his ability to adapt to the demands of life and his perception of his environment (29).

Mediation Strategies in Elementary Counseling

The counselor is making real headway when he can begin to document the success of his work through identifiable changes in behavior. Bearing in mind the four counseling models mentioned above, what are some possible counseling-mediation strategies?

Strategy and Tactics

The term *strategy* refers to long-term plans leading to goals of human development which the counselors and teachers seek. *Tactics* are the steps taken to carry out strategies. In changing children's behavior through counseling, at least four strategies can be identified. There are also a number of tactics which can be utilized with the strategies.

Behavior-Change Strategies

The four basic approaches to changing behavior are equally important and useful. The "best" approach depends upon the situation in which the tactics promise to serve the counselor's strategy. The basic strategies include:

1) *Consequence analysis* leading to personality change and done *by* or *through* children . . .
2) *Milieu mediation* or environment redesign which is done *around* children . . .
3) *Perception change* or sensitivity redesign which is done *with* children . . . and
4) *Pygmalion procedures* or direction action techniques which involve doing desirable things *to* children (35).

The array of tactics or techniques that can be mustered to make the four behavioral change strategies "pay off" are virtually infinite since they are limited only by the composite imagination of the counselor and his colleagues on the school staff. A representative sampling of tactics that can be employed is useful, however, as a means of clarifying the meaning of each of the four behavioral change strategies.

Consequence analysis involves particularly interesting tactics because it is approached *by* and *through* children. Among useful behavioral change techniques are those developed with children *so that they see cause-effect relationships and evaluate the undesirable and desirable consequences that come from these relationships.* Here a variety of sources of pleasure and satisfaction can be tapped, depending on the age and the psychological inner being or private world of the learner. Among such reinforcements are recognition, special attention, visible or status responsibilities in the school, "totems" such as a badge with the title of "School Host" and a periodic stint as a greeter of visitors, and even such familiar sources of satisfaction as a cookie or candy treat. Punishment (such as deprivation, or termination of privileges) also can be used for consequence analysis. In effect it is the reverse of positive reinforcement but generally less desirable, and under many circumstances can be totally undesirable.

Consequence analysis also includes working with children to build their insights with respect to desirable and undesirable input or stimulation from persons and things, and withdrawal tactics or stimuli reduction for the tense child.

Milieu mediation comes to a focus on activities that can be done in the personal or group "space bubble" surrounding the child or a cluster of children in a school group. The techniques used by the counselor in relation to this behavior change strategy are generally obvious ones such as physical placement, academic placement, introduction of improved sources of stimulation (or removal of overpowering stimuli), changes in pressure for performance, and varied uses of the school's resource centers.

Imaginative and creative mediation of the school milieu should, in time, eliminate discrete programs in "special" education and in "remedial" groups. The environmental mediation or intervention originally designed prior to 1970 for the physically or psychologically handicapped, or for the culturally diverse, will increasingly become part of the counselor's environmental intervention resources for *all* children.

Perception change techniques are appreciably more subtle than environmental manipulations because they are done *with* rather than *around* girls and boys. Basically, perception change is based upon the delicate counselor skills which infuse the task of redesigning the child's sensitivity. This is done through the deepening of his group-interaction insights. "Group-interaction insights" refer to a child's understandings of his personal-social status in a group. Such understandings enable him to increase his acceptance by others without loss of personal integrity. Both individual and group counseling are permeated by the quality of the transactions that the counselor seeks to encourage.

In addition to individual counseling, other long-established approaches to perception change are play therapy, role-playing, socio- and psychodrama, bibliotherapy, and experience in group processes (33,39).*

Pygmalion procedures. In ancient Greek mythology, Pygmalion was King of Cyprus and also a skilled sculptor who created Galatea—a statue so lovely that Aphrodite brought her to life. "Pygmalion procedures" carry the connotation of creating desirable changes through what the counselor and teacher *can do to children.*

The phrase " . . . do *to* children . . ." has, of course, a special connotation. For far too long a time, unfortunate things have been inflicted on boys and girls. The reference here pertains to what can be done *to* the child to change and improve his adaptation to the social and academic tasks which life in the

---

*The counselor must exercise great caution and meticulous judgment to protect children from premature exposure to ineptly planned group therapy experiences. Such groups can become outlets for structured aggression among children who are too young to cope with "encounter groups."

school demands. Among relevant tactics are 1) physical remediation if needed (e.g., eyeglasses, prosthetic devices, dental care), 2) psychological rehabilitation as needed in serious cases of disturbance or maladjustment, 3) academic analyses and making changes in the child's experiential input, and 4) social adjustment analyses followed by deliberate manipulative techniques to increase social acceptance.

Thus far we have discussed the changing of child behavior only in the context of the limited environment of the school. This limited focus is in no way intended to either minimize the importance of the out-of-school life of the child or to imply that most serious problems can be handled in the classroom. Indeed, the "life-support system" of the school is a limited one—but it *is* an area in which counselors have some measure of environmental control. Hence, it is an important realm in which to improve one's efficiency even as we speculate about ways in which counseling can improve the larger, nonschool world of childhood.

Summary

Chapter 8 deals with the breadth and with the subtlety of counseling in elementary education. After examining the increasing importance of counseling in a rapidly changing culture, the tasks of the counselor are inventoried in order to illustrate their wide extent.

Attention is given to the varied goals of elementary school counseling. These goals are identified with cognition, psychoemotional health, physical well-being, egalitarian and utilitarian goals, literacy in a socioeconomic sense, and with the skills of democratic decision-making.

Various approaches to elementary school counseling are discussed, and four models are included: psychoanalytic, client-centered, a teacher-learner model, and a behavioral model. This is followed by an examination of eighteen questions pertaining to practices in elementary school counseling. Typical questions are: "How long should a child participate in an individual counseling session?" and "Is there an optimum time for large or small group counseling sessions?"

In the last section of Chapter 8, four behavior change strategies useful in elementary education are discussed. These include: 1) consequence analysis, 2) milieu modification, 3) guiding children's perception change, and 4) "Pygmalion procedures" or direct action techniques for bringing about behavioral changes.

References

1. Allport, Gordon. "Psychological Models for Guidance." *Harvard Educational Review* 32 (Fall, 1962): 373-381.

2. Bernstein, Basil. "Language and Social Class: Research Note." *British Journal of Sociology* 11 (1960): 271-276.

3. Bordin, A. S. *Psychological Counseling.* New York: Appleton-Century-Crofts, 1955.

4. Cameron, Norman. *The Psychology of Behavior Disorders.* Boston: Houghton Mifflin Co., 1948.

5. Cash, William L. and Paul F. Munger. "Counselors and Their Preparation." *Review of Educational Research* 33 (April, 1966): 256-263.

6. Chomsky, Noam. "The Current Scene in Linguistics: Present Directions." *College English* 27 (May, 1966): 587-595.

7. Danskin, David G., Carroll E. Kennedy, Jr., and Walter S. Friesen. "Guidance: The Ecology of Students." *Personnel and Guidance Journal* 44 (October, 1965): 130-135.

8. Dinkmeyer, Donald (ed.,). *Guidance and Counseling in the Elementary School.* New York: Holt, Rinehart and Winston, Inc., 1968.

9. Drucker, Peter. "A Warning to the Rich White World." *Harper's Magazine* 237 (December, 1968): 67-75.

10. Faust, Verne. *The Counselor-Consultant in the Elementary School.* Boston: Houghton Mifflin Co., 1968.

11. _____. *History of Elementary School Counseling: Overview and Critique.* Boston: Houghton Mifflin Co., 1968.

12. Fleming, Donald. "On Living in a Biological Revolution." *The Atlantic* 223 (February, 1969): 64-70.

13. Hall, C. S. and Gardner Lindzey. *Theories of Personality.* New York: John Wiley and Sons, Inc., 1957.

14. Hansen, James C. and Richard R. Stevic. *Elementary School Guidance.* London: The Macmillan Co., 1969.

15. Hill, George E. and Eleanore B. Luckey. *Guidance for Children in Elementary Schools.* New York: Appleton-Century-Crofts, 1969.

16. Irwin, O. C. "Infant Speech: The Effects of Family Occupational Status and of Age on Sound Types." *Journal of Speech and Hearing Disorders* 13 (September, 1948): 224-226.

17. Kagan, Jerome. "The Many Faces of Response." *Psychology Today* 1 (January, 1968): 22-27, 60-65.

18. Kemp, C. G. "Open and Closed Systems in Relation to Anxiety and Childhood Experience." *The Open and Closed Mind.* Edited by Milton Rokeach. New York: Basic Books, Inc., 1960.

19. Krumboltz, John D. and Carl E. Thorensen. *Behavioral Counseling: Cases and Techniques,* New York: Holt, Rinehart and Winston, Inc., 1969.

20. _____ (ed.). *Revolution in Counseling: Implications of Behavioral Science.* Boston: Houghton Mifflin Co., 1966.

21. London, Perry. *The Modes and Models of Psychotherapy.* New York: Holt, Rinehart and Winston, Inc., 1964.

22. Mayer, G. R. and Paul F. Munger. "A Plea for Letting the Elementary School Counselor Counsel." *Counselor Education and Supervision* 6 (Summer, 1967): 341-346.

23. McLuhan, Marshall. *Understanding Media: The Extensions of Man*. New York: McGraw-Hill Book Co., 1964.

24. Meeks, Anna R. *Guidance in Elementary Education*. New York: The Ronald Press, 1968.

25. Miller, Theodore (ed.). *Theories of Psychopathology*. Philadelphia: W. B. Saunders Co., 1967.

26. Overstreet, H. A. *The Mature Mind*. New York: Copyright 1949, © 1959 by W. W. Norton and Co., Inc.

27. Patterson, C. H. (ed.). *Theories of Counseling and Therapy*. New York: Harper and Row, Publishers, 1966.

28. Peters, Herman, Bruce Shertzer, and W. Van Hoose. *Guidance in Elementary Schools*. Chicago: Rand McNally, 1965.

29. Peterson, Ronald A. "Rehabilitation of the Culturally Different: A Model of the Individual in Cultural Change." *Personnel and Guidance Journal* 47 (June, 1967): 1001-1007.

30. Rogers, Carl R. "The Characteristics of a Helping Relationship." *Personnel and Guidance Journal* 37 (September, 1958): 6-16.

31. ____. "The Interpersonal Relationship: The Core of Guidance." *Harvard Education Review* 32 (Fall, 1962): 416-429.

32. ____. *On Becoming a Person*. Boston: Houghton Mifflin Co., 1961.

33. ____. "The Process of the Basic Encounter Group." La Jolla, Calif.: Western Behavioral Sciences Institute, n.d.

34. ____. "Toward a Science of the Person." T. W. Wann (ed). *Behaviorism and Phenomenology*. Chicago: University of Chicago Press, 1964.

35. Rosenthal, Robert and L. Jacobson. *Pygmalion in the Classroom*. New York: Holt, Rinehart and Winston, Inc., 1968.

36. Sahakian, Williams S. (ed.). *Psychology of Personality: Readings in Theory*. Chicago: Rand McNally, 1965.

37. Schwab, Joseph T. *College Curriculum and Student Protest*. Chicago: University of Chicago Press, 1969.

38. Shane, Harold G. and E. T. McSwain. *Evaluation and the Elementary Curriculum*. New York: Holt, Rinehart and Winston, Inc., 1958.

39. Shostrom, Everett L. "Group Therapy: Let the Buyer Beware." *Psychology Today* 2 (May, 1969): 36-40.

40. Skinner, B. F. "Behaviorism at Fifty." T. W. Wann (ed.). *Behaviorism and Phenomenology*. Chicago: University of Chicago Press, 1964.

41. Southwell, Eugene A. and Michael Merbaum (eds.). *Personality: Readings in Theory and Research*. Belmont, Calif:: Brooks/Cole Publishing Co., 1964.

42. Stefflre, Buford. *Theories of Counseling*. New York: McGraw-Hill Book Co., 1965.

43. Taylor, G. R. *The Biological Time Bomb*. New York: World Publishing Co., 1968.

44. Thelen, Herbert. *Classroom Grouping for Teachability*. New York: John Wiley and Sons, Inc., 1967.

45. Thorensen, Carl E. "The Counselor as an Applied Behavioral Scientist." *Personnel and Guidance Journal* 47 (May, 1969): 841-847.
46. Tiger, Lionel. *Men in Groups*. New York: Random House, Inc., 1969.
47. Williamson, E. G. "Counseling as Preparation for Self-Directed Change." *College Record* 63 (April, 1964): 613-622.
48. _____. "Counselor as Technique." *Personnel and Guidance Journal* 41 (October, 1962): 108-111.
49. Winkler, Ronald C. et al. "The Effects of Selected Counseling and Remedial Techniques of Underachieving Elementary School Students." *Journal of Counseling Psychology* 12 (Winter, 1965): 384-387.

9

Resources for Studying and Guiding Human Development: Guidance Testing

Today the study of individual human development and the appraisal of the quality of learning that results from children's school experiences is an important part of the evaluation of the elementary school program.* As an integral part of his job the counselor needs to understand, use, and evaluate guidance tools and techniques to help children better understand themselves and develop the self-concepts they require in order to function effectively both now and in the future.

Evaluating human development and the effectiveness of the school program is best done in close cooperation with teachers, administrators, parents, and children. This broad involvement is necessary since the purpose of such study is to obtain, process, and interpret information about the child in the context of his total personal and educational experience. Wise use of data obtained through the study of children is necessary for better comprehension of the learner and the learning process. It is essential to the construction of children's personalized programs or "individual curriculum" and is basic to the school's total educational effort.

---

*The *Yearbook* of the National Society for the Study of Education preserves an interesting record of concern for evaluation. Between 1918 and 1969, seven of the *Yearbooks* dealt directly with measurement and evaluation beginning with *The Measurement of Educational Products* (1918) and continuing through *Educational Evaluation: New Roles, New Means* (1969) edited by Ralph Tyler. The 1969 edition describes in detail the developments in evaluation during the past thirty years.

Purposes and
Principles Involved in Evaluation

Evaluation is a broad term which refers to the accumulation of comprehensive information concerning a child's problems, abilities, and status. It is concerned with both formal and informal procedures that help ascertain 1) where the child stands with respect to academic progress in his growth continuum; 2) whether he is moving toward social-psychological, intellectual, and physical maturity in a satisfactory manner; and 3) whether the school is providing for his aptitudes and interests.

Continuity in Evaluation

Evaluation is not a periodic activity in the elementary school program. It has an ongoing quality which both extends the rim of our vision and produces continuity. Continuity may be described as the continuous outcome of a succession of learning experiences sponsored by the school and designed to improve:

1) *Self-awareness*: the child's sense of WHO he is and his place in the world (self-identity).

2) *Social interaction* skills: the attainments that enable a boy or girl to sense WHERE he is in his quest for internal integrity (self-orientation).

3) *Self-confidence*: those feelings that give the young learner a sense of direction—the sense of WHERE he is going (self-direction).

Evaluation through elementary school guidance also helps a child to answer three queries: Am I secure? Am I accepted? Can I cope?

Patently, the study of human development for guidance purposes in the 1970's is broader than the testing programs of a decade or two ago. The new program is like an automobile headlight beam illuminating the road to future possibilities for each individual child; it is not merely a rear-vision mirror revealing the old road that had been previously traveled. Let us now examine more closely some of the developments that have taken place in educational evaluation during the past years and assess their significance for guidance practices in the 1970's.

Foundations for Child Study Through Evaluation

Earlier sections of this book described many of the research studies and practices which lend strength to the structure of elementary school guidance.

However, it should also be helpful for the reader to have a succinct summary of principles which underlie the professional study of a child as he moves from the pre-primary through the secondary school years.

A number of suitable statements of principles appeared during the 1960's. Among those that have influenced the six given below are statements from the National Education Association (5), the American Personnel and Guidance Association (6), and the American Psychological Association (7). The principles presented here were chosen because they lend wholesome direction to the processes of developmental study:

Principle I: *Individual differences must be recognized.* The passing years have unequivocally demonstrated the uniqueness of the individual human being. These differences are to be found both within and between children. That is, a child "differs from himself" from day to day, just as he varies from all other beings. One of the goals of continuing evaluation is to identify, to prize, and to build on the fact of human differences.

Principle II: *Many dimensions of human development are appraised.* For years we have perfervidly acknowledged that "the whole child" had to be considered, not just his academic performance, social skills, physical abilities, or other single components of his matrix. So, too, in elementary school guidance, evaluation must focus on the total complex of available data rather than on discrete parts. For instance, achievement or aptitude tests, sociograms or attitude scales can only be interpreted in the context of all our accumulating knowledge of a girl or boy.

Principle III: *An understanding of the changing individual is indispensable.* An ancient Greek writer noted that one cannot step into the same river twice. It is equally true that one never sees exactly the same child twice! While certain physical characteristics may be more or less permanent from birth or from early childhood, and certain "characteristic" reactions are influenced early in life, human development is in an emergent state of flux throughout one's life. Obviously, then, evaluation must be an ongoing process if the school is to have an accurate, on-the-spot or "polaroid" picture of the child at a given moment. Keep in mind that his past achievement, attitudes, interests, and so forth are constantly undergoing change.

Principle IV: *One must recognize the limits of analyses.* Not only are there limitations inherent in all instruments used for the assessment of developmental changes, but the counselor and teachers have personal-professional limitations as well. In practice, this means that the ethical professional working in education is careful to use and to interpret only those scales, tests, and other devices or procedures which he has been specifically prepared to use.

Group encounter techniques, for instance, can be dangerous to some participants at any age level and can be devastating to young children, unless a
highly prepared, mature therapist is orchestrating the experience.

Principle V: *The concept of confidentiality must be honored.* The integrity of the elementary guidance program depends on the degree of protection
provided for the children who are the subjects of continuing developmental
study. What is learned about a child or his milieu is privileged information, not
the subject of coffee-break gossip. At the same time the counselor needs to
recognize that he has certain professional, legal, and moral obligations which
may mandate that pertinent data be shared with other professional workers or
authorities. There is no real substitute for *un*common good sense in these
circumstances.

Principle VI: *Emphasis must be placed on a positive approach.* When
making a developmental assessment of a child, the counselor should emphasize the strengths which manifest themselves. We often tend to stress what is
wrong or negative, thus doing damage to the child's self-concept. Damaging
concepts can be minimized or eliminated if the positive, too, is accentuated.

Records and Record Keeping

Records in themselves do not guarantee the success with which developmental analyses are made, but it is nonetheless impossible for a good guidance
program to exist without carefully preserved child study data.

School Records and Record Keeping

An old joke, cobwebbed with the passing years but still relevant, asks the
question, "How can the counselor ascertain when a youth is ready to be
graduated?" The predictable answer: "When his stack of cumulative records
is as tall as he is." To an increasing number of administrators and counselors,
the aged punch line really isn't funny anymore—if it ever was. They are harassed by paper work, often lack seasoned secretarial assistance, and are confronted by a growing variety of forms and reports as increasing federal funds
and more generous state support bring with them a variety of funded educational opportunities too good to pass by despite applications to be made in
quintuplicate.

The problem of record-keeping spills over on the teacher, too. In the past
decade, who has not heard his classroom colleagues wailing (with considerable
reason) about the way in which their noninstructional duties and tasks have
increased. Reports of all kinds—attendance forms, test scores, health data,

anecdotal records, and "critical incidents"—merely skim the formidable and frequently overlapping rosters of written forms to be maintained. Also, as the types and sources of data proliferate, errors, illegibilities, omissions, and misplaced dossiers seem to be on the increase. Frequently even experienced teachers and counselors are not always aware of the scope of pupil analysis records on file someplace in the school.

Despite the work that accompanies the compilation and maintenance of the records necessary for studying human development, their importance justifies whatever effort is needed. Records are indispensable if the counselor and teacher are to respect the six principles presented immediately above and also to develop the individualized structure or continuum toward which philosophy and psychology inevitably seem to direct the elementary school. Let us first examine the child's cumulative record, the most basic of guidance tools.

The Child's Cumulative Record

The cumulative record is, essentially, an accumulation of many records. It is a master record which continuously grows by accretion from many and varied sources and serves as a repository for information which is essential to guidance. It is the basic reference when decisions are to be made regarding child study and the guidance practices to which it points.

The cumulative record at the elementary level is designed to collect certain detailed information over the educational span which begins in early childhood and eventually merges with secondary school data. While the general types of information included may vary to some extent, Robert L. Gibson and Robert E. Higgins concluded, after inspecting actual practices, that cumulative records are likely to preserve information about:*

1) Personal characteristics
2) Out of school milieu
3) School background, including anecdotal data
4) Academic records
5) Attendance records
6) Health and physical development information
7) Guidance test findings
8) Expressions of educational and vocational interests and plans
9) Significant out-of-school experiences
10) School activities
11) Social status and sociometric data
12) Special comments, interpretations, "critical incidents," summarizations, and follow-up statements (8).

*From *Techniques of Guidance* by Robert L. Gibson and Robert E. Higgins. © 1966, Science Research Associates, Inc. Reprinted by permission of the publisher.

Cumulative records are likely to take a number of different forms ranging from plain filing folders with various inserts to single record cards. Examples of representative cumulative records of this type, used in most public schools, can readily be found in the literature available. There also is a trend toward automated record keeping which may replace many of the old handwritten inserts and the tedium of updating materials each year. Some of the merits of automated data processing that are described below seem to presage many changes in recording behavioral and academic data.

Automated Data Processing

Any discussion of records and record keeping for the 1970's must call attention to the powerful impact which automation has had not only on record keeping but on all forms of data processing and their virtually unlimited potential for the future. The arrival of UNIVAC and the numerous, more sophisticated models which followed has presented us with "computer talk" and new languages such as FORTRAN and ALGOL.

Other more permanent and far-reaching effects are also becoming evident. Although education has been sometimes slow to respond to change, it seems likely that the "automation revolution" will bring many rapid changes. For example, the automated data processing (ADP) potential for pupil accounting, analysis, and program planning is something that all educators, including counselors, are examining seriously. Potential values in these new electronic developments include these identified by Alvin Grossman and Robert Howe:

1) *Speed*: For example, it is possible to alphabetize 1,000 names in eight minutes; to list 1,000 names in six or seven minutes on conventional punched-card equipment, and in two minutes on new electronic equipment; to convert and make statistical summaries of eight test scores for 2,500 students in two hours.

2) *Accuracy*: Most electronic data processing systems include self-checking devices; but even when they do not, increased accessibility of data makes verification easier and more positive. Given correct instructions, not only will the machine make fewer errors than even the most conscientious clerk, but machine errors will be more easily detectable.

3) *Reproduction*: A test score, once it is punched on a card or recorded on magnetic tape, may be converted to a normative score and then used in a statistical summary, listed, posted on records, reproduced at other points, and collated with supplementary data—all from a single source.

4) *Accessibility, internal and external*: Data stored in machine data processing systems, unambiguously coded, may be located

rapidly and easily by those who need them. In addition, such data are readily available for conferences, historical review, or transmittal.

5) *Collating:* Pupil test data, school marks, teacher ratings, and many other types of data can be rapidly assembled in convenient form from a variety of sources for any special purpose; mechanical reference to norm tables reduces errors in test-score conversion and makes possible the multiple use of tables. Class registration lists may be collated with test scores and other data to provide teachers with information relevant to their students.

6) *Compactness:* Data may be stored, transmitted, and referenced in a highly condensed form; reels of magnetic tape or magnetized discs can be used to store information that would otherwise require many cubic feet of storage space. Identification codes can be used to effect additional compression.

7) *Automatic processes:* Although it takes time to develop programs and other automated processes for handling data, once the process has been designed, it is repeatedly reusable and can be shared by other school districts. Programs for processing student data can be used in hundreds of school systems on repeated occasions without additional developmental cost. Automation not only makes it easier in the performance of traditional tasks, but also makes feasible a number of tasks formerly considered impossible, or perhaps not even conceived.

8) *Dividends:* Under this general heading must be included all the readily obtainable by-products of data processing systems. The processing of semester grades is more efficient in a mechanized system than it is in a manual system; in addition, it makes possible more effective summaries of marks by course, grade, department, teacher, or school and permits facile pursuit of research studies. Similarly, the availability of the punched-cards that are needed to describe the course registration makes possible additional uses of the same cards for grading, attendance, mailing lists, special groupings, selection and placement systems, the maintenance of essential student records, and the analysis of curriculum needs (9).

It seems likely that the advantages cited are important ones for the elementary school counselor. For example, automatic control systems can improve program management, increase effectiveness, and make possible more rapid and effective research. The rapid assembly, synthesis, and processing of data germane to individual children should encourage and stimulate much needed progress in child study by guidance personnel who have been limited by mechanical (as distinct from electronic) data-interpretation resources.

Possible Futures for the
Computer in Elementary Education

Although their applications in elementary school counseling were by no means clear by 1970, several writers had begun to discuss possible computerized approaches and even to experiment with a computer-based automated counseling simulation system (1,13). Within the next several years it seems probable that computer-based counseling systems will be in use in some secondary schools. If so, attempts at extending them to the middle or intermediate school years, and later to the primary years, are likely to be made.

At present, a three-level system for classifying or describing computer assisted systems has been proposed (14). At the *first* level computers serve as data processing tools for the counselor. They perform conventional information processing (such as test scoring chores) but presumably do so more reliably and faster than human hands. At the *second* level, systems begin to substitute themselves for parts of the counselor's tasks. For instance, they can provide a substitute for or a supplement to the counselor's memories.

At the *third* level, it is possible that the computer may, in the intermediate future, begin to serve as a substitute counselor. A "catharsis system" or talk-it-out session, and a "leading question" session (which is taped) between computer and counselee are technically possible at this level. So is a "behavioral reinforcement" system (14:33-34).

Until much more investigation has taken place, however, it seems wise to avoid either great enthusiasm or extreme pessimism in regard to computer assisted guidance activities involving children. While machines already have infinite patience and great discretion (they never gossip about their counselees), they are limited by their programming and—at least for now—cannot bring to the counseling relationship either the warmth of a pat on the back or a genuine interest in their clients. Almost incredible innovations of the last 20 years make it unwise to underestimate what the computer one day may do, however.

Record Utilization

Neither the form of the record nor the method used in processing its information is an end in itself. The collection of volumes of information about boys and girls in the elementary schools and their subsequent organization into the most effective retrieval system possible will not guarantee the enhancement of counselors' and teachers' understanding of children. It is predominantly through the utilization of collected and organized pupil information that guidance insights are facilitated. In this regard, the elementary counselor needs to become aware of those school situations in which the faculty and administrative staff can effectively change their behavior in the light of such information and its accurate interpretation.

Guidance Testing

Of the various tools of individual, behavioral, and developmental appraisal, few, if any, are more popular in actual usage and more likely to be more misused or abused than those of testing for guidance purposes. Alas, we continue to hear a few teachers and counselors make such statements as "With an I.Q. like that he's sure to be a dropout." Or "Howard's aptitude test shows he should be an engineer." Or "How could he score only 102 on his I.Q. test when he's doing so well in math class?"

While abuses and over-emphases are sometimes the concomitants of standardized psychological testing, it is foolish to suggest abandonment of such helpful instruments for individual analysis. It is, however, the counselor's responsibility to have a thorough knowledge of the test he uses and the ability to interpret the test results. In addition, he should be able to communicate these understandings to those who can cope with and utilize test results with prudence and a feeling of security, with teachers, parents, and children—to the degree appropriate and in a language they can understand—all within a matrix of the six professional analytical principles.

Uses and Misuses of Tests

Any discussion of tests and test results is complicated by the fact that "uses" and "misuses" often are difficult to separate. In practice, the "proper" use of a testing instrument depends on the competency and the understanding of the user. An *able* counselor may use, let us say, the results of an academic aptitude test for placing a particular boy in a group and do so very effectively. An *inept* counselor may look at the same test results but make a faulty interpretation and poor decision. Both men have the same kind of data, but one *uses* it while the other *abuses* it. Recognizing this limitation then, let us examine some of the more common potential uses of test results.

1) *Test results may measure factual input.* Standardized tests can give an indication of the information a child has accumulated at the time of testing in relation to the items covered by a particular test. A measure of input may be obtained with a minimum of teacher effort, and the results usually are not subject to teacher bias.

2) *Test results may indicate ability.* Some tests may provide an indication (not an absolute measure) of the extent to which a child may have a particular ability or general capacity. Such findings can be of value in selecting classroom strategies for guidance decisions and in planning a child's individual curriculum.

3) *Test results may measure the rate and extent of academic progress.* Standardized tests may provide a reasonable indication of a particular child's academic progress *in a subject matter area* over a period of time. Such indications can provide useful clues as to the probable rate of achievement of the individual, as well as the level of achievement he has reached at the time of testing. Again, these results can be of value in curriculum development, in designing classroom instruction, and for guidance of the individual pupil.

4) *Test results may provide opportunities for comparison.* Standardized guidance testing can provide for a variety of comparisons. Care must be exercised to make sure that these do not become invidious, however. For example, it is possible to compare a child's rate of progress during two different periods of time. If done ethically—with due regard for the six principles on pages 231 to 232—children may be compared with one another. Objective information will also enable classroom teachers to make group comparisons. Finally, the actual levels of child achievement may be compared with anticipated levels of achievement as determined from prognostic tests.

5) *Test results may indicate personal characteristics.* The testing of group personality, or social characteristics, and of interests is in the process of development, hence such instruments are to be used cautiously. The experienced counselor and teacher can obtain valuable clues to pupil's interests, attitudes, social understandings, and comparable characteristics from these tests. Results from such tests also provide clues for counseling, for improved teacher-child relationships, and for increasing parental understanding of the elementary school child.

6) *Test results can complement other sources of data.* An important value of many types of guidance or psychological testing lies in their contribution to greater understanding of the individual pupil. The interpretation and interrelating of test results—their use in association with other pupil data—is a practice which increases the validity of the interpretation of the tests themselves.

Teachers and counselors alike need to be sensitized to the limitations of testing instruments that are now in common use. The following are some of the more common limitations or misuses which are found in testing programs:

1) *Test results may be overemphasized.* Frequently a single test score may become the major determinant in arriving at a decision which governs the placement of a child in a group, or to the decisions regarding his "success" or "failure." Such practices assume that test results are infallible and that other pupil information is of little value. Illustrative of this point would be a situation where students, regardless of their achievement on teacher-made tests and other assignments throughout the school year, do not move ahead with their group or repeat a grade because they scored below an arbitrary point on a standardized subject matter achievement test administered at the end of the academic year.

2) *Test results may lead to pupil "labeling."* Test results can be damaging to pupils if they lead to categorizing or to labeling pupils as "slow," "maladjusted," or "underachievers." In such instances boys and girls frequently find it difficult to escape these labels once they have been bestowed. An example of the most pernicious manifestations of this practice is found in the attitude of teachers who, regardless of a child's attainment in the classroom, will reduce his grades because of a recorded low score on an academic aptitude test.

3) *Test results may be misinterpreted.* Examples of test misuse through misinterpretation are so plentiful that they could easily comprise a book in themselves. One of the most common fallacious assumptions is that test results are permanent and unchanging. When teachers fall into this error, a child of 12 may still be appraised on the basis of testing done when he was eight or ten years of age. Furthermore, test results are sometimes used as a basis for prediction when, in fact, they may not have any predictive validity whatsoever. Interest tests also often are misinterpreted on the assumption that they indicate pupil aptitudes. Likewise, paper and pencil group tests of academic aptitude often are misinterpreted through the failure of the counselor or teacher to consider the child's reading level. Some academic aptitude tests are virtually tests of reading ability.

Then there are conspicuous errors of misinterpretation resulting from the failure of faculty members to understand testing terminology. For example, it is by no means rare to find unsophisticated persons who confuse *percentile* with *percentage*. In a few instances the results of tests are even applied to situations in which they are not appropriate—when a teacher or a counselor judges the "ability" of a culturally different child only on the basis of standardized test scores. Other users of test results are guilty of drawing unwarranted conclusions or of overgeneralizing from a *single* test score.

4) *Test results may be used to reinforce a bias.* Where test results are used selectively to substantiate the prejudices of the faculty, a basic principle of pupil analysis is obviously violated. Fortunately, such occasions arise infrequently. However, the counselor must be alert to safeguard the pupils accordingly.

5) *Test results may be inappropriate to pupil level, background or learning experiences.* "Standardized" tests are rarely standardized in the strictest interpretation of the word. For example, a test may have been "standardized" on the basis of a sample of a particular socio-geographic group, or with respect to a particular group with an experiential background not typical of groups subsequently assessed with the same instrument.

6) *Test results may be invalid as a result of errors in administration.* When the testing directions have been violated, the results obtained from the measurement instrument used are obviously invalid. The most frequent examples of this misuse are characterized by: 1) a failure to give directions exactly as stated in the manual; 2) giving excessive assistance or examples; 3) inaccurate timing; 4) inappropriate conditions for testing; and 5) crude errors in scoring.

7) *Test results may be influenced by "teaching for testing."* When the achievement of children on standardized tests is used as an index in evaluating teacher effectiveness, it is almost inevitable that some teachers—especially those who are insecure—will "teach for the test." In other situations where test results have been used as a criteria for determining children's progress, sympathetic teachers sometimes emphasize known or anticipated test items in their classrooms. Excessive coaching in the "techniques of test taking" obviously can contaminate the achievement scores which children make on standardized tests.

Employing the
Techniques of Educational Measurement

The elementary teacher or counselor who is charged with the interpretation and utilization of guidance test results needs an understanding of widely used testing terminology and basic statistical concepts through which test data are commonly summarized. While there is no substitute for a well-designed course in statistics for teachers and counselors concerned with the performance, attitudes, and abilities of children, there are certain broad and relevant guidelines which are useful.

1) The counselor should refresh his memory or acquire information about measurement and statistics by studying texts such as Clinton Chase's *Elementary Statistical Procedures* (4). All counselors should understand basic statistical concepts and terms and should be able to interpret test results.

2) Carefully examine the current *Mental Measurement Yearbook* edited by Oscar K. Buros (3). This volume is designed to help persons locate, select, and use tests with greater discrimination and ease. Be certain to read the preface and the introduction in *Tests in Print* also edited by Buros (2). The book presents a comprehensive bibliography of tests and serves as an index and supplement to the *Yearbook* series.

     The latest *Encyclopedia of Educational Research* edited by Chester Harris, and the 68th *Yearbook,* National Society for the Study of Education, *Educational Evaluation: New Roles, New Means,* edited by Ralph Tyler, are also excellent sources of information (10,21).

3) Read the manuals provided for the type of test you plan to administer. Examine the tests themselves as well as the checking, tabulating, and summarizing procedures. Note what qualified reviewers have stated about each test.

4) Peruse professional journals that deal with educational research, developments, and opinions. Besides the journals published under the auspices of the APGA, these journals are also helpful.
     Review of Educational Research
     Research Quarterly
     School and Society
     Journal of Educational Research
     Psychological Abstracts
     Educational and Psychological Measurement

5) A good foundation for evaluation and measurement depends upon a broad professional background that encompasses the many fields and disciplines that have a bearing on education. Become familiar with major developments and studies in the behavioral sciences.

6) Develop skill in the creation of teacher-made tests so that instruments may be tailored to unique aspects of the instructional program.

Test Selection, Administration, and Utilization

Guidance testing in the elementary school has only one main purpose: to improve the quality of teaching and learning. Therefore, the degree to which any standardized testing program is successful lies in the usefulness of the results. This usefulness will be determined by:

1) general considerations for guidance testing
2) the appropriateness of the tests considered
3) the accuracy of their administration
4) the correct interpretation and utilization of results.

General Considerations for Guidance Testing

Prior to planning any guidance testing program the counselor should consider the questions raised in the section below.

How can a program of guidance testing complement or aid in the achievement of objectives of the school's instructional program? Tests given merely for purposes of compiling little-used records are not justified. Nor is it desirable in the school assessment program to make analyses of child performance if the appraisals do not lead to action. *Testing* should lead to improved practices, not merely provide sterile, passive records of presumed performance levels.

In what areas and at what levels will guidance testing be most valuable? It would be a rare situation in which all areas or even most areas of guidance testing would be useful with the wide range of children served by the elementary school. A well-conceived program of appraisal is not based on the sheer quantity of tests administered but rather on the appropriate utilization of the findings. Ideally, testing should occur when teachers and counselors agree that a need exists for such information. Professional judgment rather than the season of the year should govern policies. Testing *all* children *only* at specific intervals is impossible to defend. Good appraisal is comprehensive and continuous, hence evaluations based on instruments are *ongoing* evaluations.

Is the test appropriate in terms of the characteristics of the pupils to be tested? As previously indicated in the paragraphs discussing test norms, it is important that the test be a fair and meaningful measure for those tested. There are great differences in the range of "normal" in childhood. Membership in certain subcultures, already noted, may lead to cultural bias being reflected in the scores made by girls and boys. Since tests do not generally allow for cultural, social, economic, and other differences, the teacher and counselor must make due allowances when interpreting children's responses to individual test items and in studying overall test scores.

Is the test appropriate to the experiences provided by the curriculum guides used in the school? Tests must be congruent with the children's experiences or the results may be virtually meaningless. Thus the teacher's role is an exceedingly important one in determining which of the many instruments might be chosen for use in a particular school.

Test Selection

The appropriateness of the tests selected must be determined by both technical and practical considerations. From a technical standpoint, the test user must, first of all, determine that he has selected instruments which have a degree of validity and reliability suited to the particular purposes and norms appropriate for the group being tested.

Validity information indicates the degree to which the test is capable of accomplishing certain aims according to Buros who lists these four types of validity (2:340).

1) *Content validity* is concerned with the sampling of a specified universe of content.

2) *Concurrent validity* is concerned with the relation of test scores to an accepted contemporary criterion of performance on the variable which the test is intended to measure.

3) *Predictive validity* is concerned with the relation of test scores to measures on a criterion based on performance at some later time.

4) *Construct validity.* More indirect validating procedures, which we refer to under the name *construct validation*, are invoked when the preceding three methods are insufficient to indicate the degree to which the test measures what it is intended to measure.

The basic idea of reliability is reflected in the words *stability* and *consistency*. One would expect an individual to consistently score at the same level if he repeated the test within a few days or an equivalent test. According to Robert Thorndike and Helen Hagen, "A measurement is reliable then to the extent that an individual remains nearly the same in repeated measurements." (20:175)

A consideration of *norms* is also important in test selection because they represent the tested characteristics of the group on which the instrument has been standardized. This information is important in determining the appropriateness of an instrument and its usefulness for comparative purposes. Counselors and teachers should first concern themselves with the characteristics of the norming group. Are they similar in age, background, and school experiences, for instance, to the group being tested? Or if not, are they representative of individuals with whom the pupil may at some later date have to compete or with whom he may be compared?

Many well established standardized tests for elementary school age children not only provide national and regional norms; they sometimes provide state and even local norms. A well-informed counselor can help teachers determine which comparisions will be most meaningful for child guidance and appraisal.

It is essential that the counselor make a careful examination of any technical reports and manuals available for any instrument that he is considering using. It is also urged that each elementary school guidance office have on its shelves a copy of the latest edition of the *Mental Measurements Yearbook* which provides technical reviews by recognized experts in the field. *Tests in Print* contains an excellent section on recommendations for the use of psychological tests and diagnostic techniques.

Practical educational considerations are also of importance in test selection and must not be overlooked. Here the counselor must consider: 1) the per pupil cost for a particular test, 2) the method and amount of time required for scoring, 3) the time required for administering the test, and 4) the quality of the printing and the test format. The services which the publishing company offers schools are also worth investigating since some companies have test correction services, some have consultants available to work in schools, and some have test interpretation data available in booklet form.

Test Administration

Ease of administration and interpretation are also important and should be discussed. Test administration may be considered in two phases: pre- and ongoing test adminstration and post-test scoring and recording.

The directions for administering most elementary school standardized tests are almost invariably easy to understand and uncomplicated in their application. However, this does not lessen the responsibility of the test administrator for scrupulously adhering to these guidelines. The potentially most valid instrument when carelessly administered loses its validity. The following guidelines for administering standardized tests are suggested for the teacher and counselor to contemplate:

1) Become thoroughly familiar with the specific directions for administering the test and examine or re-examine the test itself prior to the actual testing.

2) Establish conditions for effective test administration to children of the age group involved. A comfortable and uncrowded classroom with safeguards against interruptions is a minimum requirement.

3) Be certain that all necessary materials are at hand: a stopwatch if needed, ample supply of test booklets, extra pencils, and other special items.

4) Follow the directions for administering *exactly* as prescribed in the manual. This means that on nearly all types of test instruments, only those explanations and examples that are specified can be made. *No deviations are permitted.* When required, *all timing must be exact to the second!*

5) Collect all materials immediately after the testing period ends.

The second phase of test administration concerns itself with the scoring and recording of results. In the primary years, consumable hand-scored test booklets will usually be used. In the upper elementary years machine-scored answer sheets frequently are available. In either case, scoring should proceed as soon after test completion as possible. Here again, accuracy is essential. To provide an adequate safeguard, both machine scored and hand scored tests should be "spot checked" for errors especially where formulas, such as rights minus wrongs, are a part of the scoring procedures. These, too, should be checked for accuracy. Recording should be neat, accurate, and preserved in a consistent form.

Interpreting and Utilizing Test Results

When tests have been selected, administered, scored, and recorded, the results are ready for preliminary interpretation and for application in program improvement and in guidance practices. Three important questions may be raised at this point:

1) Who is entitled to share in the findings?
2) When should data and conclusions be shared?
3) How shall data and interpretation be shared?

In principle at least, pupils, parents, and teachers are all entitled to information, including interpretations of results related to a child's progress in school, his potentials, and ways in which he can be helped to move toward greater maturity. In including these persons in the group entitled to share in information, note that the key to this particular principle stresses that the emphasis is placed on *interpretation* rather than on *test score*. The problem of invidious comparisons should be avoided. Understanding of a child is the goal, not separating children into "bright" and "dull" groups.

Test results should be interpreted at the earliest appropriate opportunity following test administration and scoring. This presumes that a test is administered for a particular purpose and that such a purpose is served most effectively when followed up in the shortest possible time. Furthermore, the results of a test are never more valid than on the actual date the test is given. This is to say that the closer to this date that results can be interpreted the more valid the interpretation is likely to be.

Interpretations of the results to teachers or parents should be expressed in relation to a particular purpose or purposes and stated in terminology that is without ambiguity. In addition to interpreting in view of the particular purposes of the test, there are instances where results seem to contradict or appear to be in conflict with other information. For example, a child may make a high achievement test score yet do poorly in his classroom achievement. Obviously, under such circumstances, conferences are preferable for interpreting test results.

Testing the Disadvantaged

As has been indicated in earlier chapters, many groups of people—in schools, colleges and universities, the federal government, and foundations—have indicated increased interest and concern for children having special needs.* All are involved in attempting to work more effectively with those children who are sometimes called culturally different, culturally deprived, disadvantaged, or who are members of minority groups. To enhance these children's opportunities to succeed, teachers and counselors must be aware of particular problems and needs that inhibit children's ability to do well in school.

Therefore, it seems appropriate at this juncture to point out some of the insights needed when administering tests or using other types of instruments. First, it is important for the counselor to know that many widely used tests

*The amount of material available on the culturally disadvantaged has increased greatly during the past several years. The ERIC Center on the Disadvantaged at Columbia University is an excellent source for current materials. The reader is also referred to the *Current Index to Journals in Education* prepared through the ERIC Clearinghouse which indexes on a monthly basis articles from over 200 education and education-related journals.

are flawed by cultural biases which discriminate against young learners who did not grow up in white, "middle-class" environments. For example, a reliable sample of things being learned by most disadvantaged children is not included in many tests. Also, the language used in these tests is unfamiliar to many culturally different children. As such, they do not understand what they are asked to do. In some instruments, this bias is reflected not only on "what is being measured" but on "how it is being measured." The language and coping style expected if one is to make a satisfactory score simply does not jibe with the experiential input or the language of the culturally different.

Psychological factors also may inhibit the performance of the members of certain minority groups. Such inhibition may occur when the child views himself as competing against or with an in-group of which he is not a member, or when his self-concept presents an image of inadequacy in a given situation. It is also likely that some boys and girls from minority groups are not as sophisticated in dealing with pressures in testing situations as are others who have experienced greater security. The interpretation of test results to children often can be difficult due to a counselor's lack of understanding of a particular cultural background or by the child's inability to sense the counselor's meaning in his milieu.

In large numbers of elementary schools at present, there seems to be little attention given to the pupil's comparative standing with children of his own or similar backgrounds. Even the interpretation of so-called culture free tests may be misleading if the instruments are used for measurement or placement purposes in programs which are based on certain cultural orientations. Thus, while standardized testing may be useful in the further understanding and study of children from different cultural backgrounds, there are many conditions and inhibiting factors of which the elementary school counselor must be aware and consider in planning any school-wide testing program (11,12,15,17,18,19,22).

Areas of Guidance
Testing in Elementary Schools

Four broad categories for classifying guidance tests in elementary education may be identified. These are: 1) aptitude tests (including measures of academic aptitude), 2) achievement tests, 3) interest tests, and 4) personality tests. Of these tests, aptitude and achievement tests are by far the most extensively used in the primary and middle schools. A brief discussion of each of these basic guidance tests is presented in the paragraphs which follow.

Aptitude Tests

Aptitude testing seeks to measure a characteristic or characteristics which promise to indicate an individual's potential for learning or for acquiring certain measurable skills. Of the various areas of aptitude testing, academic aptitude is most frequently the subject of scrutiny in elementary schools. Academic aptitude tests are utilized as indices of the individual's potential for learning in conventional school situations. Other types of aptitude tests such as readiness tests may also be useful in verifying or identifying talents not clearly ascertained through other means. Only a limited number of areas, including art and music, have developed instruments with norms applicable to elementary school children, and these are less well defined and less fully developed than are the scholastically oriented aptitude tests. A sampling of general academic aptitude tests appropriate for the elementary school are inventoried below (2,3).

1) *California Short-Form Test of Mental Maturity.* Grades kgn-1, 1-3, 4-8, 7-9, 9-13, 10-16, and adults; 1938-58; 7 scores: spatial relationships, logical reasoning, verbal concepts, language, nonlanguage, total. Elizabeth T. Sullivan, Willis W. Clark, and Ernest W. Tiegs. California Test Bureau. (Revised in 1963.)

2) *The Henmon-Nelson Tests of Mental Ability, Revised Edition.* Grades 3-6, 6-9, 9-12, 13-17; 1931-61. Tom A. Lamke, M. J. Nelson, and Paul C. Kelso (college level). 3 scores for college level: quantitative, verbal, total. Houghton Mifflin Co.

3) *Kuhlmann-Anderson Intelligence Tests, Sixth Edition.* Grades kgn, 1, 2, 3, 4, 5, 6, 7-8, 9-12; 1927-52. F. Kuhlmann and Rose G. Anderson. Personnel Press, Inc.

4) *The Lorge-Thorndike Intelligence Tests.* Grades kgn-1, 2-3, 4-6, 7-9, 10-12; 1954-59. Irving Lorge and Robert L. Thorndike. Houghton Mifflin Co.

   a) *Nonverbal Battery.* Grades kgn-1, 2-3, 4-6, 7-9, 10-12.
   b) *Verbal Battery.* Grades 4-6, 7-9, 10-12.

5) *Otis Quick-Scoring Mental Ability Tests.* Grades 1.5-4, 4-9, 9-16; 1936-54. Tests for grades 4 and over are revisions of *Otis Self-Administering Tests of Mental Ability.*

6) Arthur S. Otis. Harcourt, Brace and World, Inc. (English edition; ages 7-10; nonverbal section of (a) only; 1936-39; tests identical with American edition. George G. Harrap and Co. Ltd.)

   a) *Alpha Test.* Grades 1.5-4; 1936-39. 3 scores: nonverbal, verbal, total
   b) *Beta Test.* Grades 4-9; 1937-54.
   c) *Gamma Test.* Grades 9-16; 1937-54.

Tests of Achievement

Achievement tests seek to measure the level of pupil attainment in specific subject-matter areas. Standardized achievement tests offer more or less objective comparisons which are not otherwise available. As noted earlier, standardized achievement tests should not be viewed as substitutes for well-constructed teacher-made tests since the latter will with few exceptions provide more satisfactory indices as to what a given group has learned from a particular teacher during a specified period of time. The well-balanced school testing program will, therefore, be designed to encompass both standardized achievement test results and the teacher created variety. Résumés of some representative achievement batteries and particular subject-matter achievement tests are presented herewith.

1) *California Achievement Tests, 1957 Edition.* Grades 1-2, 3-4, 4-6, 7-9, 9-14; 1934-59; 11 scores: reading vocabulary, reading comprehension, reading total, arithmetic reasoning, arithmetic fundamentals, arithmetic total, mechanics of English, spelling, language total, total, handwriting; tests in language, arithmetic, and reading available as separates. Ernest W. Tiegs and Willis W. Clark. California Test Bureau.

2) *Iowa Tests of Basic Skills.* Grades 3-9; 1955-56; 15 scores: vocabulary, reading comprehension, language (5 scores), work-study skills (4 scores), arithmetic skills (3 scores), total. E. F. Lindquist, A. N. Hieronymus, et al. Houghton Mifflin Company.

3) *Metropolitan Achievement Tests* (1960 Edition). Grades 1.5, 2, 3-4, 5-6, 7-9; 1960, © 1958-59; subtests in arithmetic, reading, science, and social studies available as separates. Walter N. Durost, Harold H. Bixler, Gertrude H. Hildreth, Kenneth W. Lund, and J. Wayne Wrightstone. Harcourt, Brace and World.

   a) *Primary Battery I.* Grade 1.5; 4 scores: work knowledge, word discrimination, reading, arithmetic concepts and skills.

   b) *Elementary Battery.* Grades 3-4; 9 scores: word knowledge, word discrimination, reading, spelling, language (usage, punctuation and capitalization, total), arithmetic (computation, problem solving, and concepts).

   c) *Intermediate Battery.* Grades 5-6; 11-13 scores: word knowledge, reading, spelling, language (usage, parts of speech, punctuation and capitalization, total), language study skills, arithmetic (computation, problem solving and concepts), social studies skills (complete battery only), social studies information, science.

d) *Advanced Battery*. Grades 7-9; 12-14 scores: same as for intermediate battery plus kinds of sentences under language.

4) *SRA Achievement Series*. Grades 1-2, 2-4, 4-6, 6-9, 1954-58; subtests in language arts, arithmetic, reading, and work-study skills available as separates. Louis P. Thorpe, D. Welty Lefever, and Robert A. Naslund. Science Research Associates, Inc.

Reading Tests

Over the years a number of tests have established themselves as standard gauges for measuring the ability of children to read. While like all testing instruments these are not infallible, they have remained popular with elementary teachers. However, it is always important to keep in mind that the health, happiness, and physical condition of a child can bias the best of tests! Some standard titles are listed below.

1) *American School Achievement Tests*. Covers sentence, word, and paragraph meaning for grades 2-3, 4-6, and 7-9. The Bobbs-Merrill Co., Inc.

2) *California Reading Test*. Part of the *California Achievement Test Battery* but available separately from the California Test Bureau for grades 1-2, 3-4, 4-6, 7-9, and 9-14. Vocabulary and comprehension are tested. (1957 edition with 1963 norms.)

3) *Gates-MacGinite Reading Tests*. Six separate tests for vocabulary, speed, and comprehensive are available for grades 1, 2, 3, 2.5-3, 4.5-6, and 7, 8, 9. Columbia University. Teachers College Press, 1965.

4) *Iowa Tests of Basic Skills*. The reading test is part of the total basic skills testing program. Vocabulary and comprehension scores may be obtained for grades 3-9. Houghton Mifflin Company.

5) *Nelson-Lohmann Reading Test*. Measures the student's grasp of central ideas, word meaning from context, and ability to integrate ideas. Part of the battery, coordinated scales of attainment are available separately for grades 4-8 from Educational Test Bureau, Educational Publishers, Inc.

6) *SRA Achievement Series*. Comprehension and vocabulary are checked for grades 1-2; 2-4; and 4-9. Three separate batteries

are included with subtests for curriculum areas. Science Research Associates, 1964.

7) *Stanford Achievement Tests.* Each of 5 separate batteries contains subtests on reading. Grades 1-2.5, 2-3, 4-5, 5-6, and 7-9. Harcourt, Brace and World, Inc., 1964.

Interest Inventories

Interest inventories are "tests" that seek to measure one's likes, dislikes, or indifferences toward various activities. Many of these inventories are vocationally oriented although they are apt to reflect individual's avocational interests as well. They are most commonly utilized at the secondary school level, and, as a matter of fact, are usually appropriate for administration only to adolescents or older individuals. As a rule, the elementary school counselor will want to use the following interest tests with caution.

The most popular of the interest inventories for secondary schools is the *Kuder Preference Record.* Two other commonly used inventories are the *Strong Vocational Interest Blank* and the *Lee-Thorpe Occupational Interest Inventory.*

1) *Kuder Preference Record-Occupational.* Grades 9-16 and adults; 1956-59; 43 scores. G. Frederic Kuder. Science Research Associates, Inc.

2) *Kuder Preference Record-Vocational.* Grades 9-16 and adults; 1934-56; 2 forms. G. Frederic Kuder. Science Research Associates, Inc.

   a) *Form B.* 1934-46; 9 or 10 scores: mechanical computational, scientific, persuasive, artistic, literary, musical, social service, clerical, masculinity-femininity (optional).

   b) *Form C.* 1934-56; revision of Form B; 11 scores: same as for Form B plus outdoor, verification.

3) *Strong Vocational Interest Blank for Men, Revised.* Ages 17 and over; 1927-59; 60 scoring scales (50 occupations, 6 occupational group scales, and 4 nonvocational scales). Edward K. Strong, Jr. Consulting Psychologists Press, Inc.

4) *Strong Vocational Interest Blank for Women, Revised.* Ages 17 and over; 1933-59; 31 scoring scales (30 occupational scales and 1 nonvocational scale). Edward K. Strong, Jr. Consulting Psychologists Press, Inc.

5) *Occupational Interest Inventory, 1956 Revision.* Grades 7-16 and adults, 9-16 and adults; 1943-1956; 10 scores grouped in

3 categories: fields of interests (personal-social, natural, mechanical, business, the arts, the sciences), types of interests (verbal, manipulative, computational), levels of interests. Edwin A. Lee and Louis P. Thorpe: California Test Bureau.

Adjustment and Temperament Inventories

Adjustment inventories and temperament inventories usually seek to assess various personal characteristics of the individual. The results may be presented in the form of a personality profile or in degrees of adjustment or maladjustment. Although these types of instruments are discussed here, it is important that the elementary school counselor and teachers recognize that group administered personality tests for elementary school children are of doubtful value. The lack of appropriate instruments for this age level may be attributed to such factors as: 1) the inability of many children to analyze themselves; 2) the unreliability of responses to self-analysis questions; 3) the nebulous nature of personality itself; and 4) a lack of psychological and psychometric background for personality test interpretation found in most teachers and many counselors.

While it is important to identify behavioral patterns indicative of social-emotional maladjustment as soon as possible in the elementary school, it is equally desirable to use other methods of assessment. In this regard, it is appropriate to mention that individually administered personality tests of a projective nature may, in the hands of one trained in their administration and interpretation, be quite useful. When the counselor feels it is necessary, he refers the child to the proper professional colleague.

However, personality inventories of a nonprojective nature may be useful. For students of elementary school age, the number of instruments available is limited but the following may be useful.

1) *California Test of Personality. 1953 Revision*. Grades kgn.-3, 4-8, 7-10, 9-16, adults; 1939-53; 15 scores: self-reliance, sense of personal worth, sense of personal freedom, feeling of belonging, withdrawing tendencies, nervous symptoms, total personal adjustment, social standards, social skills, anti-social tendencies, family relations, school relations or occupational relations, community relations, total social adjustment, total adjustment. Louis P. Thorpe, Willis W. Clark, and Ernest W. Tiegs. California Test Bureau.

2) *SRA Junior Inventory*. Grades 4-8; 1951-57; 5 scores: school, home, myself, people, health (Form A), general (Form S). H. H. Remmers and Robert H. Bauernfeind.

Summary

This chapter has discussed the assessment of human development as a fundamental activity of the school's educational program and its related guidance services. Careful appraisal is important in order that teachers and counselors may better understand the nature of each child in their charge.

It is essential for the school guidance program to provide effective individual counseling, to insure insightful group guidance, and to achieve understanding of both the ecology of childhood and the syntax of learning. This knowledge is likewise important to the child himself in developing self-understanding.

The school's program of guidance testing is enhanced when carried out within the framework of six principles:

1) recognizing the fact of the individual differences
2) focusing on the total individual
3) understanding of the changing individual
4) recognizing of the limits of analyses
5) honoring the concept of confidentiality
6) emphasizing a positive approach

Guidance testing offers opportunities for objective assessment of children's attitudes and of their subject-matter achievement. Also, certain instruments offer clues to their other personal characteristics.

References

1. Bahn, Martin J. Jr. and Donald E. Super. "The Computer in Counseling and Guidance Programs." *Educational Technology* 9 (March, 1969): 29-31.

2. Buros, Oscar K. (ed.). *Tests in Print*. Highland Park, N.J.: The Gryphon Press, 1961.

3. ____ . *The Sixth Mental Measurements Yearbook*. Highland Park, N.J.: The Gryphon Press, 1965.

4. Chase, Clinton. *Elementary Statistical Procedures*. New York: McGraw-Hill Book Co., 1967.

5. *Code of Ethics of the Education Profession*. Washington, D.C.: National Education Association, 1963.

6. "Ethical Standards—American Personnel and Guidance Association." *Personnel and Guidance Journal* 40 (October, 1961): 206-209.

7. "Ethical Standards of Psychologists." *American Psychologist* 40 (January, 1963): 56-60.

8. Gibson, Robert L. and Robert E. Higgins. *Techniques of Guidance*. Chicago: Science Research Associates, 1966.

9. Grossman, Alvin and Robert Howe. "Human Economy and Data Processing." *The Personnel and Guidance Journal* 43 (December, 1964): 343-347.

10. Harris, Chester (ed.). *Encyclopedia of Educational Research*. New York: The Macmillan Co., 1970.

11. Kagan, Norman. "Three Dimensions of Counselor Encapsulation." *Journal of Counseling Psychology* 11 (Winter, 1964): 361-365.

12. Leacock, Eleanor. "The Concept of Culture and Its Significance for School Counselors." *Personnel and Guidance Journal* 46 (May, 1968): 844-851.

13. Loughary, John W., Deloss Friesch, and Robert Hurst. "Autocoun: A Computer Based Automated Counseling System." *Personnel and Guidance Journal* 45 (September, 1966): 6-15.

14. ____ and Murray Tondow. "Computers as Substitute Counselors." *Educational Technology* 9 (March, 1969): 33-36.

15. Mathis, Harold I. "The Disadvantaged and the Aptitude Barrier." *Personnel and Guidance Journal* 47 (January, 1969): 462-472.

16. *The Measurement of Education Products*. XVII *Yearbook*. National Society for the Study of Education. Chicago: University of Chicago Press, 1918.

17. Rude, H. Neil and Donald C. King. "Aptitude Levels in a Depressed Area." *Personnel and Guidance Journal* 43 (April, 1965): 785-789.

18. Schwebel, Milton. "Learning and the Socially Deprived." *Personnel and Guidance Journal* 43 (March, 1965): 646-653.

19. Snider, James G. "The Linguistic Content Variable in School Counseling." *Personnel and Guidance Journal* 52 (February, 1964): 577-587.

20. Thorndike, Robert and Helen Hagen. *Measurement and Evaluation in Psychology and Education*. New York: John Wiley and Sons, Inc., 1964.

21. Tyler, Ralph (ed.). *Educational Evaluation: New Roles, New Means*. LXVIII *Yearbook*, Part II. National Society for the Study of Education. Chicago: University of Chicago Press, 1969.

22. Washington, Benetta B. "Growth and Cultural Conflict." *Vocational Guidance Quarterly* 12 (Spring, 1964): 153-158.

10

The Assessment of Human Development: Non-Testing Techniques

In the present chapter, attention is directed toward ways other than testing through which counselor and teachers may come to know children better. The result of failing to study children carefully is preserved in a faulty human product, and the consequence of such ineffectiveness should be obvious to all educators.

Many schools today have accepted a substantial amount of responsibility for providing an education for children in terms of their individual needs. If teachers and counselors are to pay more than lip service to this important goal, however, it is necessary that they have a thorough understanding of the status of the knowledge, capacities, interests, and background of each young learner.

Although many teachers do not hesitate to admit that physical, psychological, and educational factors may interfere with or inhibit learning, often nothing is done to expose the damaging influences that are involved and to make the proper adjustment in the school program for individuals needing help. More often than not the focus of attention rests predominantly on standardized testing—particularly tests of mental ability and tests of achievement. Once testing is completed, frequently the same standard of success is set for *all* children. The results of this arbitrary approach to appraising learning are reflected in children's dislike, disinterest, and failure in school—all of these being outcomes which take their toll in unhappiness and in maladjustment. Too frequently it is forgotten that mastery of subject matter is only one of several of the school's objectives.

Studying Children

In educational planning and practice, counselors and teachers need not only be aware of what a child's capacities are, but they must also realize that they, too, can tremendously influence his development. As Ira J. Gordon puts it, they must understand that there is a "... circular way of conceptualizing 'potential'," and that what teachers and counselors do when working with a child can influence his development along unpredictable lines (16:3). To elaborate on Gordon's point, "... a teacher's [or counselor's] behavior is modified by his moment-to-moment dealings with his pupils just as much as their behavior is only understandable in relation to his."

The Teacher Influences Development

According to Gordon one of the main tasks of the school is to bring about readiness and enhance intelligence. If this is to be accomplished, then teachers must understand the factors under their control which may influence development. Gordon suggests the following set of concepts that illustrate newly recognized tasks that teachers face:

1) In any phase of development, such as the cognitive, the learning behavior of the child is a function of the structure and organization he has already developed, the nature of the immediate learning task, and the manner in which the task is presented to him.

   a) If the task is required of the child that does not "match" the child's already developed structure, he will not actively engage in the mastery of the task.

   b) Failure of the task to engage the child may be due to mismatching in several dimensions.

      1) Cognitively, the child and task may be mismatched because the task goes beyond the child's structure (too "hard" for him), or because it may have already been incorporated into his structure, and fails to challenge his competence motivation (too "easy" for him).

   c) If the task is presented at a time when the child's structure is matched to act upon it, and it is seen by him as being in keeping with his level of aspirations and goals, he will engage in mastering it.

   d) Thus, both the cognitive and affective aspects of the child are continuously involved and interacting in his behavior, learning, and development.

2) Mastery of a new task modifies the structure of the child.

   a) Intellectual structure, that is, the complex organization of concepts, is built upon the successive mastery of learning tasks presented by the environment.

b) Self-esteem, the view of oneself as competent, is also built from the mastery of learning tasks (16:4).

Minimal Factors and Processes

Some time ago the American Council on Education prepared a report giving the minimum range of factors and processes that must be taken into consideration when studying children. This report still offers a great deal to both the teacher and to the counselor in helping them look at the transactional process as the teacher helps plan the learning experiences and the counselor assists in the total development of each boy and girl.

The following statements should help the counselor conceive of the child as an integrated being—not one artificially separated into social, emotional, intellectual, and physical dimensions.

1) *Physical factors and processes*—including health and nutrition; characteristic rate of energy out-put and normal rhythm of activity and rest; rate of growth and level of physical maturity achieved; coordination of movements and management of the body; physical handicaps and blemishes; attractiveness of physique and grooming.

2) *The climate of affection in which the child lives*—including the child's relationship to his mother, father, and siblings; other adults; the teacher; best friends; and the parents' relationship to each other and other family members.

3) *Peer-culture and group status and processes*—including the child's knowledge of the codes and customs of his maturity-level peers; his own abilities and interests in relation to activities esteemed by his peers; the roles he actually plays in peer group activities; and the status accorded him by his peers.

4) *Social background and dynamics*—including the particular cultural patterns of knowledge, attitude, and action operating in his family and community and already internalized by him; the relationships between these cultural patterns and those carried on by his peers and his teachers; the cultural aspirations of the child and his family; the cultural conflicts occurring in the child's community; and the impact on the child of events in the community, nation, and world.

5) *Self-developmental potentialities and processes*—including the child's capacities and aptitudes; experience background; knowledge and skills; his interests; his attitudes; his values; and his short-term goals and long-term aspirations.

6) *Self-defensive and adjustive processes*—including what situations and experiences create pleasant and unpleasant emotions in the child; how the child acts when he is emotional; what mechanisms operate as he defends, reassures, or comforts himself; whether his concepts, attitudes, goals, and aspirations are

consistent with each other and constitute a well-knit organizing core (30).*

Observation
Techniques and Observation Reports

Observation is a technique that almost everyone has employed at one time or another. Often upon meeting a person for the first time, we begin to analyze him on the basis of what we see. Occasionally we do even this when observing strangers riding beside us on a bus or sitting next to us at a ball game. In the same way, we watch entertainers in movies, on the stage, or on our television screen and draw conclusions—albeit often inaccurate ones—about the type of person we think he is. Indeed, it would seem that if "practice makes perfect," we would only need to use the technique of observation for any planned program of child study. Certainly most people make extensive use of such techniques however amateurish such efforts may be.

Checking Observational Skills

The effectiveness of casual observation, quite naturally, is open to question. Because observing "comes naturally" to all of us, and because we are constantly absorbing visual impressions, we tend seriously to over-estimate the accuracy of random or unsystematic observations. For instance, the play-back of films has given us proof in recent years that even highly trained observers such as baseball umpires, football officials, and racing judges, conscious of the need for accuracy in their observations and viewing the scene from a vantage point, do sometimes err in their observations. Frequent examples also may be found in the conflicting versions that witnesses to the same event or incident will, in all sincerity, report. Perhaps we can offer convincing proof by asking that the reader indicate how many of the following road signs he can identify merely by their shapes:

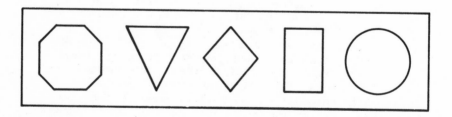

*For another useful reference dealing with human development, cf. Gordon Bronson (9).

To check responses, look at the bottom of the page.* If still convinced of his observational powers, the reader should try these additional questions:

1) Whose pictures appear on $5, $10, and $20 bills?
2) What are the colors on the top and bottom stripes in the United States flag? (See the bottom of the page.)†

The accuracy and completeness of our recall of observations usually tends to depreciate rapidly with the passage of time. Secondly, it is difficult to compare or verify undirected observations because individuals are seldom making their observation within the same frame of reference. (For example, what one man might describe to his associates as a "striking blond," his wife might describe as a "washed-out peroxide type.") Also, we frequently look for only those things in our observations of others that reinforce a bias or preconceived concept we have toward a given individual or object. Another common weakness is the analysis of an individual after observing his behavior in only one type of situation—say in the classroom during a discussion of space travel. Finally, even in the same setting, two observers may take note of or have different values; hence, reach conflicting views of the same situation.

The limitations of observation procedures as a means of studying behavior are not intended to suggest the elimination or downgrading of this technique. Rather we are endeavoring to point to the need for guidelines and for instruments which will increase the accuracy and objectivity of any observations that are recorded (2,8,10,19,20,37).

Observing Nonverbal Behavior

As Irving J. Lee once noted, "Details must be missed as observation goes on. A blade of grass as well as a three-ring circus defies coverage at any instant." (24:56) Since even the most advanced of our skills in science do not permit us even to begin to make *full* observations of physical and chemical phenomena, *really* meaningful observation of complex human beings by the counselor poses a great challenge.

Some of the important and relatively new procedures for assessing human development in the guidance field are related to the feedback which counselors and teachers can extract from *non*verbal communication. A number of writers have begun to take note of the importance of nonverbal communication in observing and drawing inferences from children's behavior (7,12,14,

*"Stop," "Yield," "Warning," "Information," and "Railroad Crossing."
†Abraham Lincoln, Alexander Hamilton, and Andrew Jackson. The top and bottom stripes are both red.

15,18,28,34). As the name suggests, nonverbal communication is a mode of behaving which provides meaning through gestures, demeanor, and expression.

> It can be symbolic or nonsymbolic, spontaneous or managed. It can be expressive, transmitting emotion; or it can be informative, transmitting facts. It can be as specific as a gesture or as general as the atmosphere of a room. It can be either dynamic or static (14:37).*

The counselor interested in assessing human behavior through nontesting techniques will find nonverbal phenomena of great value. Important clues are mirrored or reside in the way a child uses or responds to space, his gestures and expressions, the muscle tone reflected in his posture and so on. Nonverbal feedback often helps the teacher and the counselor to become aware of the child's physical well-being, the status of his social relationships with others, possible home problems, and the myriad nuances of silent meaning that bespeaks his happiness or possible maladjustments.

As stated earlier, the challenges of the silent language of the child and of the school are major ones. They acquire further importance because children in or from problem situations are most likely to provide for teacher or counselor the first "leads" to a need for guidance by what they *do* rather than by what they *say*.

Galloway has suggested and described several nonverbal expressions of behavior. An understanding of such phenomena as the sampling below is an important personal resource for counselor and teacher alike.*

> *Substitute Expression.* A child shrugs his shoulder in an "I don't know" manner after being accosted in the hallway for running. Probably this means he feels guilty at being caught, yet he hesitates to engage the teacher in a verbal debate. This is especially true if his verbal defense is likely to be employed against him later in the conversation. One of the places events like this occur repeatedly is in inner-city schools, where children are already conditioned to express their frustrations and defiance in a nonverbal way.
>
> *Qualifying Expression.* Ann says, "I don't sing well," but what does she mean? Stated one way, it suggests that she *does* sing well; or it may mean that she *would like* to sing well; or, that she truly *does not* sing well. The intent of verbal remarks is usually qualified through intonation and inflection. Facial expressions and gestures also qualify verbal language.
>
> *Nonverbal Symbolic.* John observed the teacher watching him. Now he is painting with large dramatic strokes, one eye on the teacher, hoping she will look his way again. When we know we are being observed, our behavior is designed to have intent or purpose for the observer. It symbolizes our thoughts or intentions.

*Reprinted from *Instructor* © April 1968, The Instructor Publications, Inc., Dansville, New York 14437.

Eyes alone may beckon or reject. Many gestures and facial expressions symbolize our deepest feelings.

Nonverbal Nonsymbolic. You are watching a child who is observing another child, totally unaware that you are watching him. His behavior is considered nonsymbolic since it is free of overt intent. When you observe the unobserved observer, it is a profound process—for his reactions are genuinely his own with no desire to create an impression. Observing a person who is unaware of one's presence is both informative and fun.

Attentive or Inattentive. Your students are pretending to listen while their minds wander in fields of fantasy, and when they respond it is in a bored fashion. Nonverbally they are being inattentive. As an experienced teacher, you are able to detect such reactions and use them to change the pace and direction of what is being taught. Observing when students are involved and interested and when they are not is a skill that teachers learn. But teachers vary widely in their ability or willingness to use these pupil reactions as directions for their own behavior (14:38ff).

There are other nonverbal occurrences, but these are good ones with which to start.

Helpful Observation Techniques

Most counselors and teachers can develop more accurate observation techniques through attention to and practice of the following fundamental principles of observation:

1) *Observe for a purpose.* Observation becomes meaningful and the results more relevant when one observes for a reason. Techniques and criteria may then be developed which serve the objective of the observations.

2) *Observe for specifics related to the purpose.* The accuracy of observation is enhanced when directed towards specific situations, individuals, groups, personal characteristics, or events. It also is helpful to single out specific objectives for observation. The validity of observations is increased when the number of observers is expanded and their impressions are combined.

3) *Observe long enough and over a period of time.* Observations should be conducted over a sufficient period of time to insure that the reporting is reliable rather than atypical. Verification of initial impressions or the substitution of more appropriate ones can result.

4) *Observe objectively.* Observations should be made without bias. When the observer has specific items or behaviors to observe, there is less likelihood of his personal biases influencing his viewing and subsequent reporting.

5) *Observe total behavioral fields.* While observation may be directed at an individual pupil, this does not suggest that he be viewed in isolation or out of context with the field in which he is carrying on transactions with others.

Accurate interpretation of what is observed requires a recognition and understanding of the total setting in which a boy or girl is observed.

6) *Record data immediately.* As has been indicated, the accuracy of observations, planned or otherwise, deteriorates rapidly with the passage of time. The results of an objective and well planned observation may be largely wasted if the observer does not immediately—within the hour or at least on the same day—record his viewings.

7) *Make behavioral interpretations longitudinally: study records as they accumulate.* Observation reports, like all other information gathering techniques, are most meaningful and valid when analyzed in relation to all data pertaining to the individual over a period of time. Avoid over-emphasizing "critical incidents."

Reporting Observations

The most popular form for reporting observations in the school setting has, for a number of years, been the anecdotal record. By providing guidelines for recording and reporting observations, this technique encourages objectivity and exact descriptions.

The Anecdotal Record

An anecdotal record is an objective description of an event or episode that a teacher or counselor has observed and feels significant enough to record in writing. These recorded events or episodes are called anecdotes or behavior descriptions.

In writing anecdotal reports, the experienced counselor or teacher is most careful to record *objectively* the behavior description of the event. He must not 1) include inferences; 2) mix fact with opinion; 3) write to verify a predetermined judgment; nor 4) seek to justify a preplanned course of action. While interpretations and recommendations for action are important and give meaning to the factual description of behavior, they should be distinctly separate from the event being recorded. Remember all episodes do not justify an interpretation, and many are simply indicative of trends in the growth and development of the individual. It is a *series* of anecdotal reports that is likely to provide meaningful behavioral clues and insights. A final suggestion should also be given—due consideration must be given to the background or setting of the incident or the record is not complete and cannot be interpreted correctly.

There are values in the use of anecdotal records, but there also are limitations and cautions to be observed in their preparation. The values of well-written anecdotal reports include the following:

1) They contribute to an understanding of the basic personality pattern of each child; substitute specific descriptions for vague generalizations; and direct teachers' attention from the group to the individual child.

2) They provide information for the counselor to use with pupils in self-appraisal; for the formulation of individual self-study programs; and for encouraging evidence of growth in these respects.

3) The qualitative statements supplement the interpretation of qualitative data; aid in clinical services; indicate a need for curriculum construction, modification, and emphasis; and encourage teacher understanding of larger school problems (39:133-134).

The limitations and cautions in the preparation of anecdotal reports include:

1) An anecdotal report is valuable only if the observation is accurately recorded, written with objectivity, is nonjudgmental in nature, and not used to defend the person making the report.

2) Care must be exercised that the behavior incident is not divorced from the social setting in which it occurred, that a small number of anecdotes is not accepted as valid evidence of the total picture, and that unfortunate behavior incidents (preserved in anecdotal form) do not reflect a teacher's prejudice of the moment and mirror a type of behavior that is no longer typical.

3) The adoption of a system of anecdotal reports is time consuming and must be continued over a long period of time to be effective.

4) Anecdotal reports can tend to emphasize the negative rather than the positive if the staff is not educated to observe and record evidences of growth that are positive as well as negative. Care should be exercised also so that atypical episodes are not the ones most frequently recorded.

To illustrate some of the points that have been mentioned above, some fictitious anecdotal reports are included in Figures 15 through 18.

Even a casual reading suggests that the anecdotal record prepared by Jane Ryan includes personal bias, arbitrary judgment, and inference. For example, Miss Ryan used phrases such as "below standard in all work," "can't be depended upon," "wasted her time," "did mean little things," "is spoiled at home," and "is incapable of assuming any responsibility." Note that she recorded her *reactions* to a situation; she did not provide *data*. We might ask Miss Ryan, "Is Barbara below standard in *everything* she does?" "Are you considering her capabilities *now* or are you comparing her with others in the

ANECDOTAL REPORTS

Pupil **Barbara Wiley**   Date **March 24, 19 —**

Grade **4**   Time **10:30 a.m.**

Setting: Friday morning when children were studying word lists prior to taking the weekly test.

Anecdote: Barbara, who is below standard in all her work and can't be depended upon, wasted her time during the period for studying spelling words. As usual, she did mean little things to the children around her.

Comment: Barbara is so spoiled at home that she is incapable of assuming any responsibility.

Jane Ryan
Teacher

Figure 15.   Anecdotal Record Form Reflecting Personal Bias
and Arbitrary Judgment

ANECDOTAL REPORTS

Pupil _John Robinson_   Date _September 24, 19—_

Grade _6_   Time _9:30 a.m._

Setting: _The beginning of the physical education class when baseball teams were being chosen._

Anecdote: _John was the last person selected as a member of a team. After he struck out, he threw the bat toward the pitcher, then punched the catcher as he returned to the bench._

Comment:

Helen Harvey
Teacher

Figure 16. Anecdotal Record Form Which Reports a Behavioral Incident Without Personal Bias

ANECDOTAL REPORTS

Pupil _John Robinson_   Date _October 5, 19—_

Grade _6_   Time _8:30 a.m._

Setting: The children were entering school in small groups as buses arrived from different areas.

Anecdote: John brought a catcher's mitt to school with him. He showed it to Robert, the captain of his team and said, "Now I can be the catcher on the team!" Robert replied, "Not on my team you can't. You're a poor loser." Then Robert walked off to join some other boys. John threw his mitt on the floor and began to read a book.

Comment:

Helen Harvey
Teacher

Figure 17.   Factual Data in an Anecdotal Record
(Second Example)

ANECDOTAL REPORTS

Pupil _John Robinson_   Date _October 10, 19 —_

Grade _Grade 6_   Time _2:00 p.m._

Setting: *A planning session when children were working individually and in small groups on special projects.*

Anecdote: *I asked Robert to work with John in helping to select some stories about well-known athletes. John smiled and said he would like to do this. When they finished, I thanked both boys and complimented them on their choices. They seemed pleased with their efforts also and walked off together.*

Comment: *Perhaps other opportunities like this for John will help him become friends with some of the other boys.*

Helen Harvey
Teacher

Figure 18. Anecdotal Record Entry Illustrating Teacher Follow-Up of Incidents Described in Figures 16 and 17

group?" "What was she asked to do that she didn't do?" "What mean little things does she do?" "How has she failed in assuming responsibility?" In fact, most of Miss Ryan's comments were not only subjective reactions but they were so general that they meant almost nothing at all.

Miss Harvey, however, has begun a series of meaningful behavior descriptions that can be useful to her in evaluating both John's and the group's development. As she continues to observe, she should be able to set up some hypotheses about John's behavior including both the positive and negative dimensions. Then, on the basis of her data, she should be able to arrive at some tentative conclusions as to why John behaves as he does. For example these statements are meaningful: "John seems to want to belong to a group, particularly with the boys on the baseball team. Although he gets attention from them, they seem displeased with his behavior and tend to avoid him."

Then she might consider a recommendation—which is kept separate from both the anecdote and the interpretation—for further action. "The counselor might talk with John about his relationships with the other children and discuss ways in which their interaction might be improved before the situation becomes any worse." Miss Harvey is well on her way to *studying* children's behavior rather than *labeling* it.

Rating Scales and Observation Checklists

The rating scale and observation checklist are instruments designed to offer guidelines and to encourage more specific and comprehensive approaches to classifying and evaluating what is observed. The *Vineland Social Maturity Scale* and the *Haggerty-Olson-Wickman Behavior Rating Schedule* are examples of two frequently used scales which have been used for decades. Since the 1950's the use of such has lessened however, and many are out of print.

In their simplest form a teacher-made instrument might consist of a series of items such as this.

5. To what extent does the pupil participate in sports?

1	2	3	4	5
No Participation		Occasional Participation		Frequent Participation

Figure 19. Example of Simple Rating Scale (Sports)

These scales attempt to provide an approach to obtaining comparable data from several sources both by directing attention to designated items for observation and by providing a scale for recording the response. Rating scales can be used in conjunction with other forms of reports dealing with pupil's academic performance, school adjustment, attitudes, or general personality traits.

It is important to remember that rating scales and observation checklists are tools which should only be used to help assess more accurately the meaning and nature of a child's behavior. *The teacher's or counselor's estimates are not used to determine what is "good" or "bad" or "true" about a child's supposed traits. They serve as foundations for teacher-counselor discussions which are intended to deepen their mutual understandings regarding a particular six- or eight- or eleven-year-old.*

As the reader examines these instruments, he should be aware that they do not present an adequate picture of the individual. While tools of this type may seem "easy" to use, only the very naive would believe that behavior can be indicated and interpreted by means of a checkmark. These and other instruments for reporting observations are merely diagnostic assessment *devices*. They *may* help us to appraise the individual, but only when used appropriately. They should facilitate the integration of observable pupil traits into the total and developing picture of the individual. But no rating scale can be treated as if it were a "true" and "complete" portrayal of a child. The isolated interpretation of an appraisal instrument actually can be a threat to the successful analysis of a child. If such scales are to be used at all, they should only be used after careful study and by persons whose professional competencies and personal standards insure that children's behavior is not misrepresented.

Sociometric Techniques

The many aspects of getting along with other people and understanding man's relationships with his fellow human beings have long been a fascinating area for speculation and discussion. Interpersonal behavior also is important because our understanding of other people is essential to our personal and social happiness and success and perhaps even to our long-term survival.

Increasingly, since the 1930's, the school has placed stress upon the social adjustment and the social development of the individual. Research by many experts—psychologists, sociologists, mental health and human development specialists—has emphasized the importance of social relationships in the development of personality, the influence of the group on the learning and behavior of individuals, and the importance of being accepted by others in making successful personal adjustments. Indeed, an understanding of the social microcosm that is reflected in both the class group and the total school group is one of fundamental concern to the counselor as he studies the emotional and social adjustment of boys and girls.

Since the 1930's there has been a great deal of interest in what is called *sociometry.* Here counseling is indebted to J. L. Moreno for his work in developing techniques for determining the internal social structure of a group (26). Sociometry has provided a basis for an objective approach to studying and improving social relations within the classroom. Through *sociometric devices* or procedures the approximate nature and quality of social relations among members of a group may be gauged.

Sociometry in the Elementary School

The following example of the use of sociometry and sociometric devices is provided to illustrate how they may be used in the elementary school and to introduce the reader to some of the terminology that is used (17:3-6).

Sociometric tests are frequently used to obtain some indication of an individual child's *sociometric status* or *group status.* His sociometric status is determined by the number of choices he has received from his peers. For example, a sociometric test asks children to select other persons with whom they would like to associate in some type of group situation or activity. This is done by having children reply to questions such as these:

1) Who are three children with whom you would like to work?
2) Who are three children with whom you would like to play?
3) Who are three children you would like to sit next to you?

The basis for the children making a choice is called the *sociometric question* or the *sociometric criterion.*

The data are then tabulated and often presented in the form of a matrix table as shown in Figure 20. Notice that the boys' and girls' names are arranged alphabetically, and that they are separated by both horizontal and vertical lines so that cross-sex choices may be easily discerned. The diagonal line cuts through squares that are not used since children do not select themselves on sociometric tests. The diagonal line also serves as a guide for identifying mutual choices. As might be inferred, *mutual choice* indicates two individuals who, on the basis of the same sociometric question or criterion, have chosen each other. Mutual choices are circled on this table.

At the bottom of the tabulation is recorded the number of choices each child received in terms of members of the same sex and members of the opposite sex. As was noted previously, the number of choices received determines the child's sociometric or group status. From these tabulations, one can obtain such data as these:

Star: A child who receives a large number of choices. i.e., boys 6 and 7; girls 11 and 12.

Isolate: A child who receives virtually no choices. i.e., boy 1 and girl 2.

MATRIX TABLE FOR TABULATION DATA

Name		1	2	3	4	5	6	7	8	9	10	11	12	13	14	15	16	17	18	19	20
												Pupils Chosen									
Paul A.	1		3				1	2													
John B.	2			(2)				(1)		(3)											
Bill D.	3		(3)				1	(2)													
Pete D.	4					(1)	2		3												
Jim G.	5				(1)		2	3													
Bob J.	6							(2)	(1)		(3)										
Tony M.	7		(2)				(1)			(3)											
Charles N.	8						(1)	3		(2)											
Ed W.	9		(2)	(3)				(1)													
Joe Z.	10						2		(1)	3											
Mary C.	11												(1)		(3)				(2)		
Eileen D.	12											(1)			2				(3)		
Donna F.	13												2				(1)	(3)			
Julie F.	14											(2)	1								(3)
Pearl P.	15											1	2		3						
Arlene P.	16													(2)					1		
Helen R.	17													(1)			3				
Robert R.	18											(2)	(1)		3						
Linda A.	19											2	1	3							
Jane T.	20												1		(2)				3		
Opposite Sex		0	0	0	0	0	1	0	0	0	1	1	0	0	0	0	0	0	0	0	0
Same Sex		0	4	2	1	1	7	7	3	3	1	6	7	3	5	0	2	2	3	0	1

Figure 20. Matrix Table for Recording Sociometric Data

A more detailed analysis of data is also possible. When such an analysis is made, or if the sociometric question asks individuals to indicate children whom they least prefer, these terms are sometimes used.

Neglectee: A child who receives relatively few choices (8,17).

Rejectee: A child who receives negative choices.

The Sociogram: As selections are made among individuals, a pattern of choices becomes apparent which shows the network of the groups interpersonal relations or the *sociometric structure* or *group structure*. Usually this sociometric structure is graphically portrayed in the form of a model known as a *sociogram*. While there are several ways in which sociograms may be prepared, the following illustration will serve to show how the presentation of sociometric results graphically makes it easier to understand the social relations of a group of children than only using the matrix tables (see Figure 21).

Two other terms are illustrated by this sociogram.

Sociometric cleavage: A lack of sociometric choices between two or more subgroups. For example, the boys have seldom chosen girls, and the girls have seldom chosen boys.

Sociometric clique: Individuals who chose each other but give few choices outside their close groups. For example, Karen, Jean, and Sally.

The Values and Limitations of Sociometric Tests

As with any testing device, there are both advantages and disadvantages to using sociometric techniques. Norman E. Gronlund suggests that their value lies in helping:

1) *improve the social adjustment of individual pupils.* It identifies children needing help in their social relations, it indicates an individual's drive for social interaction, and assists in evaluating the development of social maturity.

2) *improve the social structure of the group.* The sociogram presents the group's pattern of interpersonal relations and provides an objective basis for identifying and improving group members' interpersonal relations.

3) *organize groups.* Groups can be arranged or rearranged on the basis of sociometric results. The social structure of the group and the social adjustment of the individual can be improved. Sociometric grouping can increase working effectiveness and promote therapeutic values.

4) *resolve special school problems.* Sociometric measurement contributes to the study of many school problems. They can be simply constructed and briefly administered. The results serve specific purposes and considerable research on their application already exists (17:12-20).

Gronlund also discusses certain limitations and cautions that must be observed before sociometry is enthusiastically applied in the schools:

1) *The kind of information provided is limited.* The sociometric test measures the extent of individual acceptance by others and

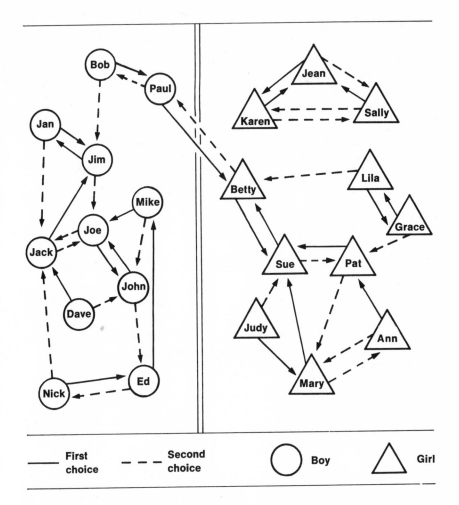

Figure 21. Sociogram Illustrating First and Second Choices of Friends

shows the group's internal structure. It does not indicate why people are chosen, nor the reason for the choice, nor how the social structure may be improved. The results reveal status and structure with regard to a specific test and specific group.

2) *The users of the sociometric test must be cautious both in its construction and administration.* The criteria of choice must be carefully selected, and the interpretations of results are limited by the directions and administration procedures followed.

3) Common misinterpretations can occur when sociometric results are interpreted and applied. Frequently, the star is considered well adjusted and a leader. Being an isolate is equated with maladjustment, and the rejectee is characterized as having undesirable personal qualities (17).

He concludes that sociometric techniques do have value and can be helpful in assessing group climate. However the limitations in a person's knowledge
as to *how* to use the sociometric test rather than the technique itself can pose
real problems if it is to be used effectively in helping children and in improving
daily school living.

Child Participation Techniques

Other means which the counselor can use to understand the inner
world of the child are the child's oral and written expression. The interview is
the most widely used, systematic means of utilizing the resource of oral
language.

Gathering Information Through the Interview

While an interview with a child can have many uses, and some of these
may be therapeutic, the emphasis here is placed on the interview as a
technique for gathering information.

Arthur E. Traxler has provided the following suggestions for conducting
interviews so that information is obtained and pupil's "privileged communication" is protected (39:37-39).

1) The counselor should carefully plan for each interview and
have definite questions in mind.

2) Rapport should be established early in the interview, and the
counselor should strive to maintain an informal and cordial
setting.

3) Questioning should not take the form of an inquisition but
should seem to arise naturally as in the course of a pleasant
conversation.

4) Following the interview, the counselor should write a summary of the information he has obtained.

5) Ethical standards require that information given in confidence
be considered "privileged communication."

Interviewing children and at the same time respecting the points Traxler
describes calls for skill and diplomacy on the part of the counselor. Yet the
results can be very rewarding and the counselor's insights into children's concerns and insecurities can be greatly increased if he is able to encourage them
to talk freely about what they feel is important.

In interviews with children of elementary school age, one of the authors asked children what five questions they would like to have answered if no one would 1) know who asked the questions, 2) laugh at the questions, or 3) think the questions stupid or "dumb." The following questions asked by children of different ages illustrates the wide range of problems that children encounter and feel are important. Reflected in these questions is evidence in another form of the fantasy so many adults hold of childhood—that it is a happy time, one of few or no problems, and that children do not see, hear, or comprehend many things in their environment.

Girl, Age Six

1) Why when I come home from school is my mother always so grumpy?

2) I get the feeling I'm not in the world, how did I get in it? My mother makes me wonder, why am I in the world?

3) I wonder about music, how they invented such a thing, such a great noise and pretty sound?

4) I can't understand what the word *brace* means in a song. I know about braces for teeth. One of my friends said it meant they got married.

5) Why do I always laugh even when my mother slaps me and my father hits me with a strap?

Girl, Age Seven

1) How does a baby come out of the mother?

2) How long will I have to wait until I get married?

3) God made us, but who made God?

4) I wonder whether I'll quit after high school or go on to college? The teacher gives such hard work.

5) I wonder why the kid next door is so mean to me?

Boy, Age Eight

1) How much does a Cadillac cost?

2) Why are parents so mean sometimes?

3) Why are we so bad all the time or most?

4) Why can't I go to sleep at night?

5) A boy in our class got hurt bad but when he came back to school, he looked the same as ever. How could he look the same?

Boy, Age Nine

1) Why did my mother get killed?

2) Why do I have to stay at other people's houses. I know I can't stay with my father because he works.

3) I wonder about my brother. When can I see him? When can I play with him?

4) I worried about speaking to Americans when I first came here. I know nothing. I wondered if they would laugh?

5) Why did the Russians have to come in? Every time they come, they start a war.

Girl, Age Ten

1) How much allowance do you think a girl my age should get?

2) I like to read about school subjects, fiction, and non-fiction. Do you think I should read as much as I can?

3) Do you think a typewriter would help me in my studies?

4) I don't have many friends. Could you give me a good system of making friends?

5) I have one sister who sometimes makes me angry. Could you help me figure out a good way to hold my temper?

Girl, Age Eleven

1) I wonder if boys really hate girls like they say?

2) Why don't some people want very old people to live with them?

3) What is life from when you're born until you die?

4) How come some people are pretty?

5) What would cause you to bite your finger nails?

Boy, Age Twelve

1) How come people get bad habits and can't stop them?

2) Why do my parents have to die?

3) Why do people sell whiskey when the policemen don't want reckless driving?

4) Why are some people dumb and some smart?

5) How can you keep out of trouble?

Boy, Age Thirteen

1) Should girls and boys our age date? Why or why not and how and when?

2) How do we think? What makes our brain function?

3) What makes people think as they do? Why do they become prejudiced or self-conscious or feel inferior or superior?

4) How does one influence people well or poorly? How are opinions formed? What makes people popular?

5) How do we know our ideas and ideals are right?

The Personal Questionnaire

The questionnaire, as the term is used here, is an instrument designed to collect specific kinds of personal information from children that is also self-revelatory. Questionnaire techniques may be employed to: 1) secure initial information for subsequent transfer to a child's cumulative record folder; 2) to collect general supplementary information for insertion in a personal record folder; or 3) to collect information for a specific purpose. Information of the last kind might be concerned with a list or description of school activities in which a child is interested or in which he is participating; it might also include background information about where he has lived or traveled.

This is an instrument which is economical to use but which can nonetheless furnish useful information to an astute counselor or teacher. In the design of questionnaires for elementary school age children, allowance should be made for the differences between and within a group of children with special regard being given to the level of their reading and other language skills. Questions should, as a general rule, be stated so as to obtain answers which are both brief and factual. Also it is well to avoid prying queries which are unethical to ask and/or which a child may not want to answer honestly if at all. Under some circumstances, it may be desirable to have unsigned responses based on a checklist. Both the questions and the instrument itself should be as short as possible.

The following is an example of a questionnaire used to solicit information about children's interests and how they saw themselves. Figure 22 shows the responses made by a child whom we will call Joey when he was in grade 3.

The Autobiography

As the title implies, the autobiography is a summary of certain phases of a child's life story as he views his past and present experiences. As a guidance technique, it offers the elementary school teacher and counselor an opportunity to understand more clearly the child's insights and self-concepts; his motivations and personal relationships. It may also contribute to improved self-understanding on the part of the young writer.

In the elementary school, the autobiography often may be most effectively employed in the middle school years although there may be some notable exceptions at the primary level. Actually a child's ability and willingness to express himself are the prime prerequisites. Also his power to recall and to understand the influences and events in his life and to organize them for meaningful reporting are other limiting factors to be considered.

One of the valuable qualities of the autobiography when used in the elementary school is its flexibility. It can touch on many points which a teacher might otherwise miss. Also there is the interest, even enthusiasm,

Personality and Interest Inventory, Elementary Form

By Gertrude Hildreth

NAME......*JOEY*.. Age ...*9*... Grade ..*3*.... Date ..*MAY 22*...

Things I Like to Do
Best in School

Drawing and painting
(Reading)
Going to assembly
Arithmetic
(Gymnasium)
(Recreation)
(Writing stories)
Spelling lessons
Writing lessons
Acting in plays
Cooking
Free work period
Building things
(Science)
Library
Shop
Music
Recess
Modeling
Studying
(Talking about things)
Making plans
Sewing
Geography
(History)

Books I Like

Name of book   Why I like it

LANDMARKS   THEY'RE INTERESTING
SIGNATURES   BOOKS

Name of book   Why I like it

CHILDHOOD OF YOUNG AMERICANS
THEY'RE INTERESTING BOOKS

Magazines I Like

Name of magazine   Why I like it

NATIONAL   GEOGRAPHIC

Boys and Girls I Like

Name of boy or girl   Why I like the boy or girl

Name of boy or girl   Why I like the boy or girl

ANDY K.
LEX V.   ANDREA V.

What I Like to Do on Saturday or During Vacation

Study	Sew	Take care of pets
(Play outdoors)	Take care of children	Work in garden
Go camping	Play music	Work to earn money
Listen to the radio	Paint or draw	Go to dancing lessons
(Ride a bicycle)	Write stories	(Work with electricity)
(Swim)	Build things	Cook
Skate	(Ride horseback)	Practice music lessons
(Climb trees)	Ride in an atuomobile	Help mother
(Work on stamp album)	(Do science experiments)	(Go hiking)
Visit museums	Make scrap-books	Play with dolls
Go to movies	Play games inside	
Go to concerts	(Play games outside)	

Figure 22. Elementary Form of the Hildreth Personality
and Interest Inventory

Games I Like

Tag
(Baseball)
Tennis
(Basketball)
Checkers
Parcheesi
Marbles
Hopscotch
(Authors)
(Hockey)
(Football)
Jacks and ball

Rook
Flinch
Pirates
Cops and robbers
Lotto
Horseshoe
Dominoes
(Chess)
Backgammon
Bridge
Anagrams
(Ping-pong)

Others....................................

....

When I Grow Up I Plan To Be

DOCTOR   LAWYER   ACTOR....................

....

People at Home I Like

Name   Why I like them

TIMMY LEWIS   JEANY LEWIS
LEX GLEN   CHUCK   LESSIE ANDY
MOTHER FATHER   BERNARD JIMMY
Name   Why I like them

ANDY   DONALD....................

....

Things That Tell About Me

Tired most of the time
Afraid of many things
(Like my teachers)
Usually a little late
(Like to obey the rules)
Don't like what we have to eat at home
(Like to save my money)
(Finish a job if I once begin it)
Never take things without asking
Like to go to parties
Don't like to go to school
(Like to get up early)
Often have bad dreams
Read many story books
Like to set fire to things
Do what my mother asks me to
(Tell them I did it if I break something)
Like to buy things for other people
Hit back if a child hits me accidentally
Would like to go away from home for a long time
Take things and tell people afterwards
(Try to help other people)
Think the rules in school are silly
Am the leader in my class
(Clean up my things after working)
Usually stay up late
Hungry most of the time
Like to go with a gang
(Sleep well at night)

Have many headaches
Run away if I break something
Hate to go to parties
Get good marks in school
(Have trouble in some school subjects)
Hide if I break something
(Often absent because of sickness)
Eat almost everything
Hide during a thunderstorm
Go to the movies often
Am smarter than most children
Like to be quiet most of the time
Would rather be alone
(Like to be with my mother most of all)
Fight back if I don't like anyone
Afraid of dogs
(Usually go to bed early)
Help my brothers and sisters
Like to stay at home
Obey the rules
(Don't often say cross things)
(Try to be on time)
(Am polite to older people)
Have many friends
Am usually the leader
Am afraid of my father
Get tired easily if I work very long
Cry about something nearly every day
Often fight with other children

Tell anything else about yourself here..

....

....

If I could have my wish for anything I like it would be *BE GOOD AT EVERYTHING*

....

PUBLISHED BY BUREAU OF PUBLICATIONS, TEACHERS COLLEGE, COLUMBIA UNIVERSITY
COPYRIGHT, 1936, BY LINCOLN SCHOOL, TEACHERS COLLEGE, COLUMBIA UNIVERSITY, REVISED, 1939
Printed in U.S.A.   10M: 6-55

Figure 22.   Elementary Form of the Hildreth Personality
and Interest Inventory (cont.)

with which most young children approach the opportunity to write their "life's history." Furthermore, to increase the usefulness of this type of revealing document, it is helpful in the elementary grades to suggest some structure for writing. Such an outline might be organized as follows:

1. My life before I entered school
   a) Where I lived
   b) Who I lived with
   c) Who I played with
   d) What I enjoyed doing
   e) My most interesting experiences
   f) Other things I would like to write about
2. My school years
   a) Where I've gone to school
   b) What I've liked most in my school
   c) What I've liked least in my school
   d) My school friends
   e) My studies
   f) Other things I would like to write about school
3. My future plans
   a) Going to school
   b) Kinds of work I think I'd like to do
   c) Other things I hope to do in the future

The sensitive teacher and counselor will be likely to agree that unstructured, stream-of-consciousness, or creative writing of an autobiographical nature can, for some boys and girls, be a more valuable source of information than the methodical statement outlined above. The following autobiography written by Joey, the same boy who replied to the *Personality and Interest Inventory*, illustrates this point. Places, names, and dates have been changed to protect the identity of the writer. Joey wrote this story about his life when he was in grade 5.

Meet Me

If you have seen a boy four feet six inches tall, who weighs about 68 pounds and who has brown hair, brown eyes, and is extremely handsome you will know rightaway that it is I, Joey Cook. This is my story.

On March 18, 19—, at 3:20 p.m. Joseph Harper Cook was born. I have a twin named Robert Olson Cook. He is ten minutes younger than I. Bobby weighed four and a half pounds. I weighed four pounds. Within twenty-nine days I weighed three pounds. Bobby weighed four pounds. At the end of the year I weighed twenty one pounds and Bobby weighed thirty pounds.

My first home was in Dayton, Ohio. It was there that Bobby and I crawled into our neighbor's yard and ate all of their flowers. The red tulips were the best. After that our father built a high wooden fence around our yard to keep us out of their garden.

Our next home was in Columbus, Ohio. One day Bobby and I decided to have some fun so we got into our bathroom and drank a whole bottle of some stuff that was supposed to make the room smell better. Our mother found us and didn't know what to do. She couldn't call Daddy because he was in the clinic. Finally she got him. She thought the deodorant was poisonous. Our father assured her it wasn't. She tried to call up and find out but she couldn't because it was Sunday. Our father told her to try and make us throw up. She carried me over to the toilet and put her finger in my mouth, hoping I would throw up. I didn't like this so I bit her. "Ow," she screamed, and nearly dropped me in the toilet. She decided not to make Bobby throw up because he was bigger than I. Our mother still carries the scar on her finger. In case you are wondering, we lived.

Another adventure I had was when we were at the zoo. I was eating a Dixie cup when I got generous and decided to give some to the rabbits. So I got some ice cream and put it on my spoon and put my hand in the rabbit's cage. I said, "Here wabbits, have some." The rabbit missed my ice cream, and he bit me on the finger. I dropped the ice cream and pulled my hand from the cage. The rabbit's teeth had gone right to the bone. I started to scream.

My parents rushed me to the hospital. By this time I had stopped screaming and was perfectly calm. I heard something about a rabies shot. At the time I didn't know what they were talking about. Anyway I didn't care to know because I was very happy. The doctor gave me a shot and we went home. I only regret that I never did feed that rabbit.

Another time Bobby and I got thirsty. We found a bottle of red wine. We drank the whole bottle and got very drunk. Our parents found us rolling over the floor. They tried to catch us but we rolled underneath a bed. Our Mother got on her hands and knees on one side of the bed and scared us over to the other side where our father caught us. After this we didn't get drunk again.

Our next home was in Chicago, Illinois. It was here that our parents were invited to Blue Island which is on an island in Canada that our grandparents and our aunts and uncles bought for a vacation place. Since it was an island and I was still a baby you would think it would be hard to get into trouble, but leave it to me to get into trouble. First Bobby and I raided our grandmother's room. There she had a drawer full of candy which she used to give us when we were good. We ate all of the candy, and then we got started squirting perfume all over the floor. We also got into a box of powder and spilled it all over the floor. You can imagine how it looked. There were broken pieces of candy all over the floor, with perfume stinking up the place and powder on top of everything in sight. But to top it off, two little babies with candy smeared all over their faces then began to jump on the bed.

Our grandmother came in and caught us as we were tearing the sheets off the bed. We were severely punished but that didn't stop me.

The next day I got lost in the boat house and drove everyone mad trying to find me. They thought I had drowned. When they did find me they decided never to let small children come to Blue Island again.

Our next home in Chicago was only a few blocks away from our former one. Very shortly after we moved there we had our third birthday. Also we bought a female collie. We named her Suzy. We bought her when she was three months old. She was the runt of the litter. Now the owner of the kennel from which we bought her wanted to buy her back and use her as a show dog.

When we were three years old we went to Camp Tapaho for a month, and it rained twenty-eight days. Our parents slept in a cabin and we slept in a tent. Our mother thought we would be scared sleeping alone at night in a tent so she came out to sleep with us. When she came into the tent the second night we asked her what she was doing. She replied that she was going to sleep with us again. We said, "Do you have to?" And from then on we slept alone.

This was our first camp experience, and it proved an unpleasant one because it rained all of the time; however, we returned to the same camp for four more years.

When I was four years old, I went to Nursery School. One day when I was leaving, I said very politely to one of the teachers, "Goodbye, you headache, you." From then on I never went to that school again.

Nothing particularly happened from then to when I was eight except I started Kindergarten when I was five years old. But at the end of the second grade, when I was eight years old, we went to Europe.

In Europe we went to England, France, Switzerland, Italy, and Greece. I liked Greece and Switzerland the best. We came home on the Queen Elizabeth which was one of the largest passenger ships in the world.

When I was nine I went on a ten day canoe trip with Bobby and my parents. At ten I went on another canoe trip. Suzy, our dog, went on both canoe trips. Suzy is still living today.

I am now ten years old, and I am in fifth grade. I am outstanding in all my subjects and in school because I have the best teacher in the school. I am interested in the Civil War, and I am well off physically and mentally. I am ambitious partly because I have the thrill of competition with my brother and sister. Also because I want to live up to my dreams.

I hope to be a doctor, an author, or an historian when I grow up. I am content with my life now and hope to be content always with what I have.

Creative writing can also prove interesting and revealing if it is done in a free environment where children are encouraged to express their thoughts. This story was one of a series of stories that Joey wrote during the year. These stories were to become part of a book that he hoped to have published later in the year.

The Saga of Eddy Rushmore

It was a hot sunny day. The sweat poured down my face. I stopped plowing the field and with the back of my hand, wiped my forehead and sighed. I wished I were a dashing red-haired man with blue eyes. I pictured myself with a large saber in my hand and mounted on a horse as black as a cooking kettle. That was the life for me. But alas, it's all a dream. I ain't never been much for looks. I'm five feet seven inches tall. I have a long broken nose, brown hair, and brown eyes. I'll someday run away and join the rebel army, I thought. I was just seventeen, old enough to be my own boss. I ain't going to take orders from that humpback foster mother of mine.

"Oh, Eddy," my foster mother's sharp voice interrupted my thoughts. "Oh, Eddy come get your dinner and don't forget to unharness the horses and rub them down."

"Yes, Mom, I'm coming." Horseshoes! Orders, orders, orders, all the time. I'll get even sometime with her.

"Eddy," cried my mother in an excited voice. "Come right now before I take a switch and learn you good."

"I'm coming." Blast this heat. I sure wish it would cool down. Plowing that field is hard work.

After I unhitched the horses and rubbed them down, I ran to the rickety old hut we lived in. The door was open and Martha, my foster mother, was waiting for me. Her brown curls were bobbing on her forehead. When I was eating my dinner which was mush and rabbit stew, I looked up. There my mother stood with such a sorry look on her face it brought a tear to my eye. I quickly brushed it away with my hand. When she saw I was looking at her, she hurriedly pretended she was working.

When I was through with my dinner, I quietly walked to a stream in the woods nearby. I looked at my reflection in the pond. I threw a small stone in the pond and watched a ripple in the water. A robin was singing a lovely tune on a branch over my head. It brought tears to my eyes when I remembered my real mother and how we used to play together when I was young.

My thoughts vanished when a metal knife whizzed over my head and stuck in a tree nearby. I couldn't move. I was stunned. Then I got to my feet and ran. I didn't know where, but my main thought was to move fast. With every step I took, it seemed I was getting nowhere. Behind every tree and bush I thought I saw a face peering at me. I was stumbling and falling constantly. My head was hot with fear. I kept looking back over my shoulder, then I would go forward and increase my speed.

My foot got caught under a root. I fell headlong to the ground. This time I couldn't get up. I lay there struggling to get my foot free. With every ounce of energy I had left, I pulled backward till my head rested on the ground. I lay there looking at the sky piteously. My leg was throbbing with pain. My head felt like a stream overflowing. I closed my eyes. It was bitter cold. I bit my lip to keep from screaming, but soon I fell unconscious.

When I woke my leg was the size of a horse's head. I wondered where I was and what had happened. Then I remembered. I looked at my leg. I was free. I started to get up but fell back. I howled like a dog would if it were stuck by a porcupine quill. My head was hot. The sun was beating down on me. I ripped my shirt off and threw it away. There was a stream a hundred feet from me. There was shade there, too. I had to get there or I would probably die.

I outstretched my arms and with my belly on the ground, I pulled myself forward. I wanted to stop. Only self preservation pushed me on. Ten feet to go, then five. I stopped. I couldn't go on. I was screaming at the top of my lungs. I was delirious with pain. I was panting hard. I urged myself on, four feet, three feet, two feet.

I stopped, gathered my energy and with all my might I frantically lunged for the water. This time I made it. I dunked my head in the water. Then let water drip from my hair. I splashed around like a two year old baby. I scooped up the water and threw it in the air. I drank and drank. Water had never tasted so good before. My leg felt better already.

I put my head in my arms and rested along the side of the creek.

As I lay there, I thought I heard some noises. I didn't think much of it. I assumed it was some birds in a tree. Soon I fell asleep. Again I was awakened by a noise. With my head still in my arms I listened. The noise got louder. I opened my eyes and lifted slowly. I couldn't see a thing. I turned my face around cautiously and there was a man.

The man must have been six feet tall. His face was coarse. He probably hadn't shaved in at least a month. My body started to quake when he walked towards me. I shut my eyes and then opened them. I wasn't dreaming. It was then I saw he was wearing a ragged, dusty gray uniform. He had tall infantry boots on his feet. He was a rebel. He walked with a limp.

He bent over me and in a voice as tender and soft as a mother's he asked, "What's the trouble lad?" He had a twinkle in his dark blue eyes. Somehow I knew I was safe. He saw my leg and without saying a word he bandaged it. I swallowed the lump in my throat. I tried in a calm voice like a man's to thank him. I couldn't. All I managed to utter was a meek, "Thanks."

I didn't know it then but this was the beginning of a life-long friendship.

At times Joey's poetry also reflected his interest in the War between the States. However, his most effectively written verses appeared to grow from his wide ranging interests and the experience inputs which came from his travels with his parents. The following poem about Greece is illustrative. The second poem dealing with water illustrates his skill with imagery.

Once Upon a Time

Now once upon a time
There were hills all green and the sky was clear
A place where no one knew fear
But that was once upon a time
Now the hills aren't green and the sky is gray
No one cares now whether it is night or day
Where once there was gaiety and peace
Temples now stand in ruins on hills in Greece.

The Water

Sometimes the water whistles as it rolls to and from the docks
Sometimes the water chants my name as it beats against the rocks
Sometimes the water's spray gets on every man and child
Sometimes the water is so furious I think it's wild
Sometimes the water is as gentle as a robin's song is clear
Sometimes the water is so dark and gloomy I shake with fear
But of all the ways I like to play
I like nothing better than to sit on the seashore all day.

Even a casual examination of Joey's *Personality and Interest Inventory,* his autobiography, his "Saga of Eddy Rushmore," and his poetry does a great deal to help the teacher form an opinion which, of course, should be verified through further observation and child study. Joey emerges as an unusually bright and lively child with excellent verbal skills, and his personality is revealed as a mixture of seriousness, humor, and mischief.

At the same time the seasoned teacher and counselor will recognize that children's self-expression, either oral or written, provide only a part of the understandings of children that are needed. When reading the "returns" on questionnaires, on written work, and from other child study devices, it is important to remember that the counselor-teacher focus is on *why* certain responses are made, not *what* the responses are. Also no interest inventory, school questionnaire, autobiographical statement, or creative expression is worth the child's time unless one has the commitment and the determination to do something to improve the school life and general well-being of the boys and girls for whom their work and society, too, have made the counselor and teacher responsible.

By now the reader should recognize that nontesting child study techniques are more subtle and in some ways likely to be even more revealing than conventional tests. It is by *combining* test data, anecdotal records, interviews, observation, out-of-school behavior data, and other sources of information into a case study that teachers and counselors learn how to select suitable therapeutic procedures on the basis of the signs and symptoms they identify and the underlying causes on which they are based.

Summary

A variety of tools and techniques are available for human development study in the elementary school. Observation techniques and observation reports such as anecdotal records, rating scales, and observation checklists can contribute much to the teacher's, counselor's, parent's, and child's understandings. Sociometry in the elementary school can offer opportunities for assessment of pupil's feelings as well as, on occasion, providing clues to other personal characteristics. The pupil autobiography provides a vehicle for the student to describe his life as he sees it, and the personal questionnaire provides an economical and efficient technique for collecting pupil data.

These techniques, when used electively, enable the elementary school counselor, teacher, and other staff members to construct a comprehensive and valid understanding of the child. The application of this understanding to curriculum development, overall development, and individual guidance is a basic component of the school's total effort to produce more effective, mature, human beings.

References

1. Allport, Gordon. "Crises in Normal Personality Development." *Teachers College Record* 66 (December, 1964): 235-241.

2. Ausubel, D. P. "A New Look at Classroom Discipline." *Mental Health and Achievement.* Edited by E. P. Torrance and R. D. Strom. New York: John Wiley and Sons, Inc., 1965.

3. _____. "Some Misconceptions Regarding Mental Health Functions and Practices in the School." *Psychology in the Schools* 2 (April, 1965): 99-105.

4. Baldwin, Alfred L. *Theories of Child Development.* New York: John Wiley and Sons, Inc., 1967.

5. Bandura, Albert and R. H. Walters. *Social Learning and Personality Development.* New York: Holt, Rinehart and Winston, Inc., 1963.

6. Berkowitz, Leonard. *The Development of Motives and Values in the Child.* New York: Basic Books, 1964.

7. Blumer, Herbert. "Social Attitudes and Nonsymbolic Interaction." *Journal of Educational Sociology* 9 (May, 1936): 515-523.

8. Bronfenbrenner, Urie. "The Changing American Child—A Speculative Analysis." *Journal of Social Issues* 17 (1961): 6-18.

9. Bronson, Gordon. "Critical Periods in Human Development." *British Journal of Medical Psychology* 35 (1962): 127-133.

10. Caldwell, Bettye, "What Is the Optimal Learning Environment for the Young Child?" *American Journal of Orthopsychiatry* 37 (January, 1967): 8-21.

11. Dreyer, Albert S. and Dorothy Haupt. "Self-Evaluation in Young Children." *Journal of Genetic Psychology* 108 (June, 1966): 185-197.

12. Efron, David. *Gesture and Environment.* New York: King's Crown Press, 1941.

13. Frank, George H. "The Role of the Family in the Development of Psychopathology." *Psychological Bulletin* 64 (September, 1965): 191-205.

14. Galloway, Charles. "Nonverbal Communication." *The Instructor* 77 (April, 1968): 37-42.

15. ____. "Teacher Nonverbal Communication." *Educational Leadership* 24 (1966): 55-63.

16. Gordon, Ira J. *Studying the Child in the School.* New York: John Wiley and Sons, Inc., 1966.

17. Gronlund, Norman E. *Sociometry in the Classroom.* New York: Harper and Bros. 1959.

18. Hall, Edward T. *The Silent Language.* New York: Fawcett World Library: Premier Books, 1969.

19. Haring, N. G. and R. W. Ridgeway. "Early Identification of Children With Learning Disabilities." *Exceptional Children* 33 (February, 1967): 387-395.

20. Havighurst, Robert, "Conditions Productive of Superior Children" *Teachers College Record* 62 (April, 1961): 524-531.

21. Hechinger, F. M. (ed.). *Pre-School Education.* New York: Doubleday and Co., 1966.

22. Hess, R. D. (ed.). *Early Education: Current Theory, Research, and Practice.* Chicago: Aldine, 1967.

23. Hunt, J. McVicker. "The Psychological Basis for Using Pre-School Enrichment as an Antidote for Cultural Deprivation." *Merrill-Palmer Quarterly of Behavior and Development* 10 (1964): 209-248.

24. Lee, Irving J. *Language Habits in Human Affairs.* New York: Harper and Bros., 1941.

25. Marshall, Hermine H. "The Effect of Punishment of Children: A Review of the Literature and a Suggested Hypotheses." *Journal of Genetic Psychology* 106 (March, 1965): 23-33.

26. Moreno, J. L. *Who Shall Survive?* Revised edition. New York: Beacon House, 1953.

27. Olsen, James, "Challenge of the Poor to the Schools." *Phi Delta Kappan* 47 (October, 1965): 79-84.

28. Orme, Michael E. J. *The Effects of Self-Feedback and Reinforcement on the Acquisition of a Teaching Skill.* Revision of a paper prepared by F. J.

McDonald, M. E. J. Orme, and D. W. Allen. Presented at the Convention of the American Educational Research Association, Chicago, Ill. (Mimeographed).

29. Pavenstedt, E. "A Comparison of the Child-rearing Environment of Upper-lower and Very Lower-lower Class Families." *American Journal of Orthopsychiatry* 35 (January, 1965): 89-98.

30. Redl, Fritz. "What Should We Know About a Child?" Chicago: Commission on Teacher Education, American Council on Education, 1940. (Mimeographed)

31. Riessman, Frank. "Low Income Culture, the Adolescent, and the School." *Bulletin of the National Association of Secondary School Principals* 49 (April, 1965): 45-49.

32. ____. "The Lessons of Poverty." *American Education* 1 (February, 1965): 21-23.

33. ____. "The Strategy of Style." *Teachers College Record* 65 (March, 1964): 484-489.

34. Ruesch, Jurgan. "Nonverbal Language and Therapy." *Psychiatry* 18 (1955): 323-330.

35. Seagie, M. V. "Children's Play as an Indicator of Cross-cultural and Inter-cultural Differences." *Journal of Educational Sociology* 35 (February, 1962): 278-283.

36. Siegel, Lawrence (ed.). *Instruction: Some Contemporary Issues.* San Francisco: Chandler, 1967.

37. Strom, R. D. "Family Influence on School Failure." *The Education Digest* 30 (February, 1965): 8-10.

38. Thelen, Herbert. "Some Classroom Quiddities for People-Oriented Teachers." *Journal of Applied Behavioral Science* 1 (July, August, September, 1965): 270-285.

39. Traxler, Arthur E. and Robert D. North. *Techniques of Guidance.* New York: Harper and Bros., 1966.

40. White, V. *Studying the Individual Child.* New York: Harper and Row, Publishers, 1958.

11

The Ecology of Childhood: Orientation Through Guidance

Ecology is a term which began to be used in education during the 1960's (1).* As a glance at the dictionary quickly will reveal, the term originally was associated with sociology and biology.† As used here, however, the ecology of childhood refers expressly to *the transactional relationships that exist between the young learner and certain social and cultural aspects of his environment.* The importance of the concept of ecology to the counselor was pointed out by David G. Danskin et al. who wrote that ". . . the time is ripe for us in guidance to consider the network of interactions between the [the child] and his environments." (5:131) At the outset of a discussion on the ecology of childhood, it is desirable to clarify the counselor's relationship to this dimension of his work.

As he performs his leadership role in the elementary school, the counselor is confronted by two ecologically significant questions on which he needs to be well informed. Without a clear understanding of possible answers to the queries, he is handicapped in any efforts to guide human development. The closely related questions are: 1) "Is the child predominantly the product of his heredity?" 2) "Is the child largely a product of transactions with his environment?"

*R. B. Barker used *ecology* in an educational context in 1960 when he defined the term as pertaining to entity-and-environment relationships (1).

†To the biologist, ecology is the branch of his field which concentrates on the relationships existing between living organisms and their environment. The sociologist thinks of ecology as the study of the influence of material resources on the distribution of human beings and their social and cultural patterns.

289

During most of the present century, these relevant questions have been the source of heated controversy, particularly among professional educators, sociologists, psychologists, and anthropologists. By the 1970's it has become evident that the relationships between child and environment continue to be a matter of major concern to the elementary school counselor.

Sixty or seventy years ago, much learned opinion held that the child was the captive of his chromosomes. Presumably he was predestined (with a few exceptions that baffled scholars) to be a peasant or an aristocrat because of his genetic history—his "blood lines." Indeed, "Blood will tell" is an old saying which implies that there were "superior" and "inferior" families, and that it was a fluke of nature when someone of peasant European background managed to display the talent or competence of the upper classes.

In the early decades of the century, the concept of inherent genetic differences among races also was widely accepted. Some "racial" groups, even within the narrow geographical limits of Western Europe, were thought to be "more honest," "more stolid," "more reliable," "more excitable," "more talented," and so on, due to their membership in Alpine, Mediterranean, or other presumed subdivisions of Europe's peoples. By 1928 the matter of heredity versus environment had become known among educators as the nature-nurture controversy. The conflicting opinions of the time were preserved in an influential and widely read two-volume *Yearbook* of the National Society for the Study of Education for which Lewis M. Terman was chairman (25).

Research and speculation since the 1930's have established the point that there are interrelationships between heredity and environment. *Both* have come to be recognized as influential elements. However, the environmental input which children experience *in their early years* has begun to be recognized as being of particular importance. Studies which have influenced thinking range from the 1930 Skeels and Skodak data regarding the influence of environment on intelligence to Krech's more recent research and hypotheses on the "creation" of intelligence through environmental mediation.

On the threshold of the 1970's the basic issue of the relative importance of nature and nurture in education remains a lively one. In fact, one of the more heated educational controversies of the late 1960's—one that carried over into the 1970's—centered around the Jensen Report (15) and the various counter-arguments subsequently advanced to disprove Arthur R. Jensen's contention that membership in the racial groups he studied had a bearing on intelligence.*

Environment, Heredity, and Intelligence. Compiled from the *Harvard Educational Review*, Cambridge, Mass.: *Harvard Educational Review*, June, 1969. The special issue contains Jensen's original article, rebuttals by Kagan, Hunt, Crow, Bereiter, Elkind, Cronbach, and Brazziel, and a reply by Jensen (7).

The preceding paragraphs may seem at first glance to be unrelated to guidance in the elementary school. *Actually, it is one of the major tasks of the counselor to provide for teachers, parents, and children certain kinds of information-orientation service which helps all three groups to understand each child's need to understand the nature of the world about him and to develop wholesome self-concepts as to his role in this immediate milieu* (17,18).

Orientation Through Guidance

Orientation services, as the term is used here, are unique to *elementary* education, not a downward extension of high school counseling. They are related to secondary school information services only in the sense that orientation of the child helps to lay a foundation for decisions in youth that may later involve appropriate occupational-educational choices and related personal-social adjustments.

The Meaning of Orientation Services

Orientation services, as is so often the case in guidance, are built upon the manifestations and evidence that the child himself provides. These give the counselor behavioral clues which enable him to help the teacher and himself—through their own deepening insights—to assist a child (and his parents!) better to understand and cope with 1) his school milieu, 2) the wider milieu of which he is a part, and 3) his role, opportunities, and responsibilities therein.

Orientation, then, is not related to a series of periodic, sequential, or perfunctory introductions to some aspects of school life as when, for example, a child enters the middle school. *It is a PROCESS rather than an EVENT.*

Orientation Differs from Assessment

It is important to make clear how orientation differs from the assessment of human development as presented in Chapters 9 and 10. Both assessment and orientation services share the qualities 1) of continuity, 2) of a focus on individual human development, and 3) of helping to create self-awareness, interactive skills, and self-confidence. The difference resides in the fact that orientation services involve action which is based on and built on the data which assessment activities are intended to provide.

The two aspects of elementary guidance under discussion here—orientation and assessment—are supportive and complementary like the two sides of a coin. Assessment provides data; orientation services draw on the data and provide feedback which, in turn, may help lend direction to the ongoing assessment activity.

Exploring the Ecology of Childhood

Since orientation services are concerned with the transactional relationships between the child and his total environment, the counselor's study of educational ecology can pay dividends in a number of ways:

1) It methodically provides insights into the in-school and out-of-school worlds of the child; worlds in which his overt expressions of behavior may differ greatly between school and home or street.

2) It helps the counselor become acquainted with problems of environmental deprivation or contamination from which some children need protection. Mental and physical health, emotional well-being, language development and intellectual development are among the qualities which can be damaged or stunted by faulty ecological relationships between child and milieu.

3) It may provide bases for or give direction to other phases of the elementary guidance program: individual and group counseling, assessment, placement, referral practices, and in-service education of the faculty to name a few.

The challenges of educational ecology, one may infer, include helping a child, over a period of time, to build defenses against the contamination caused by repeated socioculturally damaging exposures, to learn how to respect and to understand his own subculture and the subcultures of others, to improve his interpersonal and intercultural relations, and to learn how to exploit his environment for *worthy* purposes of personal-social improvement (18). It is upon such accomplishments as these that desirable orientation in childhood is based. The counselor studies childhood ecology in order to perform the task of orientation effectively.

Below is an overview of some of the elements which the counselor faces when he seeks to improve a child's interaction with the environment.

Some Dimensions of Ecology in Guidance

Helping a child begin to understand his relationships with the persons about him, and also learn how to cope with non-human things (e.g., traffic, dangerous animals, or contaminated food), should begin at the earliest possible age. Among items for the counselor and teacher to keep in mind are 1) the development of values, 2) the improvement of skills in group processes, 3) the acquisition of cross-cultural understandings with respect to U.S. subcultures as well as 4) the cultures of persons overseas, and 5) the importance of occupational and vocational perspectives. Each of these five items has relevance in the child-and-environment transactions and is elaborated below.

Developing Worthy Values

The child acquires his values from the nature and quality of the input he receives from his milieu. Each day he is imprinted more and more deeply with ideas such as that certain things are to be cherished, others ignored or reviled, and that there are inconsistencies as well as hypocrisies mirrored in the behaving of those about him (14). The good school program endeavors to protect children from undesirable behavioral expressions of values and to build up concepts which serve such general welfare concepts as sharing, taking turns, or showing mutual respect for one's fellow man regardless of the cultural differences that determine human identity.

Encouraging Skill in Group Processes

Ecological relationships are both obvious and vital targets for the attention of the counselor in situations involving *group processes* since such processes are major elements in the child's transactions with his human environment. Here the child needs to become oriented *at his level* with respect to the interaction of language and culture.* He also needs to begin to sense how language influences people—how words can heal or hurt, how they can stir or calm the emotions, how they can create in a human being either the glow of praise or the despair of rejection (21). Both counselor and teacher need clearly to understand, therefore, that there is a realm in which the language arts and the art of counseling overlap and provide mutual support and strength.

Skill in group processes is both taught and "caught" from the examples the child encounters in the school and elsewhere. Deliberate orientation in the ways of human interaction should characterize elementary guidance practices from the very beginning. Interpersonal and intergroup transactions, in other words, *should be designed to teach a way of thinking and of relating to others intelligently.*

---

*In the terminology of the linguist, the interaction of language and culture is the field of *metalinguistics. Sociolinguistics* refers to the influence of language *in* society and its relation *to* society.

Understanding and Respecting
Subcultures Other Than One's Own

In a methodical way, counseling and guidance ought to seek to orient the child to the fact that *he is a member of a subculture* and that all other members of society also belong to subgroups. One subgroup is not "better" but different from others; there are greater differences *within* rather than *between* culture groups; all are worthy of the respect of Americans.*

The initial steps one makes toward understanding, working with, and showing respect for others in foreign lands also are taken in early and middle childhood! The feeling of positive regard and acceptance of one another that boys and girls acquire in a healthy climate is the real basis for their subsequent attitudes towards persons of other nations and races. *International* understanding grows in the wholesome soil of a nation that comprehends and builds bonds of human fellowship and outreaching friendliness on an *international* basis. As counselors and teachers orient children to effective ways in which to live together with conspicuous mutual regard in the classroom, they are also building for world peace among the earth's millions.

The Teacher's
Occupational and Vocational Perspectives

Good occupational and vocational perspectives serve as our fifth example of orientation based on ecological or child-milieu relationships. Perhaps the greatest single contribution that the elementary school can make in the occupational-vocational realm is to prepare young learners for the realities of life.

A century and a half ago the United States was a predominantly agricultural nation. Society needed more professional workers, more managers and executives and more persons who would become owners or proprietors. A powerful 19th century image of the "correct" occupational choices of the bright or clever child was the result. The able student, it was assumed, would "rise above his station in life" by becoming a professional man (doctor, teacher, clergyman, engineer, etc.), an official in business or government, or "work his way up the ladder" by opening a small business or by becoming associated with a corporation or an industry. For generations U.S. teachers in the upper grades were steeped in the belief that these were *the* respectable ways of earning a living, and that any promising young person would direct his plans accordingly.†

*The counselor himself must confront the problems of his own cultural biases. Cf. C. Gilbert Wrenn, "The Culturally Encapsulated Counselor," *Harvard Educational Review,* 32 (Fall, 1962): 444-449 (27).

†Prior to 1900 very few Americans had more than an eighth grade education. (In 1892 only 25,000 young people were enrolled in high school!) As a result, informal

Perhaps in a younger America the managerial-professional-owner type of occupational goal made sense. Today this is no longer true. But many elementary teachers continue to suggest to children, directly or by their attitudes, that entry into a few professions and white-collar jobs is the only way to become a success. They consequently urge pre-adolescents whom they consider their better students to aim for these positions.

The results of an elementary teacher's outdated 19th century attitudes regarding the world of work can be harmful in the 1970's for at least two reasons. *First*, undesirable self-concepts are created in children who are not singled out as "good college material." *Second*, the changing configuration of 20th century employment has long since expanded occupational opportunities far beyond the limited professional and managerial goals of the earlier part of the century.

What is needed to orient children to the contemporary world of occupations is emphasis on the dignity and importance of all kinds of labor, whether with hand or mind. Since more than half of the population is now enrolling in some form of post-secondary education sometime after receiving a diploma, it is also absurd for teachers to continue to parrot unrealistic advice about entering one of a few professions or management positions. We must anticipate an era, already coming into existence, in which one is respected for what he *is* rather than for what he *does*. This understanding is an important orientation task that begins when children first enter school.

The Elementary School
and the Child's Occupational Future

The point has already been made that there is no counterpart to traditional secondary school information services when one deals with guidance in elementary schools. Nevertheless, the elementary guidance program, many aspects of the curriculum, and the "climate" or "tone" of the primary and middle school have a direct relationship with attitudes and values children acquire toward occupations and what it means to earn a living.

Role of the Elementary School

Few if any educators would contest the point that the elementary years, including pre-kindergarten experiences sponsored by the schools, are of great importance. They are formative years, years of inquiry and curiosity, of exploration, and (at the beginning) quite free of the prejudices which adults eventually pass along to their offspring. As one result, the elementary school

occupational advice was generally given by middle grade teachers. Even as late as 1939-40, only half of the U.S. adult population had gone beyond eighth grade in school.

is an important place for the child to have experiences that subsequently will enable him to make suitable educational and occupational decisions as he moves into adolescence.

Counselors of young children will rarely if ever discuss how girls or boys will plan their future education or specifically prepare to earn a living.* What the counselor does do is strive to strengthen the personal qualities of the learner so as to increase the likelihood of his success in any line of endeavor to which choice or chance may lead him. Children in the U.S. today have many exciting possible futures. How well they succeed will be greatly influenced by the kinds of persons they are helped to become as a result of their school experiences.

Guidelines for
Educational-Occupational Decision Making

What are some of the principles that the counselor should respect as he works to help children understand personal-ecological relationships and their bearing on personality development? A half-dozen suggest themselves:

First, the school environment should not create undesirable biases with respect to possible educational or occupational futures. As Donald E. Super notes, the elementary school years can be very important since children have not as yet attached financial and social status to unskilled or semi-skilled jobs. They are more concerned with the intrinsic nature of work and with the social contribution of the worker, and they are able to take in facts to serve as a basis for an accepting attitude toward unskilled and semi-skilled work as they grow older (23).

Second, positive responses toward the school and toward the worth of education should be created and cultivated. Far too frequently the aspirations of the child are blighted by the absence of sufficient counseling or no counseling at all. Again, a stultifying school environment can make even the most eager youngster a cynic at seventeen. Note the deterioration of educational morale as well as the changing signatures in the following excerpts from themes written on the topic, "Going to School," by the same girl when eight, fourteen, and seventeen years of age (9:165-166).

Age 8 excerpt:

I like my school very much and my teacher is Miss Berry who is the best teacher in the whole school. I can hardly wait to get to

---

*Older preadolescents and young adolescents do, however, begin to have vocational preferences. Cf. Stanley Krippner, "Junior High School Students' Vocational Preferences and Their Parents' Occupational Levels," *Personnel and Guidance Journal*, 41 (March, 1963): 590-595 (16).

school in the mornings, especially when it's my turn to call the roll or read the morning bulletin. I like all my school work, although I'm not too good in arithmetic I still like it. I like to read stories in history best. I think I could go to school forever.

Mary

Age 14 excerpt:

I have been going to school a long time but I am not sorry as we need an education to get along in the world today. Our Junior High is O.K. and being a 9th grader means something too. I have some nice girl friends that I take most of my classes with and that makes it nice. Most of the teachers are O.K. Most of my classes are O.K. too but none of them really send me. I think we should have a class in dancing, then we could learn something really worthwhile.

Mary Eleanor Jones

Age 17 excerpt:

They keep telling us to act like seniors but they treat us like infants. I think it's the teachers in this school that need to grow up. The only course I really enjoy is journalism and that is giving me some practical experience working on the school paper. I suppose that's what I'll take in college since my parents seem dead set on my going. Me, I've had enough school to last me two lifetimes—and when will they stop sticking us in these history and English classes! Maybe they don't get tired of teaching it over and over again but we students sure get tired of taking the same old thing all the time.

Jo- Jo Jones

Third, children need to develop self-understanding so that they neither over- nor underestimate what they can accomplish at a given time. The best foundation for insightful and prudent decisions in adolescence or later adult life is childhood experiences in making value-choices and in subsequent decision making—both individually and in groups. The child should not be told what decisions are best, but should have controlled opportunities even in early childhood to make choices *and to learn to interpret the consequences of his decisions.*

Fourth, it is appropriate for school experiences to help children learn to work together harmoniously by considering the general welfare of the group when classroom projects are planned and carried out. Industrial research and educational research support the view that most problems in offices, schools, factories, and so on do not come about because people are incompetent workers but because they are unskilled in human relations! Children who *live* together effectively in the present also are learning to *work* together comfortably in later life.

Fifth, as they progress along their individual growth continuums boys and girls need opportunities to begin to sense how education and vocation are related to one another and to the various ways one lives as an adult. As a rule, this is learned by inference rather than through didactic approaches. Also, it is often the teacher rather than a counselor who helps to see that this particular principle is observed.

Sixth, it is necessary that a child begin to understand where he stands on his personal educational continuum. While invidious comparisons should be avoided with care, it is equally unsound to permit a child of 12 or 14 to live in a dream world built around unrealistic future educational aspirations.

The six guidelines should be considered in the context of previous chapters in the book. The sixth guideline, for instance, is meaningful to the reader only if he already has read Chapters 5 and 6 dealing with the concept of an unbroken continuum of progress toward social and educational maturity.

Theories Pertaining to Educational-Occupational Choices

Over the years a number of theories have developed with respect to how sound educational-occupational thinking and decision-making best can be handled by the elementary counselor (19). At the outset it must be recognized that in the primary school years almost nothing should be done by teacher or counselor to guide or predispose a child toward certain educational or occupational goals. Instead, as implied earlier, a wholesome attitude toward others and a respect for the value and dignity of all forms of labor should be cultivated.

Beginning in the middle school years, at first only rarely, then with increasing frequency, the elementary school staff (including the counselor) is confronted by questions and occasional problems related to future educational plans and even possible vocations. Sometimes these matters come up because of boys' and girls' interests during the years of middle childhood. Again, educational or occupational discussions may be opened up by uneasy or eager parents who begin to push their child toward certain jobs or certain types of postsecondary education while he is in the 10- to 14-year-old range.

With rare exceptions the counselor should follow two policies: 1) try to postpone any premature commitments by children or their parents to a particular college program or job, and 2) encourage them to assess realistically the capabilities and personal qualities they have or should seek to develop for *all* types of effective participation in later life.

With these points made, attention is directed toward useful background information for the counselor. This is presented in the form of an evaluation of four types of theories bearing on educational-occupational choices. This discussion should help to clarify when—if at all—the counselor should become involved in such choices.

Ginsberg and others came to the conclusion that choices as to educational-occupational futures were part of a process; one which involved stages or steps that children and young adolescents go through. These included *fantasy*, *tentative*, and *realistic* choices. For most of the elementary years, children are in the fantasy-tentative stages. Ginzberg et al. also wrote that:*

> First, occupational choice is a process which takes place over a minimum of six or seven years, and more typically over ten years or more. Secondly, since each decision during adolescence is related to one's experience up to that point, and in turn has an influence on the future, the process of decision-making is basically irreversible. Finally, since occupational choice involves the balancing of a series of subjective elements with the opportunities and limitations of reality, the crystallization of occupational choice inevitably has the quality of compromise (10).

P. M. Blau, J. W. Gustad, R. Jessor, H. S. Parnes, and R. C. Wilcock developed the process theory which proposes that choices regarding one's future are akin to a chain of constantly modified preferences and expectations. They identified eight factors determining entry into an occupation. Four of these characterize occupations: demand, technical (functional) qualifications, personal (nonfunctional) qualifications, and rewards. Those characterizing individuals were information about an occupation, technical skills, social characteristics, and value orientations (2:531).

At the elementary level, Blau's "chain" concept can better be described as a series of transactions between child and milieu on the basis of which concepts in early adolescence are built.

As the name indicates, developmental choice theories relate human development and the timing or pacing of educational-occupational decisions. Super points out that, as in other aspects of development, vocational development may be conceived of as beginning early in life and as proceeding along a curve until late in life (24). Such a concept of vocational development leads logically, according to Super, to that of "vocational maturity" denoting the

---

*Edward S. Borodin, Barbara Nachmann, and Stanley J. Sega have prepared a critique and elaboration of Ginzberg, et al. (3).

degree of development reached on such a continuum. Super and his associates point out elsewhere that one's occupation makes possible the playing of
a role appropriate to the self-concept of the individual (22).

Robert J. Havighurst, whose developmental task concept was reviewed in
Chapter 7, has described vocational development as a lifelong process of six
stages from childhood to old age (11). Each age period has characteristic
tasks which must be successfully achieved if the individual is to achieve
happiness and success with tasks appropriate to the vocational stages which
follow. Havighurst's stages are shown in Figure 23. Only the first two are
directly related to elementary education, but all six are given to show the
total configuration.

Stages of Vocational Development	*Age*
I. *Identification with a Worker*	5-10 years
Father, mother, other significant persons. The concept of Working becomes an essential part of the ego-ideal.	
II. *Acquiring the Basic Habits of Industry*	10-15 years
Learning to organize one's time and energy to get a piece of work done. School work, chores. Learning to put work ahead of play in appropriate situations.	
III. *Acquiring Identity as a Worker in the Occupational Structure*	15-25 years
Choosing and preparing for an occupation. Getting work experience as a basis for occupational choice and for assurance of economic independence.	
IV. *Becoming a Productive Person*	25-40 years
Mastering the skills of one's occupation. Moving up the ladder within one's occupation.	
V. *Maintaining a Productive Society*	40-70 years
Emphasis shifts toward the societal and away from the individual aspect of the worker's role. The individual sees himself as a responsible citizen in a productive society. He pays attention to the civic responsibility attached to his job. He is at the peak of his occupational career and has time and energy to adorn it with broader types of activity. He pays attention to inducing younger people into stages III and IV.	
VI. *Contemplating a Productive and Responsible Life*	70+ years
This person is retired from his work or is in the process of withdrawing from the worker's role. He looks back over his work life with satisfaction, sees that he had made his social contribution, and is pleased with it. While he may not have achieved all of his ambitions, he accepts his life and believes in himself as a productive person.	

Figure 23.   Vocational Development: A Lifelong Process

"Chance" Theories

Some writers in the field of guidance suggest that, in the last analysis, chance governs the educational levels and occupational goals eventually attained by the child in later life. Caplow, for instance, has indicated that accidental or unforeseen factors tend to make a difference in what one does with his life (4). Again, an impulse or sudden emotional reaction may force a choice with respect to a career.

If there is anything of relevance for elementary counseling in the somewhat murky realm of "accident" or "impulse," it is that as early as the middle school years, children who are *ready to do so* should be helped to begin assessing themselves so that in years to come they plan for rather than merely await the future.

A Composite Theory

Hoppock, drawing from influential theories of occupational choice, presents a suggested "composite theory for school counselors." The ten major points of his theory are:

1) Occupations are chosen to meet needs.

2) The occupation that we choose is the one that we believe will best meet the needs that most concern us.

3) Needs may be intellectually perceived, or they may be only vaguely felt as attractions which draw us in certain directions. In either case, they may be influential choices.

4) Vocational development begins when we first become aware that an occupation can help to meet our needs.

5) Vocational development progresses and occupational choice improves as we become better able to anticipate how well a prospective occupation will meet our needs. Our capacity thus to anticipate depends upon our knowledge of our selves, our knowledge of occupations, and our ability to think clearly.

6) Information about ourselves affects occupational choice by helping us to recognize what we want and by helping us anticipate whether or not we will be successful in collecting what the contemplated occupation offers to us.

7) Information about occupations affects our occupational choice by helping us to discover the occupations that may meet our needs and by helping us to anticipate how well satisfied we may hope to be in one occupation as compared with another.

8) Job satisfaction depends upon the extent to which the job that we hold meets the needs that we feel it should meet. The degree of satisfaction is determined by the ratio between what we have and what we want.

9) Satisfactions can result from a job which meets our needs to-day or from a job which promises to meet them in the future.

10) Occupational choice is always subject to change when we believe that a change will better suit our needs (13:111-112).

Implications for
Elementary School Guidance Programs

In elementary education, a composite theory seems most viable when teachers or counselors help older children deal with plans for the years ahead.

It seems reasonable to accept the ideas that children move from fantasy to reality (process theory) and that there also are stages of vocational insight (developments theory) through which children and adults make their way. But the basic role of the elementary school is that of providing a suitable input of experience so that "process" and "development" operate in a favorable manner and so that chance and impulse are not the predominant factors in deciding the extent of one's formal education and lifetime career. Learning to use one's time wisely, understanding others through role-playing or psychodrama, group discussions, and many similar activities of the child thus become, in the primary and middle years, the amalgam out of which desirable, realistic decisions eventually are made.*

Examples of contemporary thinking with respect to contributions that can be made to elementary school programs have been suggested by Jack M. Thompson. He includes the following four specific objectives of a career development program for the elementary school:

1) to help the child appreciate all kinds of work in our society.

2) to develop the concept of flexibility in the work role.

3) to provide a wide base of experience regarding occupations rather than to place emphasis upon early decision-making.

4) to stress the importance of effective use of leisure time (26).

Encouraging Children's
Personal-Ecological Insights

Many teachers, perhaps even a majority, are less interested in theoretical guidelines than in what to do about improving and increasing the child's under-

---

*For an heuristic theory, cf. John L. Holland (12); for a self-concept approach, cf. Frank L. Field, Chris D. Kehas, and David V. Tiedeman (8).

standing of his environment—that is, of his personal-ecological understandings. Let us look at this practical matter more closely.

Personal-Social Adjustments

Prominent among these are school-sponsored experiences that lead to the development of satisfactory personal-social relationships in what might be called the "human environment" (6). One of the skills that children need to learn in the human environment is that of accepting and adjusting to certain degrees of independence on the one hand and to limitations and restrictions on the other. Of equivalent importance are adjustments related to praise, criticism, acceptance, rejection, reward, and punishment—all of which are found to some extent in every school setting.

In developing these learnings the counselor shares responsibility with teachers, just as it is shared in so many other ways. Examples of understandings through which the child's ecological insights may be improved include the following: improving one's grooming and personal appearance; personal hygiene; observing social conventions in various situations; ways and means of becoming acquainted with others and strengthening friendship patterns; accepting physiological changes; and coping with problems of rejection. Activities for increasing these understandings often include provisions for the experiencing of various roles, participation in social activities, role playing, and group discussions.

Educational Adjustments

Helping pupils to understand the educational environment is another important orientation service in which the counselor may work cooperatively with both the individual faculty member and the school staff as a whole. This orientation may require adjustments on the part of both pupils and faculty. Students need to acquire an increased understanding of "what school is about," and teachers and counselors need greater insights into pupils' conceptions of education and their expectations—both pleasant and fearful—of what the coming school year will bring.

Particularly among young children there is a great deal of concern about being able to read. Indeed, some alarmed kindergartners temporarily have resisted entry into the primary school because they had not yet learned to read. Failure to learn to read can have a depressing effect upon the child's psychological adjustment to learning (20). It is crucial that counselors and teachers work effectively together to help children acquire this skill, and in doing so, see that children find reading pleasant as well as something they can master with a feeling of achievement.

Occupational-Vocational Information

There are many ways in which occupational-vocational information can help in facilitating pupil understanding—an understanding both of himself and of other people. For example, recurring curricular and paracurricular experiences can be planned that deal with products, production, and ways of living both in the United States and other countries. Understandings of the interdependence of workers from the processing of raw materials to the finished product can be made clear. Trends in occupations and forecasts for the years also can be discussed, including the increasing number of service and technical positions needed in the immediate future. Through such discussions as these, interesting explanations of qualifications for various kinds of work can evolve. The points made above are merely illustrative. Other learning with a bearing on occupations is woven into the fabric of the curriculum over the six or eight years in which most children are a part of the elementary school.

Once the faculty and the guidance staff have identified and agreed upon insights and materials related to children's ecological understandings, the counselor should take appropriate steps to see that books, films, magazines, and other media are available since teachers build their work *around what is conveniently at hand*. It is equally important for a counselor to see that suitable changes are considered, particularly for the 11- to 14-year-olds' programs and experiences, when curriculum guides are written or updated.

Procedures for Developing Ecological Insights

There are a number of procedures and techniques which elementary school counselors can use that further the child's personal-ecological insights— that is, his understanding of his surroundings and how he relates to them. A sampling of these activities is presented below.

Individual Counseling

The counseling process offers elementary pupils an opportunity to increase their self-understanding and decision-making techniques for coping with the vital occupational-vocational decisions they will confront in their later school years. While the techniques of counseling are discussed in Chapter 8, emphasis at this point is placed on the occupational information materials that may be useful in the counseling process. The following principles should be observed when such materials are used:

a) Occupational materials are used only when they directly relate to the goals of counseling process.

b) Materials are used to inform not to encourage or bias the child in the making of a particular decision.

c) Materials are prepared in advance of the counseling interview, at least insofar as possible.

d) The natural flow of counseling should not be interrupted by the reading of materials. Verbal explanation of the materials may be made however.

e) Informational materials are not used to limit or restrict counseling to a particular vocational or educational concern. While counseling may, according to the dictates of the situation, have a vocational or educational emphasis, the categorizing of counseling as vocational counseling, educational counseling, or personal counseling is too limiting.

f) The principles and ethics of counseling are always followed.

It is well to bear in mind when counseling that the principles above are relevant only with respect to older elementary school children; that is, those usually in the 12 to 14 age range.

Orientation Activities

An elementary school counselor can be particularly helpful to children by helping to orient them to the new and unfamiliar environment they confront when they first enter school. This does not involve just the physical orientation to the school plant and facilities; psychological orientation is important also.

A knowledge of the physical environment is usually obtained quite simply by arranging school tours for new kindergarten or primary children. These short journeys can take them to the administrative, guidance, and other offices of the school where they will meet personnel and hear simple explanations of their functions. Other visits might be made to classrooms and special areas (the gym, music room, and so forth) and to meet the nurse, custodians, and other school employees.

Psychological orientation is much more complex since it seeks to develop positive attitudes toward school, feelings of security, an interest in the program, and understandings of the educational process. Psychological orientation may include talking individually or in small groups with children, having older children meet with those who are younger, or using "get acquainted" films or filmstrips. Of the most importance, however, is the interest the teacher and counselor show in each child and their own display of positive attitudes toward education in general and toward the child in particular.

During the last year or two children spend in elementary schools, a presecondary sequence of experience often can be designed to bring into focus the educational and vocational decisions and choices that, in some cases, are greatly influenced by the programs a child follows in grade nine or above.

Orientation to the high school years, however, is not something to cram into a week or two. It should not be just a trite, "one-shot" type of secondary school visitation but should be a continuing experience that might include a sequence such as this (the timing is approximate):

February: Weekly visits to the elementary classrooms by former pupils now in high school or the middle school who share their experiences and discuss topics selected by elementary school children.

March: Visits by teachers who will be working with incoming students during the next few years.

April: Visits by personnel performing special services; a principal, a guidance counselor, coach, student council representative, and so on.

May: Several visits to the new school with follow-up discussions and planning for the coming autumn.

The elementary and secondary school guidance staff should plan carefully to ensure that continuity is maintained and that the articulation gap between the two schools and their programs is successfully bridged for children.

Field Trips

Field trips provide the elementary age child with an opportunity to secure occupational-vocational information through his first hand observations. Such trips can include dozens of places such as libraries, local government offices, industries, transportation centers such as airports, railroads, and bus stations, or technical schools and universities.

These field experiences can enable the student to broaden his knowledge of the world of work in general and gain clearer insights into the nature of certain occupations. Plant tours may also create an awareness of the vast range of occupations and the variety of jobs involved in an industrial plant.

Educational information of current usefulness can be obtained from trips to libraries. A base for future planning can result from visits to technical schools, universities, hospitals, and government offices.

Simulated Work Experiences

Elementary school children usually enjoy role playing, and the school can offer certain opportunities to imbue this role playing with the realism of simulated job experiences. Even in the primary years, children can find pleasure in, as well as learn from, assuming a role in a simulated television program, or in the selling and buying of merchandise in a classroom "store." These and similar activities which the teacher and elementary counselor can suggest easily can be created. For youngsters in the intermediate school, more realistic experiences may be provided through a school paper, radio or television program especially where intercoms or closed circuit television are a part of the school's facilities. A school council, the safety patrol, clerking in a school store, making traffic surveys, helping teachers of nursery-kindergarten age children, operating projection equipment, or serving as a telephone attendant are other examples of this kind. Such service opportunities are limited only the the teacher's or counselor's imagination.

Simulated Personal-Social Experience

The role playing of personal-social experiences has appreciable value when linked to activities which demonstrate manners, courtesies, and common social skills. From their first months in school, children may engage in the role playing of individual and group introductions, show their knowledge of acts of courtesy and their general awareness of behavior in situations which involve interpersonal relations and suitable behavior during luncheon and other social gatherings. How one guides personal-social experiences, quite naturally, varies tremendously from an inner city school to a small rural elementary school or one in a suburban area.

The elementary school child at any age has personal-social problems which he wants and needs to discuss with others. Carefully nurtured peer group and child-teacher relationships both in the primary and middle schools can be made conducive to group discussions of common problems. Such discussions offer opportunities for group guidance, for relief of pupil tension, for the study of behaviors, and for identifying group attitudes, as well as helping in the search for possible solutions to individual problems. Other personal-social activities which can provide useful information and meaningful experiences are hobby or other special interest groups, hobby shows, simple assembly programs, cooperatively prepared bulletin board displays and exhibits which reflect the classroom work or interests of children.

It should be stressed that none of the procedures and techniques for helping children understand their relationships with their environments are prescriptions for counselors and teachers to follow. Instead they are intended to encourage creative planning that is unique to a particular school and to the unique groups of boys and girls that are characteristic of U.S. elementary education.

Summary

The years a child spends in the elementary school provide important opportunities for counselors and other faculty members to study clues which children themselves provide and which permit the school (on the basis of these clues) to help boys and girls become better oriented to their environments. The counselor in particular needs to understand the ecology of childhood: the transactional relationships existing between each young learner and various phases of his sociocultural environment.

Chapter 11 reviews how teachers and counselors can help children attain a realistic understanding of their relationship to their milieu and—in the six to eight or even ten years spent in elementary schools—begin to develop wise educational and occupational concepts. These understandings are presented as an important prerequisite to later and more firm educational and vocational choices made in adolescence.

Several theories bearing on educational-occupational choices are examined. These serve as a basis for a subsequent discussion of the development of the child's personal-ecological insights; his beginning grasp of his interaction with others in the sociocultural "envelope" or matrix surrounding the personal space bubble in which each learner has his being. Procedures are suggested for nurturing and guiding children's personal ecological insights. At the same time, stress is placed on the fact that such guidance is uniquely personal. Techniques can be described, but what actually is done by the counselor and teacher to help a child grow toward maturity remains a complex network of creative decisions which can be made only on the basis of their professional judgment.

References

1. Barker, R. B. "Ecology and Motivation." *Nebraska Symposium on Motivation*. Edited by Marshall R. Jones. Lincoln, Neb.: University of Nebraska Press, 1960.
2. Blau, P. M., J. W. Gustad, R. Jessor, H. S. Parnes, and R. C. Wilcock. "Occupational Choice: A Conceptual Framework." *Industrial and Labor Relations Review*, July, 1956.

3. Borodin, Edward S., Barbara Nachmann, and Stanley Sega. "An Articulated Framework for Vocational Development." *Journal of Counseling Psychology* 10 (Summer, 1963): 107-116.

4. Caplow, T. *The Sociology of Work.* Minneapolis: University of Minnesota Press, 1954.

5. Danskin, David G., Carroll E. Kennedy, Jr., and Walter S. Friesen. "Guidance: The Ecology of Students." *Personnel and Guidance Journal* 44 (October, 1965): 131.

6. Dos, A. K. "Social Responsibility as a Means of Promoting Better Adjustment in School Children." *Elementary School Guidance and Counseling* 2 (March, 1968): 227-228.

7. ____. *Environment, Heredity, and Intelligence. Harvard Education Review.* Cambridge, Mass.: June, 1969. (Special reprint of the winter and spring [1969] issues.)

8. Field, Frank L., Chris D. Kehas, and David V. Tiedeman. "The Self-Concept in Career Development: A Construct in Transition." *Personnel and Guidance Journal* 41 (May, 1963): 767-771.

9. Gibson, Robert L. and Robert E. Higgins. *Techniques of Guidance: An Approach to Pupil Analysis.* Chicago: Science Research Associates, 1966.

10. Ginzberg, Eli, S. W. Ginsburg, S. Axelrod, and J. L. Herma. *Occupational Choice: An Approach to a General Theory.* New York: Columbia University Press, 1951.

11. Havighurst, Robert J. "Youth in Exploration and Man Emerged." Henry Borow (ed.). *Man in a World at Work.* Boston: Houghton Mifflin Co., 1964.

12. Holland, John L. "Some Explorations of a Theory of Vocational Choice: One-and-Two-Year Longitudinal Studies." *Psychological Monographs* 76 (1962).

13. Hoppock, Robert. *Occupational Information* (3rd edition). New York: McGraw-Hill Book Co., 1967.

14. Hunt, J. McVicker. "The Implications of Changing Ideas on How Children Develop Intellectually." *Children* (May-June, 1964).

15. Jensen, Arthur R. "How Much Can We Boost IQ and Scholastic Achievement?" *Harvard Educational Review* 39 (Winter, 1969): 1-123.

16. Krippner, Stanley. "Junior High School Students' Vocational Preferences and Their Parents' Occupational Levels." *Personnel and Guidance Journal* 41 (March, 1963): 590-595.

17. Landes, Ruth. "An Anthropologist Looks at School Counseling." *Journal of Counseling Psychology* 10 (Spring, 1963): 14-17.

18. Leacock, Eleanor. "The Concept of Culture and Its Significance for School Counselors." *Personnel and Guidance Journal* 46 (May, 1968): 844-851.

19. Lonsway, Rev. Francis A. "The Developing Literature on Occupational Choice." *The High School Journal* 5 (February, 1969): 260-270. The first part of this article presents a succinct historical background statement on theories of occupational choice for which a substantial bibliography is appended.

20. Panther, E. E. "Prediction of First Grade Reading Achievement." *Elementary School Journal* 68 (October, 1967): 44-48.

21. Snider, James G. "The Linguistic Content Variable in School Counseling." *Personnel and Guidance Journal* 42 (February, 1964): 577-587.

22. Super, Donald E., et al. *Career Development: Self-Concept Theory*. New York: College Entrance Examination Board, 1963

23. _____. "Group Techniques in the Guidance Program." *Education and Psychological Measurement*. Autumn, 1959.

24. _____. *The Psychology of Careers*. New York: Harper and Row, Publishers, 1957.

25. Terman, Lewis M. (chairman). *Nature and Nurture: Their Influence on Achievement*. XXVII *Yearbook*, Parts I and II. National Society for the Study of Education. Chicago: University of Chicago Press, 1928.

26. Thompson, Jack M. "Career Development in the Elementary School: Rationale and Implications for Elementary School Counselors." *The School Counselor* 16 (January, 1969): 209.

27. Wrenn, C. Gilbert. "The Culturally Encapsulated Counselor." *Harvard Educational Review* 32 (Fall, 1962): 444-449.

12

Influencing the Syntax of Learning in Childhood

There is a particular sequence to the words spoken in the English language. This order must be followed if a speaker is to convey his meaning to a listener. The way words are arranged to show relationships among phrases, clauses, and sentences is called *syntax*. If the syntax is changed, then meaning is lost, distorted, or otherwise changed. "The fox chased the rabbit," for instance, is totally different from "The rabbit chased the fox."

Just as there is order in our language, so there is a systematic "syntax of learning" in childhood. Boys and girls must learn how to read before they can begin fully to explore the resources of the school library. They need to know how to add before they can cope with a multiplication problem with two or more digits in the multiplier. Dozens of similar illustrations could be given to demonstrate what is meant by the syntax or orderly sequence in which one learns most effectively.

Guidance and the Syntax of Learning

The school counselor is in a position to exert a benign and useful influence on the planning of the sequence in which each child encounters the flow of educational experience we call the curriculum. The counselor does this in three general ways.

First, through helping teachers determine how the child's maturity, motivation, and previous input of experience suggest that his learning should be guided or paced;

Second, through ongoing study of the child's progress in learning situations established by the school;

Third, through research activities designed to validate, or at least to explore, the effectiveness of the child's educational syntax and the success with which both his progress and the broad goals of guidance have been attained.

It is with these three strands that Chapter 12 is concerned: the sequencing of learning, the continuous "quality control" of children's experience, and both the validation of past decisions and analytical study of probable future decisions through research.* A fourth strand also should be interwoven with the first three. This is the counselor's task of assisting the teachers to understand their roles in influencing children. The vitality and importance of this influence has already been delineated in Chapter 10.

Mediating the Syntax of Learning

In most previous chapters, discussion has dwelled upon the fact that each child is unique and that when exposed to an experience he interprets it diversely and benefits differently from it than does any other child. This uniquely personal nature of the learning process implies that the nature and sequence of what is learned should vary from child to child, too.

While our elementary schools probably would collapse from the weight of the burden of having a totally different syntax of learning for each child, *programs can be personalized for children* as was illustrated in detail in Chapters 5 and 6. Let us examine now how the guidance specialist can contribute to the process.

Sequencing Learning Through Guidance

Counselors can be helpful in the sequencing of learning experiences in a number of ways without either threatening the teacher or attempting to assume functions that the primary or middle school faculty members are best

---

Sequencing and *quality control* functions in elementary education are distinctly different from "placement" and "follow-up" functions of guidance as these terms have traditionally been used by secondary school counselors. To these persons, *placement* is concerned with the identification of appropriate work opportunities and with career guidance that directs some youth into post-secondary education. *Follow-up* is identified with the process of ascertaining what happened to former high school graduates or dropouts, respectively, in their advanced study or occupations. Much secondary level "research" has consisted of the compilation of data deemed relevant: the study of cumulative records, analyses of assessment programs including testing, longitudinal counseling data, post secondary employment histories, college records—in fact, just about everything that could be used to document the success, or lack of it, in high school guidance programs.

qualified to perform. Among the ways in which the guidance program can contribute are:

1) Helping faculty members to determine whether the rate of progress made by individual children in the curriculum continuum is appropriate and whether the nature of the content is suited to his maturity and ability.

2) Evaluating (with the teacher) the success with which a child has been grouped with others for instruction, activities in special fields, for help from academic clinicians, and so forth.

3) Designing, in cooperation with teachers, a child's participation in paracurricular activities: socializing, after-school sports, work in programs or on special projects, socially useful work (as when a 12- or 13-year-old assists in the nursery school), etc.

4) In consultation with teachers, helping to find short-term or part-time employment for an older child who needs the work for financial or for development reasons (6:206).*

5) Particularly in the middle school years, laying a foundation for secondary level curricular program decisions and selections with a bearing on educational and occupational futures. This does *not* imply that the elementary program should be warped to fit high school requirements. Rather, it implies helping boys and girls live intelligently, richly, and pleasantly in the elementary school years so that they are accustomed to making wise choices at any time, including the occupational or educational ones encountered in later years.

Each of these five aspects of sequencing, pacing, and directing learning is now considered.

Determining the Rate of Individual Progress

In determining how best to pace a child's stream-of-learning input, both counselor and teacher are necessarily influenced by the particular interpretation of "curriculum" which has been accepted by the faculty. In a traditional *graded* school, the rate of a child's progress tends to center around the question of whether a child is to "pass" or to "fail" when he confronts the annual promotion hurdle. The flexibility (or lack of it) in the program, the social adjustment and emotional status of a child, his physical health and size, and

---

*According to G. R. Kaback, who conducted a 1968 study in the greater New York area, *elementary* school counselors felt that occupational and educational information service ". . . is one of the most important in their guidance programs."

his previous record as determined from assessment data reviewed in Chapters 9 and 10 are among the spectrum of factors which should influence decisions pertaining to the rate of progress of boys and girls, even in the more conservative type of school.

It is desirable for the counselor constantly to examine assessment data and to be prepared to do everything within the scope of his official and unofficial influence to nourish child intelligence, to minimize unjustified conclusions about a child and the unwise actions to which they can lead, and to match the child to his emerging social, emotional, and cognitive tasks. For example, in a graded school, the academic performance of a fourth grade boy as shown on a standardized achievement test may be expressed in a test profile which suggests that his 2.8 overall scores were those of children in the eighth month of second grade. Does this score for a nine- or ten-year-old doom him to repeat grade four? Quite possibly not, depending on the answers that counselor and teacher reach to such cogent questions as these:

1) Will this boy's experiences, if he is obliged to repeat grade 4, be significantly *different* another year, or will he merely encounter the same sequence of work in which he "failed" this year?

2) *Why* did he do poorly during the present year? Was he ill? Often absent? Harassed by other children? Culturally different or disadvantaged? Upset by home problems? In view of data pertaining to these and similar questions, what might happen if he repeats grade 4? If he continues in grade 5?

3) What is the possible emotional effect of failure on the boy? If he repeats a grade, how will his presence influence the younger children with whom he would be placed?

4) What are the implications of the boy's anecdotal or other behavioral records kept by the teacher? Will retention increase or decrease his sense of security, his coping behavior, his self-concepts?

Careful, comprehensive discussions centered around points such as the four mentioned are too frequently neglected. Now and then a tired teacher working on year-end records due in the office on Monday (and hoping to start his summer vacation or university graduate work on Tuesday!) may make arbitrary decisions in a few moments time and hastily determine the fate of a youngster for the coming year. Children deserve a better deal—and counselors should be on the job to see that careful judgment rather than snap judgment influences outcomes. In order to do this, discussions with teachers must begin early and extend throughout the year, and the sequencing and pacing of learning (day by day over a period of time) should reflect the view that "promotion" is not an *annual hurdle* but a *continuous process*—a direction in which learning is guided.

As Ira J. Gordon phrased it, the teacher should be provided ". . . with some of the operational tools and underlying concepts that will assist him in analyzing and diagnosing where children are with respect to their development and intelligence, so that the new concepts of the child may become functional in the classroom." (5:5)

In genuinely nongraded or continuum schools, the rate of individual learning is simplified because the artificiality of age-grade distinctions is reduced or removed. The primary and middle school sequences of approximately three years each are of great help in this regard.

From a guidance theory point of view, the continuous progress or curriculum continuum approach which a growing number of schools are exploring seems to be the most promising one. In such a structure the sound psychosocial placement of the learner is an integral part of pupil progress since *all* learners move individually rather than in groups.*

Grouping for Better Learning[†]

Some form of grouping is used in all elementary schools. The assignment of children to a teacher by chronological age was one of the earliest and most basic forms of grouping in the U.S. and is still probably the most prevalent. Millions of youngsters begin their school experience with others of age five or six simply because their birthdays occurred, say, before the first of December. Short-term grouping of children in a nongraded or continuous progress type school is a relatively recent development—and an example of versatile educational thinking.

In conventional schools, as of the early 1970's, most teachers in the primary years continued to be assigned "self-contained" classrooms in which they were responsible for nearly all teaching done during the school day. The counselor's opportunity to help teachers base grouping on human development principles is an important one here since much grouping below grade four has heretofore usually been done in terms of assumed reading ability. In offering help and advice, guidance specialists should strive for four things: 1) flexibility, 2) frequent changes in intraclassroom groupings, 3) careful checking of teacher decisions regarding reading group placement, and 4) investigation of causality when children are thought to be "slow."

*For a statement describing a workshop "designed to help youngsters improve their self-concepts by sensitizing teachers to the various elements of self-theory," cf. George E. Leonard, John T. Pietrofesa, and Irene M. Bank (8).

†Grouping is a topic on which the beginning counselor in elementary education needs to inform himself quickly. The Appendix lists many types of grouping "plans" or labels that have appeared in the literature. Also see Chapter 11 references for useful material on grouping.

Although some schools continue to have self-contained classrooms through grade six, departmentalized elementary school structures are also a widespread type of organization and frequently serve as a basis for grouping in the middle grades. In departmentalized fourth, fifth, or sixth grades a teacher may find himself instructing 100 to 150 different children in five or six mathematics or language arts classes each day rather than assuming responsibility for the same 25 or more children for five or six hours.

In departmentalized schools, it is not unusual to find so-called ability grouping used. For instance, if 100 children are enrolled in grade five, they may be divided into three or even four subgroups on the basis of their I.Q. scores or their cumulative grade point averages.

Ability grouping, sometimes called "homogeneous" despite the fact that no two children are ever really homogeneous, can be a source of numerous problems for insightful elementary school guidance workers when they attempt to group children for better learning. Test scores used for "ability" placement may be old or otherwise unreliable. Again, the teacher's image of a child may be inaccurate, or culturally biased due to a youngster's membership in any one of several U.S. subcultures with respect to which the teacher is uninformed or unsympathetic. Or the child's cultural background may have created some distortion in his test responses. Furthermore, test reports or the records of transfer pupils may be lost, incomplete, or incompatible with those used in the school district to which he has moved.

For these and comparable reasons which could be cited in depth and in detail to the point of tedium, counselors need to exercise a great deal of caution when they are obliged to help group children on the basis of such arbitrary yardsticks as achievement test scores, subjective anecdotal records that lack clarity, I.Q. scores, or cumulative grades based on teacher-made tests. It is also important to attempt to counteract the feeling of being stigmatized which many (if not most or all) youngsters experience when they are placed in so-called slow groups. As matters now stand, in a large segment of American schools, counselors probably are justified if they decide that it is appropriate and humane to begin working gradually to eliminate departmental programs that are based on doubtful "ability" groupings or even on what appear to be reasonably valid and reliable I.Q. or test scores. There are too many variables which influence learning to permit grouping on such limited bases.

In recent years, various kinds of flexible and short-term groupings have begun to supersede the types criticized in the preceding paragraphs. The newer trends likewise offer more interesting ways for the guidance worker to provide service. In nongraded or continuum schools, child groupings are frequently built around three or more members of a teacher unit or teaching team in the primary and middle years. When this occurs, there is an increase in opportunities for a counselor to suggest ways of matching teachers and children to help secure optimum interaction (12).

Also, in nongraded and continuum schools, the interpretations of "grouping" and "group activities" are considerably broader than those permitted by either primary reading divisions or departmental programs in the middle grades. Interest grouping, multi-age grouping, groups established to carry out special projects or activities, cross-age groups as in art, music, or physical education, and analogous types of work group combinations to intermix young personalities recently have been devised and introduced. In these newer, more informal, and often ephemeral human clusters, the counselor and a team (or other combination) of teachers have an almost unlimited range of ways to help children become welcome, contributive, and accepted participants.

Guidance in School-Related Activities

School-related or paracurricular activities are those which accompany or parallel the familiar academic and expressive activities found in elementary education. They include such things as school-sponsored clubs, service activities (such as serving periodically as host in the school foyer when visitors arrive), educational trips, holding elective office in a school council, older children serving as baby-sitters during afternoon programs for parents, the operating of audiovisual equipment, manning a school store or lost-and-found, and personalized individual activity such as music lessons. There are a number of similar items that could be included to expand and to characterize the myriad of paracurricular happenings that elementary schools sponsor or for which they provide encouragement in the form of housing.

The role of the teacher-counselor team in bringing an educationally sound syntax to paracurricular activities is a reasonably clear one. It both parallels and complements the sequencing of learning which transpires in the classroom.

However, some difficulties, and occasional confusion, can arise in relation to paracurricular activities because of socioeconomic and cultural differences which continue to permeate much of society in the U.S. There may be certain fee payments, clothing, or costly equipment involved in some school-sponsored activities. If so, how do counselors and teachers help children who lack the money needed if they are to participate? And what about the schedule problems that seem inevitably to crop up in schools that are on shifts or to which children are bussed in both rural and inner city schools? Under these conditions a counselor may find himself trying to devise all kinds of arrangements to help create, sequence, or pace school-sponsored experiences of which some youngsters seem likely to be otherwise deprived.

Nor should one overlook other selective requirements in paracurricular activities. The counselor may find himself working to help children who are barred from competitive interschool or intramural athletic teams for which coaches want the physically mature, coordinated, husky type of child.

Another special problem is the occasional disbarment from some school-related activities of the disturbed, the physically handicapped, and the frail child.

**Bringing Educational Values to
Children's Part-Time and Seasonal
Work Experiences and to Career Development**

Occupational placement in the elementary school, except in rare instances, is limited to part-time employment. The elementary school counselor will find occasions, however, when children of perhaps ten or older will need or will seek part-time employment for either financial, family, or personal reasons. To meet such needs the counselor should—in cooperation with appropriate community agencies, service clubs, and local merchants and business leaders—seek to identify part-time or temporary, non-hazardous occupational opportunities for which elementary pupils might be qualified and in which they would find satisfaction as well as money. These could include work as newspaper carriers or delivery boys, car washing, baby-sitting, light housework, or lawn and garden work. The school itself may provide some limited opportunity for work in the school cafeteria, school store, administrative offices, or in assisting the custodial staff.

George E. Leonard and Ellen Stephens have described an "Elementary School Employment Service" for fifth and sixth graders operated in Detroit under the auspices of the Developmental Career Guidance Project (9). The opportunity to apply for various jobs was later extended to fourth graders, too. The employment was *within* the schools in the Project: safety squad helpers, library assistants, audiovisual aides, office helpers, auditorium assistants, and so on (9:14). One is led to infer from the Leonard and Stephens report that in-school jobs can be made educationally valuable as well as useful services.

Any part-time out-of-school employment should be limited in scope and in the time it demands so as not to interfere with a child's academic progress. In this regard, the importance of appropriate follow-up procedures must be emphasized. The counselor does not merely open up opportunities; an even more important task is that of gauging the impact of the work on a child's *behavior*, and guiding him to greater success and satisfaction on the job if need be.

Career Development. The small but growing body of literature in elementary guidance began to direct attention to career development in the 1960's. Among persons stressing the importance of vocational experiences and occupational experiences were L. O. Eckerson and H. M. Smith (1962),

W. Norris (1963), M. E. Bennett (1964), and Jack M. Thompson (1969) (1,2,10,13). Notable in Thompson's statement was the growing recognition that "career development" was not a formal experience, but a flexible attempt to mediate the attitudes and behaviors of youngsters by:

1) helping the child appreciate all kinds of work in our society
2) developing the concept of flexibility in the work role
3) providing a wide base of experiences regarding occupations rather than to place emphasis upon early decision-making
4) stressing the importance of the effective use of leisure time (13:209).

Elsewhere in his commentary, Thompson carefully pointed out and emphasized that

> . . . career development focuses upon the importance of providing adequate exposure and experience for children from the time they enter school, which in turn will enable them to make more adequate decisions regarding their work role at points of actual decision-making. This concept does not [imply] placing pressure upon children to make earlier vocational choices . . . . The rationale for career development is that it is a developmental process which should begin in elementary school and continue throughout a person's lifetime (13:208).

Essentially, these views seem reasonable ones, especially if the "developmental process" that Thompson mentions is congruent with the concepts of personalized guidance of the child's progress from immaturity toward maturity in a seamless continuum.

The Development of Good
Articulation with Secondary School Programs

The secondary school, whether its teachers are happy about it or not, is inevitably fated to accept the preadolescents and young adolescents who enter secondary education by the millions each year. Both elementary teachers and counselors have an important obligation, therefore, not only to provide a suitable product, but to do what can be done to insure that the initial planning of the syntax of a pupil's learning in high school is carefully studied and well-designed.

For many years now, secondary education, or at least the opportunity to *begin* work therein, has been almost universal in the U.S. Equally widespread has been the social loss, the major human loss, caused by the dropout problem.

In this group we have a few children and many adolescents who for environmental, physical, academic, or other reasons fail to complete the latter years of public education (7).

Most people are inclined to think of the dropout as a predominantly high school phenomenon and problem, which is not exactly the case. Not only do millions of children fail even to enter grade nine; the roots of the dropout problem often are to be found in the elementary years during which children who later break contact with formal education have had all or most of their school experience. The counselor has an especially useful function to perform in the upper elementary years in anticipating and, when possible, salvaging youngsters on the verge of making the decision to leave school prematurely.

Problems of the potential dropout often are complex, and may range from home pressures through classroom frustration to matters of physical or emotional health. By the time a young adolescent or pre-adolescent reaches high school, he may already be predisposed to failure because of faulty counseling or due to a lack of guidance in the middle school years. It is for this reason that the *elementary* guidance specialist is an important figure! The high school counselor may discover that he has come on the scene too late to help adolescents who have not had suitable experience in their first six or eight years of schooling.*

Secondary school program choices which begin to be made in the later elementary years should be made with great care for all children. The syntax of their learning experiences, and much of the success of the disadvantaged *and* the advantaged adolescent, is strongly influenced by the elementary counselor. Among factors to be considered in preliminary program placement decisions are such items as the following:

1) Are anecdotal and other records accurate and honest? Were the records made by persons who were competent and insightful?

2) Are records as complete as possible? Can additional data, especially for recent transfer students, be obtained?

3) What are the implications of parental or family attitudes? What allowance should be made for parental indifference, or for the overly ambitious parent, and so on?

4) Have *several* teachers who know the child been asked to weigh the program choices that he might make?

5) What inferences should be drawn from the most recent assessments of the child's work—preferably from tests administered in the months during which secondary school programs were being projected?

*For a comprehensive treatment of this broad problem, cf. Daniel Schreiber (ed.), *Guidance and the School Dropout* (11).

6) What can be done through personal contact with a given child to assay his interests and motivations on the threshold of his high school years?

7) Can conferences be arranged with the secondary counselors to permit clinical discussions of children about whom they need to be especially well informed?

One last point here. The task of guiding secondary level program choices is not one to be begun in the last year before a child or young adolescent leaves the elementary school. Data of relevance should be compiled during all of a youngster's years in school. Also, the best way to prepare him for tomorrow in the secondary school is to see that he lives as richly as possible *today* in the primary and middle school years.

The Syntax of Learning as a Unique, Personal Challenge to Counselors

Both the counselor and the university program of counselor education at the elementary school level must face an important fact of life in the 1970's; a unique personal challenge. This is the challenge to prepare graduate students well enough to permit them to deal with the syntax of learning and with the related dimensions of elementary counseling. Not only must the guidance worker who seeks to mediate childhood experiences understand the counseling process, but he must have a background in the elementary curriculum, in directing learning activities, in paracurricular activities, and in human development. Indeed it is even necessary to become acquainted with the 10- to 14-year-old part-time and summertime employment market!

It is the authors' conviction that a deep sense of commitment plus extensive professional study and experience in *elementary* education as well as in guidance is essential. This is the personal challenge to elementary counselors. Love for children, an interest and background in guidance, and a dedication to better teaching and learning are not enough. The nature of a good education in childhood must be understood too.

Validating the Syntax of Learning Through the Guidance Program

Once an accumulation of decisions has been begun regarding the breadth, the sequencing, and the pacing of children's experiences in school a nagging question enters the picture. "How do we really know that the best possible choices were made?" It has become customary in an increasing number of schools for the counselor methodically to gather data and opinions which help to illuminate the question.

Validation Through Follow-Up Activities

There are a number of "textbook answers" as to how the counselor can determine whether he and the teacher have devised a suitable syntax for the children with whom they work. Most follow-up techniques are similar to those reviewed or discussed in Chapters 9 and 10 which treated assessment and testing: observation, interviews, rating scales or behavior records, sociometric techniques, or achievement tests to name a few.

But unlike general assessment procedures, follow-up is concerned expressly with 1) the counselor's success in deciding on the proper sequencing and rate of learning experiences and their scope, 2) determining the apparent success of the mediation, and 3) modifying procedures used with a child in the future in view of the apparent success or shortcoming of the treatment previously used. One may designate follow-up activities, then, as the selective use of assessment techniques in order continually to modify the syntax of learning and the progress toward the goals of human development for children which the counselor pursues.

Some Mechanical
Problems in Follow-Up Procedures

Even in the best-run and most generously supported elementary schools there are some difficulties of a mechanical or operational type that need to be overcome. In less-favored elementary schools there may be numerous problems to be methodically attacked and reduced, even if they cannot immediately be eliminated.

One frequently encountered impediment to long-term follow-up is that inaccurate or incomplete records may have been kept by the teachers—or that useful records have been carelessly filed or lost by the file clerk in the principal's office. Procrastination by seasoned teachers who fail to make records, or who do not make them promptly and while their memory is reasonably clear, is another source of trouble. So is lack of orientation to the guidance program when newly employed teachers report for duty. Unless they are helped and advised many beginners and transfer teachers can not be expected to keep reliable records.

A follow-up program can be very little better than the records that are preserved for periodic study and for guiding future decisions.

Teachers need to be urged to avoid making fragmentary or misleading entries and to avoid statements that reflect bias. Efforts also should be made, when feasible, to obtain records and information that are as complete as possible on the transfer student. These may not mesh with either the record forms or with the terminology used in another school. In some instances no records at all are sent to the school to which a child is transferred, and special requests are necessary if they are obtainable at all. In other cases, some counselors or administrators misconstrue "confidentiality" to mean that no data whatsoever, except for the child's scholastic record and grade level, should be transmitted from one school to another.

The importance of pupil personnel records to all forms of counseling, including follow-up, and the many errors and omissions that can occur suggest that most record keeping can best be handled by having the elementary guidance office or center serve as a repository. Two exceptions to this rule are: 1) official records such as daily attendance which generally are filed in the administrative offices, and 2) the current behavior and performance records kept for children—records which only the teacher can keep and which he must have at hand in order to make entries, to serve as a basis for parent, teacher-teacher or counselor conferences, and for his own reference.

When there is a separate guidance office file, the counselor, by supervising the guidance secretary, personally can make certain that records are as complete and as up to date as possible. He also can spot and attempt to help teachers correct garbled, biased, or fragmentary statements before they accumulate in large stacks. Lastly, he can keep himself informed in the process of supervising record keeping.

If it is not possible to set up a central repository for follow-up work with records, or where a program is so new that there has not yet been time to establish a center in the building, it is important for the counselor to budget his time so that record handling is properly controlled. Once the situation gets out of control, it is doubly difficult to organize files of old data and to keep abreast of current record analysis and storage.

Much remains to be done in exploring better storage and retrieval of records. Hopefully, in due time, better technical procedures at reasonable cost can be developed to help counselors deal with the world of paper on which much of their contribution depends.

Human Relations in Follow-Up Conferences

Experienced guidance workers would probably agree that success in the follow-up conferences, which are designed to learn whether children's learning has been optimal, is closely linked to their ability to deal with the personality flaws and faulty values which occasionally may be found among the ranks of an exasperating minority of teachers.

Here are four examples of problems to which the counselor needs to be alerted. They indicate how colleagues' attitudes need to be taken into account when the sequencing, pacing, and breadth of a child's experience are reviewed to determine whether his progress is satisfactory in retrospect, and what can be done to guide him in the future.

Problem 1: Particularly at the secondary level, a few counselors have tended to equate success primarily with academic performance and graduates' placement in the "right" colleges. A substantial conflict may develop over theory and practice when an elementary counselor is human development oriented and his high school counterpart is academically achievement oriented. To avoid this difficulty, the guidance worker who specializes in work with younger children needs constantly to demonstrate why he concentrates on the *many* aspects of human development, not just on the nurture of intellectual growth as reflected in test scores. High school guidance staffs, as they begin to understand the broad ranging interest of the elementary school in following up graduates, can provide many valuable kinds of pertinent social, emotional, and physical data, as well as indices of academic success. One must avoid threatening an occasional insecure counselor with ideas and arousing his dislike or disapproval of the goals of elementary *developmental* follow-up as distinct from traditional secondary *academic* follow-up. *Both* are important.

Problem 2: Within the confines of the elementary school, the counselor's fitness in follow-up activity (to validate the syntax of learning) may be tested by teachers who lack intercultural understandings. Their attitudes may range from prejudice toward children who are not in their preferred subculture to the opposite extreme—*reverse* prejudice. Reverse prejudice refers to the tendency to make so many allowances for the deprived or the culturally different child that he is developmentally weakened by being kept in an overly protective or "educational greenhouse" type of climate. Both prejudice and reverse prejudice have deep emotional roots, so it requires both tact and ability to help biased teachers begin to learn how to make *accurate* appraisals of the progress children have shown as a result of experiences they had previously planned with the counselor.

Problem 3: A third example of the human relations problems with which counselors occasionally come in contact is provided by the rare but troublesome colleague who harbors grudges against children. Such unreasonable, negative attitudes may have begun when a boy or girl repeatedly nettled the teacher during a year or more of abrasive classroom contact. The resultant "grudge reaction" needs to be identified and discounted lest it invalidate the conclusions the counselor is trying to reach. In addition to grudges, some teachers favor a "pet" child and exaggerate his successes or belittle his problems when follow-up conversations are held. Since both the grudge and "teacher's pet" phenomena are likely to be indicative of a teacher's unmet personal needs, the counselor once again needs to be most tactful in discussing children with them.

Problem 4: One more example suffices to illustrate how follow-up activity is related to interpersonal relations. As indicated in Chapter 8, a counselor needs to know how to deal with the problem of petty gossip or invidious remarks which sometimes enter the conversation in a teachers' lounge and even some parent-teacher conferences. Upon occasion, a primary teacher will comment unfavorably on what a middle school teacher or team is doing to "his" group from the year before. Under such circumstances, one must try to clear the atmosphere of pettiness, yet avoid needlessly turning the gossipy or malicious teacher into an enemy, and at the same time strive to obtain an accurate concept of children's progress.

In honesty, it must be acknowledged that some of the counselor's faculty associates occasionally may be incapable of making impersonal follow-up analyses. Under these circumstances, sometimes the counselor can do no more than treat them with courtesy while looking elsewhere for more valid information than they are capable of providing at the time. On other occasions group counseling with teachers can help them develop new insights and understanding of children.

Research as a Guidance Function

The word *research* is sometimes uttered with considerable veneration and awe, as was pointed out in Chapter 3. There are even those who view it as a panacea for most educational ills, vexations, and issues—an optimism which is not entirely justified. While research has distinct value in elementary guidance programs, virtually no wide-scale studies were done at this level prior to the 1960's and much experimental work remains to be done in the 1970's. The April, 1969, *Review of Educational Research* illustrates this point (14). Not one of ten chapters in this 151 page review was expressly concerned with the elementary field! And out of a total of some 50 references cited by H. B. Gelatt, who prepared Chapter 2, "School Guidance Programs," only four dealt directly with elementary education (3:151-153).

Needed Research in Elementary Guidance

Needed research probably will eventually seek to answer many queries for which data are now lacking. Here are some examples of topics begging for attention:

1) What instruments for use with children can be created to measure interest, motivation, and other "intangibles" of importance to counselors?

2) What are the counselor's most effective roles in elementary schools?

3) What do teachers want and expect of the guidance program?

4) At what age can children engage in valid self-referral?

5) What educational practices are most suitable for preparing counselors of younger children?

6) What substantive and professional content does the elementary counselor need to acquire?

7) What organizational structures are most suited to elementary guidance programs?

8) What is the status of elementary school guidance: theory, programs, services, and research in progress?

9) What are some of the current group counseling practices found in elementary schools?

10) What is the value of counseling for underachievers, the deprived, the advantaged, and the gifted child?

In view of the 10 questions listed above there seems no need to labor the point that much experimental research must be done in both the university and in the public schools before available information even remotely approximates the fund of elementary school data in such fields as mathematics or the language arts. At present most guidance workers need to concentrate on developing on-the-job research *services* in elementary schools as well as begin to speculate as to how they can engage in experimental or "pure" research.

Research Services

Teachers seek information in the autumn when they first meet a group of children. They also often want specific material for parent conferences, for preparing reports, and on a dozen similar occasions. Principals, consultants, and others with administrative and supervisory duties also frequently may request pupil personal data on an individual, a group, or an all-school basis. It is in order to provide suitable input for teachers, parents, and administrators that counselors perform many of their guidance research services—many of which are not so much "research" as they are "search" activities. The *really* important purpose of any such services is to provide whatever facts and opinions are necessary for placement and follow-up activities as these terms are used in Chapter 11.

Interpreted broadly, "research services" include such contributions as these:

1) Providing teachers with material pertaining to groups of children they will be meeting for the first time.

2) Advising teachers with respect to work with individual children from problem situations.

3) Interpreting to teachers the implications of human development research, research in the behavioral sciences, and its application in the classroom.

4) Helping teachers select and use appropriate nontesting instruments for classroom research.

5) Administering and helping teachers interpret tests of mental ability, reading skill, general achievement, and so forth.

6) Engaging in designing and developing projects with teachers in special education, in special fields, or areas of study.

7) Making retrospective analyses and future projections of developmental data in the guidance center files.

8) Providing up-to-date library materials dealing with research methods and current investigations.

9) Conducting alone and with others original inquiries in the realm of guidance and counseling.

From the list presented, an even clearer meaning of elementary guidance and counseling research services can be inferred. The emphasis, in rank order, is first on *service involving research* and the ability to help others *to interpret and use data*, and only second on research based on experimental designs. The amount of work needing someone's attention in elementary guidance and counseling is presently too great to permit any other rank order of priority, even in well-supported programs.

Teacher Evaluations of Guidance Services

The guidance counselor, and, in larger schools or districts, the guidance staff, should from time to time seek to obtain forthright and rather detailed evaluations of the program. Counseling, orientation services, sequencing, assessment—all should be reviewed in order to obtain the input from faculty members that keeps guidance services both dynamic and relevant.

Since elementary schools vary greatly in size, in community settings, in support, and in leadership, no uniform questionnaire, interview form, or opinionnaire could be used to obtain teacher/child/parent/administrative viewpoints even if they were available. It is suggested that counselors would do well, therefore, to prepare some type of original instrument specifically constructed for gauging the attitudes of their colleagues and perhaps others in the community such as parents and the part-time employers of preadolescents.

It is easy to lose oneself in a few minutes in the many duties of the moment, and in the pressures of the day. When this happens, even a highly competent and sensitive counselor can drift away from the reality of others' wishes and feelings. Conversations do not provide enough linkage with reality—and some teachers tend to be kind rather than blunt if asked how the program can be improved. A methodical policy of written program evaluation is far more likely to pull from teachers the fresh sense of direction that program development constantly demands.

An example of a teacher evaluation questionnaire that has been used successfully* is presented in Figure 24. Figure 25 presents a short evaluation checklist built around various activities and characteristics of the guidance program. (See pages 329-332.)

Summary

A basic guidance program is concerned with the syntax of learning: the sequence, the pacing, and the scope of experiences which promise best to promote the individual child's uniquely personal development. Grouping for instruction and child guidance in paracurricular or school-related activities also may be viewed as ways in which guidance specialists can contribute to the quality or tone of elementary school living.

In addition to mediating the syntax of learning, counselors need to develop and to coordinate follow-up activities in close cooperation with teachers. Such activities are necessary to verify that the pace and the scope of learning have been adequately selected and directed.

Research services round out the functions of the counselor as portrayed in Chapters 8 through 12. There is much need for research in elementary guidance, but research services to the school will take priority over experimental research for some time because of the heavy demand for classroom assistance from the guidance specialist.

The need for periodical evaluation of the counseling and guidance program, evaluation by one's colleagues, children, and the community, is essential to the guidance program.

*Cf. Robert L. Gibson, "Teacher Opinions of High School Guidance Programs." (4)

Teacher Opinions—General Information	Yes	No	Not Sure
1) In your opinion, does the guidance program make a positive contribution to the school instructional program?			
2) Has the guidance program of your school ever been explained, described, or outlined to you for your information?			
3) Could you tell the parents of a new student entering your school what most of the guidance services and activities are carried on in this school?			
4) Do you feel that the guidance staff in the school is identified with the administration?			
5) Should the direction of the school guidance program be the responsibility of the chief school administrator?			
6) Should the guidance staff in the school be identified with the teaching faculty?			
7) Do you feel that the school guidance program is adequately interpreted to the community?			
8) Should teachers have more responsibilities in the school guidance program other than those that are performed within the classroom?			
9) Do you feel that an in-service training program in guidance for the teaching staff would be worthwhile?			

10) Of the following activities, check those which you think should be the responsibility of the school guidance personnel. Designate the three (by number) that you feel are most important.
    Educational and occupational information
    Attendance checking and recording
    Discipline
    Test administration and interpretation
    Administrative duties other than those of the guidance program
    Individual counseling services
    Coordination of the school activities program
    Group orientation programs
    Coordination of field trips
    Curriculum placement			

11) Do you feel pupil cumulative records do help you with students more effectively?			
12) Are pupil cumulative records available and accessible to the teacher at any time?			

Figure 24. Teacher Opinions Regarding Counseling and Guidance Programs (4) (cont. on p. 330)

	Yes	No	Not Sure
13) Do you feel free to ask the guidance department to interpret information contained in the pupil cumulative record?			
14) In your opinion, does the school adequately utilize guidance test results in pupil guidance?			
15) In your opinion, should the school utilize test results in providing a richer and more meaningful curriculum?			
16) Should the teacher participate in administering, scoring, and recording standardized tests?			
17) Are you usually informed of those guidance tests results that would be appropriate and useful to you?			
18) Do you feel these test results were adequately interpreted?			
19) Of the following areas of guidance testing, please number the three (3) that you feel are the most valuable in order of their importance.			

Achievement
Vocational Aptitude
Intelligence and Academic Aptitude
Interest
Personality

Teacher Opinions—Counseling

20) Do you feel that the classroom teacher is encouraged to confer with the counselor regarding the problems of students?			
21) Do you use the counselor as a referral agent when the student's problem is beyond your training or scope?			
22) Is it desirable for the counselor to furnish a review of a student interview to the teacher who made the referral?			
23) Should the teacher share his knowledge with the counselor that he may receive from the parents of students?			
24) Do you feel that the guidance department should assist the classroom teacher in handling problems of discipline?			
25) Should the counselor be the one to administer punishment to the students if it is necessary?			

Figure 24. Teacher Opinions Regarding Counseling and Guidance Programs (4) (cont. on p. 331)

Teacher Opinions—Occupational and Educational Information	Yes	No	Not Sure
26) Do you feel the school guidance program makes an adequate contribution to pupil occupational understanding?			
27) Do you feel the school guidance program makes an adequate contribution to pupil educational understanding?			
28) Do you feel that the teacher should acquaint students with the "world of work" through his classes?			
29) Do you feel that the teacher should help students make educational plans?			
30) Should the securing, organizing, and dissemination of occupational-educational information be the primary responsibility of the guidance staff as opposed to the instructional staff?			
31) Do you think that testing and other guidance activities and their planning disrupt the school too much?			
32) In your opinion, should the school guidance department identify pupil interests and assist or direct the organization of group activities appropriate to these interests?			
33) Should the school guidance department identify, record, and if necessary limit the extent of pupil participation in pupil activities?			
34) Do you believe the school guidance staff should act as faculty sponsors for certain pupil activities?			
35) Should the guidance department conduct periodic follow-up studies of the school's former pupils (graduate and dropouts)?			

Figure 24. Teacher Opinions Regarding Counseling and Guidance Programs (4)

Indicate your evaluation of the following activities and characteristics of your school guidance program by ratings as follows:

5 = Superior   3 = Average   1 = Poor
4 = Excellent   2 = Below average U = Unknown or not appropriate
                                    N = Not necessary

Rating: Item:

_____ 1. A philosophy of guidance which complements the school's objectives

_____ 2. Coordination of the guidance program with the total educational effort of the school

_____ 3. Informs the school faculty of guidance activities

_____ 4. Informs pupils of school guidance activities

_____ 5. Informs parents of school guidance activities

_____ 6. Administration of the guidance program

_____ 7. Works cooperatively with the instructional staff for the optimum development of the pupil

_____ 8. Maintains and interprets to faculty adequate pupil guidance records

_____ 9. Has developed a program of guidance testing to aid pupil analysis

_____ 10. Interpretation of guidance test results to those concerned

_____ 11. An organized program for disseminating appropriate pupil educational information

_____ 12. An organized program for disseminating appropriate pupil information

_____ 13. An organized program for disseminating appropriate pupil social-personal information

_____ 14. Provides opportunities to pupils for individual counseling

_____ 15. Provides opportunities for parent conferences to discuss pupil development and adjustment

_____ 16. Provides opportunities and works cooperatively with faculty in assessment and solution of pupil adjustment problems

_____ 17. Assists faculty or assumes responsibility for facilitating pupil referrals to clinical agencies when needed

_____ 18. Assists faculty in pupil groupings for interest, activity, or instructional purposes

_____ 19. Involves faculty in guidance program planning and development

_____ 20. Makes consistent effort to improve the guidance program

Figure 25. Short Form Evaluation Checklist

References

1. Bennett, M. E. "Strategies of Vocational Guidance in Groups." In H. Borrow (ed.). *Man in a World at Work.* Boston: Houghton Mifflin and Company, 1964.

2. Eckerson, L. O. and H. M. Smith. "Guidance in the Elementary School." *School Life* 44 (1962): 16-20.

3. Gelatt, H. B. "School Guidance Programs." In Carl E. Thoresen (ed.). "Guidance and Counseling." *Review of Educational Research* 30 (April, 1969): 141-153.

4. Gibson, Robert L. "Teacher Opinions of High School Guidance Programs." *Personnel and Guidance Journal* 44 (December, 1965): 416-422.

5. Gordon, Ira J. *Studying the Child in the School.* New York: John Wiley and Sons, Inc., 1966.

6. Kaback, G. R. "Occupational Information in Elementary Education: What Counselors Do—What Counselors Would Like to Do." *Vocational Guidance Quarterly* 16 (March, 1968): 203-206.

7. Lacy, Charles L., "Identifying Potential High School Dropouts." *The School Counselor* 16 (September, 1968): 36-40.

8. Leonard, George E., John T. Pietrofesa, and Irene M. Bank. "A Workshop for the Improvement of the Self-Concepts of Inner City Youngsters." *The School Counselor* 16 (May, 1969): 375-379.

9. ____ and Ellen Stephens. "Elementary School Employment Service." *Vocational Guidance Quarterly* 16 (September, 1967): 13-25.

10. Norris, W. *Occupational Information in the Elementary School.* Chicago: Science Research Associates, 1963.

11. Schreiber, D. (ed.). *Guidance and the School Dropout.* Washington, D.C.: The National Educational Association and the American Personnel and Guidance Association, 1964.

12. Thelen, Herbert A. *Classroom Grouping for Teachability.* New York: John Wiley and Sons, Inc., 1967.

13. Thompson, Jack M. "Career Development in the Elementary School: Rationale and Implications for Elementary School Counselors." *The School Counselor* 16 (January, 1969): 208-210.

14. Thoresen, Carl E. (ed.). "Guidance and Counseling." *Review of Educational Research* 39 (April, 1969): 2.

13

Administering the Elementary Counseling and Guidance Program

Any treatment of the administrative coordination of an elementary school guidance program is also a study of educational leadership. The management of the program can best be studied with respect to the role of the elementary guidance counselor and the general leadership principles that lend integrity to his work (18,23,39).

Some years ago in Rome a thin, middle-aged man presented himself at a physician's office. He complained of being tired, nervous, and depressed. The doctor examined him carefully and concluded that his problem was mental rather than physical. "Take time from the work you are doing," the physician advised. "Enjoy life more. Why not go to see Grimaldi tonight? The famous clown makes everybody laugh!" The elderly patient's face worked with emotion. After a long pause he spoke. "Ah, but my God, Doctor, *I am* Grimaldi!"

The administrative leader, as in the case of the great Grimaldi (but in a *very* different context), has an important responsibility for looking after the welfare and happiness of others. Like Grimaldi, he has responsibilities and pressures which may sometimes weigh heavily on his shoulders. The next few pages review some of the tasks of the administrator of counseling and guidance services and present a self-evaluation scale which—if it can be answered largely in the affirmative—suggests the probable success of a person if he seeks a leadership role. A negative score, conversely, may imply that (like Grimaldi's) the role of serving others could be a difficult one.

Principles and Backgrounds with a Bearing on the Administration of Guidance

Every dimension of education has certain principles or guidelines which shape policies and govern professional behavior. These guides to behavior may be either implicit or explicit.

Leadership Principles

Here are a dozen principles which provide a sense of direction for the counselor as he administers a guidance program.

1) The effective guidance program has a reasonable and clear set of goals to be attained, and it is the purpose of administration to insure their attainment.

2) The administration of the program is clearly recognized as a *means*, not as an *end* in itself.

3) The administration of counseling and guidance services is marked by both continuity and flexibility.

4) The processes of administration are consistent with sound guidance processes and reflect similar values.

5) The counselor-administrator understands what it means to coordinate an elementary school program. He also recognizes that coordination does not require blind conformity from teachers or a high degree of uniformity in the curriculum.

6) Administration of the program shows awareness of the fact that good interpersonal relations are created by the counselor's *example* rather than by *precept*.

7) The administrator of the guidance program recognizes that his success resides in the desirable changed behavior and the effective classroom accomplishments of his colleagues.

8) The leader's effectiveness is partly measured by the quality of the people who work with him.

9) Insofar as possible, teachers and other persons in the guidance program should be consulted and, when possible, share in making decisions by which they are to abide.

10) The counselor sees his associates as co-workers and peers rather than as subordinates and followers. The administrator differs from teachers because of his skills and special knowledge, not by the authority of his rank.

11) Carefully planned experiences that foster personal growth rather than dictatorial orders are recognized as the bases for changing behavior in the staff.

12) The counselor-administrator recognizes the importance of understanding the art of sometimes reaching a consensus by means of honorable and viable compromises.

It would be naive to assume that mere knowledge of the dozen principles above is sufficient to insure the success of a counselor charged with the task of operating a strong elementary school program. In addition to administrative know-how, there are a few simple but important personal attributes which leaders ranging from Pericles to Winston Churchill have possessed. These important human qualities are 1) a strong willingness to accept the satisfactions and frustrations of responsibility, 2) self-confidence, 3) well-developed communication skills, 4) a broad grasp of many kinds of professional and general information, and 5) reasoned opinions on a wide range of topics.

The general tasks and responsibilities of an administrator for elementary counseling and guidance services which are given below rather clearly indicate why the five personal qualities are needed as a basis for implementing the twelve leadership principles stated above.

General Tasks and Responsibilities
of Administrative Leadership in Guidance

The specific functions of the counselor-administrator in guidance are tremendously varied because guidance itself covers many dimensions of education in the elementary school. Nevertheless, an inventory of some of the more general responsibilities and tasks of the leader can be made.*

Three important tasks of the counselor are conventional administrative responsibilities: *executing, coordinating*, and *supervising.* The leader in a guidance program also has responsibility for *advising, mediating, evaluating,* and *motivating.* Finally, his general functions include serving as an *expert,* an *interpreter,* an *example,* and as a *future-planner.*

At first glance the counselor interested in administration is likely to raise a quizzical eyebrow at the scope of these eleven points. They do, indeed,

*For a scholarly, research-based treatment of leadership in various fields of human endeavor, cf. Fred E. Fiedler, *A Theory of Leadership Effectiveness* (14).

suggest a wide-ranging and varied body of responsibilities. However, if any one task or responsibility is deleted the counselor's ability to contribute is sharply diminished. It also should be kept in mind that *a new concept of administrative tasks and supervisory responsibilities to be assumed by counselors in elementary schools is being presented.* This concept is based on the assumption that counselors are capable of cultivating leadership qualities similar to the five general characteristics of leadership identified above: personal responsibility, self-confidence, communication skills, broad knowledge, and carefully reasoned and broad ranging opinions. With these qualities it is likely that the eleven tasks and responsibilities can be carried on.

A Self-Evaluation Scale for the Administrative Leader in Elementary Guidance Programs

At this point it may be of interest for the counselor who is contemplating administrative responsibility to check himself on an informal rating scale designed for persons who are seriously thinking of a leadership career which involves administrative responsibility. The scale below assumes that there are at least three levels of leadership in guidance. These include *potential* leaders who are just beginning to perform limited guidance and counseling functions, *maturing* leaders who are well on their way, and *mature* leaders. Their qualifications correspond approximately to the *Level I*, *Level II*, and *Level III* guidance specialists. The *mature* leader presumably is one who can give an affirmative answer to all, or nearly all, of the points which follow. (See Figure 26.)

A self-appraisal made with the check list in Figure 26 obviously cannot guarantee that a person who can give 15 affirmative answers will be a first-magnitude success! At the same time, the points illustrate the need for thoughtful self-analysis if one is interested in administering a guidance program. They also are intended to suggest that an able person in this field should be representative of the most superior types of human beings that contemporary U.S. culture can produce.

Attention now is directed toward some of the emerging concepts embedded in managerial responsibility for elementary counseling and guidance.

A Résumé of Trends in School Administration: Implications for Guidance Services

As a matter of being well-informed, the counselor charged with responsibility for administration of elementary school guidance services should have

Personal Quality or Professional Competency	Do I Possess This Quality?	
	Yes	No
1) Do I have the intellectual and emotional security essential for mental health?		
2) Am I personally honest and do I have the integrity on which candor, courage, and sincerity are based?		
3) Do my recreational activities satisfy my personality needs and help to satisfy those of my associates?		
4) Do I participate in civic and professional activities of social importance?		
5) Do I have physical health which is reflected in vigorous, motivated work habits?		
6) Am I able to feel sympathy for the problems of others without becoming emotionally involved in them?		
7) Are my expressions of opinion carefully reasoned and free of demagoguery?		
8) Am I well-informed with respect to socio-economic and political trends so that I can contribute to my community environment as an effective citizen?		
9) Do I have faith in education and work to support it as an indispensable component of a democratic social structure?		
10) Can I identify and use, without harmful exploitation, the human and material resources of the community that are needed for a broad guidance program?		
11) In retrospect, have I steadily increased my general cultural background methodically, deliberately, and adequately?		
12) Have I carefully built up my personal resources with respect to skills in group interaction and decision making?		
13) Do I recognize the importance of group processes and decisions by persons who are directly concerned?		
14) Do I have an examined, workable, democratic philosophy as it applies to education?		
15) Have I developed a grasp of the principles of human development and kept up to date with regard to new knowledge?		

Figure 26. Self-Evaluation Scale: Administrative Leadership in Guidance

some knowledge of trends in professional administration. This background information helps one to understand the interplay of ideas which has led to contemporary concepts of leadership.

Early Beginnings

The idea of selecting someone to assume managerial responsibilities in U.S. schools developed about 150 years ago. The term "manager" or "school visitor" was in use around 1826 and apparently referred to a head teacher (36:144). Cleveland and Baltimore had begun to employ school managers by the 1840's, but the concept of educational leadership in the modern sense of the term was yet to develop (29).

After 1870, as education became more complicated in the cities of the U.S., members of boards of education began to be faced with a growing number of problems. Their lack of administrative competence, inability to assess the instructional program, and lack of time to give to school matters inevitably led the decision to employ some supervisory-managerial person to coordinate and to direct the work of head teachers in individual schools. By 1890, there were 380 "superintendents" in the 420 U.S. cities with 5,000 or more inhabitants. During the same era (1875-1900) the employment of supervisors for special fields such as music and art was begun (1).

Modern School Management and Supervision Begin

Many duties performed by administrators and by supervisory personnel at the present time had begun to become established by the 1920's. This was also an era in which influential leaders in administration and specialists in administrative theory gave new directions to leadership.* Supervisory theory and practice also were coming of age, and by 1922 W. H. Burton was able to classify basic functions of supervision as follows: the improvement of teaching, directing in-service education, establishing the relationship between educational goals and content, testing and assessing, and teacher rating (4).

Changing ideas regarding "good" or "effective" supervision and management between 1920 or 1930 and 1970 are of great relevance to leaders in guidance and counseling. In the 1920's much administrative leadership was influenced by the idea that efficiency was an important goal. "Efficiency" was identified with production-line speed and economy, and an authoritarian, military "line and staff" type of structure as a basis for school organization was commonly recommended by writers until the 1930's.

*Among "great names" of the period: J. C. Morrison, E. P. Cubberly, Ward Reeder, I. L. Kandel, George Strayer, Sr., and N. L. Engelhardt.

During the 1930's efforts were made to make education more democratic, and new values emerged with respect to what constituted a good "human climate" in the schools. Among influential developments were:

J. L. Moreno's ideas (1934) regarding sociometry with its focus on the nature and quality of group relationships

The idea (*ca.* 1940) that democratic school climates were superior to either laissez-faire or authoritarian ones as suggested by Ronald Lippitt and Kurt Lewin

The popularity of "group processes" after 1947, particularly under the sponsorship of the Association for Supervision and Curriculum Development

A new literature, especially at the elementary school level, stressing the vitality and importance of behavioral changes in teachers and children created through applying democracy in school administration (8,15,21,22,37,38).

As a result of the points briefly made above, both administrative and supervisory theory supported a benign, pleasant setting for teaching and learning in most elementary schools during the 1960's, although practice sometimes differed sharply from theory. A humane atmosphere (one that is congruent with accepted guidance and counseling constructs) is gradually becoming more prevalent despite the academic pressures generated in the late 1950's by critics of education and despite increased emphasis on substantive content in the 1960's due to the stress placed on excellence.

Implications for Guidance

The humane trends described above have an important implication for the field of guidance. As administrative processes have become more sensitive to human values, to participation and to desirable behavioral change, these processes have come into closer alignment with the goals and activities of the top-flight "mature" or *Level III* type of guidance worker described earlier. The qualifications of a superior guidance counselor in the elementary school are beginning to resemble more closely those of persons, such as the principal or team leader, with administrative and program development responsibility in the elementary school. Fortunately, the reverse also is true: principals and team leaders are expected to be sensitive to the human values which the insightful counselor accepts.

Elementary education is on the threshold of an era which is likely to become more and more deeply imbued with the concepts developed in earlier chapters. Contemporary interpretations of effective educational leadership are indicating more and more clearly that administrators must be persons who understand guidance. As a concomitant, top level workers in guidance are becoming logical choices for major leadership duties in the operation and management of many aspects of the elementary school program.

We now come to a basic question: if the counselor's values and skills qualify him for leadership, how is an effective counseling and guidance program to be administered, and what are the relationships among various guidance functions, services, and elements in the elementary school?

The Administration of Elementary School Guidance: A Point of View

It may be poor tactics to begin this section on the administration of elementary school guidance with a *negative* statement. But it also seems strategically important to reiterate once again the point that guidance procedures in the elementary school must *not* be based on a transposition of conventional secondary school programs or procedures to the primary level or to the middle school years. Benign administrative leadership in the guidance program should be uniquely developed to serve the children, to improve the milieu in which they learn, and to promote the reasoned purposes which good guidance serves. There are almost no conventional guidance policies or practices at the high school level that can be transferred to or grafted on the elementary program. The counselor-administrator must focus on how a program designed for children can be developed, so as to direct their optimum progress through the seamless curriculum continuum; the unbroken flow of desirable learning experiences.

Guidance Services and Functions are Different in Elementary Education

If the services and functions of guidance in elementary schools are instituted as watered-down versions of 1) appraisal, 2) placement, 3) referral, 4) follow-up information services, or 5) counseling as developed in recent decades for young adolescents in secondary schools, then the "victory" achieved by infusing guidance into the child's first six to ten years in school will be a disastrous one. Indeed, even in the high school several of the five labels are becoming obsolete.

Before beginning an examination of leadership in program development it is important to review our interpretations of elementary guidance.

Placement in the elementary program refers to the continuing professional study of the syntax of learning—the child's progress through an unbroken continuum of educational experiences. It involves carefully developed decisions which the guidance specialist helps teachers (or teams of teachers) to make with regard to the sequence and the design of individualized learning, grouping for instruction, and the rate at which a given child moves through the sequence of experiences we label the curriculum.

Referral has to do with bringing the individual child into contact with the human resources (and the tools they command) that are available to the school for maximizing his social, physical, intellectual, and emotional growth.

Information services become *orientation services* in elementary schools. They pertain to orienting a child to his milieu in school, to certain wider ecological understandings of his own subculture, of other subcultures, and to similar important personal social insights. Only incidentally and casually—if at all—is the child formally introduced in the classroom to "occupational information" and the "world of work." When this is done it is only to help him understand his world, not for the vocational purposes that enter in during later years.*

Appraisal or assessment functions at the elementary level become a part of the ongoing processes of determining how a child is maturing in relation to the many forms of human growth and development in which the school has an interest. Broad evaluation, rather than testing or narrow forms of assessment, is involved. Cumulative records are maintained primarily to deepen a teacher's understandings. The development of a "statistical biography" of a child for the school's convenience is actually of secondary importance despite its utilitarian values.

Counseling involves helping teachers learn to work closely and insightfully with boys and girls much more than it mandates a counselor-child or a counselor group contact or activity. It is aimed at creating greater self understanding of the child by teachers, by himself, by the child's peers, and by adults.

Follow-up and *research*, in the parlance of elementary school guidance, are terms which refer to the longitudinal study of a young student's behavioral responses and measurable performance. "Research," in the sense used here, is an especially valuable service in that it is a means of providing data on which to base discussions and decisions that are germane to replacement, referral, information service, appraisal, and counseling.

There is a real question as to whether the seven italicized terms reviewed above, terms which originated in the secondary school, should be used at all in elementary school guidance. If traditional meanings cling to them then these labels should be dropped immediately insofar as early and middle childhood

*The absence of *formal* occupational counseling in the elementary school does not, of course, preclude helping children find actual part-time employment as proposed in Chapter 12.

and pre-adolescence are concerned, and replaced with more applicable terms. If, on the other hand, they can be used by guidance workers in the connotations given here, then they may become acceptable for use with young learners during the 1970's. Words acquire the meanings with which people endow them and are never inherently "good" or "bad," "clean" or "dirty."

Granting that guidance does have unique meanings and qualities in the elementary school, why do we reiterate this point when it is implicit or explicit in virtually all of the foregoing chapters? Because it is these unique concepts of guiding human development in childhood that help to support the view that the counselor who is also highly knowledgeable in the elementary field merits increased leadership responsibility in the educational tomorrows toward which U.S. schools rapidly are moving.

Guidance Permeates the
Total Structure for Teaching-Learning

Since the points made about the unique contributions of elementary guidance are valid ones, the work of the counselor should permeate the entire instructional program from the time of the child's first contact with the school until he leaves the middle school or junior high school to move into secondary education. Under these circumstances it becomes highly important that guidance services—*and their administration or management*—be as comprehensive and unifying as they can be made.

It is the need for coherence, this need for authoritative*ness* in guiding children's development, as distinct from mere authori*ty*, that provides a basis for vesting major administrative responsibilities in the domain of the qualified elementary school guidance specialist. The nature and extent of such responsibility are variables. What might be advisable in New York, Chicago, or Los Angeles probably would differ sharply from what would be effective in Sundance, Wyoming, or Kennebunkport, Maine. The "best" policies likewise would differ for Kenosha, Kokomo, El Paso, or Miami Beach. They would also vary *within* each community.

Despite such variations among any list of communities, one conclusion seems to be a likely one for the years immediately ahead in most school districts. The direction of elementary guidance programs should become a strong, clearly delineated administrative responsibility assigned to a coordinator of guidance services.

Responsibilities for the
Coordinator of Elementary School Guidance

Since comprehensive guidance services, by definition, permeate the program, what are the elements to be coordinated by a specialist? Since school districts vary so greatly, let us select as an example either a very large elementary school* or a small school system with from four to six schools that have a pre-primary continuum or four- and five-year-old kindergartens and programs extending through the middle school or junior high school years. Let us further assume that the mythical school of our choice has financial resources sufficient to pay for a substantial array of student personnel services. Then, once these resources have been identified, let us suggest which among them the guidance specialist might coordinate.†

Here is a list of possible human and material resources which should be available for work with children in an unusually well-supported school.††

Human Resources

Principal
Curriculum director
Guidance coordinator
Teaching staff; teaching teams
Paraprofessional corps
Educational materials specialists: Librarian; educational media
School health staff: School nurse, doctor, dentist
Guidance staff: Counselors, school psychologist, psychometrist, psychiatric school worker
Special education personnel: Education of the deaf and hard of hearing, emotionally disturbed, blind and partially sighted, physically handicapped, etc.
Academic clinician
Special areas staff: Art, music, physical education, etc.
Non-certificated personnel

The material resources which are listed below obviously have a close relationship to the human resources above. It seems useful, however, to list them separately for purposes of clarity.

Material Resources¶

Academic clinic and equipment
Special education clinic, rooms, and equipment

*While the authors do not advocate large (1000 to 1500 pupils or more) elementary schools, their existence is a reality with which guidance services must cope.

†For a stimulating treatment of changing tasks in administration and their implications for in-service preparation, cf. George B. Brain, "Emerging Challenges and Designs for the Preparation of Other Educators." (2)

††Certain important nonschool resources such as the public library, city health department, and other agencies have been eliminated. While they often work closely with the schools at present most of them are not generally included in the school district budget.

¶School kitchens, multi-purpose rooms, teachers' lounge, auditoriums, conference areas, and certain other material resources have been omitted to simplify the presentation.

School library, including professional references

Special area rooms: Art, physical education, etc.

Health services suite

Computer-simulation center

Self-realization/inquiry center

Individualized programmed learning service area

Department of developmental guidance (including evaluation and assessment hardware and software, record keeping equipment, and an area for the human relations/anthropology specialist who concerns himself with the subcultures represented in the school)

Educational media center (deploys and operates media; works in close articulation with the library and pupil inquiry center)

Materials development center (operates as an integral part of the media center, but specializes in creating to order such items as transparencies for overhead projectors, charts, or original music for special-purpose use in the classroom)

In a small school district of 4 to 8 elementary schools, a number of the human and material resources listed could serve all the schools but would not be housed in each school. For example, special provisions that are made for the blind or partially sighted probably should be concentrated in one school in the district to which the handicapped boys and girls would be transported. Other services that might be centralized for a cluster of schools include medical-dental clinics, the materials development center, and the computer-simulation center, although each presumably would have branch offices or rooms or comparable linkages to individual schools.

It is also likely that it would be more economical, and no less efficient, to have a central Department of Developmental Guidance serving from four to a dozen elementary buildings. Indeed, this is probably the only way in which staff members (such as the human relations specialist) could be justified. It is also the only physical set-up in which a large investment in hardware (e.g., computerized records; test-correction equipment) could be defended.

A detailed examination of elementary school guidance services is facilitated through the use of a model depicting relationships among personnel and functions in a large school or a district with four or more buildings. Figure 27 presents an attempt to delineate such relationships. It also serves as a reference to the administration of elementary guidance activities and is discussed in detail.

Note from Figure 27 that an *administrative team* approach is used to illustrate the operation of either a large elementary school or a cluster of smaller ones with from 300 to 600 enrolled in each. Presumably, in a majority of school districts, one coordinator of guidance and one curriculum director would be teamed with four or more principals to make up an administrative team.

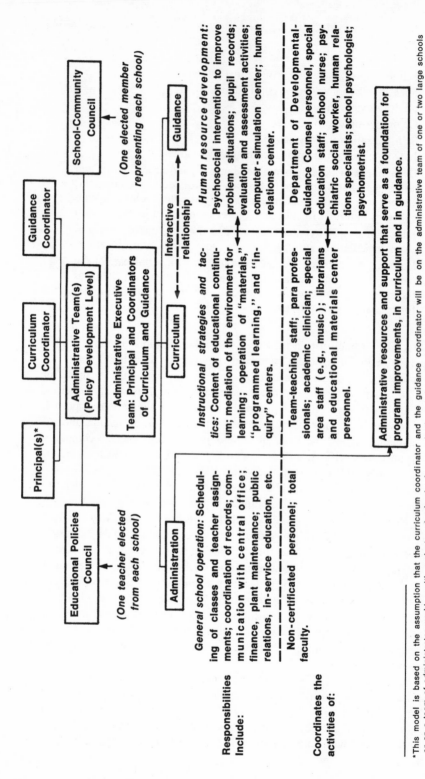

Figure 27. A Model of Personnel Relationships in the Administration of an Elementary School Guidance Program

The following text appears within the figure:

Principal(s)*

Curriculum Coordinator

Guidance Coordinator

Educational Policies Council

(One teacher elected from each school)

Administrative Team(s) (Policy Development Level)

School-Community Council

(One elected member representing each school)

Administrative Executive Team: Principal and Coordinators of Curriculum and Guidance

Curriculum ← Interactive relationship → Guidance

Administration

Responsibilities Include:

General school operation: Scheduling of classes and teacher assignments; coordination of records; communication with central office; finance, plant maintenance; public relations, in-service education, etc.

Instructional strategies and tactics: Content of educational continuum; mediation of the environment for learning; operation of "materials," "programmed learning," and "inquiry" centers.

Human resource development: Psychosocial intervention to improve problem situations; pupil records; evaluation and assessment activities; computer-simulation center; human relations center.

Coordinates the activities of:

Non-certificated personnel; total faculty.

Team-teaching staff; para professionals; academic clinician; special area staff (e.g., music); librarians and educational materials center personnel.

Department of Developmental-Guidance Counsel personnel, special education staff; school nurse; psychiatric social worker, human relations specialists; school psychologist; psychometrist.

Administrative resources and support that serve as a foundation for program improvements, in curriculum and in guidance.

*This model is based on the assumption that the curriculum coordinator and the guidance coordinator will be on the administrative team of one or two large schools or on a team of administrator working with a cluster of schools. As a result, the number of principals on a team would vary.

The purpose of the model is not only to show some of the relationships that exist among personnel; it also is intended to show how the functions of a personally competent, highly educated elementary guidance coordinator support a new concept of organizing responsibility which bring added importance and dignity to his role.

The Administration of Elementary School Guidance: Some Applications to a Point of View

It has been proposed that the developmental concepts and programs which are appearing in elementary guidance are creating a demand for a new, more responsible leadership role for the counselor—a role so new that only a few schools had begun to contemplate it in the early 1970's. In the immensely more sophisticated U.S. school systems which present trends suggest are almost certain to develop in the later 1970's and 1980's, new tasks and responsibilities will be mandated by the knowledge we are now acquiring as to how improved environments can "create" intelligence in young children for example, or how biochemistry can improve learning, or how anthropology and linguistics can deepen and widen educators' understandings of culture and communication.

It is this era of increasing educational responsibility that is illustrated by the model on page 346.

New Structures for New Times

Education already is reaching downward to encompass work with children of two and three years old as a standard component of public education.* Within a decade persons also seem likely to begin to return to school in their forties and in their sixties to be "retreaded" with new knowledge, to develop leisure-time pursuits, and to qualify for new jobs to replace old ones that have been eliminated by change. What is more, with life spans extending, the man or woman of 60 who "regraduates" from a functional post-secondary school experience may have 20 or 25 useful and healthful working years before him (34). In other words, the school is extending *upward* and *downward* and already is offering complex services and performing tasks not even contemplated by visionaries of the early 1960's. As Howard A. Miller, phrased it, "As knowledge increases and work becomes more technical . . . as automation advances and new industries replace old, learning will not be regarded as ending with graduation from school, but will become a way of life for everyone." (34:3)

---

*Cf. the entire March, 1969, issue of the *Phi Delta Kappan* which deals with early childhood education. The magazine shows the sweep of change created by our new respect for the importance of the early years of life (10).

Programs simultaneously are beginning to become more complicated both internally and externally. New hardware—new applications of the computer, refinements in programmed learning—all of these are symptomatic of internal change and mirror the complex skills educators must begin to acquire. Closer connections with social agencies, deeper involvement as a change agency, and increased awareness and participation in the urban milieu represent the accelerated trend toward outward extension of the school.

In view of these dynamic movements and of the powerful winds of change, the conventional concepts of the principal, the curriculum coordinator, and the guidance specialist are no longer adequate. No one person such as a principal—regardless of his professional competence, energy, and personal qualities—has the time to give personalized "attention-in-depth" to the universe of activities partly illustrated by the model in Figure 27.

The administrative team, or a suitable variation of this administrative approach to shared authority, is a promising possibility. In any case, it is sound to think about disparate but closely meshed responsibilities for all three persons in elementary education: principal, curriculum coordinator, and guidance specialist (13). While the limitations of space preclude an analytical study and rationale for the administrative and curricular dimensions of the model, attention must be directed here toward new structures and relationships that are suggested by changing times.

The Guidance Specialist's New Elementary-Level Opportunities

It is reasonable to develop three-man teams for leadership purposes in larger elementary schools or in clusters of smaller elementary schools. This team, at the policy-development level, would profit from receiving advice from an "Educational Policies Council" made up of elected representatives of the teaching staff and from a "School Community Council." The latter group might be made up of elected representatives from parent or neighborhood groups in each school's attendance district.

At the executive level where policy is transformed into programs and various other forms of action, it seems eminently reasonable to allocate to the highly prepared guidance coordinator or counselor special responsibilities and opportunities not all of which are presently thought of as components of his work with children of middle school age and below. If this is done, the specialist becomes, in effect, the person most responsible for a majority of the human resource development activities carried on under the school's auspices.

This major developmental function is justified if one accepts guidance as a function ". . . *concerned with the professionally skillful deployment of all available human and material resources at the school's command . . .*" This definition clearly brings under the aegis of guidance such activities as psychosocial intervention to improve problem situations, maintenance of pupil records, evaluation-assessment activities, decisions regarding the wise use made of the computer as an educational aid; and any human relations services that are built around disciplines such as anthropology.*

School system employees who might logically become those for whom the guidance expert assumes certain administrative and leadership responsibilities in view of the definition cited above include personnel in the Department of Developmental Guidance (other counselors and clerical personnel). A strong case also can be made for including coordination of the tasks of the school psychologist, psychometrist, psychiatric social worker, human relations specialist, and the school nurse except where matters of physical illness are involved (7). It is also likely that the guidance coordinator or senior counselor on the administrative leadership team should coordinate the efforts of teachers working in special education with the deaf, hard of hearing, and other handicapped children.†

The responsibilities proposed here for the guidance coordinator may at first seem cosmic in scope. Upon closer examination they appear broad largely because they depart from customary practices in today's elementary schools. Actually, there are excellent reasons for each suggestion. These reasons become more apparent as our examination of the administration of guidance is continued in Chapter 14.

Summary

In years past, major administrative responsibilities have rarely been delegated to guidance workers in elementary schools. Educational changes that are occurring and sociocultural forces that are increasing the importance of guidance services in childhood suggest that the administration of guidance is becoming a new and important component of the counselor's work.

General principles of administration are presented in relation to the guidance program, followed by an informal self-appraisal instrument presented as a means of helping a guidance counselor evaluate his potential as a leader in elementary guidance and as a coordinator of services for the younger child and the pre-adolescent.

Trends in educational leadership are examined, particularly with respect to their bearing on guidance. These trends are followed by a proposal for organizing the elementary school so as to enhance the ability of the counselor

---

*For a good account of the nature and scope of problems of the inner city, one written by an anthropologist, cf. Jacquetta H. Burnett, "School Culture and Social Change in the City." (3)

†In view of the broad responsibilities envisioned for a guidance expert, it seems likely that he would, in school districts of appropriate size, have a title such as Assistant or Associate Superintendent of Guidance and Pupil Personnel Services.

to contribute to program development. The enhanced importance of guidance is reflected in a model which portrays the guidance coordinator as an integral part of an administrative team with responsibility for program development shared among the principal, curriculum director, and the guidance coordinator.

On the basis of the model, the scope of the coordinator's guidance responsibilities and opportunities for leadership is described. It is further suggested that many persons concerned directly with the analysis of human development in elementary schools might work effectively under the leadership of the counselor-administrator.

References

1. Ayer, F. C. and A. S. Barr. *The Organization of Supervision*. New York: D. Appleton-Century Co., 1928. Chapters I-IV.
2. Brain, George B. "Emerging Challenges and Designs for the Preparation of Other Educators." Edgar L. Morphet and David L. Jesser (eds.). *Preparing Educators to Meet Emerging Needs*. Denver, Colo.: Designing Education for the Future: An Eight-State Project, 1969.
3. Burnett, Jacquetta H. "School Culture and Social Change in the City." *Educational Leadership* 26 (October, 1968): 12-16.
4. Burton, W. H. *Supervision and the Improvement of Teaching*. New York: D. Appleton-Century Co., 1922.
5. Cleveland, David I. and William R. King. *Systems Analysis and Project Management*. New York: McGraw-Hill Book Co., 1968.
6. Cubberly, Ellwood P. *Public School Administration*. Revised edition. Boston: Houghton Mifflin Co., 1929.
7. Demak, Leonard S. "Impact of Social Forces on Public Schools in Cities." *Educational Leadership* 26 (November, 1968): 177-185.
8. Dewey, John. "Democracy for the Teacher." *Elementary Teacher*, 1903.
9. Downing, Lester N. *Guidance and Counseling Services*. New York: McGraw-Hill Book Co., 1968. Note especially Chapter 17.
10. "Early Childhood Education–Special Issue." *Phi Delta Kappan* 50 (March, 1969): 389-433.
11. Elsbree, Willard S., Harold McNally, and Richard Wynn. *Elementary School Administration and Supervision*. New York: American Book Co., 1967.
12. Englehardt, N. L., N. L. Englehardt, Jr., and Stanton Leggett. *School Planning and Building Handbook*. New York: F. W. Dodge Corp., 1956.
13. Fench, Edwin and Robert E. Wilson. *The Superintendency Team*. Columbus, Ohio: Charles E. Merrill Books, 1964.
14. Fiedler, Fred E. *A Theory of Leadership Effectiveness*. New York: McGraw-Hill Book Co., 1967. Appropriate attention is given to current "organizational engineering" in both education and general mangement.
15. Hanlon, James M. *Administration and Education*. Belmont, Calif.: Wadsworth Publishing Co., 1968.

16. Hatch, Raymond and Buford Stefflre. *Administration of Guidance Service*. Englewood Cliffs, N.J.: Prentice-Hall, Inc., 1965.

17. Hicks, Herbert G. *The Management of Organizations*. New York: McGraw-Hill Book Co., 1967.

18. Hill, George E. and Eleanor Braun Luckey. *Guidance for Children in Elementary Schools*. New York: Appleton-Century-Crofts, 1969.

19. Hummel, Dean L. and S. J. Bonham, Jr. *Pupil Personnel Services in Schools: Organization and Coordination*. Chicago: Rand McNally, 1968.

20. Kandel, I. L. *History of Secondary Education*. Boston: Houghton Mifflin Co., 1930.

21. Kimbrough, Ralph B. *Administering Elementary Schools—Concepts and Practices*. New York: The Macmillan Co., 1968.

22. Koopman, G. R., Alice Miel, and P. J. Misner. *Democracy in School Administration*. New York: Appleton-Century-Crofts, 1943.

23. Kowitz, Gerald T. and Norma G. Kowitz. *Operating Guidance Services for the Modern School*. New York: Holt, Rinehart and Winston, Inc., 1968.

24. Morphet, Edgar L. and David L. Jesser (eds.). *Preparing Educators to Meet Emerging Needs*. Denver, Colo.: Designing Education for the Future: An Eight-State Project, 1969.

25. Morrison, Henry C. *American Schools: A Critical Study of Our School System*. Chicago: University of Chicago Press, 1943.

26. Mosher, Ralph L., Richard F. Carle, and Chris D. Kehas. *Guidance, An Examination*. New York: Harcourt, Brace and World, Inc., 1965.

27. Peters, Herman and Bruce Shertzer. *Guidance Program Development and Management*. Columbus, Ohio: Charles E. Merrill Books, 1963.

28. Reeder, Ward G. *The Fundamentals of Public School Administration*. 4th edition. New York: The Macmillan Co., 1958.

29. Reller, T. L. *The Development of the City Superintendency of Schools in the United States*. Philadelphia: published by the author, 1935.

30. Riccio, Anthony C. and Garry R. Waltz (eds.). "Forces for Change in Counselor Education and Supervision." *Counselor Education and Supervision*, Special Issue 6 (Spring, 1967).

31. Roeber, Edward C., Garry R. Waltz, and Glenn E. Smith. *A Strategy for Guidance*. London: Collier-Macmillan Ltd., 1969.

32. *Scope of Pupil Personnel Services*. Washington, D.C.: U.S. Department of Health, Education, and Welfare, 1966.

33. Shane, Harold G. and June Grant Shane. "Inventing Educational Tomorrows through *Future*-Planning," *Viewpoint*, (February, 1969): 11-12.

34. Squibb, Andrew, Jr., "Year 2000: Education from [the] Crib." *Target* (June 14, 1968).

35. Strayer, G. D. and N. L. Englehardt. *Problems in Educational Administration*. New York: Teachers College Press, 1925.

36. Suzzalo, Henry. *The Rise of Local Supervision in Massachusetts*. New York: Teachers College Press, 1906.

37. Wiles, Kimball. *Supervision for Better Schools*. New York: Prentice-Hall, Inc., 1950. (3rd edition, 1967.)

38. Yauch, W. A. *Improving Human Relations in School Administration.* New York: Harper and Bros., 1949.

39. Zeran, Franklin R. and Anthony Riccio. *Organization and Administration of Guidance Services.* Chicago: Rand McNally, 1962.

Part
THREE

14

Creating a
Good Environment for
Elementary School Guidance

Anything that can be done at all in the field of elementary guidance can be done better and perhaps more simply than it is now being done. This is just one way of saying that although many gains have been made in the last decade or two, much more can still be accomplished. Furthermore, most members of our culture continually aspire to higher levels of excellence which they envision being accomplished through education. Under these circumstances, it is important that the school's guidance environment be appraised to determine what are the most effective learning settings and what are the priorities that must be established in the processes of educational change.*

"Environment" is a word having many connotations and nuances of meaning. These meanings, in recent years, have increased both in subtlety and in significance. Developments in ecology, for instance, have added to the fund of sophisticated knowledge now available with respect to the web of interrelations existing between the biological organism and its environment. Current research further serves to highlight the extremely important role that the milieu apparently plays in "creating" whatever ability or quality it is that we measure as intelligence when I.Q. tests are administered.

*For background reading cf. Warren G. Bennis, "Theory and Method in Applying Behavioral Science to Planned Organizational Change." (1).

Because of the vital nature of the setting in which behavioral changes are fostered, Chapter 14 analyzes both the human and the material dimensions of the young learner's school world. Actually, of course, the school environment is all of one piece. However, for purposes of presentation it is convenient to discuss separately the people and the things with which the counselor works. The more important of these two—the human environment—is considered first.

The Human Environment

The Need for Artistry in Guidance

As much as any person employed in elementary education, and probably more than most of his colleagues on the faculty, the counselor needs to bring a special artistry to the development of interpersonal relationships or human traffic patterns around which the human environment is each day rebuilt (24). Unlike the relatively stable physical or material setting provided by classrooms or clinics, the human environment is one which constantly changes, appears in new sociometric configurations, and has all the unpredictability of the designs that come to life when one rotates the bits of glass in an old-fashioned kaleidoscope.

A child may come to school in a happy or unhappy frame of mind—rested or tired, hungry or stuffed with a good breakfast and vitamin supplements, angry at his best friend or warmly pleased with a new one. The possibilities for variety in attitudes, health, security, or morale in the under-the-skin world of even one child at eight o'clock on a Tuesday morning are almost infinite.*

The same generalization applies to the teacher or anyone else connected with the school environment. They may be sad or light-hearted, newly in love or bitter with family quarrels, the winner of a new car in a raffle or short of funds in the family checking account. The interplay of personalities under the influence of a thousand such tangibles and intangibles is so involved, so bound up in our human strengths and weaknesses, motivations and aspirations, as to defy and defeat any attempt at neat categories. Yet we have no choice but to learn more about how to deal with these protean qualities found within every elementary school.

The "Emotional Powder Charge" in Guidance

The human environment in which the counselor functions contains a heavy charge of "emotional dynamite" made up of feelings and emotions.

---

*For more detailed information, cf. Robert Theobald, "Planning With People," in William R. Ewald (ed.), *Environment and Change* (27).

Among the explosive elements in a school situation are parental aspirations, or parental disinterest; the child's quest for security and the improvement of his self-image or his attempts to withdraw from a frustrating world; and the teacher's insight and compassion or the lack of these qualities when working with a child.

Mature counselor behavior is measured by the quality and extent of the artistry which he can bring into play so as to reinforce his efforts to help each boy and girl move a little nearer each day to the greatest self-realization and most comfortable self-image of which they are capable. To serve this purpose it is extremely important for the counselor himself to understand how deeply the feelings of most people are involved in the interplay of personality which determines at a given moment what the human environment will be.

What are some of the understandings of this human setting that the mature counselor needs to acquire through his formal preparation and his practical experience? Many approaches might be made to answer this query. Two have been selected as exemplary: 1) the counselor's understanding of the "personality" of the community; the way in which each unique school setting requires a unique program, and 2) his understanding of interpersonal traffic patterns; the configurations or patterns in human relations which are an important part of his daily tasks (4). Each will be considered in turn.

The Personality of the Community

Each town, village, or city has a civic personality. Some are of sober mien, some lively; some are gracious, some rough and ready. Inquiry also quickly reveals that in many communities the socio-economic differences and discrepancies and the temperament of their neighborhoods are as great or greater *within* these communities than *between* them.* The counselor needs, as rapidly as he can, to acquaint himself with the personality or civic profile of the community in which he is employed so that he can begin to work to good effect with his colleagues in the shared task of creating a professionally tailored program.

In general, the profile of a community is shaped by such elements as 1) its educational traditions, 2) its size, and 3) its socio-economic characteristics. The *educational traditions* of a community reflect the sum of the citizens' judgments as to what is educationally good or bad in the way human affairs can be conducted. Their attitudes have a direct bearing on support that is given to or withheld from a guidance program for children of elementary school age.

The *size* of a school district has certain obvious bearings on the programs offered. There are assets and liabilities in a small enrollment as well as

*A 1968 report distributed by the Ford Foundation casts considerable light on urban educational problems (7). Reprints are available from the Ford Foundation, Office of Reports, 320 East Third Street, New York, New York, 10017.

advantages and disadvantages in a large one. While a big school often can support a large, diversified group of non-classroom personnel to work in human development activities, the sheer size of the larger school units with their wide-ranging problems can appreciably complicate elementary school guidance functions.

Educational Traditions

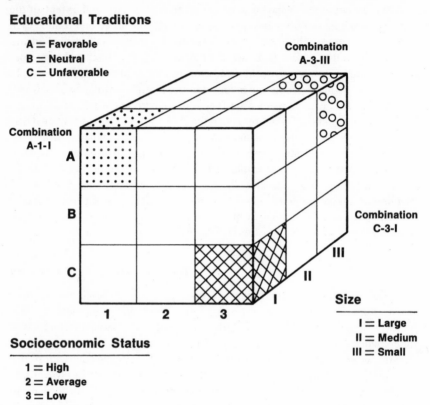

A = Favorable
B = Neutral
C = Unfavorable

Combination
A-3-III

Combination
A-1-I

A

B

Combination
C-3-I

III

C

II

I   Size

1   2   3

I = Large
II = Medium
III = Small

Socioeconomic Status

1 = High
2 = Average
3 = Low

Figure 28. Model of Environmental Factors in the Community with a Bearing on the Elementary Guidance Program

Socio-economic characteristics, as used here, refer to the nature of the local power structure and to social class configurations, both of which vary a great deal among the thousands of school districts in the U.S.

Although it has some of the dangers inherent in any simplistic interpretation, Figure 28 should help to make clear some of the combinations of the "civic personalities" which the coordinator of guidance may confront. Three illustrative variables which contribute to the personality or profile of the community are: FIRST, various educational traditions (lettered A, B, and C); SECOND, high, average, and low socio-economic status (numbers 1, 2, and 3);

and THIRD, school size (shown in Roman numerals). It is the purpose of the model to suggest that even with only three levels of three variables there are 27 possible school profile combinations such as A-1-I, A-3-III, or C-3-I.

As brief examination of Figure 28 will reveal, an A-1-I type of school combines "favorable traditions," "high socio-economic status," and "large size." Presumably, such a community milieu would be an easier one in which to operate an elementary program, including guidance services, than would be a C-3-I combination (one with unfavorable educational traditions, low socio-economic status, and also of large size). A professional assessment of the school-community setting in which he finds himself employed can be of considerable value to the counselor.

Interlacing Patterns of Human Relations in Guidance

At least equally important, and often appreciably more important than the community setting, are the interpersonal traffic patterns within the school: the structure and interfaces of human relationships. Many configurations of human personality influence the elementary school day. Along with the elementary principal, and perhaps even more than the curriculum coordinator, the counselor finds himself deeply involved in the human environment of the school. There are several ways in which the elementary counselor's role in a human relations context might be approached. It could be presented in view of certain publications and of research findings, in terms of the authors' subjective judgment related to inter-personal relations, or with reference to counseling and guidance concepts (12-17,19,22,23).

But perhaps the most simple, practical, and explicit approach to a careful look at the human environment of the school is to consider in turn the various groups of persons with whom the counselor is most likely to come in contact. These encompass five clusters:

1) parents and other school patrons, as well as representatives of certain social agencies: *the non-school cluster*

2) *the classroom cluster*: children, teachers and paraprofessionals

3) *the cluster of administrators and supervisors*

4) *the cluster of specialists in fields other than guidance*: special area staff, educational materials, remedial, health, and curriculum personnel

5) *the guidance-related cluster*: associated counselors, psychometrists, guidance paraprofessionals, school psychologists, and social workers.

In the following paragraphs certain subtleties in the school counselor's interaction with each of the five clusters will be discussed in order to suggest some of the ways in which common sense in human relations not only can facilitate guidance services, but also have a salutary influence on the human environment of the entire school.

The Non-School Cluster. One of the characteristics of the persons and groups outside the school with whom the school counselor works is their great diversity. Parents are inclined to have a highly personal attitude toward the school. More likely than not it is colored by the success their child experiences in school. Rarely is a parent concerned about an elementary program being "too liberal," "too expensive," "too conservative," or "too poorly financed" if *his* boy or girl is happy and is reportedly experiencing success.

Conversely, the parent with a child who is performing poorly or who is confronted by difficult social adjustments can rarely be convinced that the school is all that it should be regardless of its level of support and of excellence. In the human environment of the parent, then, three important points to which the counselor should be sensitive are: 1) the link between parent and child, 2) the need to assay the quality of parent and child relationships, and 3) the importance of evaluating the home setting. Each has a significant bearing on the pupils' in-school progress.

Patrons of the schools who are not parents, or who do not have children in school, present to the guidance specialist in the elementary school a different facet of the community than do parents. Contacts with such citizens, although sometimes less frequent than parent contacts, may at least be equally important especially in terms of long range support for the guidance program. In general, these lay citizens are interested in three matters directly related to broadly conceived child guidance policies.

1) What is the quality of learning? Are the children acquiring the social and academic skills which adults in their particular subculture prize?

2) Are school policies sound with respect to such varied items as the music program, team teaching, grouping, or promotion policies?

3) Are the values which the school directly or indirectly inculcates strengthening such virtures as self-discipline, honesty, respect for hard work, and democratic goals?

While parents also share these kinds of concerns in varying degrees, often depending on the socio-ethnic cultural subgroup in which they have membership, the *non*parent school patron is often more likely to be interested in the school program as a whole than in one particular child. In human traffic patterns with the nonparent, the counselor is challenged to think through *what* the school is endeavoring to do and *why*, and to develop poise and skill in interpreting the program clearly, with integrity, and with the conviction of a person who has examined what he believes and who has decided what he needs to do to improve human development.

The Classroom Cluster. Children, teachers, and paraprofessionals have been identified as individuals in the cluster of personalities brought into relationship because of their assignment to the same school. Nothing more need be said here about the association between boys and girls and the counselor since most of this book already has concerned itself with his role in helping them to find security, happiness, an ability to cope, and various similar satisfactions which add up to optimum self-realization. Teachers and paraprofessionals are further discussed here.

In general, teachers cover a spectrum of performance in their ability to help children develop. The positive and negative contributions they make range from being actively or passively *helpful* to being passively or actively *harmful*. Each of the four types of plus and minus behavior poses different opportunities for the counselor to help improve the human environment of the school. The precise ways in which he can contribute can be determined only as the counselor applies his professional judgment, but some broad generalizations readily can be made.

The "actively helpful" teacher poses one of the more appreciable challenges because it is so easy for a counselor to do little or nothing to be of assistance to persons who already are striving to reinforce his work in guidance. Just as the bright, friendly, secure child is often left to himself because he poses no conspicuous problems and creates no disturbance, so it is equally easy to ignore or overlook the able teacher. The counselor is especially challenged here to see that the teacher is not left to do a merely good job when he might do an excellent one if provided with more of the counselor's expertise.

The "passively helpful" teacher is one with welcoming attitudes toward the purposes and practices of guidance. At the same time, he tends too much toward being dependent on guidance personnel for the performance of tasks that he, by himself, with advice and suggestions often could perform equally well or better. Under such circumstances the guidance coordinator needs to use his knowledge of motivation in stimulating the teacher to participate more fully in meeting individual pupil-needs and in general program development.

Teachers who are "passively harmful" include those who lack confidence in a guidance program, feel that it calls on them to do too much work, or who have unsatisfied personal needs of their own which impair the skill needed in guidance work with children. The "actively harmful" teacher has many of the same attitudes and personal problems, but aggressively seeks to block the guidance program or to impede change and the processes of innovation on the basis of any pretext. In working with "harmful" types it is especially important for the coordinator to avoid personal-emotional involvement and situations in which paranoid behavior can be expressed. Teachers as well as children are human challenges and the procedures followed in unsnarling faulty human traffic patterns are usually analogous ones for young and old alike. The well-prepared coordinator already has the insights and the know-how needed for his own coping behavior. His particular task is to avoid being angered, upset, or caught off balance, thus letting himself become ego-involved and no longer capable of doing the very job he has been prepared to do by reason of educational preparation and past experience.

The paraprofessional in a number of schools has become more than a mere pair of helping hands and in the future probably will often have one or two years of college preparation for his duties. Insofar as the paraprofessional is concerned, the counselor interested in improved intraschool relationships needs to remember that these classroom personnel cover the same gamut from "harmful" to "helpful" that teachers cover and need to be approached in the same way and with the same spirit of respect and of assistance. Para-professionals with children in school or who are local residents also may be in the "parent" or in the "local citizen" categories mentioned above.

It is especially valuable for the guidance coordinator to find ways of furthering the strength of the program and its resources by arranging basic in-service activities for paraprofessionals so that they develop useful skills to bring to the overall guidance activities of the school. For example, they can learn to operate test scoring equipment, to do routine typing, to issue and file guidance materials, or help to maintain some of the records kept in the guidance center.

The Administrative Cluster. The cluster of administrative personnel with whom a counselor comes in contact generally includes the principal and his assistants, supervisors or consultants (often serving more than one school building), and the leaders of teams or of cooperating teacher units in those schools which have team teaching units with designated head teachers. The human equation encountered in the administration cluster is a difficult one to describe because, in a number of respects, it is greatly influenced by the principal. An able, energetic, and well-prepared principal can create a pleasant, businesslike, and positive school climate. The weary, cynical, poorly-informed titular "leader" who has become a principal through mere seniority often generates a negative atmosphere.

In a positive climate, the counselor finds his work supported, his associates friendly, and opportunities for program development limited only by the resources that the school district is able to provide. The negative school atmosphere often is characterized by impediments to counseling, by mutual suspicion, and by a power struggle for funds, recognition, and salary increments.

While no specific packaged advice can be offered the counselor working in a negative administrative environment, several common sense suggestions come to mind. *First*, when coping with ineffectual principals, consultants, or team leaders, remember that the counselor can not afford the doubtful luxury of losing his temper, of playing politics to get his own way, or of withdrawing to the small enclave of the guidance office to await referrals or requests for assistance that are unlikely to come in any large numbers. *Active* solutions to the negative environment should be sought.

Second, when seeking improvements the counselor should remember that what he has learned about human development, motivation, relations, and needs is just as applicable to administrators or to consultants as it is to teachers and children. It is suggested that the counselor try to study the cluster and subsequently endeavor to help these professional associates through the maturity and judgment he has acquired. Human nature is both caused by and capable of modification. Therefore, the human environment of the administrative cluster is subject to modification.

Consultants, team leaders, and principals need and want to be accepted, respected, appreciated. What can be done to move them toward these goals through wholesome involvement in the guidance program development that provides satisfaction?

The Specialists' Cluster. The growing support provided elementary education has led to an increase in specialized personnel: curriculum workers, school nurses and physicians, librarians and audiovisual directors who often share an educational materials center, etc. When working with other specialists, the guidance counselor finds himself in a peer relationship in which the key concepts are cooperation, persuasion, and shared mutual goals. With respect to *cooperation* the counselor needs to look for ways in which the program he heads can draw on the capabilities of other specialists. Most of them are eager to see an increased need and respect for their contributions because of involvement with guidance activities.

As to *persuasion*, specialists need to be convinced that their programs and financial support for their areas are not threatened, but are strengthened by the services and functions of the counselor.

Insofar as *shared mutual goals* go, the astute counselor quickly recognizes and points out that *all* special areas have basically similar purposes in guiding and maximizing human development and that in their unity there is increased stability and power to do good for all.

The Guidance-Related Cluster. The approaches that a counselor might make to improving the human environment in which he works with his immediate associates depend upon the combination of persons and functions found in a guidance center or department of developmental guidance such are depicted in Figure 27 (Chapter 13).

For purposes of examining the patterns of human relationships that become interlaced in the department, it is assumed that it is a large one with two or more counselors, a psychometrist, paraprofessional and clerical assistance, a school psychologist, and a part-time social worker assigned to the school by a civic agency or employed by the school.

Just as cooperation was one of the key themes in working with specialists from other areas, so clarity of function, job satisfaction, and intra-group reinforcement are important to the department of developmental guidance, regardless of whether two or ten persons are employed.

The larger a counseling and guidance corps becomes the more important *clarity* of function becomes. The senior counselor needs to avoid friction by being sure that responsibility is clearly delegated and that it is spread fairly among his associates. Job *satisfaction* depends upon fair play, recognition for ability to contribute, and the feeling that one has a future compatible with realistic levels of personal aspiration.

Intragroup *reinforcement* is indicative of high morale and is reflected in mutual support, ethical behavior, a willingness to share in work to be done, and in the absence of snobbishness with regard to the importance of "my" job in the department of developmental guidance.

Although their important roles are not discussed here, mention should be made of the great importance of secretaries, custodians, bus drivers, cafeteria workers and other noncertificated personnel employed by school districts. Suggestions made and advice offered with regard to the five clusters mentioned above are equally applicable to *all* employees working in the elementary program.

Understanding Interpersonal Traffic Patterns

The discussion of the five human clusters found in elementary schools has reminded the counselor of the importance of understanding the interpersonal relations that are an integral part of school keeping. There is probably nothing more important to the success of the guidance program than the counselor's ability to understand the invisible web of human traffic patterns.

The wellsprings of man's behavior, as Bertrand Russell noted years ago, are fed by ". . . some desires which are, so to speak, infinite, which can never be fully gratified, and which would keep him restless even in Paradise." (25:27) Even in the quiet cloisters of the best ordered elementary schools many persons are motivated by acquisitiveness, rivalry, vanity, and an urge to acquire power. Love of excitement, hate, and fear also long have been in man's blood. Fortunately, so have been sympathy, compassion, and the ability to rise above the self-interest of naked apes! The maturing counselor is one who is learning to respect his colleagues, to build on man's conscience and morality, and yet able to be understanding when less admirable traits appear. He also needs the compassion that tells him that in the human environment many of the problems which occur are the relics of man's diminishing savagery, not the portents of his coming cultural decline.

Behavior of the various individuals in the school clusters can be almost infinitely improved and the counselor needs the faith which tells him it can be done and the knowledge to bring to the task.

Finally, in working with human equations, the counselor should recognize the limits of his art and knowledge. As yet we are just beginning to learn the art of contributing to optimal human development through guidance and must not expect too much too soon. If we were to do so it would be like asking the Wright brothers on one of their early flights also to make an aerial survey of North Carolina!

The Physical Setting
for Guidance and Counseling

The "open universe" guidance philosophy or point of view has distinct implications for the physical setting for learning. These implications encompass the elementary school as a whole as well as the specialized territory of a department of developmental guidance. Even though the focus in Chapter 14 remains on guidance, it becomes necessary first to examine briefly the overall setting of the school in which counselors and teachers foster human development. Guidance functions are not confined to a center, but permeate the entire school.

The School House as Shelter

Until the late 1930's the school was looked upon as but little more than a structure that protected children from inclement weather. Most classrooms were of about the same dimensions and when children were not present, only the size of the furniture enabled a casual visitor to distinguish between grade one and grade six.

By 1940 a few educators and architects were convinced that the school plant should be designed for the program rather than obliging the faculty to warp or adapt the curriculum to fit the space available in a building. At that time, however, and for 20 years thereafter teachers kept on thinking of the program in terms of grade levels, uniform time blocks, of bells to announce when school began and to indicate when groups of children moved from room to room, of uniformity and conformity in instruction, and of subject matter skills to be absorbed. Well into the 1960's elementary schools continued to be thought of as shelter modified to permit a few special activities in art, music, physical education, and science.

By the mid-1960's, the term "flexibility" had become a fashionable one to use when one spoke of a modern school plant. In the new school of the 1960's there were large spaces, carrels or electronic learning cubicles, folding interior walls (or no walls at all), specially designed areas for team teaching, here and there a language laboratory, and an occasional work-and-inquiry room. During this period, interesting ideas regarding schoolhouses began to spring up like mushrooms. For the first time the nature of modern teaching *procedures* began to be reflected in the school plant.

By the end of the decade, *avant-garde* architects and educators had expanded the meaning of flexibility to include:

Expansible space to allow for ordered growth
Convertible space to be economically adapted to program changes
Versatile space that serves many functions and
Malleable space that can be changed "at once and at will." (6:15)

As has been cleverly stated by william Caudill ". . . our schools have exercised a Procrustean constraint on educational imagination and innovation. Now, with education in an unprecedented phase of questioning, changing, and experimenting, Proteus may at last replace Procrustes." (6:15)

The School as an Enabling Environment

The concept of what a school house ought to be has moved from mere shelter to housing designed to facilitate teaching the content of the curriculum. In its third evolutionary step the plant was adapted to encourage modern teaching practices in a flexible setting. The logical next step, one likely to occur in the coming decade, is one through which:*

1) *The school becomes media*—an enabling environment
2) *The school becomes a biosocial nutrient* which strengthens the health and social skills of children
3) *The school is designed to mediate experience*, to encourage carefully reasoned intervention or "appropriate interference" in the flow or input of children's experiences.

For this next step to occur easily, the idea of the school becoming a responsive resource for teaching—just as the good teacher is today—must first be accepted on its merits. Then prototype structures need to be created,

---

*For stimulating conjectures about possible future developments, cf. Harold E. Moore (ed.), *Planning for Education in Litchfield Park in 2000 A.D.* (18).

not by architects alone, but by a team of educators, media specialists, engineers and technologists, architects, and behavioral scientists thinking, planning, and then creating a superior psychophysical environment.

The school that results should not be a huge teaching machine, since no machine or thing has an interest in its products or in how it affects humanity. Rather it should be a mechanism that responds to humans—to teachers and children—so that the interaction of both is strengthened and improved.

A Physical Setting for Guidance and Counseling

The brief, preceding overview of the architectual consequences of emerging educational concepts leads up to the heart of the matter with which this part of the chapter is concerned: What is a good physical setting for guidance and counseling? (8,28)

A global answer to this question is that such an environment is one in which the counselor's goals are most easily met with respect to 1) creating a guidance continuum, 2) facilitating individual and group counseling, 3) accurately assessing human development, 4) orienting children, and 5) mediating the sequences and pacing of learning experiences. In the school as a whole, these five counseling goals suggest that classrooms should have a pleasant and relaxed atmosphere, be uncrowded, varied, suited to team teaching, and built with the idea of expansible, convertible, versatile, and malleable spaces in mind. Good guidance practices *are* greatly assisted by a good all-school atmosphere.

There are in this school spaces where children can be by themselves, care for pets, receive special attention, and work or play in small groups or in large. There are areas where work in art and music are encouraged, where materials can be prepared, and where teachers can think together. It is the composite of resources such as these that make the elementary school *biosocially nutrient*; renewing and refreshing environments in which the biological, social, and mental aspects of human development can be fostered.

Highly important in the responsive and enabling school are the uses made of media so that the increased sensory extension of children can occur (21). Among media resources are educational TV for individual and group use, terminals that permit the use of computer-assisted instruction, retrieval systems which permit individuals to obtain films for personalized viewing, responsive teaching machines, facsimile reproduction of printed materials, and sources of recorded information.

The guidance center itself, in the school which is an enabling environment, has ample space including: 1) an automated records and storage room, 2) large conference and counseling area, 3) office space for both professional and clerical personnel, 4) reception area, 5) small (one to one) conference-counseling cubicle, 6) a room that can be used for play therapy, and 7) either a small space used as a professional library or files and shelving along the walls in other areas, such as the large one used for conferences, which permit up to 10 to 15 persons to be present.

In addition to space, the center should insure privacy as needed and have the comfortable atmosphere which tasteful furnishings can help to create. In all of the school plant and especially in the guidance center, attractive furnishings including carpeting are not frills but a part of the constructive psychosocial atmosphere that is sought.*

Whenever possible—as when a school is built or remodeled—thought should be given to the matter of a physical environment not only for guidance personnel but for such associated staff members as school psychologists, psychometrists, teachers working with the handicapped, and the school nurse. The many transactions that take place among the personnel mentioned suggest that the close physical proximity of their work areas is desirable. When architecturally feasible, it often may be desirable also to have the administrative offices and educational materials suites in the vicinity.

Especially since adequate guidance services are a quite recent innovation in those elementary schools that have them at all, the comprehensive physical resources described have heretofore rarely been available.

Beginning the Program

If a program in elementary education is being begun for the first time, priority efforts should be made to obtain certain indispensible physical resources: an office area which can also be used for individual and group counseling or conferences, and an adequate secretarial area including space for records and testing files. These constitute a minimum space for a guidance program and the counselor is severely handicapped without it. A secretary-clerk is also imperative. Lacking such help, half or even more of the elementary counselor's time can be consumed by interruptions which diminish or destroy his usefulness in helping to guide human development.

The Transitional Program. Once a program is functioning smoothly, the office described above should begin to transform itself into a center or a department of developmental guidance. First priorities here should go to personnel in most situations (an associate counselor, psychometrist, or other employee depending on what is needed to complement the senior counselor's special competencies). However, at this point Chapter 14 is concerned with the school plant rather than with staffing patterns. What material resources should be added first?

*For an expansion of these points, cf. W. J. Dickson and F. J. Roethlisberger (5).

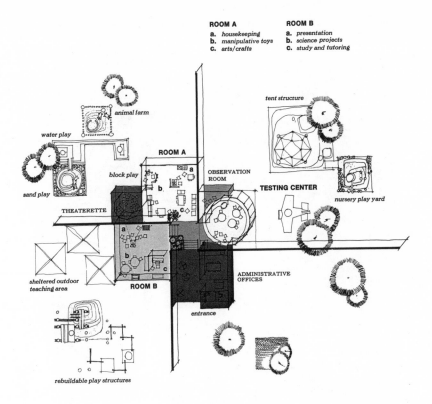

ROOM A
a. *housekeeping*
b. *manipulative toys*
c. *arts/crafts*

ROOM B
a. *presentation*
b. *science projects*
c. *study and tutoring*

Figure 29.   A Pre-Primary School Floor Plan Which Illustrates
a Benign Environment for Guidance

The "best" decision invariably depends on the layout of the space in a particular school, but in most instances priority should be given as follows. First, to private office and conference/counseling space or to a flexible area that lends itself to the counseling of individuals and of small groups and to professional discussions with parents, with teachers, and with other staff members. A combined guidance library and records area comes next on the list of needed material facilities. A records area should be one wired to permit the use of test-scoring equipment, and an automated record layout should be an eventual possiblity for this area.

The Optimal Center. The idea of an "optimal" center is likely to be misleading! The dynamics of change strongly indicate that what is an optimum physical setting today begins to become obsolescent immediately. One is reminded of the aircraft corporation engineer who commented just before the

Figure 30.   Observation Room

test-flight of a supersonic jet, "Even if the darn thing flies like a dream, it's already obsolete because of what we learned while we were building it!"

With this story in mind, two generalizations about the physical setting can be made: 1) the *best* guidance center is always in process rather than complete, 2) each center has unique "first needs" in school plant development, and these are most properly identified by applying intelligence, values, and the process of reason to cooperative decision making.

Relationships Among
Counselors and Non-School Agencies

A sometimes neglected part of the counselor's wider school environment is made up of resource persons in the community who are employed privately, in other schools, or by various agencies such as local welfare, police, and health departments. A partial roster of agencies and individuals usually found in middle-sized (50,000 to 200,000 people) cities and large ones (200,000 and up) with whom the counselor may work often includes:

School-Related Personnel

1) Counselors in other schools
2) Central administrative personnel (including system-wide supervisors, consultants, and district deputy superintendents)
3) State department personnel, especially Office of Public Instruction staff members
4) Federal educational employees; e.g., from Regional Offices of the United States Office of Education
5) University personnel in nearby schools of education

Personnel Not Directly Engaged in Education

1) Physicians, including psychiatrists
2) Consulting psychologists
3) Clergymen
4) Public librarians
5) Social workers
6) Law enforcement groups, including police specializing in juvenile problems
7) Clubs and analogous youth groups; e.g., the YMCA, Boy Scouts and Girl Scouts of America, Community House Groups
8) Community Mental Health Centers and Child Centers
9) Welfare agencies

Counselors usually will find these resource persons remarkably helpful and supportive, although there is no way to tell what combination of individuals or agencies will be most valuable to the guidance program at a given time. Among them may be a hard working librarian who has made a hobby of bibliotherapy, a clergyman in an inner city church, a pediatrician interested in a school program for two- and three-year-olds, or, under certain circumstances, a parent with time and energy who serves 10 or 12 hours a week without pay as an unofficial and unpaid paraprofessional in the guidance center.*

---

*Great caution must be exercised when, and if, volunteer parental help is utilized in the guidance center. In many instances it is prudent to avoid using parents' help, and all pupil personnel data such as test scores must be recorded and filed by regular workers in the center.

Since there are few if any hard and fast rules to go by when looking for helpful human resources, the counselor should discount none of them. Also, he should avoid "turning in on himself," of developing an "ingrowing" program or department by spending nearly all of his working hours inside the confines of the elementary school. Since there is always service to be given, it is easy for the dedicated counselor to concentrate almost exclusively on laboring in the immediate milieu of the center or department of developmental guidance rather than budgeting time to explore and to exploit more fully the larger environment's potentialities.

In addition to mining human resources, the counselor has the reverse obligation to be socially useful himself in the larger community; to be a small part of its resources for others. Unlike many members of the elementary faculty who participate in service clubs, church work, and the like for social or religious reasons, the counselor has an added professional motive. It is through well-developed participation that he becomes acquainted with and opens doors to resources for improving the education of boys and girls in his own school setting—and contributes in return to others.

This is the era of the atomistic family described in Chapter 1; an age of psychological *apartheid* for many who live in the brick and concrete canyons of U.S. cities, even among the members of the same subculture groups. Some of the emotional frost that so quickly can form on people today can be thawed by counselors who bring outreaching friendliness for others in their personal quest for mutually advantageous relationships with non-school agencies.

Summary

The milieu which each elementary school provides has two dimensions, the human environment and the physical setting. Of the two, the former is by far the more important since it has the greater impact on children and also tends to determine the nature or at least the tone of the physical plant.

The variety and subtlety of the human environment makes it of prime importance to the counselor. He needs to have insights into behavior that help to explain what transpires in this environment. He further needs to understand that there is a powerful "emotional powder charge" in guidance because of its close linkage to problem situations in which the feelings and personalities of parents, children, and teachers can become profoundly involved.

Chapter 14 points out that the community is organic because it is composed of people rather than brick and mortar, then goes on to suggest (through the use of a simple model) that cities develop a "civic personality" because of the traditions and values that their citizens respect and reject.

"Human traffic patterns" in the school are examined, and five human personality clusters with which the counselor works are discussed.

The last half of the chapter deals with guidance in the physical setting for learning provided by the school. The development of the contemporary school plant is sketched to demonstrate that in four evolutionary steps the schoolhouse has changed from mere shelter into a responsive, enabling environment. Also treated is the matter of priorities to be considered in creating the physical setting for a guidance center.

The closing pages of the chapter direct attention to the counselor's relationships with the wider environment of non-school agencies with which he invariably comes in contact.

References

1. Bennis, Warren G. "Theory and Method in Applying Behavioral Science to Planned Organizational Change." *The Journal of Applied Behavioral Science* 1 (1965): 337-359.

2. Berelson, Bernard and Gary A. Steiner. *Human Behavior: An Inventory of Scientific Findings.* New York: Harcourt, Brace and World, Inc., 1964.

3. Boles, Harold W. *Step by Step to Better School Facilities.* New York: Holt, Rinehart and Winston, 1965.

4. Chin, Robert and Kenneth E. Benne. "General Strategies for Effecting Changes in Human Systems." Warren G. Bennis, Kenneth D. Benne, and Robert Chin. *The Planning of Change.* New York: Holt, Rinehart and Winston, Inc., 1969, pp. 32-59.

5. Dickson, William J. and F. J. Roethlisberger. *Personal Counseling in an Organization: A Sequel to the Hawthorne Researches.* Boston: Harvard Business School, 1966.

6. Educational Facilities Laboratories. *Educational Change and Architectural Consequences.* New York: Educational Facilities Laboratories, 1968. William Caudill.

7. Fantini, Mario D. "Alternatives for Urban School Reform." *Harvard Educational Review* Winter, 1968.

8. Goodlad, John. "Learning and Teaching in the Future." *Today's Education* 57 (February, 1968): 49-51.

9. Green, A., et al. *Educational Facilities with New Media.* Washington, D.C.: Department of Audiovisual Instruction, National Education Association, 1966.

10. Jennings, Helen H. *Sociometry of Leadership.* Sociometry Monograph No. 14. New York: Beacon House, 1947.

11. Jung, Charles and Ronald Lippit. "Utilization of Scientific Knowledge for Change in Education." *Concepts for Social Change.* Washington, D.C.: National Education Association, National Training Laboratories, 1967.

12. Lewin, Kurt. *A Dynamic Theory of Personality.* New York: McGraw Hill Book Co., 1935.

13. _____. "Group Decision and Social Change." G. E. Swanson, et al. (eds.). *Readings in Social Psychology.* New York: Holt, 1952.

14. _____. Ronald Lippit, and R. K. White. "Patterns of Aggressive Behavior in Experimentally Created 'Social Climates'." *Journal of Social Psychology* 10 (1939): 271-299.

15. _____. "The Social Climate of Children's Groups." R. Barker, J. S. Kaunin, and H. F. Wright (eds.). *Child Behavior and Development*. New York: McGraw-Hill, 1943.

16. Lippitt, Ronald. "An Experimental Study of Democratic and Authoritarian Group Atmospheres." *University of Iowa Studies in Child Welfare* 16 (1940): 43-195.

17. _____ et al. *Dynamics of Planned Change*. New York: Harcourt, Brace and World, Inc., 1958.

18. Moore, Harold E. (ed.). *Planning for Education in Litchfield Park in 2000 A.D.* Educational Services Bulletin No. 21. Tempe, Ariz.: Bureau of Educational Research and Services, College of Education, Arizona State University, 1967.

19. Moreno, J. L. *Who Shall Survive?* Scranton, Pa.: Nervous and Medical Diseases Publishing House, 1934.

20. *NCSC Guide for Planning School Plants*. Columbus, Ohio: Council of Educational Facility Planners, 1964.

21. Neagley, Ross L., N. Dean Evans, and Clarence A. Lynn, Jr. *The School Administrator and Learning Resources*. Englewood Cliffs, N. J. Prentice-Hall, Inc., 1969. Chapters 3, 5, 6, and 7 are particularly germane to the uses of media.

22. Plant, James. *Personality and the Cultural Patterns*. London: H. Milford, 1937.

23. Prescott, Daniel A. *Emotion and the Educative Process*. Washington, D.C.: American Council on Education, 1938.

24. Rogers, Everett. "What Are Innovators Like?" *Change Processes in the Public Schools*. Center for the Advanced Study of Educational Administration. Eugene, Ore.: University of Oregon, 1965.

25. Russell, Bertrand. "The Springs of Human Action." *The Atlantic* 189 (March, 1952): 27.

26. Thelen, Herbert A. *Dynamics of Groups at Work*. Chicago: University of Chicago Press, 1954.

27. Theobald, Robert. "Planning With People." William R. Ewald (ed.). *Environment and Change*. Bloomington, Ind.: Indiana University Press, 1968.

28. Wiman, R. V. and W. C. Meierhenry (eds.). *Educational Media: Theory Into Practice*. Columbus, Ohio: Charles E. Merrill Publishing Co., 1969.

15

Epilogue:
Broadening Concepts
for Counseling and Teaching

Since his first years as a civilized being, man has devised systematic plans for sharing his hard-won wisdom and skills with his children. In a hostile world, in which an uncompromising nature was his foe, early man needed to educate his offspring for survival. It was necessary for man-cubs of 10,000 years ago to learn how to match wits with a harsh environment if they were to survive beyond early childhood. Hence, the central purpose of education was to stay alive.

By the time Greece had shed the light of her intellect throughout the Mediterranean world, the saber-tooth and cave bear had long been dead in their tar pits or silted river bottoms. Man, however, still needed to educate his children. Survival was pushed at least partly aside as the main purpose of schooling as art, politics, music, and rhetoric found a place in the Greek *agora* where scholars met their pupils. The student who was systematically educated in the Athens of 350 B.C. was prepared as a literate man of the world.

During the Middle Ages, when the light of learning burned feebly in the inhospitable corridors of cathedral schools and medieval universities, the purpose of formal education turned to creating a man of God. After the Renaissance, during which schools often produced worldly men of God, education began to assume a more contemporary mien.

By 1850, elementary schools provided basic skills in the three R's, and secondary education was planned for the minority who were to attend college. The university concentrated on the instruction of a few who were planning to enter one of the professions, such as law or the ministry, or to acquire a classical education suited to the cultured gentleman who, by reason of his ancestry and wealth, potentially was in a leadership position. By 1920, mass education at the secondary level was being achieved in the United States. Its central purpose was, in general, that of preparing all children and youth to live as effective citizens in a manner consistent with the Seven Cardinal Principles set forth by a Commission of the National Education Association.

To summarize the changing purposes of education, man moved from a survival-oriented education to one which was actually designed, in the Western world at least, to help young learners live effectively in a society of potential abundance—with opportunities for self-realization and with responsibilities for enlightened participation in democratic society. Between 1920 and 1970 the sense of direction and purpose which has sustained education went awry. Old institutions and practices no longer seem suited to new times, and much has been written about the need to relate education more closely to the life of the times.

The Rediscovery of Purpose

Although educational goals in the past were not always consistent with the general welfare, education during the last several thousand years *did* have purpose. Even when schooling strongly favored an aristocratic or an élite group, it tended—during any given period in history—to eventuate in some type of social order in which man was able to keep alive and through which he eventually moved forward into what *should* have been the most promising of eras—the 20th century.

Along with religion, government, and similar institutions, however, education seems to have floundered because of conflicting or lost purposes. Especially since mid-century this uncertainty has been reflected in a considerable loss of faith in the church, in a credibility gap between what the public thinks governmental leaders *say* and what they *do*, and in an appreciable lack of public confidence shown in education. Each of these agencies needs once again to find broad goals that genuinely serve mankind. The remaining pages of this book are directed toward the rediscovery of the purposes of education and the relevant functions guidance can make to the elementary schools in the context of these purposes.

From Survival to Survival

Education was essential for the survival of man in an environment that was very dangerous. In view of developments that have occurred during the past thirty years of exponential change, *the central purpose of education now seems to have come full cycle and returned to survival.*

The accompanying model in Figure 31 suggests, in a simplified form, what has happened. After 10,000 years, man has moved from the need to survive the battle with an implacable nature as his foe to the need to survive an inimical environment of his own making.

Whether we like it or not—the destructive power of nuclear warfare, the population increase which threatens the earth with a return to medieval poverty, the long erosion and heedless use of natural resources, and the growing danger from pollution and waste accumulations clearly indicate man's present inability to protect himself from himself. In view of the global scope and magnitude of these four problems, it is not only reasonable but essential that society assign schools the critical task of educating children and youth to cultivate and share the earth wisely so that there will be a twenty-first century in which life is worth living.

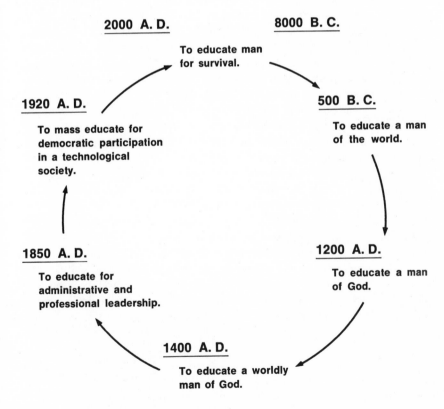

Figure 31. A Model of Changing Purposes of Education
Over a 10,000 Year Interval

The Restoration of Relevance

There is nothing that can be done in the remaining years of the 1970's to make education more relevant than that of producing a tough-minded yet compassionate generation committed to human survival. This must be done even at the cost of a sharp curtailment of sensate pleasures and in contrast to the self-indulgent lives led by many of our present generations. *What could be more relevant than learning how to go on living in a world which is remaking itself into a desirable place for humans.*

The Hardest Task—Ever!

In aiding children and young people to rediscover ways in which man may avoid his present suicidal inclinations and practices, education will encounter the most difficult job it has ever had. For generations we have made a fallacious axiom of the "right" to exploit one's property as he sees fit. As Thorsten Veblen pointed out in 1899 in *Theory of the Leisure Class*, conspicuous waste and conspicuous display had long been the hallmarks of success in ecologically naive societies. With equivalent intercultural naiveté, man has deliberately denigrated races, religions, and social groups other than his own when characterizing them to his children.

Past human frailties and "self-interest" practices must not only change *but be reversed* if children are to obtain a reliable "survival kit" in the form of new concepts from public education. The next generation should be schooled to recognize and accept the possibility—the probability—that their lives must be less hedonistic. They should also be helped to accept and to prize the idea that a more simple, even relatively austere, and responsible way of life will be more rewarding than the frustration and frenzy, the extravagance, and the frequent moral degradation that have remained characteristic of broad segments of the American scene in the 1970's.

The reversal of established patterns of human behavior which have helped create the four great problems of pollution, garbage and poisonous wastes, instant destruction, and overbreeding will be peculiarly difficult, because in many instances counselors, teachers, and parents *themselves* will need to make a 180° shift in the course of their thinking. It will be especially desirable if their social intelligence rather than belated ecological panic motivates the change.

Guidance Concepts for Counselors and Classroom Teachers

In many respects, *Guiding Human Development* has been permeated from its first chapter with an implicit concept for both the counselor and the teacher; the concept that through commitment and intelligent self-directed preparation, through basic acceptance of and trust in others, and through a sense of personal responsibility for creating a better human environment the school could become an important outpost on the exciting frontiers of desirable sociocultural change.

By possessing certain socially important commitments, counselors and teachers can bring an increased measure of dignity and importance to their work. These commitments also provide a base on which to begin building better tomorrows *now*.

A Concept for Guiding Human Development

The points numbered below are an inventory of desirable attitudes and practices summarizing the contribution which counselors and teachers can make through improved educational environments.

The educators' willingness to work to achieve these or similar improvements in what is emphasized in our schools is as important as his knowledge of how teaching takes place, and how learning occurs. It is important because a genuine dedication to better lives and experiences for children *now* should help to increase the odds in favor of the world remaining a decent, comfortable, or at least habitable place to live.

1) Schools, insofar as is possible, need to assume greater responsibility for total human development, recognizing that this development includes mental and physical health, and that the merely informed human being is capable of doing an extended amount of harm if his knowledge is not directed by moral and ethical standards.

2) Children shall develop a respect for the processes of inquiry and the skills of group action necessary to make decisions based on inquiring.

3) The education of children who will help to reverse man's growing threat to himself must be *individually* appraised, diagnosed, and guided since educational uniformity and human differences are irreconcilable.

4) Cooperative and enlightened home-school child guidance policies must be sought since each can undo the work of the other at a time when the maximum efforts of both are needed to increase survival odds.

5) Continuous evaluation of the child's personal-social needs is mandatory since each boy and girl is, to some degree, a new child each morning he comes to school.

6) Academic assessments should be made in depth, not so much to make a searching scrutiny of a child's attainment as to determine how his learnings are mediating his behavior.

7) In keeping with individual appraisal and guidance concepts, the progress of children should be construed as continuous in a seamless curriculum; progress thus being recognized as a *direction*, as distinct from the hurdle of promotion.

8) Attention is centered on the *normalness* of children rather than on *deviate* behavior in recognition of the fact that the "normal" child is a myth, a non-real statistic; that *all* "normal" children deviate from the average, and that each normal child perforce *must* present a deviate behavioral configuration to counselor and teacher.

9) The normal "gifted" child shall be challenged by demanding but interesting and relevant potential learnings, and by his responsibility to society and to himself.

10) The normal "slow learning" child shall be kept from frustration created by premature demands or unreasonable requirements which it is normal for him *not* to meet.

11) The wide range of normal performance of children is looked upon largely as the result of differences in experiential input—especially in the early years of life—rather than as primarily inherent differences in native intelligence.

12) What has generally heretofore been known as "special education" must undergo a creative metamorphosis and re-emerge as the kind of personalized education that *all* children require; the special educationist thus becoming a resource for the total school population.

13) Research in human development mandates flexible curriculum planning and new concepts of content through which attitudes and values expressed as behaviors become of coordinate importance with the knowledge and skills on which children draw as they seek to satisfy their psychosocial and physical needs.

14) The education of teachers and counselors shall embody the same concepts as those used in guiding the human development of children and youth so that tomorrow's educators will learn their roles more through *example* and less by *precept*.

Our future as a nation, and perhaps even as an inhabited planet, depends on the quality of judgment, the conviction, and the motivation which directs adults during the years immediately ahead. Research and careful observation blended into the writers' professional experiences suggest that the viewpoints—the concepts for counselors and teachers—expressed here have much merit as a basis for the educational leadership which will be an important part of the total adult judgment which the U.S. will display.

A cluster of concepts, however, is something that cannot be imposed. It must be examined and accepted. May the reader's own living and experience, therefore, lead him to reach wise, humane conclusions and develop personalized insights to guide his behavior as he performs the guidance-related tasks which are becoming even more important as education rediscovers its broad purpose.

List of Figures

Appendix

Grouping for Instruction: An Annotated List
of 42 Grouping Schemes*

Introduction. For over a century of U.S. education diverse grouping plans have been initiated, discarded, modified, or gradually accepted on a widespread scale. Here is an overview, with annotations, of some plans and programs that have been introduced in U.S. schools or discussed by educational writers.

1) *Ungraded groups.* Originally found in the 17th century Dame school and 18th century "district" school, ungraded groups were taught by one teacher who handled all subjects in the first eight grades. One-room ungraded schools are still commonplace in many areas, but have decreased sharply since the 1940's.

2) *Primary-intermediate grouping.* When the one-room school grew too large for a single teacher to handle, it often was split into a two-room establishment with children in grades 1-4 and grades 5-8, respectively, assigned to two instructors.

3) *Grade-level grouping.* Introduced around 1848 in Boston's Quincy Grammer School, the graded-type organization permitted one teacher to work with a given grade group. In practice, this is the same as chronological age grouping or heterogeneous grouping. (See 4 below.)

4) *Heterogeneous grouping.* Essentially, this is the absence of an especially structured plan. Children when entering grade one are assigned to a given teacher irrespective of such factors as intelligence, social maturity, or achievement that might have been scrutinized at the kindergarten level. Individual differences may be dealt with through such means as program enrichment, accelerated promotion, or interclassroom grouping as in primary reading.

5) *Homogeneous grouping.* A misnomer for *ability* grouping, this approach frequently uses intelligence test data, reading ability, or generalized achievement scores as a basis for placement in a given classroom.

6) *XYZ grouping.* A form of ability grouping in which "X," "Y," and "Z" refer to levels of intelligence, or to three levels of assumed potential performance in such a subject as arithmetic. Teaching procedures are modified to allow for differences among the three groups.

7) *Intrasubject field grouping.* This plan is generally used in departmentalized junior and senior high schools. (See "departmental grouping" below.) For example, in the New Trier Township (9-12) High School (Winnetka, Illinois), a student may be in an "advanced" ability group in English and in a "middle" ability group in mathematics. As many as five levels have been used in such groupings.

8) *Departmental grouping.* The practice of having pupils move from one classroom to another for instruction by teachers in each subject field. A departmental program is the antithesis of the unit classroom program in which one teacher handles all, or nearly all, instruction in subject fields. Rarely used below the intermediate grade, departmentalization becomes most commonplace in grade 7 and above.

*Revised and expanded in 1970 from a list originally compiled for an article by Harold G. Shane which appeared in the *Phi Delta Kappan* 41 (April, 1960): 313-319.

9) *"Vestibule" groups.* The label here suggests the idea of an anteroom or small entrance room or hall into which one comes before entering the main rooms of a house. To illustrate, in some school systems such as Chicago, there are "1-c" groups in which less mature children are enrolled prior to entering "1-b" and "1-a" classes in first grade. Thus without "failing" or repeating, certain pupils spend one and one-half semesters in grade one. "Vestibule" groups also have been used at the threshold of high school to help slow learners and children with cultural flaws to increase their prospects of success in secondary education. That is, students may spend four and a half or five years in progressing from eighth grade to the high-school diploma.

10) *Hosic's Cooperative Group plan.* Originally conceived by James F. Hosic in the 1920's, this plan calls for *teachers* to work in small cooperative groups under a group chairman. It is a novel twist, since nearly all other plans involve grouping *children.* Under it, staff members were in charge of special rooms (e.g., a literature, composition, storytelling, reading, and spelling center) but were not so much "subject specialists" as specialists in teaching children. Work for a given group of children was planned at frequent intervals by the "cooperating group" of teachers, who sought to extract from their special area rooms the contributions that each center might make to a unified learning experience.

11) *Winnetka Plan grouping.* Pupil progress in Winnetka has been influenced for many years by self-instructional materials and what might be called an "individual-within-the-group" approach to instruction. The basic classroom unit in grades 1-6 in Winnetka is heterogeneous, but individual progress continues to be personalized by the use of record forms or "goal cards," which encourage optimum academic growth by each child. Thus, in a sense, individual progress within the group constitutes a grouping device which has many of the merits of ability grouping without some of the problems of so-called homogeneous groups.

12) *Dalton Plan grouping.* The classic Dalton Plan was based upon individual progress, group interaction, and a time-budgeting "contract plan" to facilitate individual achievement. Subject matter was grouped in two component parts, the academic and the physical-social. The former was presented predominantly by individualized instruction, the latter by the whole-class method. The work for each grade was laid out in the form of "contracts," which described work to be done over a period of weeks.

13) *Multiple-track grouping.* This is a type of ability grouping in which children of varied ability complete a given number of units or topics at different rates of speed, their progress being contingent upon individual ability. An historically important multiple-track plan was developed late in the 19th century by Preston W. Search in Pueblo, Colorado. In brief, the multiple-track plan permitted some children to finish eight years of elementary school in seven years, while others (on a slower track) might take up to nine years to complete the same tasks. Thus three ability levels were involved, and the *amount,* not the *nature,* of requirements were "scaled down" for slower learning children in a given year, though all children presumably completed the basic requirements before leaving the elementary school.

14) *Platoon grouping.* Platoon grouping goes back to 1900, when it was devised by William A. Wirt for use in Bluffton, Indiana. In broad terms, this plan sectioned children into two groups (platoons) so scheduled as to have one group studying fundamental subjects in classrooms while the second

group used special rooms for activities. As originally conceived, the plan was designed to encourage efficient use of the school plant and to achieve balance between academic and social activity or creative work. The platoon plan also was known as the Gary Plan (since it was best known for its application in Gary), and as the "Work-Study-Play" plan.

15) *Social maturity grouping.* A rather loosely defined concept, this one suggests that grouping be heterogeneous but that children be grouped when they leave kindergarten, for example, into three first grade rooms on the basis of social development and friendship patterns rather than on the basis of ability or of sheer chance. This plan implies the exercise of professional judgment and the use of available test data in assigning boys and girls to "well balanced" groups, with the most mature and the least mature assigned to separate classrooms.

16) *Developmental grouping.* Another term used loosely, this one apparently connotes an approach to grouping roughly comparable to "social maturity" grouping.

17) *Organismic age grouping.* Also a loosely used term, organismic age grouping was apparently coined by persons attempting to apply Willard Olson's concept of organismic age to the grouping of children at varied levels of maturity. In practice, the term probably implies policies similar to those associated with "social maturity" grouping, plus study of various indices of organismic age as determinants of group structure.

18) *Social maturity-teacher personality grouping.* This refers to "social maturity" grouping coupled or linked to a consideration of teacher personality in the assignment of children to a given classroom. It recognizes that teachers as well as children vary as individuals and implies recognition of the assumption that some teachers are more effective with less mature children and that some are most effective with the more mature children in an ungraded primary or "social maturity" grouping situation.

19) *Ungraded primary groups.* This term may be used to describe a situation in which grade levels as such are abandoned at the primary level and where children work together in an environment conducive both to individual and to group progress without reference to precise grade level standards or norms. The teacher in the ungraded primary may work with the same group for two and occasionally three years. It is her purpose to help children progress as far and as fast as they can with less regard for conventional minimum essentials than for total human development.

20) *Ungraded intermediate plan.* Not widely used, the ungraded intermediate approach to grouping involves assigning a group of children in, say, grades 3-5 or 4-5 to one teacher. The program or curricular design is appreciably influenced by teacher-pupil planning. As distinct from the split or "hyphenated" group (see 21 below), the ungraded intermediate grouping is intended to enrich and to improve learning rather than merely to compensate for uneven distribution of pupil enrollment.

21) *Split grade or "hyphenated" groups.* The "hyphenated" or split group is one enrolling children from two and occasionally three grade levels. As a rule, groups are split in smaller schools when, for instance, there are too many children in the fourth and fifth grades for efficient instruction, yet too few to justify dividing both grades. When this situation occurs, a division may be made as follows:

1970-71
3rd grade — 40 pupils
4th grade — 40 pupils
Total   80

1971-72
4th grade — 30 pupils
4-5 grade — 20 pupils
5th grade — 30 pupils
Total   80

The "hyphenated" grouping plan is obviously an administrative-organizational device for securing smaller classes while adding one rather than two new teachers.

22) *Intra-classroom grouping.* A number of teachers make use of various schemes for grouping within the classroom. This is especially true of primary teachers, who create two or more groups when teaching reading. As a rule, intra-classroom grouping is "part-time ability grouping," designed to permit the teacher to work with youngsters of roughly comparable ability. (See also 25, "grouping through teacher-pupil planning.")

23) *Inter-classroom grouping.* Some schools have developed the idea of grouping children not within the classroom but within a given grade or grade range for instruction in a particular subject field (commonly reading), presumably to allow for individual differences. This type of grouping requires that all three teachers in grade five, for instance, schedule reading at the same hours. Then each of the three fifth grade teachers works with the children who remain in or come to her room (on the basis of reading ability) for instruction in reading. Frequently several grade levels are involved in this temporary inter-classroom grouping. For example, all children may, at a given time, exchange rooms for reading activities, the children going to the classrooms which presumably correspond to the level of their reading ability, e.g., the fourth grade child reading at the third grade level would report to the third grade room.

24) *Inter-grade ability grouping.* This is very similar to inter-classroom grouping (described above) and to departmentalized grouping, but is limited exclusively to shifts made within a single grade. For example, three fifth grade teachers may schedule their mathematics period for a given hour daily, then shuffle their enrollment according to ability so that one teacher works with the children in the top-achieving group, one with the middle-, and one with the slow-achieving section.

25) *Grouping within the classroom through teacher-pupil planning.* Such grouping involves the creative or emergent planning of experiences with children in such ways as will eventuate in the selection of various pupil activities to be developed and pupil responsibilities to be carried out. Once a topic, project, or unit has been selected, the teacher and children discuss: a) What do we already know about this topic? b) What do we want to find out? c) How shall we go about it? At point c) various class committees or groups are formed, each of which assumes certain responsibilities for assembling information, for construction work, etc. Teacher guidance is essential to insure that the children volunteering for or assigned to these temporary groupings are challenged by the committee work on the one hand, yet are not frustrated by a too-difficult task on the other.

26) *Self-selection grouping.* This term is rather closely related to 25 above. It implies the creation of a rich environment which is also diversified so as to provide a variety of activities or projects from among which children can "self select" work in which they will engage (individually and/or in

groups) in conjunction with a topic or subject which promises to be a sound "center of interest" or "group interest" compatible with the developmental levels in the group.

27) *Extra-curricular activity grouping.* Especially in the upper grades, many children may be involved in such activities as band, orchestra, or sports. This type of grouping is designed to group children (especially in semi-departmental or departmental programs) so that those in, say, the orchestra can be free to rehearse or practice at the same hours during the week. To serve this purpose, children in the school orchestra, for instance, have their programs so designed as to free them for rehearsal at the same hour of the day.

28) *Special grouping for the gifted.* In schools with large enough enrollments to permit it, there may be special groupings for high I.Q. children which go beyond the provisions of mere ability grouping and which segregate these high I.Q. pupils in special programs or even in special schools or centers. Such groups usually are derivatives of one of the plans already mentioned.

29) *"Opportunity Room" grouping for the slow learning or mentally handicapped.* For many years, the educable mentally handicapped or trainable mentally handicapped child has, in some schools, been placed in special ungraded groups with small teacher-pupil ratios. Special instruction and training are provided, usually for children with I.Q.'s of 70 or below.

30) *"Self-Realization Room" grouping for the gifted.* The S-R room is the reverse or antithesis of the so-called opportunity room for the slow learner and, indeed, is a "grouping" plan only in a very broad sense. In brief, the S-R room is one presided over by a highly capable teacher, well-equipped with study and research aids, and open during the day for gifted children in grades 1-6 or 1-8 to use as they see fit. This plan is based on the assumption that the gifted will be placed in the regular classroom but will also be free to supplement their personal-intellectual development under expert guidance when they have completed basic work with their peers or age-mates. In a school of 500 or 600 pupils, perhaps twenty to thirty would have S-R room privileges and responsibilities. That is, only from one to three youngsters would be likely to come from each grade level.

31) *Ungraded four and five year old kindergarten grouping.* A few places have introduced "ungraded" kindergarten programs for four and five year olds. Depending on his social and intellectual maturity, the child may spend from one to three years at the kindergarten level. This approach to grouping is designed to reduce the range of individual difference.

32) *The Woodring Proposal.* A plan for reorganizing the American school system advocated by Paul Woodring in 1957 has certain features which involve grouping. In brief, Woodring envisioned grouping aimed at helping both the slower and faster pupils in a manner somewhat reminiscent of the multiple-track and other historically interesting proposals. Woodring suggested that the K-8 organization be divided between an ungraded primary school and a middle elementary school. The more able children would spend as little as two years in the primary, moving to the middle school as early as age seven. The less able might remain in the ungraded primary through age nine. He envisioned the bright children leaving elementary school at age 11, the dull leaving at, perhaps, age 13. Woodring created no entirely new plan, but developed a synthesis of the ungraded, multiple-track, homogeneous, and individualized concepts (6).

33) *The Trump Proposal.* Described in a report of the National Association of Secondary School Principals (9), the Trump Proposal advances the

idea of a limited amount of large group instruction coordinated with small classes and individually guided independent study at the high school level.

34) *The Newton Plan.* A proposal from the Newton (Mass.) Public Schools suggesting some class groups of from 50 to 200 students. It is somewhat similar to the Trump Proposal, and involves classes of varied size, restructuring of teachers' time schedules, changes in space and equipment utilization, and curriculum modification to meet individual differences (1).

35) *The Rutgers Plan.* Formulated by teachers of English meeting on the Rutgers campus. Designed so that ". . . no English teacher need ever meet more than twenty-five students at a time except by choice." (2) Other components of the plan include one day per week for each (English) teacher without scheduled classes, bi-weekly class periods, testing and self-correcting homework periods, outside reading and increased independent study, and the use of college-educated but non-certificated personnel as readers.

36) *Grouping through team teaching.* In recent years there has been a good deal of interest in the kind of grouping made possible through team teaching. In general, this type of grouping can best be described through an example. In a conventional school, say, at the third grade level, each of three teachers may teach classes of 30 children or a total of 90 in all. The team teaching approach is one in which one of the teachers commonly is designated as a team leader and, with his two associates, coordinates the experiences of all 90 children. Essentially, each of the teachers brings his particular skills and abilities to all 90 boys and girls rather than working with 30 of them all day long. For example, if one person is particularly good in science or in mathematics, he may work with all 90 of the children in these fields, while another member of the team with strength in the language arts or social sciences may assume responsibilities to an enhanced degree in these fields. To sum up, team teaching is a pooling of effort on the part of several teachers working with youngsters at approximately the same age level in such ways as will maximize the teachers' personal and academic contributions. The grouping that results is flexible, often changes from day to day, and grows out of cooperative planning among the teachers involved.

37) *The Dual Progress Plan.* First received wide attention when a book with this title by George D. Stoddard appeared in 1961 (7). The plan divides content between "cultural imperatives" (language arts, social studies) and "cultural electives" (science, arts, music, etc.). A core (the "imperatives") is taught by a classroom teacher and specialists work in the other fields, on a vertical basis with the children.

38) *"Self-contained" classroom grouping.* The "self-contained" classroom approach assigns a group of children to the same teacher for all or most of the day. This plan is the same as 4 above (heterogeneous grouping) and can be done on an ability or so-called homogeneous basis. See 5.

39) *Non-graded grouping.* Reference has been made to *un*graded groups (see 1 and 19-20), hence a distinction should be made between *un-* and *non*-graded grouping. As noted, *un*-graded groups (as in a one-room rural school of the past) are composed of children of a wide-ranging age spectrum (e.g., from grade 1-4 or 1-8) working together or in rotation with the same teacher. The *non*-graded school abandons the strictures of graded organization and is linked (by Goodlad and Anderson) to the "continuous progress" concept listed below (3).

40) *Continuous Progress plan.* This is difficult to separate from the nongraded school and often there *is* no distinction other than a semantic one. Essentially, there are no grade level lines through which one is promoted in the continuous progress school. Rather, one moves through a K-12 continuum at his own rate. Breakneck progress is reduced by lateral enrichment, and slow learners receive special attention, to keep them with age-mates insofar as possible.

41) *Transactional grouping.* Based on the concept of the learner operating in an "open universe" in which "potential is creatable through transaction with environment." (4) Grouping here is conceived of as flexible and ephemeral, motivated and developmental. The child is not *grouped* but works in peer or cross-age *groupings* which change as child-milieu transactions change.

42) *Continuum grouping.* A form of progress in which decisions by teacher, child, and special personnel such as the elementary school counselor, guide an unbroken or "seamless" flow of experiences through a continuum from as early as age 2 through school leaving age. Based on interactive and transactional concepts.

The list of 42 plans and proposals sketched above, while by no means comprehensive, serves, by its impressive length, to emphasize the many ideas that have been voiced for purposes of personalizing teaching and recognizing individual differences during more than a century of U.S. educational history. Patently, the challenge of human individuality has engaged the attention and stimulated the imagination of scores of educational leaders.

References

1. Bissex, H. S. "Newton Plan Challenges Traditions of Class Size." *The Nation's Schools* 65 (March, 1960): 60-64.

2. Diederich, P. B. "Rutgers Plan for Cutting Class Size in Two." *English Journal* 49 (April, 1960): 229-236.

3. Goodlad, John I., and Robert H. Anderson. *The Nongraded Elementary School.* New York: Harcourt, Brace and World, Inc., 1959. 248 pp.

4. Gordon, Ira J. "New Conceptions of Children's Learning and Development." *Learning and Mental Health in the Schools.* 1966 Yearbook. Washington, D.C.: ASCD, 1966.

5. Otto, Henry J. *Elementary School Organization and Administration.* New York: Appleton-Century-Crofts, Inc., 1954.

6. Shane, Harold G. "Grouping in the Elementary School." *Phi Delta Kappan* 41 (April, 1960): 313-319.

7. Stoddard, George D. *The Dual Progress Plan.* New York: Harper and Bros., 1961. 225 pp.

8. Thelen, Herbert A. *Classroom Grouping for Teachability.* New York: John Wiley and Sons, Inc., 1967. 274 pp.

9. Trump, Lloyd J. *Images of the Future.* Washington, D.C.: The National Association of Secondary School Principals, NEA, 1959. 48 pp.

10. Woodring, Paul. *A Fourth of a Nation.* New York: McGraw-Hill Book Co., 1957.

Name Index

Adams, G. Donald, 130, 151
Adler, Alfred, 13, 39, 76, 80, 86
Agranoff, Bernard, 42
Aikin, W. M., 77, 86
Alexander, Carter, 64
Allen, D. W., 288
Allport, Gordon, 77, 80, 86, 193, 225, 286
Anderson, Robert H., 37, 53, 118, 161, 177, 178, 388, 389
Anderson, Rose, G., 248
Armstrong, Robert J., 29
Asbell, Bernard, 53
Astor, Martin H., 186, 202
Ausubel, D. P., 286
Axelrod, S., 309
Ayer, F. C., 350
Ayres, Leonard P., 74, 86

Bahn, Martin J., Jr., 253
Baldwin, Alfred L., 286
Bandura, Albert, 286
Bank, Irene M., 315, 329
Banmen, John, 202
Barker, R. B., 31, 289, 308
Barnes, Keith D., 206
Barr, A. S., 350
Barr, John A., 15, 29
Basedow, Bernard, 189
Bauernfeind, Robert H., 252

Beauchamp, George A., 127, 151
Beck, Carlton E., 184, 202
Beck, Robert H., 151
Beers, Clifford, 9, 29, 74, 86
Beggs, David W., III, 161, 177
Benedict, Ruth, 13, 53, 76, 86
Benne, Kenneth, 373
Bennett, M. E., 319, 333
Bennis, Warren G., 355, 373
Bereiter, Carl, 53, 290
Berelson, Bernard, 8, 29, 59, 86, 160, 177, 373
Berkowitz, Leonard, 286
Bernstein, Basil, 41, 53, 226
Bestor, Arthur, 19, 80, 86
Bijou, Sidney W., 217
Binet, Alfred, 39
Bissex, H. S., 389
Bixler, Harold H., 249
Blau, P. M., 299, 308
Blocher, Donald, 15, 29, 180, 181, 184, 186, 188, 202
Bloom, Benjamin S., 80, 83, 86
Blumer, Herbert, 286
Boaz, Franz, 40
Bobbitt, Frank, 75, 86

Bode, Boyd, 76, 86
Boles, Harold W., 373
Bonham, S. J., Jr., 351
Bordin, A. S., 226
Borodin, Edward S., 299, 309
Bossard, James H. S., 13, 30, 78, 86
Bossing, Nelson L., 127, 151
Boulding, Kenneth, 4, 30
Boykin, J. C., 30
Brain, George B., 344, 350
Brameld, Theodore, 182, 183, 202
Brazziel, William F., 290
Bronfenbrenner, Urie, 287
Bronson, Gordon, 258, 287
Brooks, John, 53
Bross, Irwin D., 6, 30
Brown, Stanley B., 62, 63
Brownell, John A., 126, 152
Bruner, Jerome, 22, 82, 87
Bryan, William J., 75
Buffie, Edward G., 161, 177
Bunzell, Ruth L., 54
Burk, Frederic, 11, 30
Burke, Arvid J., 64
Burnett, Jaquetta H., 349, 350

Subject Index